RECREATION TODAY

SERIES IN HEALTH, PHYSICAL EDUCATION
PHYSICAL THERAPY, AND RECREATION

Charles A. Bucher, *Editor*

RECREATION TODAY
Program Planning
and Leadership

Richard G. Kraus

Teachers College, Columbia University

New York
APPLETON-CENTURY-CROFTS
Division of Meredith Corporation

668-3

Library of Congress Card Number: 66-22191

PRINTED IN THE UNITED STATES OF AMERICA
E 52585

This book is dedicated to Professor Harlan "Gold" Metcalf of the State University College at Cortland, New York—a true pioneer in the field of professional preparation in recreation, and the most generous and warm-hearted of men.

Preface

As leisure and recreation have expanded on the American scene, a number of texts have been published for use in the professional preparation of recreation personnel. These books have been concerned with the philosophy, leadership, administration, or program materials of organized recreation service.

The present text cuts across several areas of concern. It examines the role and status of the recreation professional, with emphasis on leadership methodology. It provides useful examples of program activities, guides for the development of recreation programs, and a survey of the types of programs sponsored by a wide variety of public and voluntary agencies. It is therefore intended to serve as a text in three related areas:

1. Courses dealing with the principles and methodology of recreation leadership.
2. Courses providing an overview of recreation programs and program planning guides.
3. Courses serving as an introduction to the total field of organized recreation service.

In carrying out preparatory research, the author requested annual reports, schedules, manuals and similar materials from several hundred recreation administrators (in municipal, county, or school departments of recreation or recreation and parks), as well as from many directors in industrial, military, hospital, religious and other agencies. The majority replied promptly and generously. It is not possible to thank all who contributed, but it should be acknowledged that heavy use was made of materials drawn from the following communities—among many others:

Phoenix, Arizona	New Orleans, Louisiana
Vancouver, British Columbia	Minneapolis, Minnesota
Culver City, California	New York, New York
Fresno, California	Oceanside, New York
Pasadena, California	White Plains, New York
Coral Gables, Florida	Winston-Salem, North Carolina
Bloomington, Indiana	Seattle, Washington
Evansville, Indiana	Milwaukee, Wisconsin
Louisville, Kentucky	

In addition, considerable material was drawn from the reports of county recreation and park departments. Hospitals and rehabilitation centers which contributed included: the North Dakota State Hospital, in Jamestown, North Dakota; the National Institutes of Health Hospital, in Bethesda, Maryland; Hillside Hospital, in Queens, New York; and the Menninger Foundation, Topeka, Kansas. There were many other sources, particularly a large number of industrial recreation directors who submitted useful materials.

A great number of useful references were found in *Recreation Magazine,* published until 1966 by the National Recreation Association, and an outstanding source of information about current trends and program materials. To a lesser degree, the author made use of articles in the *American Recreation Journal,* published until 1966 by the American Recreation Society, and the *Journal of Health, Physical Education and Recreation,* published by the American Association for Health, Physical Education and Recreation. Within the specialized field of therapeutic recreation service, *Recreation in Treatment Centers,* published by the Hospital Recreation Section of the American Recreation Society, was invaluable.

The perceptive reader will realize that many of the figures and descriptions of program services offered here apply only to the present day. Statistics of amounts spent on recreation, of numbers of personnel employed, or of personnel standards and salaries, are rapidly climbing. Thus, such references will not apply a number of years from now. But, as of the date the reference is made, they are correct.

The author wishes to express his appreciation to those who have encouraged him in his writing, including the chairman of his department at Teachers College, Columbia University, Professor James Malfetti, as well as his close colleague on the recreation faculty, Professor Elliott Avedon. He also wishes to acknowledge the support and interest shown by his colleagues in the broader field of recreation education, by his students, by those with whom he has worked in recreation settings, and finally, by his family.

It is his hope that this book will be of real value both to those who are entering the recreation field and those who have served in it over a period of years.

R. K.

Contents

PART *I*

THE RECREATION PROFESSIONAL

Chapter 1

Trends in Organized Recreation Service

With the rapid growth of leisure over the past several decades, there has been a tremendous expansion of recreational activities on every level of society. Within the private sphere, the satisfaction of leisure needs and interests is now the basis for a sizable portion of the nation's economic well-being. Within public and voluntary organizations, the provision of organized recreation service has grown, both in scope and diversity.

At the turn of the century, recreation was seen as largely aimed at meeting the needs of children and youth, in programs heavily geared to sports and playground activities during the summer months. Today, recreation programs operate on a year-round basis, serving the varied needs of people of all ages and social classes. No longer is recreation an offshoot of physical education. It is now seen as a distinct area of professional service, requiring specialized college training, in order to insure effective leadership, supervision, and administration. When we refer to recreation professionals, we are describing individuals who are operating on a wide range of levels of authority and responsibility. These may include any or all of the following categories:

1. *Administrator*. He is the superintendent or director of recreation as a major department of governmental service (municipal or county), or in another type of program, such as a hospital, armed forces recreation center, voluntary agency, religious agency, or large industrial plant.

2. *Supervisor*. This person is responsible for a major area of recreation service, either for a particular population group within a community, for a district or geographical area, or for a special category of program service, such as creative arts or outdoor recreation activities.

3. *Center Director*. This individual, who may also be in charge of a large playground or other outdoor facility, is on a somewhat lower level of administrative responsibility but nonetheless holds a key position in the large recreation department.

4. *Recreation Leader*. This person, who is a full-time professional, may either be a generalist, working with numbers of groups in face-to-face leadership in a variety of activities, or may be a specialist in one type of activity.

5. *Part-Time and Volunteer Leaders and Recreation Aides*. These workers, who tend to hold part-time (session) or seasonal positions, tend to be in a subprofessional classification. Working under the supervision of more highly trained professionals, they number in the hundreds of thousands, and are active particularly in voluntary agencies, therapeutic settings, and youth-serving organizations.

In addition to these positions, many recreation professionals are employed today in such roles as consultants, resource specialists, city-planning experts, college union directors, research specialists, and similar varied assignments.

What are the settings in which recreation professionals work? They include the following:

1. *Public Recreation*. This term applies to public, tax-supported departments, commissions, and boards within villages, towns, school districts, cities, and counties throughout the United States. It also includes recreation specialists who are employed by State departments of conservation, parks, and recreation, and a number of agencies of the federal government which, although they do not provide direct recreation services, provide assistance to others that do. These programs cut across the board, serving people of all ages, socioeconomic classes, and recreational interests.

2. *Voluntary Recreation Agencies*. So-called because they are supported chiefly by the voluntary efforts of private citizens and because they are nongovernmental, these represent a wide range of social agencies and

organizations. They include programs like the Boy and Girl Scouts of America, the Young Men's and Young Women's Christian Association and their youth affiliates, the 4-H Clubs, the Children's Aid Society, as well as settlement houses, neighborhood centers, and a host of organizations that serve special age groups or program interests. Much organized camping, and religious and industrial recreation may be described as of a voluntary nature.

3. *Private Recreation.* These consist of a host of privately owned and operated programs, either for public amusement and entertainment or for private membership groups. Examples would include golf, tennis, or yacht clubs, boat marinas, ski centers, game preserves, amusement parks, billiard parlors, bowling centers, vacation resorts, night clubs, and motion picture houses.

In each of these categories, recreation leaders and directors are employed throughout the country. In many of them, the kinds of skills that are required relate to business management and personnel administration, rather than to direct leadership or even to the supervision of direct program services. Thus, it is no longer possible to think of the recreation professional as being primarily a face-to-face group leader. In many positions, he must have theoretical and practical competence in the processes of administration, budget-planning, public relations, personnel management, facility development and maintenance, and city government.

Beyond these qualities, however, because *recreation service* is at the core of his task, he must have a sound philosophy of leisure and recreation, and a knowledge of the history, background, and current trends of this field. An understanding of individual psychological processes and of group dynamics is essential, as well as a comprehensive understanding of sociology and social psychology. Finally, the recreation professional, whatever his level, should have a broad knowledge of program activities and leadership methods, and should have the ability to train and supervise subprofessional leaders in this field.

UNDERSTANDING THE NATURE OF RECREATION

Recognizing that the task of the recreation professional is a varied and complex one, and that he may appear in many different lights to different observers, it is appropriate at this point to examine the meaning of the term "recreation" itself. Most people—including many professionals in this field—feel they have a fairly good idea of what this is. But, when they are pinned down and asked to define the word, the results are likely to be contradictory and confused!

Traditionally, the term "recreation" was applied to those activities that provided relaxation after toil, thus helping the individual "re-create" himself. In most cases, it was viewed as having no purpose beyond that of immediate enjoyment; indeed, the presence of other goals or purposes made an activity somewhat suspect as recreation. Thus, Slavson, the noted authority on group work and social agency programs, wrote:

> Play and recreation . . . are leisure-time activities . . . motivated by pleasure, and serve as diversions from the more pressing and serious occupations of daily living. . . .[1]

The Neumeyers, distinguished sociologists who took a special interest in the field of leisure and recreation, support this view:

> Recreation is . . . any activity, either individual or collective, pursued during one's leisure time. Being relatively free and pleasurable, it has its own appeal.[2]

Even in comparatively recent texts written by authorities in the professional preparation of recreation personnel, this sort of limited view is present. Thus, Meyer and Brightbill offered the following as a definition in the second edition (1956) of their widely read book, *Community Recreation: A Guide to Its Organization:*

> Recreation is activity voluntarily engaged in during leisure and primarily motivated by the satisfaction or pleasure derived from it.[3]

In their text, *Recreation in American Life,* published in 1963, Carlson, Deppe, and MacLean state:

> Recreation is any enjoyable leisure experience in which the participant voluntarily engages, and from which he receives immediate satisfaction.[4]

In justice to the authors just quoted, it must be made clear that in their discussions of the term, following these initial definitions, they broaden the meaning of the word "recreation," when viewed as an area of social service.

The difficulty with these definitions, when taken by themselves, is that they give no immediate sense or conviction of social purpose. When recreation is defined solely in the light of the immediate pleasure to be derived from it—and in no other terms—it is difficult to view it seriously as a matter of public concern. Furthermore, these definitions do not exclude the possibility of forms of play activity or leisure involvement that are destructive or pathological for the individual or society. Gambling, excessive drinking, delinquent gang behavior or vandalism, vice, and

[1] S. R. Slavson, quoted in Allen V. Sapora, and Elmer D. Mitchell, *The Theory of Play and Recreation* (New York: Ronald, 1961), p. 114.

[2] Martin H. Neumeyer and Esther S. Neumeyer, *Leisure and Recreation* (New York: Ronald, 1958), p. 17.

[3] Harold D. Meyer and Charles K. Brightbill, *Community Recreation: A Guide to Its Organization* (Englewood Cliffs, N.J.: Prentice-Hall, 1956), p. 28.

[4] Reynold E. Carlson, Theodore R. Deppe, and Janet R. MacLean, *Recreation in American Life* (Belmont, Calif.: Wadsworth Publishing Company, Inc., 1963), p. 28.

similar pursuits might all be described by definitions that stress only the elements of *leisure, free choice,* and *pleasure.*

Therefore, a number of authors in the field of recreation have stressed that recreation, when viewed as a phase of social service provided by modern government or other agencies, must not only be voluntarily chosen and enjoyable but must also be socially acceptable, morally sound, and must have the potential for making significant contributions to the well-being of the individual and society at large. Furthermore, it must be recognized that much of what the public may conceive of as recreation deserves and receives no place in the community or agency recreation program.

This position has been well-stated by Rodney:

> Any community recreation activity or service, if it is to have real meaning to individuals, must be purposeful. It must provide people with meaningful processes or growth-producing involvements. It must be cloaked in a framework of values. Hence, it must generate intellectual, social and spiritual growth. It is not in the American tradition to use tax moneys or to provide leadership in services that are not goal-oriented.[5]

This emphasis is crucial if recreation is to continue to be seriously regarded and fully supported as an important community service in modern American society. One must recognize, of course, that people engage in many other forms of play and recreational activities, besides those that are structured and offered by social agencies. These activities may be passive or active, simple or complicated, deeply creative or superficial and dull, constructive or pathological. No one can control what people do for their private amusement—unless they are overtly breaking the law. In terms of *organized service,* however, and *community recreation,* values and purpose must predominate, along with the very important goals of providing wholesome fun and a high level of personal pleasure to participants.

The author therefore offers the following, working definition of recreation, as it is conceived of in this book:

> Recreation consists of an activity or experience, usually chosen voluntarily by the participant, either because of the immediate satisfaction to be derived from it, or because he perceives some personal or social values to be achieved by it. It is carried on in leisure time, and has no work connotations, such as study for promotion in a job. It is usually enjoyable and, when it is carried on as part of organized community or agency services, it is designed to meet constructive and socially worthwhile goals of the individual participant, the group, and society at large.

5 Lynn S. Rodney, *Administration of Public Recreation* (New York: Ronald, 1964), p. 4.

In certain situations, this definition may need to be slightly modified. Thus, in a hospital program, when recreation is prescribed or strongly indicated for a patient who may not be capable of making wise independent choices for himself, his participation may not be altogether voluntary. In other cases, the mere fact that activities have been pre-selected by a program director may reduce the degree of voluntary choice by participants. In general, however, the definition is a sound one and widely applicable.

It helps, in viewing the nature of recreational experience, to recognize that it has a somewhat evanescent quality. What is recreation for one individual may not be for another. For example, although both are playing the same game, the Little League baseball player is engaging in recreation, whereas the professional ball player is engaged in hard work. What may be recreation for an individual at one point may cease to be at another, depending on the circumstances and motivations involved. The quality of the experience, and the feeling of the participant about it, are all-important. Slavson sums this up well:

> Recreation does not consist of *what* one does; it is rather the motive, attitude and value of the doing to the individual that gives an activity a recreational significance.[6]

This is tremendously important. Because under most circumstances it is a voluntarily chosen activity, recreation must be attractive and pleasurable, if participants are to continue to take part. They must perceive it as enjoyable. No matter what social goals are intended by the sponsor, the goal of satisfaction *must* be reached by the participant—if not immediately, then not deferred for too long afterward.

RECREATION AS AN AREA OF SOCIAL CONCERN

This discussion leads directly to an analysis of the role of recreation in modern society.

What factors in the present day account for the growth of interest in recreation as a form of community service? Actually, it should be made clear that this is not a recent kind of concern. On the contrary, ancient philosophers discussed it in depth. Aristotle wrote:

> . . . we should be able, not only to work well, but to use leisure well, for as I must repeat once more, the first principle of all action is leisure. Both are required, but leisure is better than work and is its end; and therefore the question must be asked, what ought we to do when at leisure?[7]

[6] S. R. Slavson, *Recreation and the Total Personality* (New York: Association Press, 1946), p. 2.

[7] Aristotle, *Politics VIII, 1337B, 1338A,* quoted in Eric Larrabee and Rolf Meyersohn, eds., *Mass Leisure* (New York: Free Press, 1958), p. 43.

Within the last century, a number of philosophers, anthropologists, and psychologists have formulated widely read theories of play. The concern in this text is not philosophical, however. Instead, it is directly rooted in the needs of society and individual citizens, young and old, in the present day. With this orientation, one may identify the following as underlying elements in the growing concern about recreation in modern America: *Important*

1. The dramatic expansion of leisure (unobligated time) that has come about as a consequence of industrialization and automation, the shorter work week, earlier retirement, medical and social advances, and modern technology in general

2. Our "affluent society"—the continuing rise in national income and the overall standard of living, which permits ever-larger sums to be spent on leisure pursuits

3. Such social factors as the development of "urban blight," the shift of the middle-class population to suburban life, the plight of depressed minority groups, and a simultaneous concern about two sections of our growing population—the teen-ager and the older citizen

4. A general upgrading and expansion of social services directed to meeting the needs of the handicapped, aged, chronically ill, retarded, and similar groups in our population

5. A recognition of the increased importance of leisure spending in our national and local economies

6. A powerful movement toward the conservation, protection, improvement, and development of our nation's natural resources, which have been for so long ruthlessly depleted

7. The growth of interest in artistic and cultural activities throughout our society, sharply contrasted with, at the same time, the deadly conformity imposed by the mass media of communications, particularly television programing

8. A direct linkage of recreation with educational and spiritual goals, values, and programs

In the pages that follow, each of these factors will be discussed, with particular respect to its implications for organized recreation service.

THE EXPANSION OF LEISURE

The growth in the amount of leisure available to us today (time free from work or other obligations) is too well known and too fully documented to justify an extensive discussion here. Suffice it to say that from the beginning of the Industrial Revolution, we have seen a gradual but steady shortening of the work week and an increase in the number of years spent in retirement. People have more vacations and paid holidays. Because of more effective medical practices, they live longer.

In 1880, Americans worked in offices 6 days a week, from 8:00 A.M.

to 6:00 P.M. At that time, an 84-hour work week prevailed for industrial workers, and farmers often worked even longer hours. Today, a number of major unions have achieved a 35-hour work week, and electrical construction workers in New York City have won a union contract that is based on a 25-hour work week—literally a 5-hour working day!

Dr. Marion Clawson, a leading economist, has estimated that our nation will have 660 billion more leisure hours in the year 2000 than it had in 1950; other economists claim that this projection is much too conservative. Even today, it has been calculated that the average American has more leisure hours than working hours in a year: 2,175 leisure hours compared to 1,960 hours of paid work. When labor unions continue to press today for even shorter work weeks for their members, they do not do this because the work load is really too long, or oppressive, as it once was. Instead, the basic motivation is to spread the amount of available work among *more* employees. Nonetheless, this too continues to add to the amount of leisure time available in our society.

For many, even the amount of leisure they have today is too much. Several million workers have, in fact, solved this problem by taking a second job—sometimes known as "moonlighting." Others use their time in aimless forms of passive, stultifying entertainment or, worse, in the kinds of pathological play that have been mentioned earlier.

Curiously, what used to be the leisure class is no longer. Today, the white- or blue-collar worker has a short work-week, heavily controlled and set by union contracts and organizational policy. On the other hand, it is the professional, the business manager, and those in other executive posts at the upper end of the economic scale, who tend to work long hours each day, to take work home from the office, and, in addition, to assume many community service responsibilities.

The growth of automation offers a mixed blessing. Some see it as a force that is presently eliminating and will continue to eliminate hundreds of thousands of jobs each year from the labor market. Others challenge these figures and contend that millions of jobs, particularly in new service industries, are being created each year, and that these are heavily dependent on our continually developing new technologies.

To sum up, there is no question that leisure will continue to grow in availability, as Americans work less and live longer in retirement. Thus, organized forms of recreation will have to be developed increasingly, to fill the void of empty time in a meaningful and constructive way. Beyond this, as the nature of work performed by the bulk of our society continues to grow increasingly specialized and mechanical and to lose the creative values that work once provided more fully, the major focus of living will become more and more one's leisure life. We will not live to work, but to play.

LEISURE SPENDING AND THE AFFLUENT SOCIETY

Today the standard of living of Americans is higher than ever before. The *Statistical Abstract of the United States, 1964,* published by the U.S. Department of Commerce, points out that our gross national product climbed from 100.2 billion dollars in 1940, to 284.6 billion in 1950, to 585.1 billion in 1963. People have money to spend, and they are spending it on recreation—both within the public and private spheres of our economy. For example, the total amount of personal consumption spent on recreation went from 11.3 billion dollars in 1950, to 18.3 billion in 1959, to 21.6 billion in 1962. The amount of public funds spent on outdoor recreation alone climbed from 553 million dollars in 1951 to 1,151 million dollars in 1960. As another example of trends in leisure spending, 302,000 persons traveled to Europe and the Mediterranean area in 1950; in 1963, the number was 1,102,000, the bulk of whom were traveling for pleasure.[8]

What forms of leisure spending and recreational involvement have showed a steady increase? Here are some examples, in terms of sports and outdoor activities, both spectator and participant:

	Number	
Activity	*1950*	*1963*
Major league baseball attendance	17,659,000	20,725,000
Professional football attendance	2,008,000	4,209,000
College football attendance	18,962,000	22,237,000
Horse racing attendance	29,291,000	55,754,000
Ten-pin bowling, number of establishments	6,325	10,883
Outboard motors in use	2,811,000	6,390,000

The annual Sports Participation Survey of the Athletic Institute revealed that during 1965, 39,300,000 Americans had taken part in boating, 22,500,000 in softball, 20,000,000 in shooting sports, 8,000,000 in target archery, and 4,000,000 in skiing. The most popular sports activity of all was bicycling, with an estimated 57,000,000 participants.

Several years ago, *Life* magazine estimated that 40 billion dollars a year were being spent on leisure activities—including all forms of public entertainment, sports equipment, music lessons and instruments, vacation travel, hunting and fishing, arts and crafts participation, boating and water sports, hobbies, home-gardening, and "do-it-yourself" activities.

The Bureau of Labor Statistics of the United States Commerce

[8] United States Bureau of the Census, *Statistical Abstract of the United States, 1964* (Washington, D.C.: U.S. Department of Commerce, 1964), pp. 205, 211, 322, 325.

Department reported that in 1963, Americans spent almost 3 billion dollars for toys and sporting goods, roughly classified as nondurable, and 2.5 billion dollars on the durable kind (golf carts, pleasure airplanes, and the like). We spent more than 4 billion dollars for radio and TV sets, high-fidelity phonographs and records, and another 1 billion to repair them. More than 1 billion dollars was spent for flowers and plants, 2 billion to get into theaters, and 847 million dollars for club dues.

Travel has become an increasingly popular recreational pursuit, both within the United States and abroad. In 1965, it was estimated that 16 million Americans spent over 3 billion dollars traveling outside the country. Family camping in national and state parks and forests has also expanded markedly. In 1956, only 15,000 family campers or trailers used for recreational purposes were manufactured—mostly in California. In 1965, eight states produced 211,499 units worth 300 million dollars, and it was estimated that this industry would triple within another five years.

The Bureau of Labor Statistics indicates that the amount spent on recreation is greater than ever before, and the upward trend is continuing. Recent estimates of leisure-spending range as high as 60 to 70 billion dollars a year. Of this total, the greatest proportion by far is spent within the private sector of the economy—in commercial forms of recreation, in the payment of private fees or the purchase of equipment—rather than through government expenditure. But even this latter amount has grown steadily and impressively. To illustrate, according to the official year-books of the National Recreation Association, expenditures for community recreation services rose from $7,199,430 in 1920, to $33,539,806 in 1929—a period generally viewed as a "Golden Age" for the development of public recreation.

In 1948, Dewhurst, in *America's Needs and Resources* set the total figure for government expenditures on recreation at 262 million dollars. Twelve years later, in 1960, De Grazia, in his study for the Twentieth Century Fund, set the amount at 894 million dollars spent by all government agencies on recreation. To give an example of a single recent form of federal expenditure, in 1964 Congress passed the Land and Water Conservation Fund Act (H.R. 3846), which will provide a total sum of approximately 180 million dollars a year to acquire and develop, on a "pay-as-you-go" basis, land and water areas for outdoor recreation use. Since three-fifths of this is to be made available to the states on a matching basis, it may be estimated that up to 300 million dollars a year (for 25 years) will be spent on recreation through this single federal act.

Similarly, local public spending on recreation facilities and programs has been growing steadily, particularly in terms of park and recreation programs. Thus we see a reflection of the "affluent society"—and the use of available funds for leisure spending on all levels.

SOCIAL FACTORS AFFECTING RECREATION NEEDS

Here we no longer see the distinct pattern of urbanization—that is, a steady population shift from rural areas to the large cities—that was characteristic in the early decades of this century. Instead, following World War II, the trend has changed to one of rapid suburban growth outside the cities, forming a vast belt of suburbia and in effect almost connecting the major metropolitan areas in heavily populated sections of the country. Throughout these new suburban developments, the first task has been, in terms of civic development, to build and staff new schools to serve the growing youth population. Close behind, other social services have been instituted, including municipal or county recreation, or recreation and park boards, departments, and commissions.

Within the cities themselves, the picture has been quite different. In many of the largest urban centers, a so-called "blight" has developed. With the middle class moving out in large numbers, the population make-up has shifted heavily to the very wealthy, and to the poor—including in many cities a high proportion of members of racial minorities. Along with all the other problems of the cities (retaining and attracting suitable industry and business, solving traffic and parking problems, demolishing slums and building new housing), the needs of this large mass of underprivileged residents—many of whom require social assistance on a wide variety of levels—have been almost insuperable. As in the early part of this century, when settlement houses sprang up to meet the educational, social, and leisure needs of masses of immigrants who came to our cities, there is the necessity for redoubled efforts to provide educational, vocational, health, social work, and recreational services for the depressed groups in the urban population.

Recreation in particular is required to help build family unity, to open new channels of participation in constructive activities for young people, and to counteract the pathological attractions of the slum. Thus far, only a few cities have come fully to grips with this problem. In others, there continues to be a confusion of roles, a lack of coordination, and, most important, a failure to recognize fully the necessity of providing imaginative and realistic recreation services to all members of the community—as an essential social function.

Significantly, the federal government has recognized the important role of organized recreation service, as a weapon in the "war on poverty." During the summer of 1965, a number of communities throughout the nation were given multimillion-dollar federal grants (under the Economic Opportunity Act of 1964), to provide "crash" programs of recreation in poverty neighborhoods. These Community Action programs were intended not only to meet the needs of youth and adults for recreational activities, but to stimulate new processes of community organization among those served. Self-help and the hiring of indigenous personnel were stressed, and recreation was viewed as a threshold experience which helped many poor families become involved in other forms of social services. In addition, thousands of Neighborhood Youth Corps trainees were employed in recreational settings, thus gaining a sense of responsibility and community service. At the same time, there has also been a general growth of concern about the needs of certain handicapped groups within our society. Both private organizations and governmental agencies have joined together to stimulate professional conferences and workshops, demonstration and experimental projects, and increased services for the mentally retarded, cerebral palsied, homebound, aged-ill and handicapped, physically handicapped, and similar groups. Both institutional and municipal recreation departments have provided specially designed recreation services to enrich the lives of individuals in these handicapped groups, to assist in the task of rehabilitation, and, as in the case of the discharged mental patient, to provide a greatly needed form of aftercare.

It must be clearly recognized that recreation can never operate in a fully independent way in the sphere of social service. Instead, it must be an integral part of a team effort which provides *all* needed services. In the case of therapeutic recreation in the community setting, this is discussed fully in Chapter 13.

ECONOMIC IMPLICATIONS OF RECREATION

It was pointed out earlier that great sums of money were being spent each year by the American public on leisure services and activities.

More and more, civic officials and business leaders have come to realize the economic value of recreation. In many regions and states, the tourist trade, based on the availability of scenic attractions, forest and water areas, ski centers and other resorts, has developed into a primary source of income.

One of the techniques for assisting farmers and businessmen in poverty-stricken sections of the country has been to aid them in developing their land and water resources for recreational use. The Tennessee Valley Authority is a case in point. When this project was initiated, its primary purpose was to provide flood and erosion control, and to give cheap electric power to rural residents in the Appalachian mountain region. It has since developed into one of the most successful recreation regions in the country, because of the attractive lakes that have been created. Today, many farmers and landowners are being encouraged to turn their properties into hunting and fishing preserves, boating and aquatic centers, or family camping centers. Similarly, a number of American Indian tribes have been assisted in developing their lands for out-door recreation uses.

[In terms of income, a number of states have derived major amounts of tax revenue from certain forms of recreation. For example, since New York State legalized betting on horse racing, under a pari-mutuel system, it has realized almost 1.4 billion dollars of income. In 1964, the first year its legalized lottery was in effect, New Hampshire received over 2.7 million dollars for use in educational programs.

Today civic officials throughout the country are coming to recognize that having a varied and attractive recreation program in their community is an important factor in the attraction of new industry and new residents. Often, when industrialists establish new plants or seek to recruit new employees, this is a key point for consideration. A former president of the National Association of Manufacturers stated in 1960:

> Nothing is more important to the physical and emotional health of the men and women of industry than proper recreation activities. So important is this considered that few modern companies would consider locating a new plant or facility in a community without first surveying its recreation possibilities. Management knows that, in seeking competent and gifted personnel, its ability to attract and hold the men and women it wants often is decided by the little theatre, the park system, or the Little League . . .[9]

[Thus, recreation has proven to be an increasingly important aspect of the economic structure of the nation, both in its relation to other businesses, its attractiveness as a community asset, the tax revenues it provides, and the fact that large numbers of persons are today employed in leisure-centered businesses and industries.]

THE CONSERVATION OF NATURAL RESOURCES

Since the mid-nineteenth century, the federal and state governments have been actively concerned with the conservation and protection of natural resources and wildlife and, in many cases, making them available for public recreational uses. Since the establishment of Yosemite Park in 1864 and the Yellowstone National Park in 1872, such agencies as the Department of Agriculture, the United States Forest Service, the Fish and Wildlife Service, the Army Corps of Engineers, and similar governmental and private groups have been active in this cause. To a great extent, however, it has been a losing effort. We have seen a ruthless depletion of public lands, and a continuing waste of our rich natural resources in this country. With the population growing rapidly, high-

[9] Rudolph Bannow, "What is Expected of Recreation by Management," *Recreation*, January, 1960, p. 15.

ways have taken over parklands and forests, streams have become congested and poisoned, smog has filled the air over our cities, and wildlife has been destroyed on a wholesale basis, or had its natural habitats taken away. As a single example, one might cite our Atlantic and Gulf coastlines—certainly a precious national resource. This amounts to 3,700 miles in all, from Maine to Texas. Of this total, only 240 miles remain today in federal or state hands for public recreational use.

Within recent years, there has been a concerted and powerful effort by conservationists, governmental officials, and thousands of private individuals, to reverse this tide. The emphasis has been on the reclamation, conversion, and protection of land and water resources, and on making them available for intelligently administered, carefully designed public recreational uses. In the words of President Johnson:

> The first step is to break old patterns—to begin to think, work and plan for the development of entire metropolitan areas. We will take this step with new programs of help for basic community facilities and neighborhood centers of health and recreation. . . .

> In a fruitful new partnership with the states and cities the next decade should be a conservation milestone. We must make a massive effort to save the countryside and establish—as a green legacy for tomorrow—more large and small parks, more seashores and open spaces than have been created during any period in our history. A new and substantial effort must be made to landscape highways and provide places of relaxation and recreation wherever our roads run. Within our cities imaginative programs are needed to landscape streets and transform open areas into places of beauty and recreation . . .[10]

These are more than mere words. The 1962 report of the Outdoor Recreation Resources Review Commission, which provided a thorough-going analysis of outdoor recreation needs, interests, resources, and problems, made a number of specific recommendations, several of which have already been acted upon. A Bureau of Outdoor Recreation has been established within the Department of the Interior, and major legislation, as noted earlier, has been passed to enable states and the federal government to protect open lands, develop water recreation sites, establish "green belts" around our cities, and new parks within the cities.

Within this framework, the deliberate planning for healthy outdoor recreation has been accepted as a key element. The fact that so many of the available outdoor recreation resources of the nation are at a distance from the urban centers where this kind of facility is so greatly needed will undoubtedly be reflected in land acquisition and development programs in the years immediately ahead.

[10] President Lyndon B. Johnson, "State of the Union Message," *The New York Times,* January 5, 1965, p. 16.

THE ARTISTIC AND CULTURAL EXPLOSION

Another major influence on the development of the organized recreation movement in this country has been exerted by the dramatic "cultural explosion" of the 1950's and 1960's. This has involved a mass swing toward participation in activities involving artistic and cultural forms of expression, in greatly increased attendance of art classes, concerts, exhibitions and musical groups, and the building of huge new cultural and art centers, both attached to colleges and universities, and as municipal projects.

Consumer spending on the arts rose about 130 percent during the period from 1953 to 1960, about twice as fast as total spending for recreation in general and over six times as much as spending for spectator sports attendance. In 1964, for example, about 3 billion dollars were spent on all forms of artistic and cultural activity. In 1970, it is estimated that the figure will be 7 billion dollars. About 120 million Americans attend art events annually, and about 50 million participate directly in some form of artistic activity.

Why has this come about? Some have seen it as a new form of striving for status and approval. Because the arts have traditionally been the province of the wealthy, with strong linkages to superior education and high job status, many individuals have become involved in order to raise their own social level.

Whatever the motivations underlying it, there is no question that the great public surge of interest in the fine and graphic arts, literature, music, dance, theater, and all forms of cultural expression has much significance for community recreation programs. Many municipal departments have expanded their activities in these areas, have hired cultural arts' specialists or supervisors, and are exploring new forms of participation in the arts. These are illustrated and described in Chapters 7 and 8.

LINKAGE OF RECREATION WITH EDUCATIONAL AND SPIRITUAL GOALS AND PROGRAMS

Finally, it must be stressed that Americans have come to realize that recreation, far from being a peripheral or unimportant part of man's existence, is at the core of his life. It contributes significantly to his social, psychological, physical, and creative well-being and happiness.

Within the field of education, for example, the National Education Association, as long ago as 1911, passed a resolution approving the wider use of schools for social, recreational, and civic activities. A number of important presentations given at the 50th annual meeting of the NEA in 1912 had to do with leisure education and the provision of community recreation services. For example, one report, entitled "How A Community May Find Out and Pay For Its Recreation Needs," demonstrated sharply that the schools had an important role in this total effort. Some excerpts follow:

> . . . it has been found in certain cities that over one-half the children were doing nothing after school hours, neither playing nor working; that 70 per cent of the children were on the streets; that there was less for the girls than for the boys to do in the way of play; that the moving picture shows were drawing every week a number of patrons equal to twice the population of the entire city; that only from 2 to 9 per cent of the space not taken by streets and alleys was free for play, even in cities not considered very congested. . . .

> . . . much of the millions of dollars invested in our school systems is wasted owing to the fact that, outside of school, children form wrong habits due to unwholesome play conditions, and develop traits of character which make much of their school training useless. Because of the size of the task before an adequate recreation system, because of the need of a recreation system to save from loss the enormous investments in schools and other municipal services, because of the call to avoid duplication and waste in the face of this unmet need, many communities are trying to find out and to plan systematically for their recreational needs.[11]

A second aspect of the connection between public education and the growing field of recreation service developed with the statement by the Commission on the Reorganization of Secondary School Education of the National Education Association in 1918 of a number of "Cardinal Principles of Secondary Education." This bulletin discussed the positive values of recreation in modern society and concluded with a strong affirmation of the need for "education for the worthy use of leisure" as a major task of the schools.[12]

Through the decades that followed, a number of important policy statements of leading educators and professional organizations have supported this linkage between recreation and education, both in terms of the need for the schools to educate for leisure, and to sponsor or cooperate in the sponsorship of community recreation services. As recently as 1962, at the Second National Conference on School Recreation sponsored by the American Association for Health, Physical Education and Recreation, the following recommendations were emphasized:

    11 *Journal of Proceedings and Addresses of the Fiftieth Annual Meeting of the National Education Association,* July 6–12, 1912 (Ann Arbor, Mich.: National Education Association, 1912).

    12 "Cardinal Principles of Secondary Education," *Report of the Commission on the Reorganization of Secondary Education of the National Education Association,* Bulletin No. 35 (Washington, D.C.: Department of the Interior, Bureau of Education, 1918).

Education for leisure is a major responsibility of every school.

Every school, from kindergarten through college, has an obligation to provide its students with opportunities for participation in wholesome, creative activities.

Every school has a responsibility to make its facilities and resources available for recreation when needed.

The school has a responsibility to cooperate with community agencies which conduct programs of recreation or which are interested in the conduct of such programs.[13]

Again, in 1964, the Society of State Directors of Health, Physical Education and Recreation stated in a national report:

The state director of health, physical education, and recreation and his staff, working with and through the chief state school officer and the state board of education, should assess recreation developments, problems, needs and opportunities. They should coordinate leadership functions within the department, and should work with other department staff members, such as specialists in art, music, science, language arts, and school plant planning. . . .[14]

More specifically, the state director and his staff should be in a position to carry out the following functions, among others:

Provide expert consultative services on recreation matters to local school systems and to colleges and universities

Establish and maintain effective communication with other state and local recreation agencies and groups and provide appropriate services and assistance upon request . . . where appropriate, take the initiative to organize or strengthen a state inter-agency committee on recreation, or some similar medium for effective cooperation among state agencies

Work to improve the professional preparation of recreation personnel and to increase the supply of qualified recreation leaders . . . assist colleges and universities to upgrade their curriculums for pre-service and in-service education of recreation personnel . . . establish high standards for the professional preparation of recreation personnel employed by the schools

. . . encourage and assist in needed recreation research . . . establish and carry out pilot and demonstration programs of school-community recreation [15]

[13] *Twentieth Century Recreation: Re-Engagement of School and Community* (Washington, D.C.: American Association for Health, Physical Education and Recreation, 1963), p. 30.
[14] *The Role of the State Deparment of Education in Recreation Today* (Washington, D.C.: Society of State Directors of Health, Physical Education and Recreation, 1964), pp. 9–10.
[15] *Ibid.*

In hundreds of school systems throughout the country, it is the Board of Education that is primarily responsible for providing recreation services to the community at large. In over 90 percent of those recreation programs that are sponsored by municipal departments, use is made of at least one school facility. Indeed the *1961 Parks and Recreation Yearbook* indicates that, of 16,960 buildings that were reported as used for recreation purposes, three-fourths were school buildings. In the cocurricular programs of elementary and secondary schools, many clubs, sports, dramatics, publications, and similar activities are strongly recreational in nature; this is true of the offerings of college unions and social organizations and even of many adult education activities throughout the country.

Thus we see that the link between recreation and education in the United States has been strongly established, both in concept and in certain areas of practice.

RELIGION AND RECREATION

Similarly, it has been recognized that recreation, far from being a form of human activity in conflict with spiritual teachings (as it was regarded by Puritan colonists), is inextricably linked with the task of modern religion. The basic position of the major denominations today has been well expressed by the Rev. Warren Ost:

> The trinity of leisure—technology, mobility, and prosperity, has radically upset patterns of American life. What few people see is where this upset has changed their own lives. Nowhere is this lack of awareness more critical than in the whole field of leisure-recreation. The critical situation can be best illustrated by saying that the people who need the leisure, and who make the greatest contribution to society, literally do not have time for it, and the people who have all the leisure often don't know what to do with it. Leisure, recreation opportunities, and guidance are no longer identified with class, education, or training. It is the concern of every community agency including the Church to help people make the most creative and restoring uses of leisure and recreation. How can the Church talk about eternal life when many people don't know what to do with the next weekend? [16]

Specifically, this means that many religious leaders believe that the church recreation program should take its place along with the religious education program, the service program, the mission program, the music program, and the stewardship program. Clemens, Tully, and Crill have written:

> The role of recreation in enriching human life, in attracting new members, in developing and deepening fellowship, in maintaining good morale, in

[16] Warren Ost, "On Recreation Literacy," *Recreation*, December, 1963, p. 458.

complementing the whole program of the church, needs to be recognized by each church member. He needs to know the values of recreation as they affect his children, his family, and his church, as well as himself.

The awakened, responsible church member may ask himself these questions about the church recreation program: Does it reach everybody in the church; children, youth, adults? Are certain racial, economic, and ethnic groups being neglected? Are there enough recreation leaders and are they well trained? Does the church have the needed recreation facilities? Is the program financed as a part of the church budget? Do the standards of the recreation program coincide with the best interests of the church? [17]

As a single brief but convincing example of the work of a major religious denomination, today over 120 Southern Baptist churches operate well-equipped gymnasium and recreation centers, and many more such facilities are in the planning stage or nearing completion. Over 105 million dollars has already been invested by the Southern Baptists in facilities used primarily for recreation, and it is estimated that this sum will go to 146 million by 1967.

Although such statistics are impressive, the most important role of churches and temples that engage in the sponsorship of recreation, either for their own membership or the community at large, is to stress the element of moral purpose and spiritual meanings, as they may be embodied in leisure activity. It is this dimension that religious recreation leaders strive to explore, both in their own programs and in the conferences or civic councils in which many of them are influential.

PERSONAL VALUES IN RECREATION

Finally, the basic question must be asked—what are the major contributions of recreation with respect to the growth and development of its participants?

Psychological Aspects of Recreation

A number of distinguished psychiatrists have subscribed to the value of recreational experience as an essential part of happy and well-balanced living. In a Life Adjustment Publication titled *Enjoying Leisure Time*, [18] Dr. William Menninger stresses the great importance of hobbies, sports and games, and group involvement, in maintaining emotional health. He

[17] "Church Recreation Leadership," *Recreation*, November, 1961, p. 479 (excerpted from: Frances Clemens, Robert Tully, and Edward Crill, *Recreation and the Local Church*, Elgin, Ill.: Brethren Publishing House).

[18] William Menninger, M.D., *Enjoying Leisure Time* (Chicago, Ill.: Life Adjustment Publication of Science Research Associates, 1950).

points out that recreation has become increasingly recognized as an important tool, not only in the prevention of illness, but also in the total process of rehabilitation of mentally ill patients, in institutions and after discharge, in the community setting. He comments:

> It has been the privilege of many of us practicing medicine in psychiatry to have some very rewarding experiences in the use of recreation as an adjunctive method of treatment. . . . Recreation has not only played an important part in the treatment program of mental illnesses, but it has been a considerable factor in enabling former mental patients to remain well. Therefore, psychiatrists believe that recreative activity can also be a valuable preventative of mental and emotional ill health. . . .[19]

Another leading psychiatrist, Dr. Alexander Reid Martin, subscribes to this view, stressing that many forms of psychosomatic illness among the population at large appear to be directly linked to an inability to use leisure in a wholesome and creative way. Such conditions as duodenal ulcers, coronary thrombosis, asthma, migraine and certain skin diseases reflect the individual's response to the stress, strain, and pressure of modern life. Martin writes:

> . . . we find increasing annual budgets for mental disease and increasing consumption of drugs for sleeplessness of psychological origin. Thirty-six million prescriptions for tranquillizers were issued last year to the general non-hospital population of this country. Apparently, tranquillity no longer comes naturally, but only in bottles. Then we have the . . . paradox that many of the aforementioned psychosomatic conditions . . . become aggravated when the individual is on a holiday. We have the very definite entity now called the Sunday neurosis, or the weekend neurosis—conditions of irritability, restlessness, increased tension, sleeplessness—all coinciding with removal or withdrawal from the strait-jacket of work routine and schedule, and immediately disappearing when the individual returns to work. Angina pectoris, which in the old days was associated with great physical and emotional strain and prolonged effort, we now see occurring not infrequently when the individual is supposedly at leisure.[20]

When one recognizes that one's use of leisure not only expresses, but influences the nature of personality growth and self-fulfillment, and that a family climate in which parents can join with their children in a relaxed and happy involvement in leisure activities contributes greatly to healthy development, it becomes obvious that the psychological implications of recreation go far beyond its use with the mentally ill. Instead, it must be recognized as essential to the mental health of *all* individuals.

[19] William Menninger, M.D., "Recreation and Mental Health," in *Recreation and Psychiatry* (New York: National Recreation Association, 1960), p. 8.
[20] Alexander Reid Martin, M.D., "Recreation: A Positive Force in Preventative Medicine," in *Recreation and Psychiatry, op. cit.,* p. 19.

Physical Aspects of Recreation

/ Similarly, it is important to recognize that recreation in the form of sports, games, and moderately strenuous outdoor pastimes may make an important contribution to the physical well-being of all Americans, both young and old. Since World War II, we have been uncomfortably aware that American children and youth are shockingly low in physical efficiency, as a result of the sedentary, inactive, overfed lives that too many of them lead.

The Kraus-Weber tests, in the late 1940's, showed American children to be strikingly inferior to European counterparts in certain limited aspects of strength and flexibility. Later, in 1960, the American Association for Health, Physical Education and Recreation released research findings showing that American boys and girls had lower levels of performance than children in England, Scotland, Wales, and Cyprus, in almost every component of physical fitness. For example, for all tests and at all ages, British boys finished 14 percent higher than American boys. The AAHPER even found that in the test for "endurance for sustained activity," British girls in the 10 and 11 age bracket outscored American boys; in "leg power" British girls of 10, 11, 12, and 13 outscored American boys of the same ages.

/ One of the major recommendations to come out of national conferences dealing with this problem has been the expansion of community recreation programs that place a strong stress on physical activity. Specific proposals have included: (a) establishing community-wide physical fitness committees involving all recreation and other leisure-time agencies; (b) providing state and local laws, when necessary, to broaden the use of existing playgrounds, schools, and all types of facilities suitable for recreation activities; (c) providing year-round as well as summer opportunities for special physical fitness centers and sports clubs; (d) providing and expanding opportunities for daily physical activities for all ages.

While tests carried out in 1965 indicate that American school children have improved markedly in fitness, as a result of intensified physical education programs, it is important to recognize that similar results will not be achieved for the population at large by reliance on resistive exercise, weight-lifting, or rigorous calisthenics and gymnastics. While some may do them under compulsion, or as part of a brief "crash" program, most people regard such activities as dull routine, or even "punishment." Instead, activities should be functional, should provide moderate physical exercise that can be carried on through adulthood, and should be enjoyable—so that people will perform them willingly. The need for continuing physical activities that are suitable for the later years has *not* been sufficiently recognized until recently. Dr. Edward Bartz, Chief of Medical Service at Philadelphia's Lankenau Hospital, states:

. . . the exercise factor is one of the most important, and the most neglected, of the practices individuals should utilize to enjoy the added years which science is making possible. It begins to appear that exercise is the master conditioner for the healthy and the major therapy for the ill.[21]

Dr. Paul Dudley White, the eminent cardiologist, has subscribed to this view of lack of exercise as a primary cause of heart trouble. British medical researchers found that coronary heart disease occurs with twice as much incidence among the physically less active than among the active; when it does occur, the mortality is much higher among the less active. A total view of the role of recreation in providing healthy physical exercise is given by Dr. W. W. Bauer of the American Medical Association, who writes:

Most of us need more activity. Some like it in the form of push-ups, tumbling, giant swings, football, baseball, basketball—or you name it. Well and good. Each to his liking, if we are going to hew to our line of satisfying activities to make a satisfying life. But there should be emphasis, during youth, on a personal sport or activity which can be carried on when the demands of adult life render participation in team sports, or activities requiring much time, space, or equipment, impractical. Then we shall need something like walking, cycling, active gardening, swimming, rowing, golf, mountain climbing, or nature study involving field excursions, in order to get us out of the stands and onto the playing fields. This is a neglected facet of fitness.[22]

Social Aspects of Recreation

An extremely important aspect of recreation is that it can provide the opportunity for group experiences that meet fundamental human needs. The distinguished social work authority, Dr. Gisela Konopka, offers the view that even the recent concepts of dynamic psychiatry which recognize the integrated nature of man, but see him as a whole but separate entity, are no longer completely acceptable. Today, it is necessary, she stresses, to see man as a *whole individual interrelated with others.*

Man's need for food and shelter, for love and tenderness, for accomplishment, and for fulfillment of his thirst for knowledge, are all dependent on the interaction of man with man. Next to the biological necessities, man's deepest longings are to love and to be important—important to someone; it is from these that all other needs spring. An inseparable connection exists between self-respect and a freely given relationship with someone else. . . .[23]

21 Edward Bartz, M.D., "The Value of Exercise," *American Recreation Journal,* July–August, 1963, p. 4.

22 W. W. Bauer, M.D., "Facets of Fitness," *Journal of Health, Physical Education and Recreation,* September, 1960, p. 24.

23 Gisela Konopka, *Social Group Work, A Helping Process* (Englewood Cliffs, N.J.: Prentice-Hall, 1963), pp. 39–40.

This important need can be met, Konopka points out, through a healthy group life, which has the following ingredients: (a) the opportunity to identify with others in a peer group relationship; (b) provision for meaningful bonds being established with *several* persons (which is less vulnerable than when there is closeness with only *one* person); (c) freedom to be an individual, and to express one's "differentness" without apprehension; (d) freedom to choose the friends one prefers, combined with a willingness to accept others if they need to be accepted, although this may be on a more superficial level; (e) respecting the uniqueness of others; and, (f) an opportunity both to test one's independence and, when necessary, to have a degree of dependence on others.

Grace Coyle has written of the necessity for favorable group experiences:

> I believe that groups . . . if properly understood and sympathetically led, can provide for the participants a kind of social nourishment which will enhance life and encourage growth. If a group, through the interaction of the members and the guidance of the leader, is friendly, warm and accepting, it can give to its members a chance to experience mutual relationships and the diffused but significant securities that come from the sense of belonging. For different individuals, and at different age levels, this kind of acceptance will have varied meanings. For many it can contribute to emotional stability and security and can give acceptable guidance to both positive and negative feelings.[24]

Although these passages are intended to apply chiefly to social group work experiences, they are relevant also to club and small group activities when carried on as part of recreation programing. Without question, one of the most significant outcomes of constructive recreational involvement should be that of group participation.

IN CONCLUSION—A BALANCED LIFE

In each of our lives, we become involved with two broad spheres of experience—one pertaining to work or the preparation for work, and the other related to a host of nonwork possibilities.

For many, work may involve not only the job itself but studying for a career, associations with others in the same field, professional organizations and clubs, and allied interests. For a fortunate few, work itself may be extremely fascinating; so much so that even leisure is spent in activities which contribute ultimately to, or are indirectly derived from, one's job, but which are voluntarily chosen and add much enjoyment to living. For too many people, however, work in an industrial, highly mechanized

[24] Grace Coyle, *Group Work with American Youth* (New York: Harper & Row, 1948), p. 252.

society tends to be a narrow, uncreative, and unsatisfying experience. In
a recently written sociological study, this description appears:

> In a factory in Michigan that makes automobile wheels, nothing but wheels,
> wheels, wheels, I recently saw a man who sits in a high perch beside a noisy,
> endless conveyor. All day unfinished wheels glide toward him from some-
> where down the line, one about every ten seconds. He lifts each wheel from
> a conveyor, lays it down on a press, pulls a lever. The press smashes down
> on the wheel, leaving a decorative groove. The man lifts the wheel, puts it
> back on the conveyor, takes the next one.
>
> Every ten seconds, every minute, every hour, every day, for year after year.
> The man's hair is gray, his eyes are gray, his skin is gray. His life appears
> gray.[25]

For people who have such jobs—and with the increase of mechaniza-
tion and automation, their number is growing—it will only be within the
world of leisure that true personal self-fulfillment will be found. Indeed,
for all of us, a host of hobbies, games, creative pursuits, group associations, cultural involvements, entertainment, and travel are waiting to be
discovered. So flexible and varied are the possibilities that it is this sphere
of living that affords the greatest opportunity for self-discovery as a full
human being—and for becoming a real individual in a society increasingly
characterized by blind conformity.

Ideally, this should be a continuously flowing process, from infancy
through old age. Stimulated and encouraged first by parents, brothers and
sisters, and playmates, we are opened up to new skills and areas of
knowledge by education, by camp, and by group associations, until as
adults our leisure lives combine physical, intellectual, creative, and social
experiences. For some, this process is an easy one. Brooks Atkinson, the
famed drama critic, once wrote a newspaper column which humorously
debunked the need for "leisure experts" or the formal provision of
recreational opportunities and programs. For such people as Atkinson—
highly creative, resourceful and open to new experience—this sort of
criticism may be valid. They need no recreational advice or help to spend
their leisure fruitfully.

But for the mass of people, this is not the case. Faced with great
amounts of leisure, with limited skills and narrow attitudes regarding its
use, too many tend to fritter their time away with petty, meaningless tasks
or in endless staring with glazed eyes at a television screen—or worse. For
them, and for the community at large, it is essential that knowledgeable
and skilled leadership be provided to plan programs, develop facilities,
and give consultation and direction in a variety of challenging and
constructive recreational experiences. The alternative is a barren, dull,
drab existence—that could be so alive and exciting!

The function of providing recreation as an important public service

25 Bernard Asbell, *The New Improved America* (New York: McGraw-Hill, 1965).

has been accepted by America's communities large and small. The reasons are several. As cited by Butler, they include the following:)

1. Municipal recreation affords a large percentage of the people their only opportunity for forms of wholesome recreation.
2. Only through government can adequate lands be acquired.
3. Municipal recreation is democratic and inclusive.
4. Municipal recreation is comparatively inexpensive.
5. The local government gives permanency to recreation.
6. The job is too great for a private agency.
7. Recreation plays an important role in the local economy.
8. The people demand it and are willing to be taxed for it.[26]

As a consequence of the steady growth of organized recreation services, the number of publicly sponsored local and county agencies in this field had expanded by 1960 to a total of 2,762. These were broken down as follows:

Agencies administering recreation as a single function	949
Agencies administering departments of parks, park and public properties, etc.	543
Agencies administering both recreation and park services, such as park and recreation departments	466
Agencies administering recreation in conjunction with the schools, such as school boards and committees	274
Other public authorities administering recreation or park services (such as city managers, departments of public works, youth commissions, etc.)	530

Similarly, a wide variety of private and voluntary agencies throughout the country today provide impressive recreation programs, to meet important personal and societal needs of Americans. For these to be most effective, professional leadership is required.

What is the nature of the professional recreation leader's task? What is his recommended training? Under what circumstances and in what settings is he employed, and what sort of salary is he paid? What techniques, skills, and fundamental understandings must he have? All of these points, as well as actual materials for use in recreation programs, and guides for effective planning, are included in chapters that follow.

SUGGESTED QUESTIONS FOR DISCUSSION

1. Define the meaning of the term "recreation," as it applies to organized community services today.
2. Discuss the social factors that make leisure an important subject of public concern, and that promote expanded programs of organized recreation service. Which of these are most apparent in your community?
3. What are the personal values of recreational participation? Discuss these in terms of your own experience.

26 George Butler, *Introduction to Community Recreation* (New York: McGraw-Hill, 1959), pp. 59–63.

Chapter 2

The Recreation Profession Today

Clearly, with the emergence of the recreation movement in the United States today, there has also emerged a new occupation—that of recreation leadership and administration.

A number of descriptive terms have been coined to apply to this individual. Feeling that the terms currently in use described only single levels of responsibility, some authorities have proposed the word "recreator." Similar to "educator" or "doctor," this implies one who provides professional services in the field of recreation. Others have proposed the term "recreationist," apparently deriving the suffix from such words as "therapist" or "internist."

Since neither of these terms has become widely accepted or known to the public, and since there is marked disagreement regarding their use, the author chooses to use the title "recreation professional" as descriptive of all those employed on a professional level in the field today. As this chapter will demonstrate, such individuals function on a number of levels, such as: superintendent or director, center director, supervisor, specialist, or leader.

CLARIFYING THE ROLE OF THE RECREATION PROFESSIONAL

Although public understanding of this field has improved markedly since the mid-1950's, it is still safe to say that recreation is such a new form of service that it is not yet fully understood or respected. This is partly true because the recreation professional has so many varied functions and specializations, and is employed by so many different kinds of agencies, public, private, and voluntary. It is also true because many practitioners in this field have not received professional training. Indeed, the full-time, well-qualified professionals in recreation are considerably outnumbered by those who are volunteers, part-time or seasonal workers, and who must be regarded as subprofessionals.

For these reasons, and because recreation still lacks a formal certification plan to identify the fully qualified individual, many people, including secondary school guidance counselors who advise young people about occupational and professional fields, are comparatively ignorant about it as a life's work. This chapter seeks to shed light on this point, for the practitioner, the guidance counselor, the individual who is contemplating a career in recreation, and those in the field of professional preparation.

CRITERIA OF A PROFESSION

First, exactly what constitutes a profession? What are the true characteristics of a profession in any field?

Clearly, the notion that being paid for a piece of work automatically makes one a professional, is fallacious. While it may give us a useful distinction between the amateur and professional ballplayer, it does not discriminate sufficiently. The word "profession" has certain other important connotations in our society. For example, there are several major criteria that apply to the identification of a profession as such. These are: (a) general acceptance of the field; (b) a specific body of knowledge; (c) the existence of basic research in the field; (d) professional higher education; (e) certification in the field; (f) personnel standards; (g) recruitment; (h) professional organizations; and (i) a code of ethics. One might also add the point that members of a profession are generally expected to provide an important service to humanity.

Clearly, when one examines the field of recreation using this yardstick, it rates well in certain categories, and less impressively in others. In each, progress is being made.

General Acceptance of the Field

One good way to measure public acceptance of this field is to ask, "How many recreation professionals are there today? How widely is this function practiced?"

A nation-wide survey of Social Welfare Manpower was conducted in 1960, examining personnel in the fields of welfare, health, rehabilitation, and recreation, working for voluntary and governmental agencies. Over-all, the report identified 116,000 social welfare workers, including 10,450 who were classified as recreation leaders in government (64 percent) and voluntary (36 percent) agencies. It is clear that this report underestimated the number of recreation workers in at least two important respects. First, it identified only 5,487 individuals employed by state or local government in recreation capacities—much lower than authoritative figures derived by National Recreation Association studies for the same year. In addition, in a number of fields, such as therapeutic service or settlement house work, many individuals carrying out recreational functions were not designated as such, but given other titles. Therefore, the total figure of 10,450 is unquestionably quite low.

Another set of figures is to be found in the *1961 Recreation and Park Yearbook,* compiled and published by the National Recreation Association. This revealed that there was a total of 99,696 paid recreation leaders in 1960, in city and county recreation and park programs. Of this number, 9,216 were designated as full-time, year-round workers (an increase of 35 percent for the preceding decade). In addition, there was a tremendous number of volunteer recreation leaders—277,074—far more than ever before. But these statistics too, give only a partial picture of employment in this field.

Other authorities, adding available information in each of the specialized fields of recreation, have come up with estimates of between 30,000 and 35,000 currently employed, full-time, year-round recreation workers. In terms of future needs in this field, it has been predicted that between 20,000 and 30,000 new professionals will be needed within the next 10-year period, to fill newly created positions or fill positions opened up by turnover.[1]

If one adds all the types of positions (including part-time, seasonal and volunteer), jobs in the armed forces, college unions, churches, industries and hospitals, commercial recreation and camping, the figure would expand to even more impressive dimensions. In addition, those in other fields who have a partial responsibility for recreation service (such

[1] Jay B. Nash, *Opportunities in Recreation and Outdoor Education* (New York: Vocational Guidance Manuals, Universal Publishing and Distribution Corporation, 1963), p. 77.

as social workers, teachers, occupational therapists, or city managers) represent a considerable number.

The Bureau of Labor Statistics of the United States Department of Commerce supports the view that recreation is a field rapidly growing in public acceptance with the following statement, made in 1965:

> Recreation is becoming an enormous industry with vast funds and a large labor force. It is an area of job growth with few equals in the economy and has a wider range of job openings than any single industry in the nation.[2]

Professional Education in Recreation Service

The history of professional preparation in recreation is a comparatively brief one, when compared to other fields.

The National Recreation School for Professional Graduate Training was established in 1926 by the National Recreation Association to train recreation executives. It continued to be sponsored annually, until 1935. During the same period of the 1920's and 1930's, a number of college departments of physical education or youth work offered courses in the areas of play leadership, playground direction, and youth activities. During the late 1930's, a number of colleges initiated major programs in recreation, usually within departments of health, physical education, and recreation, to meet growing community and institutional needs.

During the Depression of the 1930's, about 45,000 recreation leaders were hired and trained as part of the federal recovery program in the Works Progress Administration. Working in all sorts of recreation leadership positions, including cultural activities, sports and games, and outdoor recreation services, they were required in most cases to take weekly in-service training courses. This represented a major stimulus to the field, as well as a form of professional preparation. In addition, a number of national conferences on professional preparation of recreation personnel were held: at the University of Minnesota in 1937, the University of North Carolina in 1939, and New York University in 1941.

World War II represented both a setback and a boost to the field of recreation. While many community programs were necessarily limited in their operations, the greatly expanded armed forces recreation programs, the development of youth centers to combat incipient juvenile delinquency during the wartime period, and the increase of industrial recreation programs, all spurred interest in this field. Following the war, municipal, county, and state recreation services began to accelerate rapidly. This was directly accompanied by a steady growth in the number of colleges and universities that developed major programs to prepare recreation leaders and administrators.

2 News release, New York *Post,* August 2, 1965, p. 31.

In 1963, the American Recreation Society and the National Recreation Association conducted a joint survey, which revealed 65 institutions offering a major, with 2,834 majors. These colleges and universities were found most heavily in the Midwest region (18 schools), the far Southwest (14 schools, with a large number of graduate students), and the Southeast (12 schools). Of the 65 colleges and universities responding, 55 were public institutions. Although this seemed to represent favorable progress, the fact is that enrollment in this field has failed to keep pace either with the growth in the recreation field in general, or with the growth in the college population as such. For example, a 1964 report indicated that colleges and universities expected to graduate 667 recreation majors in that year—approximately the same number that were graduated in 1956. The average number of students graduating in each institution reporting had remained almost exactly the same over the eight-year span of time.

Clearly, this does not represent healthy growth. What accounts for it? Certain factors may be responsible: (a) the quality and general reputation of professional curriculums in this field; (b) the attractiveness of the field for potential recruits, in terms of personnel standards and salaries; (c) the efforts of college and university personnel, professional practitioners, and professional organizations to recruit new students; and, (d) the necessity for having a degree in this field, in order to obtain a position.

Curricular Quality

During the first decades of growth, many recreation curriculums were subpar. In a number of cases they simply represented minor appendages of physical education departments. First-class teaching personnel were rare, and solid research in the field almost nonexistent.

This situation has rapidly changed. A number of conferences have focused attention on academic programs in this field, including one on undergraduate preparation of recreation leaders or administrators at Jackson's Mill, West Virginia, in 1948, and another on graduate study, at Pere Marquette State Park, Illinois, in 1950. During the 1950's, a concerted attempt was made in many institutions to raise academic requirements and strengthen staff. Thus, when, in 1959, the recreation curriculum at Indiana University was criticized in an article in a national magazine, entitled "Are We Making A Playground Out Of College," the Dean of the School of Health, Physical Education and Recreation, and the Chairman of the Recreation Department replied promptly and indignantly. Referring to the description in the article of their curriculum as one ". . . which allows one to become a bachelor of science without ever having to study mathematics, chemistry, physics, history or science, but *only* things like volleyball, archery, lacrosse, deep breathing, and refereeing," they wrote:

> The actual facts, as they pertain to the school of health, physical education, and recreation curriculum, are as follows:
>
> Requirements in the various curriculum options in the school of health, physical education and recreation, include history, arts, sciences, mathematics, and humanities, and range from thirty-seven to sixty-five semester hours, depending on the particular curriculum. This does not include required English courses, or electives which are most commonly taken in the arts and science college.
>
> Required science courses, in the various curriculum options in health, physical education and recreation range over anatomy, physiology, kinesiology, psychology, social sciences, botany, zoology, anthropology, and bacteriology. Other requirements include courses in business, economics, speech and theater, journalism, education and government.
>
> There are *no* courses in lacrosse and deep breathing. . . . Recreation majors, the object of . . . inaccurate remarks, are required to complete a minimum of forty-nine semester hours, in the college of arts and science and an additional fifty-nine hours, distributed among four other schools in the university. . . .[3]

This emphasis on sharply raised standards in professional preparation was reflected in a Conference on Professional Preparation sponsored in 1962 by the American Association for Health, Physical Education and Recreation. Specifically, the report of this meeting offers detailed recommendations in the field of recreation, relating to selective recruitment, admission, advisement, retention, and placement of students. It provides standards regarding faculty qualifications and skills, and makes detailed recommendations regarding the undergraduate and graduate curriculums —with emphasis on both general and specialized professional courses.[4]

On the graduate level, for example, it was recommended that a strong stress be placed on the following curricular areas: (a) philosophy and principles of recreation; (b) administration of recreation; (c) research and evaluation; (d) personnel management; and, (e) public relations.

Other professional conferences have dealt with more specialized aspects of preparation in recreation service. For example, standards in the area of recreation for the ill and handicapped were developed at a Therapeutic Recreation Curriculum Development Conference held in

---

[3] Arthur S. Daniels and Garret G. Eppley, Letter to Editor, *Recreation*, May, 1959, p. 174.

[4] *Professional Preparation in Health Education, Physical Education and Recreation Education* (Washington, D.C.: American Association for Health, Physical Education and Recreation, 1962), pp. 84–102.

1961 at Teachers College, Columbia University.[5] In the growing field of outdoor recreation, a National Conference on Professional Education for Outdoor Recreation was held at Syracuse University in 1964; it critically analyzed the growing need for specialists in the administration of park and forest recreation areas and presented principles for the construction of curriculums in this field.[6]

Professional organizations have been active in this field. The American Institute for Park Executives has sponsored a number of surveys, including one dealing with recruitment and curriculums for park and recreation personnel, which analyzed the training and special courses needed for administrators in outdoor recreation. In 1963, the Federation of National Professional Organizations for Recreation embarked on a National Recreation Education Accreditation Project,[7] intended to develop standards and evaluative criteria with which to measure the effectiveness of professional education in recreation at the undergraduate and graduate levels. When this has been accomplished, and when the National Commission on Accrediting approves the basic statement establishing the need for accreditation of institutions in this field, it will become possible to screen and designate those colleges that have solidly supported and effectively organized and staffed departments of recreation education. This will immeasurably improve professional education in this field, as it has other fields in which institutions have undergone an accreditation process. In turn, it will make certification of recreation personnel more feasible and meaningful.

Certification. Certification consists of a process which offers a means of identifying qualified personnel for work in a given field and of enforcing certain requirements that individuals must have if they are to be hired. Normally, it is carried out by having a state legislature pass a law, framed with the assistance of state recreation organizations or societies, which will establish mandatory requirements for the hiring and firing of recreation personnel. This would apply to all public agencies, and to those voluntary agencies willing to comply, or that did so as a matter of professional standards or organizational agreement. Typical of such legislation is the following proposed law framed by the Florida Recreation Association, proposing a State Board of Recreation Examiners, to be empowered to grant certificates:

> . . . to provide laws and provisions establishing the qualifications and certification of professional recreators in the field of recreation to the end

[5] *Therapeutic Recreation Curriculum Development Conference* (New York: Comeback, Inc., 1961).

[6] *National Conference on Professional Education for Outdoor Recreation* (Washington, D.C.: Bureau of Outdoor Recreation, Department of the Interior, 1964).

[7] *National Recreation Education Accreditation Project* (Tentative Final Draft of Standards and Evaluative Criteria, published for Federation of National Professional Organizations for Recreation by National Recreation Association, New York, March, 1965).

that the public shall not be improperly served by unprofessional, un-authorized and unqualified recreators, and that the public shall be protected against unprofessional conduct by persons certified as professional recre-ators.[8]

The basis for certification should include not only holding of college degrees in recreation or allied areas, but references, experience, and in-service training, good moral character, and written, oral, or practical examinations. In a sense, this is being carried out already in a number of states, where specific Civil Service requirements have been set up for professional recreation personnel in municipal or county departments. In branches of federal employ, this is also the practice.

In a number of states, a registration process has been employed to identify qualified personnel. This has been defined as ". . . a voluntary submission of one's credentials to a group, and recognition of these credentials." Criteria that may be established by state recreation organiza-tions are likely to include specific undergraduate or graduate degrees from approved institutions, as well as the character, conduct, and profes-sional experience of the individual. Although registration may provide a useful means of helping recreation agencies hire qualified individuals, it is limited in its effect since it is voluntary and there are no state-wide or national means of enforcement, as in other professions. Thus, the most meaningful identification and screening of recreation personnel will not come until colleges and universities in this field have been accredited, and until certification becomes a reality.

Recognizing that these factors will play an important part in the public "image" of recreation, it is also necessary to examine other factors that are even more important to the potential recruit to this field. These represent concrete evidences of public support and recognition—salaries and working conditions.

Personnel Standards, Salaries, and Status

One of the key concerns of professionals in the field of recreation obviously has been that of status and public recognition. These may be measured rather vividly in terms of the kinds of salaries that are paid to recreation leaders and administrators. When a field is highly regarded, it pays well and people seek to enter it. When it is poorly regarded, the reverse is true, and talented students do not seek to enter it as a field of employment.

In the past, salaries in the field of recreation have been poor, com-

8 "Proposed Florida Law for Establishing a State Board of Recreation Examiners" (Tallahassee, Fla.: Florida State University, 1963), p. 4.

pared to other fields with roughly comparable personal and educational qualifications. However, they are rapidly becoming more and more attractive. So great is the shortage of qualified recreation personnel on the supervisory and lower administrative levels that many recreation graduates are hired today for such positions, immediately after graduation. In the Middle Atlantic states, for example, June, 1964 graduates of recreation curriculums were hired in a number of cases at salaries ranging between $6,000 and $6,500. One graduate of Cortland State College of the State University of New York was hired immediately as a supervisor of Women's and Girl's Activities, at a salary of $6,925. Dr. J. B. Nash cites figures from a study of recreation workers' salaries in 880 cities in the United States in 1962 showing that the salaries of recreation workers over the previous 10 years had increased in median amounts of 39 percent for leaders, 59 percent for assistant directors, and 62 percent for center directors.[9]

Typical salary ranges in communities through the country included the following (in 1964–1965):

Winston-Salem, North Carolina: Recreation Director: $9,720–$12,240; Assistant Recreation Director: $7,680–$9,720; Supervisors: $6,780–$8,460.

Minneapolis, Minnesota: Director of Recreation: $12,252–$14,892; Assistant Recreation Director: $10,164–$12,000; Recreation Program Supervisor: $8,940–$10,440.

The State of California recently announced positions for Recreation Therapists, with a salary range of $5,832 to $7,080, and the opportunity to advance to higher grades in rehabilitation services.

The Bureau of Outdoor Recreation of the Department of the Interior has been seeking Recreation Resource Specialists to fill Civil Service positions, at salaries ranging from $6,675 (Grade GS-9) to $14,565 (Grade GS-15).

In many counties, municipalities, and state governments throughout the country, there has developed a practice of having capable recreation executives move into posts involving high levels of administrative responsibility, related to city management, county executive offices, state departments of planning, conservation, mental health, and similar posts.

These salary ranges and career opportunities in the recreation field may now be compared very favorably with teachers' salaries which, apart from extremely high ranges in certain sections of the country or wealthy metropolitan areas, are not as high as is often supposed. For example, the Research Bulletin of the National Education Association revealed in 1965 that the average salary of all classroom teachers in public schools in the United States during the preceding year was estimated to be

[9] Jay B. Nash, *op. cit.*, p. 47.

$6,222.[10] In many communities and school districts, teachers were obviously receiving far less.

Compared with these findings, recreation salaries for the same year in public and voluntary agencies were excellent. While financial remuneration is not the only consideration, it is and should be an important part of the appeal of any professional field.

Similarly, working conditions and job expectations have become much more realistic and attractive for recreation professionals. No longer should a recreation graduate expect to have to take a position where it will be demanded that he work at all hours, day and night, with insufficient time to see his own family, or enjoy his own recreation. Today, most enlightened city or agency administrators will expect a recreation director to have a working schedule similar to that of other employees on comparable levels of authority. True, much of it will be evening work, or possibly involve weekend assignments. However, this should be compensated for by free time elsewhere in his schedule. True, the recreation professional may be called upon to participate in many meetings, address civic groups, serve as a resource consultant or advisor for other agencies in the community. But, for the recreation leader or administrator who is interested in people, in promoting a sound philosophy of leisure, and strengthening the influence of his own department, these represent opportunities, rather than unwelcome chores.

Personnel Practices. Many municipal, county, or school recreation departments have developed formal codes or manuals of personnel practices. These deal with such matters as: (a) employment (needed qualifications, examinations, and application procedures); (b) required participation in in-service training courses; (c) probationary periods of employment; (d) leaves of absence, for vacation, holiday, illness, maternity, or educational reasons; (e) retirement plans, joint-contribution pension plans, disability retirement plans, death benefits; (f) legal assistance for suits related to job occurrences; (g) overtime pay or compensatory time for emergency work; (h) codes for disciplinary action when necessary; and (i) evaluation plan, with service ratings to be considered with relation to pay increases or promotions.

Both the American Recreation Society and the National Recreation Association [11] have carried out surveys and developed recommended

10 "Salaries Paid Public School Personnel, 1964–65," *National Education Association Research Bulletin* (Washington, D.C.: National Education Association, October, 1965), p. 81.

11 See "Personnel Practices for Recreation Departments and Agencies" (Washington, D.C.: American Recreation Society, 1959) and two-part study of "Professional Salaries in Local Public Recreational Agencies" and "Fringe Benefits and Personnel Practices in Local Public Recreation Agencies" (New York: National Recreation Association, 1963).

standards with respect to salaries and personnel practices in recreation agencies.

It is now clear that recreation service is rapidly moving to a position involving a high level of responsibility and remuneration for capable and professionally trained candidates.

Why, therefore, does recruitment in this field continue to lag far behind the demand for professionally trained personnel?

One of the most important tasks to be carried out is to improve public understanding of the recreation field, so that high school students, their parents, and guidance counselors will recognize it as a career field which performs an important public service, pays attractive salaries, offers real opportunity for advancement to executive levels, and provides great satisfactions to the practitioner. At the same time, it is necessary to make clear that professional training in this field is becoming increasingly important, both for initial hiring on a favorable level, as well as for future advancement.

In a recent doctoral dissertation, "Factors Related to the Recruitment of Personnel," Dr. Byrne C. Fernelius found that a high proportion of recreation majors, when questioned about negative factors that had tended to deter them from entering this field, cited ". . . the lack of information about recreation." [12]

How can this situation be remedied?

The immediate response might be—through a concentrated public relations campaign on the part of those in the profession! Actually, there is a step that must precede this.

Recruitment Goals and Techniques

The very first task is to make sure that recreational programs become as imaginative, effective, well-organized, and far-reaching as possible. No public relations effort can or should succeed unless it represents a good product, and the best advertisement for any product is a satisfied user. Therefore, the total process of organizing and carrying on recreation services—whether in public, hospital, armed forces, or other settings— needs to be constantly studied, experimented with, and improved. Evaluation and meaningful research techniques should be used to insure successful operations. Staff members need to be carefully selected, oriented to their responsibilities; supervision and in-service training must be provided to make sure that their work is of the highest caliber possible. On every level, a sense of responsibility, of ethical concern, of professional obligation to do the best job possible, needs to pervade the functioning of the recreation department.

[12] Byrne C. Fernelius, "Recruitment Factors," *Recreation*, December, 1964, p. 527.

The next task is to identify the specific audiences that must be reached and to determine ways of getting a "message" to them.

Public Understanding of Recreation

Obviously, one audience which needs to achieve a better understanding of recreation is the public at large.

The recreation professional and his national organizations must make fullest possible use of the mass media of communication: the radio, press, magazines, television, and similar outlets, both to promote awareness of specific events or programs and to improve general understanding of the recreation field. He should take every opportunity to meet with other community officials, civic clubs, and service organizations or community councils.

Public Displays. Community recreation departments often find it possible to develop special displays or exhibits in libraries, museums, schools, or even large department store windows where thousands of people pass each day. These techniques are specially useful in promoting unusual events or highlights of the recreation program.

Films and Slide-Talks. Some recreation departments have prepared color slides with which to accompany talks to luncheon clubs or other groups. Others have actually made color films which effectively describe the work of their departments, in a convincing way.

Recruitment Literature. Brochures, pamphlets, and written career guides are useful as supplemental aids, when the recreation director actually addresses a group of high school students who may be direct recruitment prospects. They offer a means of following up the personal contact with facts, suggestions for follow-up, and additional needed information.

To be most effective in recruitment, it is necessary to reach the audience that is personally concerned directly: the high school junior or senior who is planning to go to college and is considering a number of possible career fields. There are several ways of reaching him. Recruitment pamphlets, mentioned above, are one such means. Others are:

Career Days. Thousands of secondary schools sponsor such events, or clinics, each year, often as part of "American Education Week." Speakers often come to these, representing all walks of life, businesses, and professions. Recreation executives should make a strong effort to appear on such programs to give the important facts about their field, and to give advice to boys and girls who are interested and seek further information. Often these sessions, or other "career" meetings which may be arranged independently by recreation directors in cooperation with guidance counselors, are highly successful and arouse much interest.

Early Identification and Training. Since successful recreation leadership demands certain personal qualities or traits, the alert recreation administrator should make an attempt to recognize those young people who may be working in his program as summer playground aids, or in similar capacities, who give promise of being gifted in this field. With his encouragement, and after exploration of the field, they may decide to go to a college or university that offers training in it.

High School Courses. A few secondary schools have actually offered courses for credit, in the area of recreation leadership.[13] These have been extremely useful in giving early experience and theoretical training to high school boys and girls who are interested in the recreation field. Those who have a high degree of interest and ability should be encouraged to continue in a college major program.

In-Service Recruitment. Since many individuals are actually employed in recreation functions, by public and voluntary agencies, although they have not had specialized training in this field, there is often the opportunity for "in-service recruitment." This means that such workers, *if* they have the capacity for completing an undergraduate or graduate degree in recreation, should be urged to explore this possibility— as a means of improving their professional ability and gaining advancement. Some agencies arrange schedules so that their employees may attend college on a part-time basis. Others, particularly public agencies or institutions serving the handicapped, actually assist their employees by paying their tuition costs.

Throughout the recruitment process, it should be borne in mind that, although public recreation administration has traditionally been considered a "man's field," there have been a number of highly successful women recreation executives. In addition, many of the specialized fields of recreation leadership, particularly in church work, rehabilitation settings, voluntary agencies, and armed forces recreation, offer many recreation opportunities for women.[14] This factor should be strongly considered when recruitment efforts are made.

Professional Organizations

Within the recreation field, there have been a number of important organizations that have contributed to research, professional education, mobilization of community support, improvement of personnel standards, and similar functions. Chief among these have been the National Recreation Association, which, although technically a service organization, has provided invaluable assistance to professionals in recreation for many

[13] See: Yale Newman: "Recreational Leadership in Secondary Schools," *Journal of Health, Physical Education and Recreation,* March, 1954, and "Recruiting, One Town's Problem," *Recreation,* March, 1959.

[14] Marjorie B. Miller, "Help Wanted: Female," *Recreation,* January, 1965, p. 38.

years, and the more recently formed American Recreation Society. The American Institute of Park Executives and the American Association for Health, Physical Education and Recreation have also been extremely effective. Other organizations, in somewhat more highly specialized fields, have included the American Camping Association, the Association of College Unions, the National Industrial Recreation Association, and similar groups. These and several other organizations joined together during the 1950's to form the Federation of National Professional Organizations for Recreation. Since then, in 1965, five of the leading organizations most directly concerned with the profession of recreation formally merged, with the name of the new body becoming the National Recreation and Park Association. The structure and goals of this new and highly influential organization are described in Chapter 17.

In terms of a code of ethics, deemed by many to be essential for professional status, the American Recreation Society has formulated such a code. It consists largely of a statement of philosophical purpose, obligations and responsibilities, rather than a sharply stated and enforceable delineation of professional behavior and functioning.

THE WORK OF THE RECREATION PROFESSIONAL

Having considered a wide variety of aspects of the recreation leader or administrator as a professional, it now becomes logical to examine his specific responsibilities. What kind of work is he called upon to perform on various levels of authority? First, the major job categories may be outlined. The following listing is drawn from personnel standards formulated by the National Recreation Association, with a number of additional job titles drawn from the manuals of individual recreation departments in municipalities around the country.

I. *EXECUTIVE LEVEL*
1. Recreation Superintendent (may also be called Director, or Commissioner); in a joint department, may be Superintendent of Parks and Recreation
2. Assistant Superintendent of Recreation

II. *SUPERVISORY LEVEL*
1. Recreation Supervisor (General)
2. Recreation Supervisor (Specialist); may be concerned with a particular type of activity, *or* with a special population group, with unique recreation needs

III. *CENTER DIRECTOR LEVEL*
1. Recreation Center Director (term might also apply to a Playground Director, suggesting responsibility for a large facility with a comprehensive program)
2. Assistant Center Director

IV) *LEADERSHIP LEVEL*

   1. Recreation Leader (General)
   2. Recreation Leader (Specialist) (Some job specifications list program specialists with more specific titles. Others refer to Senior Leaders, Leaders, and Assistant Leaders.)

V) *TRAINEE LEVEL*

   1. Recreation Intern
   2. Student Recreation Leader, or Junior Recreation Assistant (Some departments refer to Recreation Aides, or Attendants, who may or may not be regarded as "trainees" in the sense of being prepared for more responsible work.) [15]

Rather than deal with each of these levels in detail, this chapter selects three *major* categories: executive, supervisory, and leadership, and describes their functions, responsibilities, and qualifications. These specifications are drawn heavily from those prepared by the National Advisory Committee on Recruitment, Training, and Placement of Recreation Personnel of the National Recreation Association. However, they also reflect the personnel descriptions in use in a number of American cities, including Phoenix, Arizona; Fresno, California; Oceanside, New York; Winston-Salem, North Carolina; Evansville, Indiana; and others. The organization chart of the Topeka, Kansas, Recreation Commission illustrates how these three levels of professional service fit into the total picture.

JOB SPECIFICATIONS: EXECUTIVE LEVEL

Recreation Administrator

He may be called Superintendent, Director or Commissioner of Recreation. He is the chief executive officer in charge of a recreation department or division, and its personnel. He is responsible for planning, promoting, and administering a comprehensive recreation service for the entire community. His work is performed in accordance with policies determined or approved by a Recreation Board or Commission, and/or a City Manager or other municipal authority. He must, however, exercise independent judgment and ingenuity in accomplishing program objectives and interpreting the needs and desires of the public.

In a combined Park and Recreation Department, he may be in charge

---

[15] *Personnel Standards in Community Recreation Leadership* (New York: National Advisory Committee on Recruitment, Training, and Placement of Recreation Personnel of the National Recreation Association, 1965).

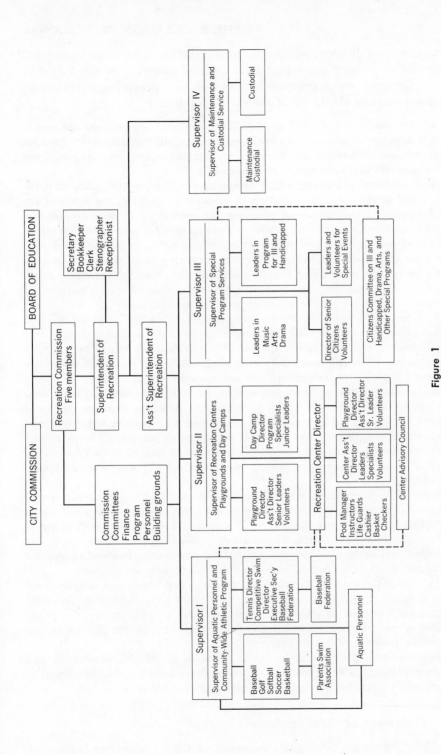

Figure 1

Topeka Recreation Commission Organization Chart, Topeka, Kansas

of a recreation division, within the total structure. In a school-sponsored department, he may serve under the general direction of the Board of Education and the Superintendent of Schools, providing a recreation program meeting the needs of the entire population.

(1) *Administrative Responsibilities:* (a) directs the total operation of the recreation department according to approved policies; (b) organizes and supervises an efficient administrative structure; (c) establishes and reviews procedures for most efficient operation at minimum cost.

(2) *Program Development:* (a) selects or approves a diversified program of activities and services, and new projects to be initiated, to meet the needs of the community; (b) supervises the planning and conduct of all program activities

(3) *Staff:* (a) develops personnel standards and employment procedures; (b) selects and employs departmental personnel; (c) assigns, trains, and supervises departmental personnel, conferring at frequent intervals with supervisory personnel who may have more direct contact with leadership staff; (d) maintains favorable attitudes and working relationships among staff members; (e) recruits and trains volunteers for subprofessional positions in department

(4) *Facilities and Areas:* (a) directs the acquisition, design, construction, and maintenance of facilities and areas under control of the recreation department; (b) requests and arranges for the use of public facilities owned by other departments, when appropriate; (c) determines policies for the use of recreation-owned facilities by civic groups and other public agencies

(5) *Evaluation and Research:* (a) prepares and presents immediate and long range plans to meet community needs in recreation, based on objective studies of local conditions; (b) uses evaluative techniques to determine effectiveness of recreation program services and staff, as continuing process; (c) keeps abreast of new developments and experimental projects in recreation field and, when appropriate, sponsors or cooperates in the conduct of research within his department

(6) *Finance:* (a) prepares, presents, and defends annual budget estimates or special financial requests; (b) directs, controls, and accounts for the expenditure of funds under approved budgetary allowances; (c) supervises the keeping of complete financial records; (d) furnishes periodic reviews of the recreation budget and outlays; (e) develops policies for establishing fees and charges for departmental services or activities, and supervises their application

(7) *Public and Community Relations:* (a) promotes and works with neighborhood or community-wide recreation councils or advisory groups; (b) establishes close working relationships with other organizations or community agencies in the field of social service; (c) interprets to the public at large the philosophy and specific program of his department

(8) *Records and Reports:* (a) maintains or supervises the keeping of complete and accurate departmental records in all areas; (b) prepares and issues annual or periodic reports for the community at large, or other uses

Statement of Qualifications

The recreation administrator needs to have comprehensive knowledge of recreation theory and philosophy, and the ability to interpret these meaningfully to others. He must possess important administrative skills relating to budgets and financial practices; training, selection, and supervision of leaders; planning, development, and maintenance of facilities; maintaining effective working relationships with representatives of other public, voluntary, or private agencies. Must possess the executive qualities of leadership, initiative, the ability to make decisions, inspire others, and communicate effectively both orally and in written form.

Minimum specific qualifications usually include a combination of the following: (a) graduation from a recognized college or university with a bachelor's degree in recreation leadership or administration, including supervised field work and/or completion of the requirements for a master's degree in recreation, or a related field, such as public administration; (b) proven successful experience in recreation supervision and/or administration, with a specified number of years according to the size of the community and scope of the recreation program involved.

JOB SPECIFICATIONS: SUPERVISORY LEVEL

Recreation Supervisor (General)

Recreation supervisors may have a general responsibility for a major district or geographical areas of service, or may have a more specific responsibility for a branch of service (either in terms of a particular kind of activity, such as arts and crafts, or sports and athletics, or in terms of serving a particular population group, such as the aged, members of a specific sex, or the handicapped). This analysis deals with the *general recreation supervisor*. He serves as a deputy to the chief recreation administrator in the planning, implementation, and administration of a comprehensive recreation program within his district. He must exercise responsible judgment in supervising the work of other employees, and reports to and receives guidance from the chief recreation administrator.

1. *Administrative Responsibilities:* (a) serves as a deputy to the recreation superintendent in all matters pertaining to recreation in his district; (b) administers the recreation program in his district, maintaining a high level of service
2. *Program Development:* (a) determines special needs within his district and recommends program services to meet these; (b) coordinates his program with that of the overall department, as well as other agencies' recreation services
3. *Staff:* (a) supervises, trains, and evaluates all recreation personnel assigned to his district through observations, visitations, meetings, and conferences; (b) demonstrates leadership skills and introduces new recreation program activities, materials, and equipment to staff members and others; (c) serves as a liaison between the chief administrator and subordinate employees
4. *Facilities and Areas:* (a) is responsible for the direct maintenance and use of all facilities, areas, and equipment in his district; (b) determines special needs

for facilities within his district and submits proposals or requests for these; (c) arranges for the cooperative exchange of facilities' use with other public and voluntary agencies

5. *Evaluation and Research:* (a) participates in departmental planning, evaluation, and research; (b) studies recreation needs and recommends action to meet them

6. *Finance:* (a) prepares budget estimates and work programs for his district; (b) carries out, according to departmental policies, the collection of, and accounting for, fees and charges that may be imposed for program services

7. *Public and Community Relations:* (a) assists in the interpretation of the recreation program to the community at large, or to his district; (b) when this is approved policy, submits releases and other publicity materials to news media; otherwise, submits them through departmental channels; (c) investigates and responds to public requests, suggestions, and complaints regarding recreation service; when necessary, forwards these to recreation superintendent

8. *Records and Reports:* (a) receives and reviews reports from subordinate staff members, taking or recommending necessary action; (b) assembles data for presentation to superintendent, for use in departmental report; (c) prepares special reports for his district, when necessary

Statement of Qualifications

The same qualifications that are applied to recreation administrators are usually applied to supervisors: the ability to interpret recreation theory and philosophy to others, to carry out a variety of administrative functions, to maintain effective working relationships with others, and, most important, to train and supervise professional and nonprofessional staff members under their jurisdiction. They are usually expected to have a higher degree of specific leadership skills, and less administrative competence and experience than the superintendent of recreation.

Minimum specific qualifications usually include a combination of bachelor's degree work in recreation leadership or administration, including supervised field work, with a minimum amount of successful professional experience. Increasingly, as pointed out earlier, recent college graduates have been hired for supervisory positions; they have, however, had a variety of summertime, part-time, and field-work experiences as part of their training.

JOB SPECIFICATIONS: LEADERSHIP LEVEL

Recreation Leader (Specialist)

Like the recreation supervisor, the recreation leader may either be a general leader or a specialist, who provides leadership services related to one program activity or a group of closely connected activities, such as arts and crafts, sports and games, performing arts, or social recreation. This analysis deals with the *specialist,* who works directly under the administrative supervision of a center or playground director, or a district supervisor. He may lead programs at one or more centers or areas, and may be responsible for overseeing the work of nonprofessional employees.

His duties are much more directly related to face-to-face group leadership than to the functions described earlier for the administrator or supervisor. He is expected to perform the following functions:

1. Promote and interpret recreation of a specific type, organizing and leading groups in this activity, and helping participants to reach the maximum values possible through successful involvement in it
2. Arrange for special tournaments, exhibitions, public demonstrations or shows in the activity, as part of local or community-wide programs
3. Recommend and assist in the optimum use of facilities and equipment necessary for the activity; maintain all needed safety and health precautions necessary for the activity
4. Advise and assist other staff members, including volunteer or subprofessional leaders, in working with this activity; may offer in-service training courses in it
5. Keep records of attendance, equipment inventories, financial charges and receipts, accidents, incidents, special programs, and other matters requiring detailed recording; submit these to center director or supervisor
6. Assist in the evaluation of program services and consult with the center director, supervisor, or administrator regarding the place of his specialized service within the total program structure
7. Substitute, when necessary, for the center director or district supervisor, acting in his absence

Statement of Qualifications

These tend to be less concerned with administrative or interpretive abilities than the positions previously described. Instead, they stress the personal ability to direct the activity successfully, to work effectively with groups at both beginning and advanced levels, to promote and organize the activity, and maintain effective working relationships with others.

Educational qualifications frequently include holding a college degree related to the particular activity field in which the leader is a specialist. Additionally, it may be required that the individual have taken courses equivalent to a minor in recreation leadership, or have had appropriate leadership experience equivalent to a three-months period of field work. The alternative of a bachelor's degree in recreation, plus special training and experience in the activity area may also be acceptable.

JOB SPECIFICATIONS IN OTHER SETTINGS

In addition to public recreation departments, there are obviously a number of other kinds of job settings. One of the widest fields of employment in recreation has to do with providing services for the ill and handicapped, in community or institutional settings.

The California State Personnel Board gives the following job specifications for the position of Recreation Therapist:

> A Recreation Therapist assists with the recreation therapy program of a state hospital; leads, instructs, and encourages patients in a program of individual and group activities of a physical, social, and cultural nature such as indoor and outdoor games and sports, dances, parties, dramatics, picnics, and special interest clubs; supervises entertainments and movies and assists in planning programs for special occasions; with the therapeutic team, plans treatment goals for specific patients; as assigned, coordinates the activities program of a group of wards including simple crafts, games, social and musical activities, and instructs ward personnel in basic activity skills; observes patients' reactions and keeps clinical notes and records; and does other work as required.

Educational requirements (for admission to the competitive examination for these positions) include graduation from a recognized college with major work in recreation or recreation therapy. The major must have included supervised field work.

In another rehabilitative setting, the National Institute of Health Hospital at Bethesda, Maryland, the following job description and statement of duties is given for the position of Recreation Specialist (General):

> Under the general direction of the Chief, Patient Activity Section, serves as a Recreation Specialist, and in this capacity is responsible for the organization, execution and evaluation of a comprehensive recreation program. . . . Is responsible for a broad range of activities designed to meet the physical and psychological needs, interests, and capabilities of adult and children patients which is consistent with the research objectives being undertaken in the Clinical Center, National Institute of Health. . . .

Specific duties are described as follows:

> . . . directing parties, musical and dramatic productions, television programs, sightseeing tours, sports, games, arts and crafts, and similar activities. . . .

> Establishing and maintaining contact with representatives of community volunteer groups, local organizations such as theatre groups, musicians unions, Armed Services bands, and other groups, working closely with them in order to integrate and utilize such groups within the planned recreation program. . . .

Organizes, executes, and evaluates specific recreation programs and activities for particular patients or patient groups who are isolated or otherwise confined over a period of time within their specific research study area. In this capacity works closely with physicians and nurses in meeting the recreation needs of the patient, adapting all possible tools to their physical and psychological capabilities. . . .

Is responsible for the ordering and maintenance of material and equipment necessary to carry out the planned recreation program. Exercises ingenuity and originality in the selection and adaptation of tools, motivation and techniques within specific settings. . . . Constantly analyzes and evaluates the overall recreation program. . . .

JOB SPECIFICATIONS IN FEDERAL SETTINGS

There are many recreation positions opening up at all times within the armed forces, for civilian employees. For example, the following Civil Service job descriptions apply to Army Special Services positions:

Service Club Program. Recreation Specialist (Social Activities) Grade 5. Female, single; minimum age, 21; degree from an accredited college (major in recreation, physical education, social psychology, social sciences, music, art, dramatics, or related areas); leadership ability demonstrated through work experience or extracurricular activities. Priority consideration is given to applicants who have at least six months of successful work experience.

Entertainment Program. Recreation Specialist (Drama and Music) Grade 8. Female, single; male, single preferred; minimum age, 21; degree from an accredited college (major in dramatics or music) and 18 months of experience in teaching dramatics or music, or in directing and supervising amateurs or professionals in such activities. Experience as an entertainer or performer is nonqualifying.

Sports Program. Recreation Specialist (Sports) Grade 9. Male, single preferred; minimum age, 21; degree from an accredited college (major in physical education); two years of experience in organizing and directing a comprehensive recreational sports program. Experience as an athlete, professional or otherwise, is nonqualifying.

On another level of federal employment, Recreation Resources Specialists who are hired by the Bureau of Outdoor Recreation of the Department of the Interior and other federal agencies have the following job responsibilities:

Recreation Resources Specialists provide technical advice, guidance, and assistance to federal, state, and local governments and nongovernmental organizations in (1) appraising needs for new or expanded outdoor recreation resources, e.g., land areas, facilities, or program developments, to meet the expanding needs or changing habits of the using public; (2) identifying and classifying existing or potential outdoor recreation areas; and (3) evaluating potential or proposed recreation resources in terms of the relative merits and long term importance of such competing demands on the area as water, soil, or wildlife conservation. . . .

They advise on such matters as legislation relating to recreation resources, facilities, and programs, and the formulation of standards and criteria for the selection and use of outdoor recreation areas. They are responsible for the coordination and integration of the efforts of separate governmental and nongovernmental organizations engaged in planning and administering broadly conceived long-range outdoor recreation programs. They evaluate and make recommendations regarding the nature and extent of federal support which should be given to such plans and programs.

Some Recreation Resources Specialists may participate in international work by attending conferences and advising foreign government or other organizations regarding outdoor recreation resource planning and program development matters.

Similarly, job descriptions might be presented for positions in industrial or union recreation departments, in voluntary agencies (religious or otherwise, chiefly in the youth-serving category), college student-life departments and student unions, camping programs, and a host of similar programs.

IN CONCLUSION: THE MARKS OF A PROFESSIONAL

This chapter has traced the development of the recreation profession, and has subjected it to careful scrutiny based on certain important criteria that must be applied to any professional field. Professional education has been described, proposals offered for more effective recruitment procedures, and job specifications for a variety of positions in several settings have been outlined. At this point, in conclusion, it is appropriate to ask—"What sort of person should the recreation professional be?" Howard Danford made an excellent statement several years ago; here are several passages from that description:

1. He is motivated primarily by ideals of service rather than by money. He is in recreation because he loves it and he would not be in any other type of work even if he could be. He believes that people, not activities or facilities, are the most important thing in the world and that the basic purpose of recreation is to enrich the lives of people. . . .
2. He is an educated man who has undergone a prolonged period of preparation for his work. . . . He knows the values which should be sought through recreation in a democracy, and he is deeply committed to democratic ideals and values. He constantly seeks to improve himself professionally. . . .
3. He voluntarily joins his professional societies or associations, pays his dues, attends meetings, and contributes both time and energy to furthering the work of his profession and elevating its standards. . . .
4. He conducts himself at all times in such a manner as to enhance the prestige

and dignity of his profession. He knows that people judge a profession by the individuals who are in it and that undignified conduct on his part will hurt his profession in the eyes of the public. His professional life and conduct are regulated by a code of behavior based on moral and ethical principles. . . .

5. The professional man seeks to exclude from the profession those who are not qualified to enter it. He is interested in the exercise by the state, or by the profession itself, or by both, of some form of control over who may enter into at least the most responsible recreation positions. He wants no quacks, frauds, or unfit individuals in the profession.

6. He is a team player, not a prima donna. He prefers cooperation as a way of life. He works with all agencies and individuals in the community on matters of common concern. . . . He is motivated primarily by the ideal of public service. . . .

7. He insists on high standards of excellence in his work; he is not satisfied with mediocrity but is constantly working to upgrade his professional performance. . . . He is motivated by a spark of divine discontent . . . he seeks perfection although he never quite achieves it. . . .

8. And finally, the professional man in recreation enjoys life. He has fun; he is no sour-puss, no stuffed shirt, no kill-joy. For how can he lead others in joyous living if he doesn't live joyously himself? . . .[16]

SUGGESTED QUESTIONS FOR DISCUSSION

1. "Recreation today meets the criteria of a profession." Discuss this statement from both positive and negative points of view.

2. What methods currently exist, and what projects are under way, to upgrade the quality of recreation professionals? Which of these do you feel are most likely to be effective?

3. Outline the major personnel levels in professional recreation service, and indicate the types of responsibilities and functions commonly assigned to each level.

4. Develop and defend a proposal for more effective recruitment in the recreation profession. Whose responsibility should recruitment in recreation be?

[16] Howard G. Danford, "The Marks of a Professional Man in Recreation," *Journal of Health, Physical Education and Recreation*, November, 1960, p. 31.

Chapter 3

Leadership and Group Dynamics

In Chapter 2, professional service in recreation was described, and the specific job responsibilities of professional workers in this field were outlined.

It was made clear that the term "leader" applies in a technical sense only to one level of worker—that is the face-to-face group leader or specialist who provides direct leadership services. People on other levels may be called "superintendents," "directors," "supervisors," or "center directors," but are not usually called "leaders" as such.

Why, then, does this book—and why do many other texts—focus on the words "leader" or "leadership" as a vital concern?

The answers are simple. First, direct program leadership represents the firing-line of any recreation agency. It is here that service is rendered to the public, and it is toward this end that all administrative or supervisory efforts are directed. Second, *all* who work in the field of recreation are called upon to provide leadership in a broad sense. For example:

1. The superintendent, or top executive, must provide leadership within the community at large, if he is to operate as an effective spokesman for his field, and gain community support. He must also exert leadership with other municipal officials on comparable levels of authority, with his advisory board or commission, and with those who work for him. So, although he is not usually directly concerned with recreational leadership of groups of participants, the administrator is a leader.

2. Similarly, the supervisor acts as a leader of others. He motivates, guides, stimulates, directs, and teaches those who work under his supervision.

3. The recreation leader—whether a specialist or general group leader—is, of course, directly concerned with groups that are carrying on activities; this is the commonest understanding of the term.

Thus, leadership is viewed as a direct concern of all levels of the recreation profession, just as it is in many other areas of business and public life, including the armed forces, industry, politics, and the sciences. Simply broken down, the leader in recreation may have two kinds of concerns: (a) involvement with task or work-oriented groups that are planning programs, developing projects, undergoing training or providing services themselves; and, (b) providing direct recreation services to clubs, groups, those on the playground or in the community center.

In each of these settings, effective leadership is essential. Research studies have shown a direct correlation between the success of a recreation program and the presence of skilled leadership in adequate numbers.[1]

Now, exactly what is leadership?

A dictionary definition suggests that a leader is ". . . a person or thing that leads; directing, commanding, or guiding head, as of a group or activity. . . ."[2]

Ordway Tead has defined leadership as ". . . the activity of influencing people to cooperate toward some goal which they come to find desirable."[3]

Two social group work authors, Wilson and Ryland, state, "Leadership is a natural phenomenon in group life, a dynamic process which emerges in the interaction of individuals, one with another."[4]

In terms of leadership within the field of recreation, Howard Danford has provided a good working definition:

[1] *The Effect of Increased Leadership and Its Relation to Interest and Participation* (Skokie, Illinois: Skokie Park District, 1961), p. 4. For a brief summary, see: Reynold E. Carlson, Theodore R. Deppe, and Janet R. MacLean, *Recreation in American Life* (Belmont, Calif.: Wadsworth, 1963), p. 322.

[2] *Webster's New World Dictionary of the American Language* (New York: World Publishing, 1962), p. 831.

[3] Ordway Tead, *The Art of Leadership* (New York: McGraw-Hill, 1935), p. 20.

[4] Gertrude Wilson and Gladys Ryland, *Social Group Work Practice* (Boston: Houghton Mifflin Company, 1949), p. vii.

Leadership is a process of stimulating and aiding groups to determine, or to accept, common goals, and to carry out effectively the measures leading to the attainment of these goals. . . . Leadership in recreation is concerned with all aspects of the situation which help make it possible to achieve the objectives important to the department and to the group.[5]

In another recent text on recreation leadership, Jay Shivers refers to leadership as:

. . . an ability which causes other people to become aware of the person attempting to lead, to recognize the information or idea which he is trying to present, and to move or act on this basis toward some predetermined end. The leader must be capable of getting other people to recognize him, to understand what he is attempting to communicate or trying to do, and to follow his advice. Further, he must provide his followers with reasons for accepting his ideas for planned or immediate action. Leadership is based upon influence, and influence is derived from understanding the needs of others.[6]

Thus, we see leadership defined first as a function, then as an activity, then a phenomenon, then a process, and finally an ability. While each of these views has merit, this text will regard leadership as *a quality, or a combination of qualities, which gives an individual the ability to work effectively with groups in a process of joint planning, decision-making, or program service.* "Working effectively" may imply in some cases playing a forceful and authoritative role, i.e., being "in command." In other cases, the nature of the leadership that is called for will be much more subtle and indirect.

Trait Theory of Leadership

The notion that leadership consists of the possession of certain personal qualities that are essential to the successful performance of the leadership task is not a new one. In essence, it suggests that there is a certain combination of traits—intelligence, courage, warmth and enthusiasm, sensitivity, energy, professional drive, responsibility, and the like—that underlies leadership within a given field, or in general. In some discussions, it has been suggested that leadership represents an inborn, indefinable trait in itself, an almost mystic quality that makes men follow the individual who possesses it. Others stress that the qualities making for successful leadership can be learned.

After a period of wide acceptance, the "trait theory" of leadership was challenged by researches that demonstrated that only a few of the

[5] Howard Danford, *Creative Leadership in Recreation* (Boston: Allyn and Bacon, 1964), p. 80.

[6] Jay S. Shivers, *Leadership in Recreational Service* (New York: Macmillan, 1963), p. 30.

traits commonly referred to as components of leadership (such as adaptability, aggressiveness, ambition, or ascendance) were found widely in studies of leadership in varied settings.[7] In a research report critical of the "trait theory," Stogdill comments:

> . . . the evidence suggests that leadership is a relationship that exists between persons in a social situation, and that persons who are leaders in one situation may not necessarily be leaders in other situations.[8]

Situational Theory of Leadership

The idea that leadership is largely a *situational* matter, and that who is (or becomes) a leader depends mainly on the requirements of the task at hand, has evolved as a theory of leadership. Jenkins points out that there is considerable evidence indicating that there is great divergence in leadership behavior in different situations. The only common factor appears to be that leaders in a particular field need and tend to possess superior general or technical competence or knowledge in that area. General intelligence does not appear to be an invariable element in such competence.[9]

As an extension of the "situational theory," it has been pointed out that leadership represents a function of the entire group, in the sense that any or all of the members of the group may perform specific acts of leadership at different times. The concept that leadership is found in what an individual *does*, rather than what he *is* as a person or what he *knows*, and that it is a widely shared function of the group, is known as the "functional theory" of leadership.

Functional Theory of Leadership

Ross and Hendry have described this theory well, in the following passage:

> In essence, the view represented is that it is in the nature of a group property. Leadership resides not primarily and certainly not exclusively in an individual leader. Rather, leadership is viewed as a function of group structure. We would do well, if we follow this line of analysis, to speak of the leadership structure of a group and not of the leader or the leaders of a group.[10]

[7] Matthew B. Miles, *Learning to Work in Groups* (New York: Teachers College, Columbia University, 1959), p. 16.

[8] R. M. Stogdill, "Personal Factors Associated with Leadership: A Survey of the Literature," quoted in Miles, *op. cit.,* p. 16.

[9] W. O. Jenkins, "A Review of Leadership Studies with Particular Reference to Military Problems," quoted in Miles, *op. cit.,* p. 17.

[10] Murray G. Ross and Charles E. Hendry, *New Understandings of Leadership* (New York: Association Press, 1957), p. 22.

Miles suggests certain criteria which may be used to judge the effectiveness of leadership acts, in terms of meeting the functional needs of groups:

> *Augmentation:* Does the leadership act augment or facilitate group members' positive search for need satisfaction? Or does it accentuate the negative—threaten people with punishment of loss of present satisfactions if they do not perform as desired by the leader?

> *Effectiveness and Efficiency:* Does the leadership act aid the group to do its work rapidly and well (effectiveness), besides improving internal working relations (efficiency)? Or does it tend to evoke a group product of poor quality and feelings of low morale and antagonism? [11]

Recognizing the value of the "situational" and "functional" theories, it is important to point out that they are based heavily on researches that were carried out in fields very different from recreational service—in many cases military units or task group experiments. The most meaningful view of effective recreation leadership would have to be one which combined elements of all three approaches.

COMPOSITE THEORY OF RECREATION LEADERSHIP

First, it must be stated that within different work-oriented or program service-oriented recreation situations, different kinds of leadership skills or approaches are called for. Thus, in different settings, leaders with varying qualities and abilities may prove to be successful.

Second, it is clear that certain recurrent functions in such groups may be carried on by the leader, *or* by different members of the group. Thus, leadership is a shared process and, at times, will be in the hands of other individuals than the formal or appointed leader.

Third, it should be pointed out that leaders within the field of recreation typically are found to possess certain qualities, and, if they are to be highly successful, must have these traits to a considerable degree. Sessoms, in a survey of leadership functions in public, voluntary, industrial, and hospital recreation agencies in North Carolina, found the following qualities to be the most important: (a) moral character; (b) awareness of democratic ideals; (c) good health; (d) professional proficiency; (e) intellectual capacities; and (f) social capacities.[12]

These suggest that needed traits may fall into three categories: general personality characteristics, attitude toward people and ability to work effectively with them, and qualities which have direct functional importance in recreation.

[11] Miles, *op. cit.,* pp. 18–19.
[12] H. Douglas Sessoms, "An Analysis of the Leadership Functions Performed within Various Recreation Agencies and Their Effect upon the Development of Recreation as a Profession" (Raleigh, North Carolina: North Carolina Recreation Commission, 1959).

1) *General Personal Characteristics.* These might include such traits as enthusiasm, intellectual capacity, initiative, imagination, personal integrity, a sense of humor, sound emotional health, and confidence.

2) *Interpersonal Relationship Traits.* Here it is important that the leader like and respect others, that he is sensitive to their needs and feelings, that he is able to work effectively with others, and that he operates well within a group or team situation.

3) *Qualities of Functional Importance.* This might include having needed skills and abilities, having a sound philosophy of recreation, the ability to communicate well, to make sound decisions, to organize effectively, and to command respect as a leader.

In terms of the leader's attitude toward members of groups with whom he must work, it is clear that effective human relations must be built upon a foundation of mutual respect and faith in the dignity and worth of human beings as individuals. Beyond this, in working with people, the leader must be intensely aware of the nature of groups and group processes; this represents a form of knowledge and interpersonal skill in which good will is not enough. Instead, effective group leadership can be learned and developed. First, the leader needs to be aware of the nature of groups as such.

THE NATURE OF GROUPS

What are groups? Krech and Crutchfield offer the following definition:

> The term group . . . refers to two or more people who bear an explicit *psychological relationship to one another.* This means that for each member of the group the other members must exist in some more or less immediate psychological way so that their behavior and their characteristics influence him.[13]

Obviously, there are many forms of groups to which most of us belong in our lives: families, groups of friends, neighborhood associations or clubs, church groups, employment-centered groups, political clubs, hobby groups or associations, as well as other broader kinds of involvements. These may be classified in different ways. A common means of classification has been to assign them to "primary" or "secondary" categories, depending on the degree of intimacy and closeness of interdependence and interaction in the group. Another type of analysis has been the *compulsory* group (in which membership is compelled), the *motivated* group (which one may join voluntarily but in which there are

[13] D. Krech and R. S. Crutchfield, *Theory and Problems of Social Psychology* (New York: McGraw-Hill, 1948), p. 18.

elements of pressure or desire for approbation), and the *voluntary* group (which one joins because of inner need or deep-seated interest).

Most groups in the field of recreation tend to be of a voluntary nature. These in turn may be classified as socially or culturally homogeneous in nature, multiactivity, single activity, or therapy-centered. In general, recreation groups tend either to be socially or culturally homogeneous, and of a social club type, *or* groups in which the activity or activities to be carried on offer the primary appeal.

No matter what the nature of the group, it is essential that the leader be aware of its inner processes. These are commonly referred to as "group dynamics."

UNDERSTANDING GROUP DYNAMICS

Simply stated, this refers to the kind and quality of the interaction among members of the group. In other words, what is the nature of acceptance or rejection of members of the group? Are there factions or constellations of the members which exclude others? How are decisions arrived at? How are problems solved? How is communication carried on? Does the group have a harmonious climate—i.e., do people accept, like and work well with each other, or is there a climate of bickering and personal antagonism? Does work get accomplished and projects get carried out, or do people refuse to take assignments or live up to their responsibilities?

The awareness of the group process is extremely important, not only in terms of how successful it is as an aggregate of people, but also in terms of its effect upon individuals. It is known that the way in which individuals learn, and their speed and retention of learning and effective problem-solving, are definitely influenced by the nature of the group experience. The group strongly influences the individual's formation of attitudes, levels of aspiration, self-perception and self-insight.

In all this, the atmosphere or climate of the group, its degree of cohesion, or interdependence, and the presence of democratic leadership play an extremely important role.

In working with groups, what are the tasks or functions of the recreation leader? First, it must be stressed that they are somewhat different from those of the social group worker. The recreation leader tends to work with somewhat larger groups which are more fluid in membership, and which are more oriented toward activity than they are toward an intensive concern with group relationships.

Nonetheless, the leader has certain functions to play, both in the task or work-oriented group, and in the activity, or program-oriented group.

Functions in the Work-Oriented Group

[In a group which is concerned with exploring problems, making plans, developing recommendations or carrying out similar tasks, the following functions may be carried out by the group leader, or may be shared by other members of the group:]

Initiating: keeping the group action moving, or getting it under way (example: suggesting steps to be taken, pointing out goals)

Regulating: influencing the direction and tempo of the group's work (example: summarizing, pointing out time limits, restating goals)

Informing: bringing information or opinion to the group

Supporting: creating an emotional climate which holds the group together and harmonizes difficulties

Evaluating: helping group to evaluate its decisions, goals, or procedures (example: testing for consensus, noting group processes) [14]

Throughout, in any such task-oriented process, the leader must do the following: (a) help the group members define the limits of the problem they face, and decide which aspect of it they intend to attack; (b) encourage and make it possible for all group members to express their ideas; (c) to maintain an atmosphere in which cooperation is stressed and tensions or fear eliminated; (d) keep the discussion or other efforts of the group focused on the work to be accomplished, moving steadily from theoretical considerations to practical outcomes and steps.

Functions in the Program-Oriented Group

When a recreation leader is in charge of an activity-oriented, or program-oriented group, his task at the outset may appear to be rather narrow, or limited. He may believe that all he is expected to do is to coach a sport, teach a craft activity, or lead the group in a dance session. He is likely to find out that even in such an assignment, there are problems of interpersonal relationships, deciding on scheduling, special events, programs or exhibitions, irregular attendance, poor morale, and similar concerns. Thus, even in an activity-centered group, group dynamics represent an important concern.

Beyond this, when the leader is working with a social group, in which the dynamics of interpersonal relationship are more important than the particular activity the group happens to be carrying on, he will find that he assumes a number of varied roles. In such a situation, the

[14] J. R. Gibb and L. M. Gibb, *Applied Group Dynamics,* quoted in Miles, *op. cit.,* p. 20.

leader may need to assume, or to help group members assume, any of the following roles:

Policy-maker: helping the group make decisions regarding questions relating to goals, membership, meeting time and place, dues and similar matters.

Planner: helping the group develop specific plans for activities, programs, trips, special events, and other projects

Organizer: helping the group evolve ways of structuring themselves, of making concrete plans for action

Resource Person: acting as a source of information, knowledge, skills, and contacts

Stimulator: inspiring the group and helping to get things going; acting as a source of ideas, suggestions, and motivation

As an adult (when working with children and youth) or as an outsider, the leader may also assume some special roles that members of the group cannot readily assume themselves:

Referee: helping the group resolve conflicts and disagreements

Disciplinarian: in a constructive sense, helping the group members develop rules and other forms of control and impose them of their own volition; exerting controls himself when necessary

Group Symbol: acting as an adult image, or model, whom group members admire and respect, and whose values and behavior they emulate

Spokesman: acting as a spokesman for the members of the group, either in the sponsoring agency, or in the community at large

When these functions of the activity-oriented recreation leader are examined, it becomes apparent that he needs to have a clear philosophical orientation, if he is to operate wisely and effectively. Sound judgment must be complemented by leadership behavior that is designed to achieve desirable goals.

How may this leadership behavior be developed? We tend to speak of the "democratic" group leader. What does this mean?

APPROACHES TO GROUP LEADERSHIP

During the 1930's and 1940's an extensive series of researches in group leadership techniques were carried on by Lewin, Lippitt, and White, among others.[15] These tended to identify three major orientations or leadership approaches: the *autocratic,* or highly authoritarian; the *laissez-faire,* or permissive; and the *democratic* approach, in which

15 Ronald Lippitt and Ralph K. White, "An Experimental Study of Leadership and Group Life," in Guy E. Swanson *et al.* (eds.), *Readings in Social Psychology* (New York: Henry Holt and Company, 1952), pp. 340–355. See also: Kurt Lewin, Ronald Lippitt, and Ralph K. White, "Patterns of Aggressive Behavior in Experimentally Created 'Social Climates,'" in P. H. Harriman (ed.), *Twentieth Century Psychology* (New York: The Philosophical Library, 1946), p. 202.

the leader offers support, advice, technical assistance, and similar forms of help but strives also to have group members take over the functions of decision-making, planning, and other group tasks.

For some years, the democratic approach was identified without qualification as the most appropriate form of recreation leadership. As the situational theory of leadership gained prominence, however, it became apparent that no single approach could apply to all group situations.

In some situations, dependent on the immediate needs or evident characteristics of the group, an autocratic or laissez-faire approach may provide the most sensible and productive plan of attack. This does not mean that the leader believes that they are desirable in terms of achieving long term goals, but that they are strategic in terms of present situational factors. For example, group members who are accustomed to strong, authoritarian controls will not react in a completely favorable way to a democratic form of leadership when they first encounter it. They are likely to misinterpret it as weakness on the part of the leader. They must gradually grow to understand and accept it, and be weaned away from autocratic leadership. Similarly, there may be circumstances when a permissive approach is the wisest one.

In general, when the group being served is a very large one, when the emphasis is on instruction in a particular skills area, or on carrying out projects successfully, or when there are problems of behavior or safety, the leader may have to veer toward the authoritarian approach. On the other hand, if the group is small, when it meets regularly with the same membership, when it is concerned with developing its own program, the leader may assume a more permissive role.

In any case, there are certain general guidelines the leader may follow, no matter what the specific circumstances of the group.

GUIDELINES FOR LEADERSHIP

1) The leader is chiefly concerned with people, rather than activities. His primary concern must be what happens to the program participants, rather than the overt successful accomplishment of program objectives stated in terms of attendance, activities consummated, etc.

2) He must have a coherent set of human values, which sees each person as an individual with dignity and worth, who needs understanding, support, and encouragement. The recreational group experience offers an opportunity to make these values meaningful in practice, and to help shape the attitudes of group members in a constructive way.

3) He must be alert to group organization and group processes. He should be ready to provide assistance when it is needed, or to withdraw when group members are able to provide the needed leadership them-

selves. This principle of alternative assistance and withdrawal, skillfully applied, helps the leader become an *enabler*—rather than a *director*—of groups.

(4) Recognizing that each person is an individual, with his own interests, personal background, needs, drives, and ways of behaving, the leader must be prepared to understand and accept a wide variety of behaviors. To a degree, he needs to be able to recognize and understand the meaning of variant behavior, including hostility, withdrawal, compulsive actions, and the like, although he is not expected to be an expert psychologist.

(5) He must start wherever the individuals comprising the group are (in terms of their attitudes, skills, and patterns of behavior) and gradually help them move in positive directions, which they understand and accept.

Within this total framework, it is helpful for the leader to establish a set of personal objectives, toward which he is constantly working. These might include the following: (a) helping group members discover new and rewarding interests, skills, and personal capacities; i.e., broaden their recreation horizons; (b) help group members gain increased social sensitivity, acceptance of others, and ways of behaving effectively and constructively in terms of interpersonal relationships; (c) help group members become capable of planning and carrying out their own programs.

GUIDELINES FOR WORKING WITH A GROUP OVER A PERIOD OF TIME

In addition to having a general philosophical orientation, or to possessing specific activity leadership skills, it is helpful to have the leader recognize a number of functions or tasks that will face him as he works with a group over a period of time. These include:

1. Getting to know the members of the group, having them begin to accept and gain confidence in him as a leader
2. Helping the group examine and clarify its goals and purposes, and to develop a logical organizational structure: meeting time, place, membership arrangements, etc.
3. Helping the program get under way, whether it consists of a single kind of activity or a mixture of social activities, discussions, trips, hobbies, and other events, which may entail providing direct activity leadership himself, helping group members take on this task, or arranging to bring in outside leaders
4. Helping the group maintain a high level of morale and interest, with regular attendance and program continuity
5. Helping the group deal with problems as they come up, including personality clashes, program-planning disagreements, relations with the sponsoring agency, or similar concerns

6. Helping the group plan special projects, trips, dances, joint meetings, or other single major events

7. Dealing with problems of discipline or antisocial behavior himself, when this can be done successfully, or referring the problem to a supervisory level, when this seems necessary

8. Helping emergent leaders within the group recognize their own capacities and take on responsibilities.

9. Helping group members evaluate their process and program, with an eye to constant improvement of the total experience

EFFECTIVE AND INEFFECTIVE LEADERSHIP: A CASE ANALYSIS

Often, guidelines and principles, when stated as such, tend to have less meaning or impact than actual case studies. It might therefore be appropriate to examine the nature of effective and ineffective leadership within a given group situation. The following paper, written by a graduate recreation student at Teachers College, Columbia University, presents such a contrast. It is presented almost in its entirety; a few minor passages have been deleted:

> One of my daughters, during her eighth and ninth years, belonged to two different Brownie troops in two different locales. Her membership in one was very salutary, but her membership in the other was unrewarding. . . . The most important element, in my judgment, was the difference in leadership. . . .
>
> The first Brownie troop was led by two women who really believed that the girls could and would have a meaningful experience, not only as Brownies, or as potential Girl Scouts, but as citizens. They both acquainted themselves with the philosophy behind scouting and felt the girls would grow as people if they themselves shared this ideology.
>
> They believed in the positive value of a group recreative experience which embodied immediate goals for the group as well as a far-reaching ideology. Both women had attended indoctrination sessions at the regional scout office and both were familiar with the history of the movement. Although neither woman had had much previous experience leading a group of children, each liked children and wanted the experience to be successful. They met frequently to outline their program and to determine in which areas one might assume dominance, and in which areas they could be equally responsible. Before the children themselves were informed that a Brownie Troop was going to be formed, they informally sounded out all the mothers of all the girls in the grade and explained why they felt a troop was appropriate and how they felt the girls could benefit.
>
> After the meeting place and the time of meeting was established, they sent an attractive notice to the three classes involved, and invited the girls who might be interested to attend a meeting, at which the purpose of the forma-

tion of the troop and a description of what the girls could expect if they became members was outlined. Although the facilities—the kindergarten school room—were not the best, they were centrally located for all the children. The schoolyard was used by many other children, but one of the mothers offered the use of her backyard for games and parties. Many of the other mothers offered either facilities or services, because the leaders had . . . established excellent public relations.[16]

The author goes on to comment that she felt that these two adult leaders possessed strong leadership qualities. They related well to each other and to the children, and were aware of the children's interests, desires, and needs. They were interested in developing the children's social and creative potentials. They met together each week, two or three days before the troop assembled, to discuss the programs that had been held, to review the responses of children to earlier experiences, and to plan new activities. They had a flair, she felt, for making the scout rituals dramatic and exciting, rather than silly or humdrum. They exercised democratic leadership by letting the children take over as many responsibilities as they could handle, and they made sure that each child had an equal opportunity to participate. They set the tone for the behavior of the group by their friendliness and interest.

They were both fair and firm. Although the group had some very lively youngsters, there were no disciplinary problems and the leaders were successful at enticing the more reticent girls to participate without coercing or embarrassing them in any way. They functioned as enablers, providing assistance to the group when the children asked for it. They understood the kinds of judgments and decisions which were appropriate for children of that age to make; they understood also which administrative duties were too difficult for the children to handle. As much as was possible, the children conducted the troop with stimulation and guidance from the adults.

So successful was the experience that the author comments, "Although we moved away from the area eight years ago (prior to the writing of this paper), my daughter still corresponds with her friends from this troop, although she retains no contact with our immediate neighbor's children. She still refers to this experience as the happiest group experience she has ever had." The author then continues:

After we moved away from the area, my daughter wanted to join a new troop. The community into which we had moved had a fine Scout House with more than adequate indoor and outdoor facilities. None of the children she knew were Brownies, and when I called the Girl Scout Council, I was told that there was difficulty in starting a troop because there was no leadership available. I did not want to be a leader in my daughter's troop, and I

[16] Hope Cramer, unpublished course paper, Teachers College, Columbia University, 1964. Used by permission.

managed to get two women to agree to lead the troop with a promise that I would assist them with the program.

I was rather uneasy from the start, but I hoped that they would enjoy the experience once the troop was formed. They did not devote much energy to public relations or laying the groundwork before the troop met. I perhaps was not forceful enough in offering my services, since I did not know them very well and was not called upon for advice. My daughter managed to spread some of her enthusiasm around, and a group of girls did meet at the Scout House to form a troop. I do not believe these women had the inherent qualities of leadership or a real interest in leading young girls. They did little if any planning ahead for the meetings, and had constant disciplinary problems. They shouted to get order and frequently contradicted each other. I attended the investiture, and felt that the spirit of the ritual had been lost completely; nor had the girls been imbued with any of the ideology of the Girl Scout movement.

When the leaders complained that they were glorified baby-sitters and that these children "don't need this experience," they reflected their inability to relate to the principles behind scouting and to the children involved. It was especially sad to me because I had pressured these women to become leaders and to assume roles for which they were unprepared as well as uninterested. As I look back, I feel that I also did the children a disservice, and they would have been better off if no troop had been formed. After several months, the troop disbanded. My daughter never again wanted to join the Girl Scouts.

I think these women failed because they lacked the necessary personality traits for leadership. They did not understand how to inculcate group morale, how to achieve cohesiveness within the group, or democratic participation in a group activity. They failed also to establish any rapport with the parents of the children, and did not develop any kind of a meaningful program which would enhance the children's recreative experiences. Children are not easily fooled, and they responded to their leaders' lack of interest and inability to develop the social and creative potentialities the children possessed. The women never seemed to me to be aware of what was happening, nor to care very much. They said that the children's behavior confirmed their original opinion that there was no need for a troop and felt justified when the troop disbanded in chaos. . . .[17]

What conclusions may be reached by the reader, based on this case analysis?

First, that there are such things as leadership traits, but, second, and more important, that these must be buttressed by thorough planning, conviction that what one is doing is important, and by a well thought out philosophy of purpose. The first two leaders were not successful solely because of intuitive skills, but because they believed in the goals of Scouting and in the potentials of the children who came to them.

[17] *Ibid.*

They had a coherent set of objectives in mind, they enjoyed their task, and they worked hard at it.

These are the ingredients of success in recreation leadership.

SUGGESTED QUESTIONS FOR DISCUSSION

1. What are three different concepts of leadership that were discussed in the chapter? Show how they apply to an analysis of the work of a recreation administrator and a recreation activity leader.
2. Discuss a group that you have belonged to, in terms of its reason for existence, structure, degree of cohesion, and influence on its members.
3. Present several guides for leadership in a recreation situation, based on the latter section of this chapter. Using these guides, analyze the leadership in a recreational group you have participated in, or have observed over a period of time.

PART II

RECREATION PROGRAM ACTIVITIES

Chapter 4

Games for Every Occasion

As the previous chapter pointed out, recreational leadership operates on many levels, but its ultimate purpose is to provide direct program service to groups of participants. This service, basically, is of two types:

1. The development of facilities or play areas that may be used by participants with comparatively little leadership, although a degree of supervision may be provided (for example: picnic areas or golf courses)
2. The provision of more direct program leadership, such as the teaching of arts and crafts skills, scheduling and umpiring of sports events, organizing of drama groups or festivals, or social club leadership.

This book is primarily concerned with the latter form of service rather than with the task of planning and developing facilities for essentially self-directed recreational use.

THE RANGE OF PROGRAM SERVICES

It is important to recognize that people, in their leisure lives, carry on many forms of recreational activity that are not part of organized public or agency programs, or that do not require formal leadership as such. Some of the most interesting or unusual pursuits of this type are either self-directed, learned through books, manuals, or magazines, or carried on in private clubs or associations.

One such interest is that of the private printer. It has been estimated that there are as many as 3,000 private printing presses all over the United States, many of which turn out superb pieces of work and have won awards for design and craftsmanship. Clearly, few public or agency recreation programs could afford to purchase the expensive equipment and provide the highly skilled leadership to make this a feasible activity for the comparatively small number of potential participants.

Another unusual hobby that has developed rapidly in the past few years is that of sports parachuting. In 1962, it was estimated that some 15,000 amateur parachutists had racked up 80,000 jumps—including many who practice "free fall" jumping (pulling the cord only after a period of free flight). While this recreational pursuit certainly is a challenging one, and must meet important needs of those who carry it on, it is not appropriate for organized recreation service—for obvious reasons.

Other hobbies? Many thousands of Americans raise fighting gamecocks and, although the activity is banned in almost every state of the union, pit their prize birds against each other in no fewer than 500 cockpits throughout the country. They support four monthly magazines, and it is not uncommon for as much as $5,000 or $10,000 to be bet on a single match, between the owners of competing cocks.

Other people spend years building their own homes (for reasons that are not primarily economic), put together extensive collections of lead soldiers and authentic miniature war machinery in order to play war games, or get together in businessmen's syndicates to build modern but faithful reproductions of nineteenth-century Mississippi river boats —or engage in a wide variety of other hobbies—all in the name of fun!

SUITABLE PROGRAM ACTIVITIES

Because of the expense, the risk involved, the highly skilled leadership required, or the values involved, such activities are not suitable for inclusion in public or agency recreation programs. What *does* make an activity appropriate? There are three important elements:

1. It must have fairly broad appeal; that is, many people, young or old, must perceive it as something that they will enjoy doing.
2. It must serve constructive purposes; it must be acceptable in terms of moral and social values, and must meet the needs of participants.
3. It must be administratively feasible—not too dangerous, not too expensive, capable of serving a fairly good sized group and of sustaining interest and attendance over a period of time.

One other element that might be mentioned is whether or not it is generally available elsewhere in the community. By and large, it is not organized recreation service's task to provide, or *duplicate,* activities that are already widely available, unless the mass of people are not able to participate elsewhere for monetary reasons or because the activity is provided for a membership group.

Based on these factors, certain broad activity categories have come to be traditional offerings of most public or voluntary recreation agencies. These include: (a) games of all types; (b) sports and athletics, including aquatic sports; (c) the performing arts—music, drama, and dance; (d) arts and crafts; (e) outdoor recreation or nature-centered activities; (f) festival, carnival, or special holiday programs or celebrations; (g) hobby clubs or other special interest groups; (h) service groups, in which individuals provide voluntary assistance in programs of social service, for their own pleasure.

Each of these categories of activity is presented in the pages that follow. Obviously, it is not possible to deal with them in encyclopedic detail. However, the attempt has been to:

1. Illustrate the kinds of activities or program services that are offered today by recreation departments and agencies
2. Present a good cross-section of each type of activity, so that a recreation leader or supervisor might be able to use this book as a *basic* source of activities—going to more specialized sources only when pursuing the activity on a more advanced level
3. Provide enough activities so that this book may be used as a text in recreation leadership courses, where practical demonstrations of leadership skills are called for

USEFUL GAMES FOR RECREATIONAL GROUPS

Games are universal in their appeal. We know from the artifacts of ancient civilization that they have been played throughout the history of mankind. We know too that people play remarkably similar games in cultures all around the world—even where it does not appear that they have had contact with each other.

What is the nature of this appeal? Huizinga, the noted Dutch historian of culture,[1] suggests that mankind's urge to play is fundamental and that, in effect, many of life's most serious rituals and activities represent disguised or sublimated forms of play. Thus, warfare was for centuries carried out as a sort of deadly game, with elaborate rules, strategies, and codes of sportsmanship. Huizinga writes of the practice of law, of art, of philosophy, of poetry, all as forms of play. In games as such, the essence

[1] Johan Huizinga, *Homo Ludens, A Study of the Play Element in Culture* (Boston: Beacon Press, 1950).

of the matter is to pit oneself against an opponent or opponents in a mock-serious situation. To try to outguess him, to perplex him, to physically master him, to defeat him through strategic improvisation—this is the task! Or, in some games, the object is to cooperate so cleverly that the coparticipant is enabled to achieve a desired goal, because not all games are highly competitive.

Games tax a variety of abilities: *physical*, in that they test speed, agility, or strength; *mental,* in terms of memory, deduction, the ability to calculate rapidly or make necessary associations; *dramatic,* in terms of physical pantomime or the ability to improvise with words; and many others.

They are useful for all ages, ranging from the highly complex to the very simple, and from the physically strenuous to the most passive and quiet forms of activity. Most games may be played by both sexes together, as contrasted with sports or athletics, in which boys and men usually have superior abilities, making coeducational participation impractical.

In the past, game playing was one of the most common forms of family or social group entertainment. Everyone played games like Ghost, Coffeepot, Twenty Questions, or, as children, Red Light, Blind Man's Buff, or Hare and Hounds. Today, the pattern of family or neighborhood participation in recreational activity has changed somewhat, and many people have become accustomed to being entertained by television (often watching *others* play at quiz games, charades, and similar contests) rather than to taking part themselves. Usually, when they are introduced to game activities—in schools, 4-H clubs, on playgrounds, in couples' clubs or even Senior Citizen's groups—people realize that it is far more fun to be actively involved oneself than to be passively entertained. Here lies the task for the recreation leader!

The games that are presented in this chapter fall into several categories: (a) active or semiactive group games; (b) social games, mixers, icebreakers, and stunts; (c) mental games, quizzes, puzzles, and paper and pencil games; and (d) table and equipment games. Each category may to a degree overlap with some of the others, but the games presented here have been placed under the headings which seem most obvious and appropriate. In addition, certain other games, such as dramatic games or nature games, have been placed in other chapters.

In general, the games selected for this book represented familiar, tried-and-true activities. A few are of recent origin, come from unusual sources, or represent interesting new variations of older activities.

EFFECTIVE GAME LEADERSHIP

What is the process of successful game leadership?

To begin with, it is most important to pick the right activity.

Gauge the ability and area of interest of the group; take their age, numbers, mental ability, physical status, and previous recreational experiences into account. Ideally, your choice (or choices, if you are planning a *session* of games) should be based on activities that you have enjoyed personally, or that you have seen work well with similar groups.

(2.) Prepare yourself. Become completely familiar with the game, so there is no question in your mind about its rules, purpose or strategy. If special equipment or materials are required, get them ready.

(3.) In presenting the game to the group, do so in as lively and enthusiastic a manner as possible. First, have them take the appropriate formation or divide into whatever teams, lines, or other arrangement may be necessary. Then introduce the activity—arousing their interest with a brief explanatory phrase or two.

(4.) Explain the game. This should be done as quickly as possible, but the basic point must be understood. Too often, a leader gets all tangled up in explaining rules, roles of different players, or strategy, without making it clear that the purpose is to catch someone, to gain the highest point total, to guess the correct answer, or complete the action. The essential purpose of the game *must* be made clear.

(5.) Briefly demonstrate the game, either yourself, or with participants carrying out the action as you tell them what to do. As soon as it is generally understood, *get started*. There should not be a long-winded delay before the game is actually played.

(6.) As the game is played, if the contestants are carrying it on successfully, do not interfere; in fact, it is appropriate in most games for the leader to play it along with the others. Only if there is confusion or disagreement, or if certain individuals are having a great deal of difficulty, should the leader step in to iron out the difficulty and help the action resume. If some players are unsuccessful in a certain role—such as the "chaser" in a tag game—the leader may quickly step in, to have roles rotate or changed.

(7.) Finally, cut the game off while interest in it is still fairly high—rather than have it drag on and grind to a dull ending.

VALUES IN GAME PLAY

Games have a great potential for achieving desirable personal or social values and outcomes, but this does not happen automatically. Children, or even adults, left to their own devices, may play a game teasingly or sadistically, or deliberately breaking the rules with short cuts and cheating. This simply reflects their previous experiences or their concept of the purpose of game-playing. Thus, it is important that the leader have a clear-cut set of purposes in mind. In terms of desired outcomes for participants, he should include the following goals. Players should learn to: (a) take turns; (b) accept boundary limits (either in a physical sense, or in terms of personal behavior); (c) accept and abide by the rules of the game willingly; (d) accept defeat or elimination in good spirit, although they should also learn to persevere and keep trying; (e) accept the decisions of others (team captain, group members, or leader); (f) learn new skills and improve existing skills; (g) improve their powers of observation and decision-making in situations that call for quick thinking; (h) develop good sportsmanship and consideration for the rights of others, as well as of their feelings; (i) develop their own leadership abilities; and, (j) develop the ability to cooperate effectively with others.

In presenting games, the leader will see that different activities impose varying kinds of group structures, or contrasting kinds of stress or challenges upon the participants. Thus, in some games, equal teams are pitted against each other. In others, one individual may be pitted against another, or against the entire group. In others, the entire group may be drawn in and out of the action, without any formal competitive structure. Similarly, some games may be quite serious in nature, and may impose a degree of real tension on the participants. Others may be clearly "just for fun," with laughter ringing out at almost every moment.

Whatever the game structure, the leader's goal at all times should be to insure that all are involved as successfully as possible, and that all are gaining satisfaction from the activity. Throughout, his own values of acceptance, friendship, and good humor should be stressed. Before long, the group should grow to understand and believe that it is the process of playing the game that is more important than the outcome and that winning—although desirable—does not overpower other goals of participation. Playing the game should be its own reward.

In some collections, games are classified rather rigidly, according to the size of the group with which they may be used and also the age category: young children, preteens, teen-agers, adults, and older persons. Since these limits are usually arbitrary, and since a game may often be used successfully on several levels, such classifications will not be presented here except in certain necessary cases. The leader should use his judgment in determining whether a game will be appropriate for a given group.

SOCIAL GAMES AND ICEBREAKERS

This section includes a number of informal social games and icebreakers which may be played with groups ranging between about 10 and 40 in number. Many of them are quite humorous, but none should cause embarrassment. A few require slight physical exertion, but none can be classified as strenuous.

Indian Chief. One player in the circle is chosen as "It" and is asked to cover his eyes. The group then selects a secret leader, or Indian Chief.

The Chief begins to lead the group in performing some action, such as hand clapping, or lightly stamping a foot on the floor. "It" uncovers his eyes and tries to determine, walking around inside the circle, who the Chief is. The Chief continues to lead the others in different actions (such as waving hands, "brushing" hair, standing up and sitting down, or similar movements) and they must follow him immediately each time, without seeming to pay too much attention to him.

"It" is given three chances to guess who the Indian Chief is. If he is successful, that player becomes "It" and the game is played again. If not, it is usually best to pick a new "It" and a new Chief.

Clumps. The group divides into two even teams. Each team draws apart from the other and chooses a captain. The captain of each team selects a player who goes out of the room. The two players who have gone out agree on some object in the room that must be guessed by those in the room. They return to their respective teams, who ask them rapid-fire questions (which must be answered by "yes" or "no") to identify the object. The first team to do this wins. Its captain chooses a player from the other team, to join his. The game is repeated several times, each time with a new player going out from each team. After a given time period, the group with the greatest number of players is the winner.

Hot Potato. This is a very easily played and familiar game that is always popular with children. They stand or sit in a circle and, while music plays, pass a ball or beanbag from person to person. The music is suddenly stopped after 15 or 20 seconds, and the child holding the "hot potato" is eliminated (a whistle may also be used as a signal). A variation of this may also be played with a player holding one hand up in the air, the first time he is caught, and being eliminated the second time.

Hidden Names. Each person is given the name of a famous person (on a slip pinned to his back). He also has pencil and paper. The object is to circulate around, read, and write down as many names of other players as possible. This would be easy if other people let him—but the object is to compile the biggest list possible yourself, and not to permit others to read the name on your back. Players therefore back up against walls, dodge around speedily, and lie on the floor to avoid having their names read. After about five minutes have passed, a signal is given, and the lists are totaled, to find the winner.

Who's That Knocking? One player stands with his back to the group. The leader points at someone who walks up quietly and taps three times on the first player's back. The first player asks in angry tones, "Who's that knocking at my door?" The one who did the knocking must reply in a trembling, disguised voice, "It is I." The player with his back turned is given three chances to guess the name of the one who tapped. As he calls out his guess, the person named (if he is in the group) answers, "No, it is not I." If he identifies the correct person, that player becomes "It," stands with his back to the group, and the game continues.

Tangled Teams. The group divides into two teams. One player is selected to be "It" from each team. He goes to the other team (they are holding hands in a circle) and, at a signal, begins to "tangle" them. This is done by winding them up, raising arms over heads, having them duck under arms—without ever letting go of hands. After about two minutes, they should be thoroughly tangled. Each "It" then returns to his own group and, at a signal, begins to untangle them. The first "It" to get his group back to the original circle is the winner.

Laughing Handkerchief. The group is seated in a single circle. The leader throws a handkerchief into the air; all the others must at once laugh boisterously. The second the leader catches it, they must stop laughing. Those who do not are eliminated, and the game continues.

Conversation Cards. This icebreaker is useful for teen-age parties. The leader makes up a list of conversational topics, placing the numbered list on two large cards or sheets of paper. The boys get one list, and each boy writes his name next to a topic. The girls do the same. At a signal, each player finds the member of the opposite sex who had chosen the same topic, and they talk for a set period of minutes with that person on the topic.

Ball of Yarn. This game may serve as a surprise mixer for teen-age or adult parties. A ball of yarn has each girl's name fixed to it with scotch tape, at intervals. Boys stand in a line and the ball of yarn is unwound along the line. Each boy gets a girl's name, and she will be his partner for the next game or dance—or for refreshments.

Sing Down. The group is divided into two teams. Each team is given a word that commonly appears in many popular song titles or lyrics. They are given several minutes to think of and list the titles or lines of songs which contain this word. Then, at a signal, the teams alternate in singing the first line of the songs they have thought of. The winning team is the one that can keep going the longest. A given song may be used only once.

The Minister's Cat. Players are seated in a circle. One player says to the person on his right, "The minister has a new cat." That person asks, "What kind of cat?" The first player must reply, using an adjective starting with "a," such as "angry"—"an angry cat." The second player then turns to the player on his right and so it continues, with a new letter being used each time: "b," "c," "d," and so on. If a player cannot quickly supply a word starting with the needed letter, he may be eliminated—or the turn may simply pass to the next player.

Problems and Solutions. Players are divided into two teams. In each team, they divide into two's or three's; in one team, each small group makes up and writes down an unusual problem or predicament. In the other team, each small group makes up and writes down a humorous solution—without knowing what the problem will be. Then, a player from one side stands up and states his problem, and a player from the opposite team states his solution, which is usually funny, whether or not it fits the particular problem. This is continued, until all the problems and solutions have been heard.

An example:

Problem: "What would you do if you ran out of gas and had a flat tire on the desert?"
Solution: "I'd close my eyes and jump backward off the pier."

Smooth Talkers. Two players who are nominated by the others for their ability to talk smoothly and convincingly are each given a slip with a humorous sentence written on it. Some examples might be, "Yes, my favorite food is walrus steak; I had it last year at the North Pole," or "That's what I like about you—your sensitivity and those big purple eyes." They then take turns in talking to each other, each one for 20 seconds at a stretch, for two or three minutes. The object is to steer the conversation quickly in their own direction, so they can say the sentence they were given, as inconspicuously as possible. When the three minutes are over, the leader asks each player if he detected the key sentence in his opponent's monologues. If he did (he need not repeat the exact words, but should come fairly close) he gets one point. If a player gets the phrase across without it being detected, he gets one point. It may be played as a team game, with each player being a "smooth talker" in turn, and trying to add to his team's total.

Tie and Untie. To play the game, four strips of cloth are needed, each about 15 inches long and about two inches wide. Players sit in four teams, each in a row on one side of a square, facing in. The first player on the left of each team is given a strip of cloth. At the signal, he ties the cloth with a loose knot around the left arm of the second player (on his right). This player quickly unties it with his right hand and ties it on the next player. So it goes until it reaches the end player on the right. He runs down the line, and ties it on the left arm of the first player. This player unties it, and the whole team stands up to show they have completed the action. The first team to finish is the winner.

Shopping. One player faces the group, sitting in a circle, and says, "I am going to Chicago for my vacation. What shall I buy?" He points immediately at any player in the circle, who must at once respond with three objects starting with the same initial as the city named—"C." Examples: *carrots, carriages,* and *cars.* He must name all three before the leader can count to 10. If he does, he becomes the leader. If not, the leader plays the game again with a new person, and the name of a new city.

Murder Will Out. Here is an unusual party stunt which shows how people often get distorted impressions of events that occur. As the group is playing another game, or simply dancing or having refreshments, have two or three players suddenly come in, engage in a violent quarrel, using a toy gun or knife, shoving some furniture around, making angry accusations and winding up with a "corpse" or two on the floor.

Immediately afterward, several players are chosen, placed on a "witness" stand and asked to describe exactly what happened. Usually, their accounts will disagree widely—an example of the effects of excitement on accurate observation. This will be even more pronounced if they are not allowed to listen to the previous witnesses.

The Long Step. This game involves a little movement, but is not at all strenuous. Players divide into two equal teams. The first player in each team (the others are standing in line behind him) stands with one foot on the starting line and places the right foot as far forward as he can without losing his balance. Immediately, the next player behind him runs forward, puts his left foot next to the right foot of the first player, and extends his right foot forward as far as he can. Each of the other players quickly does this, until the whole line is extended at maximum length.

The event is then scored: the first team to complete the action scores two points, and the team to reach the greatest length is given five points. It can be played again, or can be part of a series of stunts or contests that add up to a total score.

ACTIVE GAMES AND CONTESTS

These games all involve a certain amount of physical activity; some are quite strenuous and others only mildly so. They are therefore most appropriate for children and youth in camp or playground situations, although some may be enjoyed by adults in outdoor settings and informal recreation programs. Because they do not involve a high level of skill, they may be played by both boys and girls, and in mixed groups. Most tend to be of the "tag" or "relay" type.

Games for Younger Children

Do This or That. The leader faces the group and takes any gymnastic position or performs some action, saying "Do this." All the children must immediately imitate him. If he says, "Do that," they must not copy him. By giving them rapid-fire commands and actions, the leader makes it increasingly hard for the players to keep up with him. If they make mistakes, they may be eliminated, as in "Simple Simon," or may simply be given a point each time they "miss." At the end, if it is played this way, the child with the lowest number of points wins.

Cat and Rat. All the children join hands in the circle, but the Cat, who is on the outside, and the Rat, who is on the inside. The Cat says, "I am the Cat," and the Rat replies, "I am the Rat." The Cat says, "I will catch you," and the Rat replies, "Come, please do." As the Rat runs away, the players in the circle try to keep the Cat from getting between them. However, they permit the Rat to run freely about. If the Rat cannot be caught, two Cats may be put to work, or the roles may be reversed.

Line Moves Up. Children stand in a straight line, facing the leader, who bounces a rubber playground ball to them, one at a time, working from front to rear. Those in the line bounce it back to the teacher. If he misses, he goes to the foot of the line, and the child at the head takes his place. If any child in the line misses, he goes to the foot, and the line moves up.

Face to Face. Children stand in couples scattered about the play area, facing their partners. One child, the leader, stands without a partner. As he calls, "Face to face," or "Back to back," the others obey his directions, facing partners, or turning to stand back to back. When the leader calls, "All Change!" each child must seek a new partner. Usually, the leader is able to get a partner, which leaves another child without one; he becomes the new leader.

Meet at the Switch. Children stand in two relay teams of equal numbers; the leader stands about 15 feet in front of them, holding a beanbag or ball in each hand (Fig. 2). At a signal, the first child from each team runs to the leader, takes the beanbag, and runs back, going completely

Figure 2

around the two teams (passing on the outside of his own line to begin) and back to the leader. The player who returns his beanbag to the leader first wins a point for his team. Each child takes his turn in running up. Older children may play the game as a continuous relay.

Games for Older Children

Twenty-One. Between 10 and 20 children stand in a circle, with one player in the center. They pass the ball back and forth, using a bounce pass, and trying to complete 21 consecutive passes before the player in the center can touch the ball. If he touches it in time, the last circle player to handle it goes into the center and the game is begun again. If not, another child should be chosen to go into the center.

Tadpole. Children are divided into two equal teams of eight or ten in a team. One team stands in a circle, facing in, while the other stands in a single line with the first player about three feet from the circle. At a signal, the ball is passed from player to player around the circle, with a bounce pass. It must go around *as many times* as there are players in the circle. At the same time, the first player in the line runs around the circle, comes back to the line, tags the next player, who runs around the circle, etc., until every player in the line completes the action. The first team to complete its task wins. Then they reverse roles and the team that passed the ball runs, and vice versa.

Relays

Relays are enjoyable team contests which may or may not stress physical ability. The simplest relay, of course, is one in which each player in turn runs to a line and back, touching off the next player, until all have completed the action. Here are some interesting variations:

Stiff Knee Relay. Keeping both knees absolutely stiff and straight, each player runs to the turning line and back, in turn.

Cross-Toe Relay. Leaning forward and holding his right toe with his left hand and vice versa, each player runs (or waddles) to the turning line and back.

All-Fours Relay. Traveling on all fours, hands and feet, the player races to the turning line and back. This may also be done as "Backward All-Fours Relay," with the same hand and foot positions, but traveling backward.

Kangaroo Relay. Children race to the turning line and back, holding a playground ball firmly between their knees (not using hands) as they travel. They find that the fastest way to travel is in a series of jumps, like a kangaroo.

Over-the-Border Relay. The captain of each relay team stands behind the turning line, facing his own team. At the signal, he runs forward, takes the hand of the first player in the line; together they run to the turning line. The captain now remains there, but the first player returns to the team to bring back a new player. This continues until all players have been brought over; the first team to complete the action is the winner.

Tag Games

There are literally hundreds of variations of "tag." All are based on the idea that a player, when "tagged," is either put out of commission, or becomes "It," and tries to tag others.

Japanese Tag. This is like simple tag, except that a player, when touched, must hold the spot that was tagged with his hand, while chasing other players. If he happens to have been tagged on the leg or foot, he has quite a handicap.

Hook-on. All players take partners and hook arms to form couples, except for two children. One of these is "It" and the other is the Chaser. Couples are scattered over the play area. At a signal, the Chaser runs after "It" to tag him. To escape, "It" may "hook-on" to the free arm of one of the other players in a couple. When he does that, the other player in the couple is released, becomes "It," and is pursued by the Chaser. If he is caught, the roles are reversed, and he becomes the Chaser.

Flying Dutchman. Each player takes a partner. All of the players stand in a single circle, hands joined, facing the center, with one couple standing on the outside. The outside couple, the Flying Dutchman, runs to the right. While running, they tag the joined hands of two players standing in the circle. This couple must immediately run in the opposite direction around the outside, in a race with the Flying Dutchman to get back to the spot they have just vacated. The winning couple remains in the spot, and the other couple starts the game again, traveling to the right, as the Flying Dutchman.

True and False. The players divide into two even teams, standing on either side of a center line. One group is called the True Team, and the other the False Team. The leader calls out a statement, which may be either true or false. If it is True, the players in the True Team run across the center line and chase the False Team players toward their goal line. If they tag any of them, those players must join the True Team. If the statement is false, the False Team players do the chasing. After a set period of time (with both teams having had an equal number of chances), the team with the most players is the winner.

Games of Other Lands

As mentioned earlier, many of the games we play in the United States are similar to those played in other countries of the world. Here are several Latin American games which are similar to North American favorites: [2]

Pelota Envenenoda (Poison Ball). This game, played in Colombia, is popular throughout Latin America, and is just like our Dodge Ball. Two teams are formed. The players in one team form a circle; those in the other team stand inside the circle. The circle players throw the ball back and forth (it should be a rubber playground ball, thrown no higher than the waist) attempting to touch children within the circle with the ball. When they are hit, they are eliminated and must leave the circle. When all of the inner players are eliminated, the teams change roles.

El Gavilan y Los Pollitos (The Eagle and the Chickens). One child plays the part of the eagle. Facing him, one child is the old mother hen, and the others line up behind her, each player grasping the waist in front of him. The eagle attempts to tag any of the chicks behind the old mother hen, as the hen holds her arms out to ward him off, and others dodge about to avoid him (Fig. 3). When the eagle touches a child, he stands behind the eagle in a line. The last chicken to be tagged becomes the new eagle, as the game is replayed. This game comes from Ecuador, and

Figure 3

is much like the North American game "Mother Carey's Chickens."

Gallina Ciega (The Blind Chicken). One child is blindfolded. He then wanders around trying to tag other children, who must remain fixed to one spot, although they may move their bodies to avoid his touch.

2 Games summarized from: J. D. McAulay, "The Traveling Vegetable and Other Games," *Recreation,* February, 1962, p. 91.

When he tags one, he asks, *"Que animales tiene en su chacra?"* ("What animals do you have on your farm?"). The tagged child must name several barnyard animals. If the blindfolded child names the tagged child correctly, that player then becomes the Blind Chicken, and the game is played again. This game comes from Panama and is, of course, like Blind Man's Bluff.

MENTAL GAMES, QUIZZES, AND PUZZLES

Particularly with smaller and older groups of participants who are somewhat more intellectually inclined, games stressing mental, verbal, or mathematical ability are extremely useful. This does not mean that even little children will not be captivated by simple puzzles, "magic" stunts, or quizzes. They enjoy them—as they do all kinds of play activities. But mental games as such are most useful with groups that are less interested in physical performance but enjoy tackling intellectual challenges. Here is a varied sampling:

Teakettle. One person goes out of the room, while the others select a group of words that sound alike, but are spelled differently and have different meanings. Examples might be: *for, four,* and *fore; pare* and *pair; rain, rein,* and *reign;* or *to, two,* and *too.* When he returns, the other players engage in conversation using the word "teakettle" in place of these words. His job is to figure out the real words they have in mind. The conversation might run this way:

"Yes, we went up to *teakettle* last summer."

"Did you travel over the bounding *teakettle?*"

"No, we took the *teakettle* highway."

"If you go horseback riding when you're there next summer, hold on to the *teakettle* or you'll be thrown."

It may take a while, but he'll probably figure out that *teakettle* stands for *Maine, main,* and *mane,* in this case.

Animal, Vegetable, or Mineral. In this game, one person goes out of the room while the others think of some real or fictional person, object, place, or thing. When "It" returns, he is given the clue that the group has thought of something that is either Animal, or Vegetable, or Mineral (or possibly a combination of these). A person, an animal, or anything made of animal substance would be classified as Animal, for example. An automobile might be classified as all three, in that it might include Animal (leather seat covers), Vegetable (rubber floor mat) and Mineral (steel body).

"It" asks as many questions as he needs to identify the thing they have in mind. His first questions should establish major categories and make clear whether or not it is a real or fictional person or thing, a single object or a class of objects, in the past or present, etc. Since this game may drag on, if the choice was a very difficult one, it may be wise to set a time limit.

Buzz. The group sits in a circle. The first player calls out the number *one,* the next *two,* and so on, in rapid order. The only catch is that when *seven* is reached (or multiple of seven, or number containing seven, like 14, 17, 21, or 27) the player involved must quickly stand and say *Buzz.* If he makes a mistake, he is given the first letter of *Buzz* (B), and the game is started from the beginning. When a person is given all four letters (B-u-z-z) he is eliminated. A skillful group may go up to the hundreds, but this is rare.

A variation of this is "Fizz," a word which is used whenever *five* or a multiple of *five* appears. The game may also be played as "Fizz-Buzz," which combines the two games.

What Dropped? Some mental games involve the ability to smell, to remember, or to see. This one is based on listening ability. A group of players sit in front of a screen with paper and pencil. Behind the screen, a number of unbreakable objects are dropped on the floor, one at a time. The players must write down, one by one, what they believe the objects were, based on the sound they made when they fell. Typical objects might include: a key ring with keys, a ping pong ball, a deck of cards, a pin, a magazine, an empty can, a hammer, a shoe, and a plastic baby rattle. After all have been dropped, the correct answers are given, and players tally their lists to find the winner.

Things. Here's an easy one. Have the group decide upon four letters of the alphabet. Then have them divide into equal teams and give each about five minutes' time to write down all the objects visible to them in the room that begin with these letters. After the time is up, tally the lists to find the winner. A somewhat more difficult version is to divide into teams of two individuals. One person in each team is then blindfolded. He must name objects that he remembers being in the room to the other player, who writes them down. Again, at the end, the lists are tallied to find the winning pair.

Magazine Scavenger Hunt. Divide into teams, with no more than four or five in each group. Each group is given two or three old picture magazines, and a list of objects that would commonly be found in picture stories and illustrations—such as automobiles, airplanes, animals of various types, houses, beaches, children, articles of clothing, etc. Within a five-minute time period, each team must find and cut out as many of the assigned pictures as possible. At the end, the team with the most correct pictures wins.

Advertising Slogans. Have one or two people help in compiling a list of well-known advertising phrases or slogans, taking them from television commercials or magazines. These may include such phrases as:

"I'd rather fight than switch," "Wouldn't you rather buy a _____,"
or "_____ tastes good, like a cigarette should." The group is
divided into two teams. The leader calls out a slogan, and the first player
to call back the name of the correct product wins a point for his team.
Or it may be played with the first player of one team given the chance
to answer (if he cannot, his opponent may), and then the first player of
the opposing team has a turn—and so on down the line.

Surprise Portraits. Here's an amusing drawing game. Each player
writes his name on a small slip of paper; these are put into a hat or container which is passed around. They are mixed up, and then each player
must draw a name (not his own) from the hat. Sitting in a circle, with
drawing paper and crayon, each person must draw a likeness of the person whose name he drew. After ten minutes, each player holds up the
picture he has drawn, and all try to find themselves. When every por-
trait has been identified, the group may then vote on which two or three
pictures most resemble their subjects.

Picture Charades. Players divide into teams of at least five or six
each. Each team is given a pencil and a pad of paper. It selects an
"artist." The artist from each team goes up to the leader (who has
prepared a list of titles, famous names, proverbs, etc.). He shows them all
the first title or other phrase. They hurry back to their groups, and, without saying a word (although they may shake their heads or nod, to indicate "hot" or "cold") they draw a picture to get the idea across. The
group members keep guessing until they have the solution. The first
team to get it has its "artist" run up, and the leader gives his team one
point. The game is continued several times, until each player has been
an "artist."

Word Games

Many popular games are based on spelling, word discovering, or
deciphering skills. Here are several.

Scrambled Holiday Words. At any holiday party, the leader may
prepare a set of cards, on which he has printed, in large letters, a particular word or phrase commonly attached to that holiday. One after
one, he holds up the cards, and the players, in teams, try to identify the
words or phrases. The catch? The letters are scrambled, like this:

Halloween Words	*Christmas Words*
bogsni (goblins)	gamern (manger)
skopos (spooks)	fitsg (gifts)
nukpmip (pumpkin)	galens (angels)
chitw (witch)	Linsegnith (Silent Night)
raertikotrtc (trick or treat)	Luassacant (Santa Claus)

Depending on the group, these may be scrambled so they are more or less easy to decipher. Also, phrases with two or more words may have the words kept separate, so they are easier. Thus, Santa Claus could be: Tasan Sluac.

Words on Foot. Players are divided into teams of eight or ten each. Each group is given the same set of letter cards; let us say they include the letters—r, o, a, b, s, t, m, l, e, c. Each group, standing by itself, faces a spelling line. The leader, on the side, calls out a word using the letters that were given. At once, the players with the correct letter cards run forward, stand on the spelling line facing their teams in the correct order, and hold up their cards. The first team to spell the word correctly wins a point. They return to their groups, and the game is repeated again and again until the first team with 10 points wins.

Typical words for the above list of letters would be:

cost	cast	male	race	lest	boast
beast	steal	meal	cart	lame	clear

Super Brain. A somewhat similar word game is one in which the group divides into small teams, each with a pencil and paper. The leader gives them a two-word combination, each with five letters, like "super brain." Each team must then make up a list of as many four- or five-letter words starting with the letters found in "super brain" as it can, within 10 minutes. The team with the most correct words at the end wins.

Examples:	brine	spear	pear	pain
	spare	raise	barn	rain

Twenty-Five Squares. Here's another word-building game, and a much more difficult one. Players draw six horizontal lines, crossing six vertical lines, on a sheet of paper, thus making 25 squares. Each player then takes a turn in calling out a letter of the alphabet. Immediately, all players must print this letter in one of the squares on their paper; it must be done at once and cannot later be changed. The purpose is to build common English words (no proper names allowed), that read in straight lines (from left to right, from top to bottom, or diagonally, moving from left to right). In scoring, when the game is over and all boxes are filled up, a player may count 1 point for a *three*-letter word, 3 points for a *four*-letter word, and 5 points for a word of *five* letters or more. Words found within words (like "air" within "hair") may also count. At the end, each player counts up his total and the high score wins.

Magic Stunts and Tricks

There are many so-called "magic" puzzles and tricks which both children and adults enjoy—not the kinds of elaborate tricks that real performers put on—but simple little novelties that require only a moment's preparation. These include: (a) humorous stunts which may involve a play on words; (b) so-called mind-reading activities, based on prearrangement; (c) simple manipulation of cards, coins, or other props; and (d) paper-and-pencil puzzles, mathematical tricks and stunts. Several of these follow:

The Amazing Nut. One person boasts to the others that he will show them something they have never seen before, and will never see again. When they indicate loud disbelief, he cracks a peanut, shows them the nut—which they've never seen before—and eats it. They'll never see it again.

Poke Your Foot. The same person holds up a key ring and states that he can poke his foot—shoe and all—through it. Not likely? When others confess they don't see how it can be done, he promptly puts his forefinger through the key ring and pokes his foot—to a chorus of groans.

In Cahoots. In this "magic" stunt, one person goes out of the group. The players then select some object in the room. "It" comes back in. The leader of the group points to one object after another. When he comes to the right one, "It" promptly says, "That's it." The secret? The leader and "It" have previously agreed that the correct object would be the first one named after any piece of furniture with legs. Thus, if the correct object was to be a *lamp,* the leader would point to: a rug, a picture, a window, a *chair*—and then the *lamp.*

Magic Identification. Similarly, while "It" goes out of the room, the group picks one person whom he must identify when he comes back in. When he returns, after a moment or two of thought, "It" points to the correct person. The trick? The leader of the group, with whom "It" is in "cahoots," has his legs crossed, with the toe of his right foot pointing directly at the person secretly chosen. If this is too obvious, or if they are not sitting in convenient positions for it, the leader may have a cigarette in his hand pointing directly at the person—just as "It" comes in.

Okay, All right, Ready. In a similar stunt, three persons are chosen to stand facing the group. One of them is designated as the secret one who must be identified, while "It" is out of the room. The leader calls "It" to come in, and goes out of the room himself—so that no one can accuse him of giving the plot away. Yet, when "It" comes in, he promptly points at the right person. How? The secret is in the word the leader used to call him in. It was either, "Okay," "All right," or "Ready." Reading from left to right, the first letters of these spell "Oar," a convenient memory clue. If the word was "Okay," the secret person was the first on the left; if "All right," the middle person; if "Ready," the one on the right.

Pick the Card. This is another "magic" stunt. The leader deals out nine cards, in three rows of three each, as "It" goes out. The group selects one card, which "It" must then identify when he returns. The leader points to each card in turn, without saying a word. When he points to the correct one, "It" says, "That's it!" The secret is that when the leader points to the very first card, he touches it on one of nine spots, which indicates which card (upper left, upper middle, upper right, etc.) is the correct one. (Fig. 4.)

Figure 4

Head Through a Card. Not "magic"—and quite different from "poking" your foot through a ring—is this one. You offer to put your head through a small calling card. When the scoffing is over, and you've assured the others that you are really going to do it, you take a scissors and cut the card from alternate sides as shown (Fig. 5). When you've gently

Figure 5

unfolded it, it will open up to a sizable paper circlet that you can put your head through.

Touching Coins. Here's a real challenge. Take five coins, preferably quarters, and place them on the table top. Ask anyone to place them so that each coin touches all four of the others. Impossible? Try it this way. Two coins are put down flat, so they are touching each other. Two more are put down flat over them, so that they rest chiefly on one quarter but overlap slightly, touching the other, and also touching each other. Now, place the fifth quarter on edge, so it stands between the upper two coins and just where the lower two intersect. If you've done it right, each coin will be touching each of the others.

Turn the Glasses Over. Here's a puzzler involving three drinking glasses, which are placed on the table in a row. The first is right side up, the second upside down, and the third right side up. The task is to turn all three glasses so they are upside down, in *three moves.* Each move consists of turning two glasses over at one time. How does it work? First, turn over the second and third glasses. Then turn over the first and third

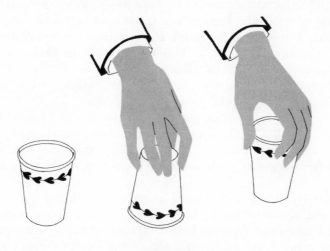

Figure 6

glasses. Finally, turn over the second and third glasses again—and you'll have them all upside down!

There are hundreds of mathematical problems of a puzzle nature, involving diagrams, number manipulations, and simple calculations. Here are a few sample ones:

Which Bills? A man bought an overcoat for $103. He paid for it with eight bills—but they were *not* five 20-dollar bills and three 1-dollar bills, which would be the easy answer. In fact, there were *no* 1-dollar bills used at all. What were they? The answer: a 50-dollar bill, two 20-dollar bills, a 5-dollar bill, and four 2-dollar bills. They're still in circulation.

Amazing Nine's. Ask the group to take any three digit number; if they will reverse it, and then subtract the lesser from the greater number, you will tell them what the middle digit will be—nine. Try it! For example, 678, when reversed, becomes 876. Subtract one from the other and the answer is 198.

The Mysterious Number. When you add 100 to a certain number, the total is actually more than if you multiply the number by 100. What is this mysterious number? The answer—one.

TABLE AND EQUIPMENT GAMES

There are many useful table games, involving homemade or specially built pieces of equipment. These are especially suited for small groups of participants, two or three at a time, in a game room, a lounge, or even in a hospital ward, where patients may not move from their beds or wheelchairs. One very popular form of fun in such settings is playing cards, of course—and it is extremely useful for a recreation leader to know a variety of simple card games, such as Solitaire and its variations, Casino, the various forms of Rummy, Concentration, War, Slapjack, Old Maid, Hearts, Fan Tan, and others which are not basically gambling games. There are several good collections of card games.

Board games are another good kind of intriguing pastime for small groups or twosomes. Such games as chess, checkers, Monopoly, Chinese Checkers, Parcheesi, Backgammon, Scrabble, and some of the more recently invented games, such as Clue or Detective, hold appeal for young and old.

Essentially, these are mental games, involving a knowledge of strategy and alertness. Other kinds of equipment games, such as Nok Hockey (a miniature form of hockey played within a box-type frame), Skittles (a game using a spinning top which knocks down pins within a box frame), Puff Billiards (a circular-table game in which players squeeze rubber bulbs to shoot a cork ball into opponents' goal pockets), and Labyrinth (a Swedish game in which a steel ball must be passed along a numbered route without falling into holes along the way), are becoming increasingly popular. These involve a high degree of dexterity, and, in most cases, excitement and a great amount of rollicking laughter.

Most of the best table-top equipment games cannot be built very easily. They can, however, be purchased from a leading company in this field: World Wide Games of Delaware, Ohio, which has produced superior games of this type for a number of years—based on folk games from all over the world.

Homemade Equipment Games

A final type of game involves simple homemade equipment, or the improvised use of readily available supplies and objects. Examples would include:

Tests of Accuracy. Contestants stand at a distance and attempt to: (1) throw beans, one at a time, into a small tin pie plate floating in a washtub of water; (2) bounce ping pong balls, or tennis balls, so they land in a container on a chair; (3) toss beanbags at a board with numbered holes (piling up a total score for the holes the beanbags go through; (4) toss quoits at an upright board with nails driven in at an angle, or onto a flat board with upstanding pegs; (5) shoot a water pistol at a flickering candle, to put it out; (6) throw darts (metal or suction-tipped) at a target; or, (7) roll balls at duck pins set up 15 or 20 feet away.

Tests of Strength. Contestants show their strength by: (1) seeing how many blows with a hammer it takes them to drive 10-penny nails into heavy plank; or (2) using a pole about 6 feet long, with several notches in it, a contestant lifts the pole with a weight of about 2 pounds suspended from the nearest notch; he then moves it to the next notch, and so on, and is finally scored according to the number of the notch on his last successful try. The pole must be held level, at arm's length.

Many other humorous games may be improvised: "Landing on the Carrier" (sailing paper airplanes so they come as close as possible to a "carrier" chalked on the floor); "Hoop Toss" (throwing hoops or quoits onto the legs of an overturned chair); "Ring the Bell" (throwing a rubber ball at a bell suspended in a 12- or 15-inch wire hoop hung at eye-level height; "Fanning Football" (teams on opposite sides of a table attempt to blow a ping pong ball across the opponents' side for a goal, *or* use folded newspapers to *fan* it across the goal line).

ORGANIZING THE GAME ROOM OR LOUNGE

A Game Room or Lounge is an area set aside for activities such as party games, table games, paper and pencil games, board games, and the like. In an Armed Forces center, or recreation center serving young adults, it may also involve informal dancing, music, refreshments, or other activities of a social nature. When it caters to children and youth, it should be based chiefly on a variety of different games: (a) games such as Nok Hockey, involving noisy competition; (b) quiet two-player games such as checkers, cards, chess, or Dominoes; (c) games requiring a larger area, like table tennis, billiard or table shuffleboard; (d) others involving targets and longer distances, like horseshoes or duckpins. In organizing the room and its program, the following guides are helpful:

1. Tables and chairs should be grouped together according to type, separating quiet games from the noisy or more vigorous ones.

2. If possible, particularly when children with a wide age spread are using the Game Room, equipment for each major age grouping should be placed in a separate section of the room, so that children have a feeling of "our" section, and do not squabble about the use of equipment.

3. Make the room attractive by displaying posters, tournament charts, pictures of game room activities and sports events, and even mimeographed or hand-printed newspapers, placed on the bulletin board.

4. Organize the program so that each group has some individual attention and guidance during the session; this can best be done if organized games for each age group are not taking place at the same time.

5. Special events, such as demonstrations or tournaments, should be used to increase interest in game participation on each age level. Tournaments of short duration, lasting for a single session or possibly one week, are often more useful and manageable than longer tournaments. For greatest interest, these should be of many types, such as checkers or chess tournaments, Nok Hockey, table tennis, top spinning, billiards—or almost any sort of game that can be played within a fairly short span of time and come up with a definite winner.

A VIEWPOINT ABOUT GAMES

Some leaders are hesitant about presenting games, particularly to teen-agers or adults, because they feel that they might be resisted or thought silly. While this might be a superficial first reaction, it rarely lasts, and games of all types are among the most useful and happily accepted activities that the recreation leader can offer. Their success, of course, depends heavily on his selection of the right *kinds* of games, and on effective leadership, based on the guides offered earlier in this chapter. But this is not a complicated matter, and depends more on the common sense and outgoing personality of the leader than any other factor.

PROJECTS AND SPECIAL ASSIGNMENTS

1. Develop selections of games suitable for use over a period of time with specific types of groups: children in a day-camp program, teen-agers in a church club, senior citizens in a community center, etc. Base your choices on age, sex, physical condition, and size of each group, and other pertinent factors.

2. As a workshop or class activity, have different individuals teach examples of the following types of games to the total group:

Social Games and Icebreakers
Active Games and Contests
Games for Older Children
Games of Other Lands

Mental Games, Quizzes, and Puzzles
Word Games
Magic Stunts and Tricks
Table and Equipment Games

Following each leadership assignment, discuss its strong and weak points, and offer constructive suggestions for improvement.

3. Develop a card file of useful games for recreation situations, including activities drawn from other books or collections, or personal experience.

Chapter 5

Sports in Recreation

Like games, sports have played an important role in human culture throughout the centuries. In ancient civilizations, mass sports and athletic events were carried on regularly as part of religious observances. In early Greece, in Mexico of the Aztec period, and in many other societies, we see this connection. Today, in the Western world, sports have lost any formal connection with religion. Yet, when one examines them closely, they still represent almost a religion in our culture.

In terms of the enthusiastic participation of children and youth, the membership of adults in sports clubs (particularly in Europe), the huge crowds that attend sports events, the extensive coverage in the press and on television, and the degree to which we idolize and reward outstanding sports figures—it is clear that sports represent a major fascination of our time. Many colleges are far better known for their football or basketball teams than they are for their academic achievements.

For the highly skilled athlete—whether professional or amateur—

sports come close to being a priesthood. He must devote himself to training, diet, rest, consecration to his task, and, to crowds of worshipers who always dog his footsteps.

In a sense, sports frequently represent a polite form of warfare. The Olympics, which were intended to match the finest young men and women of each nation in athletic competition without regard for national prestige, tend today to do just the opposite. An even more vivid example is found in championship soccer matches that have been held in recent years in Europe and Latin American countries, attended by huge audiences, and ending in mass bloody riots when the home team lost.

All this is to say that, far from being a trivial aspect of our culture, sports apparently represent something very basic in our lives. It is important that the community recreation director recognize this, and that he make every effort to understand the psychological, physical, and social aspects of sports participation. What are these?

WHY PEOPLE PARTICIPATE IN SPORTS

On a superficial level, the answer is "fun." People take part in sports because they enjoy them. Certainly too, there is an element of status. People join in pursuits which are popular and accepted things to do. But, beyond these factors, there are deeper human needs which are apparently met by this form of activity.

Psychological Aspects

Sports offer, in simple terms, an opportunity to "let off steam," to express aggression or hostility—either directly or vicariously. A noted psychiatrist, Dr. A. A. Brill, wrote that all games and sports, including bridge, Parcheesi, boxing, baseball, and tennis, spring from the same root; an aggressive component in human nature, based on the primitive urge to master others. In our modern lives, the cruel struggle for survival of the cave man no longer exists. We have, therefore, in Brill's terms, created sports and games which are mock struggles with artificial dangers. Incidentally, these activities fortunately turned out to be highly pleasurable. Brill wrote:

> . . . sports are a great and necessary catharsis, indispensable to modern man —a salutary purgation of the combative instincts which, if dammed up within him, would break out in a disastrous way. . . .[1]

Whether or not one fully accepts this notion, there is no question that sports, particularly those which are combative or dangerous (such

[1] A. A. Brill, quoted in Robert H. Boyle, *Sport: Mirror of American Life* (Boston: Little, Brown, 1963), pp. 58–60.

as boxing, wrestling, judo, bobsledding, parachute jumping, and the like) offer modern man a challenge and a form of self-testing that he cannot find elsewhere in his life. In a way, they offer a means of asserting one's manhood.

Social Aspects

Another highly important aspect of sports participation is that it provides in most cases the chance to be a member of a team—a closely knit human group—with all the reassurance and warmth that may imply. This is a particularly important factor in the present day. Many social commentators have described a growth of *alienation,* a lack of belonging and commitment, on the part of young people today. They simply do not feel connected or involved—and it is believed that this accounts for much of the psychologically disturbed behavior of today's youth, including the wild destructive riots and vandalism that have appeared so frequently in the press.

Sports, while obviously not the total answer to the problem, do provide a direct and forceful kind of identification and human contact that is the very opposite of alienation. A team under pressure is a very tightly knit group. And even when it is a nonteam sport, with a player competing against a single opponent, there is contact. The athlete identifies closely with his rival; they are sharing the same impulses, strategic concerns, pressures, and emotions. In some events, the player sees his opponent as a human being whose sweat and even blood may be mixed with his; after a grueling prize fight, the combatants often embrace each other, as the winner consoles the loser.

Physical Aspects

The need for developing and maintaining an effective level of physical fitness in our society has already been described at length. Our mechanized society is sadly lacking in this area, and too often we have the deluded idea that the proper approach to fitness is through conditioning programs that place great reliance on exercises, gymnastics, and the like. It must be reemphasized that these artificially imposed forms of activity have little value for the total needs of our society. Weiss has written:

> . . . Sports programs run on their own motivational power. Physical conditioning programs are somewhat like medicine. We take these activities not because we like them but because they are good for us. Such nonsport programs last only as long as they are required.

World War II affords a good illustration. Air Force cadets were rigorously trained in one of the most intensive physical conditioning programs ever put together. Running, grass drills, guerilla exercises, and the obstacle course were the backbone of the program. By the time of graduation, these cadets had reached their peak of condition. Then they promptly lost their fitness when, as pilots, they were no longer required to exercise.

The situation is no better in civilian life. Ask any 20 friends in sedentary occupations how much nonsport physical conditioning they engage in each week. Unless I miss my guess, most will say they do nothing. Why? Well, most of all, these exercises are boring. . . . On the other hand, sports carry their own, built-in incentive. . . .[2]

It is interesting to recognize that many other nations have discerned these important values in sports and have made far greater efforts to stimulate and encourage mass participation than we have in the United States. This includes not only national support for training and competition on a top amateur level (as a means of enhancing national prestige), but the subsidizing of facilities and leadership to serve the great mass of youth and adults, of both sexes.

SPORTS AS A NATIONAL CONCERN

In Great Britain, for example, there is a Central Council of Physical Recreation, which has been extremely influential in promoting the ideal of "active leisure and coaching" throughout the country. They train many thousands of leaders and coaches, and have built a number of major national sports and recreation centers—including the famed Crystal Palace. This is a huge new National Recreation and Sport Center, with a stadium that offers accommodations for 15,000 spectators, with three pools, facilities for boxing, wrestling, badminton, squash, tennis, gymnastics, fencing, judo, dancing, track and field, soccer, cricket, and hockey. It has a hotel which makes it possible to serve as a training center for leaders and coaches, and to host major sports conferences, amateur organizational meetings, and similar events.

In Britain, as in most European countries, there is a far higher level of participation in adult sports clubs (including gymnastics, aquatic activities, hiking, and bicycling) than in the United States. This is particularly true in the nations behind the Iron Curtain.

The Soviet Union promotes sports and athletic participation almost as a matter of patriotic obligation. From childhood, all citizens are imbued with the idea that physical stamina and sturdiness are essential both for healthful living, and for a vigorous, hardy nation. While much of the national sports program is geared toward the production of out-

---

[2] Raymond A. Weiss, "Do Sports Produce Fitness?," *Journal of Health, Physical Education and Recreation*, March, 1961, pp. 20–21.

standing athletes for international sports competition and festivals, the
basic effect is a mass-approach, across-the-board involvement. McLendon
writes:

> From the early years to older adult years, a physical culture program is being
> made available for everyone. Millions now compete for badges signifying
> athletic achievement. All participants are provided with facilities, trainers,
> coaches and—more important—opportunities for organized competition and
> awards for recognition. This is one of the most important phases of Soviet
> living and encompasses all age levels.
>
> The emphasis on *participation* in sports over *spectatorship* is noticeable.
> Public works related to the development of parks, rivers, lakes, stadiums,
> arenas, and pools are extensive, more and more modern. The populace is
> being provided with modern sports activity facilities for all individual, team,
> and recreational classifications.
>
> In the educational institutions, the physical culture leader and coach (man-
> ager) occupy equal (or better, recognized) status with other professors and
> other professions. The athletes in the republic-level and the union-level pro-
> grams are highly respected and in some instances almost revered. . . .
>
> . . . in one Republic alone, the Ukraine, thousands of juvenile sports sec-
> tions are operating under the auspices of the various sports associations;
> there are over one hundred sports schools for adolescents and youths, where
> athletes are being trained.[3]

No wonder that Russia has made such rapid progress in international
sports competition! One might ask—what has all this to do with recreation? Is this grim determination to use sports as a means for building
national strength and prestige, this rigorous competitive drive—are these
what we mean by recreation? The question is a fair one. The answer is
"no." In the United States, we have a different set of goals and purposes,
and would probably never wish to have the degree of government
sponsorship and control of athletics that is found in the Soviet Union.
And yet, what have we to learn from them, in terms of their successes
in having the great mass of people engage in desirable participation in
vigorous sports and outdoor activities? Surely we need to make much
greater efforts nationally, through state programs, as well as locally, to
stimulate sports and physical recreation.

How is it to be done? Recognizing that the job of training and that
of stimulating participation are to be shared by physical education departments and recreation agencies, one writer proposes the following:

1. We must get our youth out of the grandstand and into the arena through
   a program of amateur sports in all our schools, such as hiking, cycling, camping, canoeing, skating, skiing, fencing and gymnastics.

   [3] John B. McLendon, Jr., "The Soviet Union's Program of Physical Culture and
   Sport," *Journal of Health, Physical Education and Recreation,* April, 1962.

2. Our press should place less emphasis on horse racing, professional ball games, auto racing, and gambling on sports.

3. We should have more sports facilities such as cycling paths, skating rinks, hiking trails, canoe marinas, et cetera. Every national and state park should provide these recreation facilities.

4. Colleges and schools should show more interest in providing individual sport activities than in gate receipts from ball games.

5. The government and our schools and colleges should offer full support in the establishment of a national youth hosteling project.

6. All people should receive athletic training in schools and the armed services, not just a few promising Olympic athletes.

7. The national youth fitness committee should be composed of amateur coaches and athletes, not professional ball coaches who are more interested in filling the grandstands.

8. Our railroads and boat and bus lines should provide opportunities to the public to enjoy sports away from the crowded cities by offering cycle trains, hikers' trains, foldboat trains, skate trains, ski trains, et cetera. Over five hundred cyclists enjoyed a recent train tour offered by the Long Island Railroad.

9. Many amateur active sports have military values and should be stressed by our service schools, such as skiing, skating, cycling, mountaineering, et cetera.

10. The fitness movement should not degenerate into stunts such as the fifty-mile-a-day hikes . . .[4]

While these statements represent the point of view of a single individual and may not all be feasible, certainly they suggest the broad direction in which we should be moving, in our schools, colleges, armed service centers, and community recreation departments.

SPORTS AS COMMUNITY RECREATION ACTIVITY

The fact, of course, is that because of their great popular appeal, sports have traditionally been an important part of public recreation programs. In addition to their popularity (particularly for men and boys, and for children and youth), they have the great advantage that they can be offered on various levels of skill, ranging from the complete beginner to the advanced competitive level. While some sports activities may require close supervision or instruction, many of them almost run themselves, once leagues, teams, and schedules have been established. It is possible, therefore, to serve comparatively large groups of people with a minimum of professional leadership, in contrast to certain other recreational activities. Furthermore, in terms of advancing the positive values of recreational experience, sports offer a great *potential*. That this potential is not always achieved is discussed later in this chapter.

[4] R. C. Geist, Letter to the Editor, *Recreation*, October, 1964, p. 379.

An Overall View of Sports Sponsorship

In an attempt to discover the extent to which athletic activities are organized, supervised, or conducted by recreation departments, several hundred local and county recreation and park departments were surveyed by the National Recreation Association in 1962. Some of their findings follow:

> Athletics and sports comprise slightly more than three-fifths of the total participation in the entire recreation program of 406 departments reporting. The percentage in individual departments varies from fifteen to one hundred; in a majority of them the participation in sports exceeds the total in all other aspects of their program. The overwhelming emphasis on sports in many cities indicates that other types of activities are not receiving a proportional share in the department program. The average percentages of participation in sports as reported by the districts are:

New England	67%	Midwest	60.6%
Mid-Atlantic	60%	Southwest	55%
Southern	55%	Pacific Northwest	65.4%
Great Lakes	57.4%	Pacific Southwest	52.3% [5]

Another area of investigation had to do with the relative importance that recreation departments attached to competitive athletic activities, as compared with other phases of their programs. Recognizing that some responses did not lend themselves to easy classification, the total response was tallied as follows:

Major, main or primary importance	32
High or great importance	75
Equal—same as others	174
Secondary or minor	21

The reasons cited by community recreation departments for giving sports a high rating included the following: (a) they were cited as a most effective public relations' medium and a means for easily reaching and serving large numbers of people; (b) a useful means of providing spectator events for adults; (c) a form of activity that could meet varying needs of people of different ages; (d) they serve to motivate physical fitness, develop sportsmanship and character, and release tension; (e) they create interest in the entire recreation program; and finally, (f) they are valuable because they afford an opportunity for general participation and mass enjoyment rather than intensive competition and the development of champions.

[5] "Municipal Sports Programs and Policies," *Recreation,* May, 1963, p. 215.

Types of Sports Activities Offered

Of 28 different athletic activities listed, the average number of activities offered by a single department was 11. Only eight of the activities listed were checked by as many as one-half of the reporting departments, and these may be identified as the most popular community sports activities. They were, in the order named: *softball, basketball, baseball, tennis, swimming* and *diving, volleyball, track* and *field,* and *archery.* Other activities which were mentioned by at least a quarter of the respondents were: *bowling, regulation* and *touch football, golf, gymnastics* and *tumbling, ice skating,* and *weightlifting.* Such sports as *ice hockey, hiking, boxing, soccer, trampoline,* and *wrestling* also received strong mentions.

It is interesting to note that there are certain definite regional differences throughout the United States, with respect to certain sports:

Half the reporting departments in the Southwest provide boxing activities; very few in the Middle Atlantic and Pacific Southwest do so.

Regulation football ranks high in the Southern District; touch (or flag) football in the Pacific Southwest.

Many departments in the Midwest and Pacific Southwest offer gymnastics and tumbling.

The Great Lakes District leads in the percentage of departments providing skating, icy hockey, and scuba, and ranks second to the Pacific Southwest in trampolining.

Weightlifting is most frequently reported by Southern cities; next by cities in the Pacific Southwest, which indicates little interest in such activities as boxing and wrestling.

Winter sports lead in New England, the Mid-Atlantic, and Great Lakes Districts.

Obviously, some of these choices reflect the effect of climate or topographical characteristics of different regions. Others, particularly those which stress competitive or body-contact sports, may be interpreted as reflecting other regional characteristics or interests.

Extent of Growth of Sports Facilities

It is widely known that there has been a steady rise in the provision of public recreation facilities for such sports as baseball, golf, softball, and tennis since World War II. However, this growth has *not* begun to meet the need, based on commonly accepted standards for community sports facilities. For example, these standards call for a city to provide:

1 baseball diamond per 6,000 population
1 hole of golf per 3,000 population
1 softball diamond per 3,000 population
1 tennis court per 2,000 population [6]

Thus far, only a small proportion of American cities, particularly those with less than 25,000 in population, have managed to live up to these suggested requirements. An analysis of statistics cited in the Recreation and Parks Yearbooks of 1948, 1955, and 1960 reveals a great shortage of adequate sports facilities, especially in the larger cities.

For example, in a survey of the top quartile of cities in eight population groupings in 1960, it was found that, while 53 percent of the cities in the 5,000–9,999 category met the standard for baseball diamonds, *none* of the cities in the population group of 250,000 and over did. Again, although 100 percent of the smaller municipalities met the standard requirement with respect to golf, only 2.3 percent of the largest cities met it. With respect to tennis courts, 27 percent of the smaller cities met the approved standard, and none of the larger cities. Based on this survey, it is apparent that the majority of our communities have far to go, in terms of providing adequate facilities for even the most common sports activities.

In addition to building sports facilities and areas, what are some of the other functions of community recreation departments, within the area of sports and athletics?

Other Functions of Recreation Departments

Specifically, these include the following:

1. To survey and analyze total community needs, interests, and capabilities, in order to develop a comprehensive and diversified offering of sports activities

2. To provide direct participant services, including the following:
   a. to offer instruction on a variety of levels, from beginning skills to advanced or high-level performance
   b. to schedule opportunities for free-play, or casual participation, on playgrounds or playfields, or in afterschool centers, in those sports which can be carried on with a minimum of supervision or leadership
   c. to organize, or to assist other groups in carrying on programs of league competition, or scheduled play throughout the sports season

3. To stimulate community-wide interest and participation in sports in general, or in specific activities, by sponsoring clinics, workshops, demonstrations or other special events—including tournaments and competition

[6] "Community Sports Facilities on the Increase," *Recreation,* January, 1963, pp. 21–22.

4. To train and develop leadership in the form of leaders and coaches, both within professional staff and the community at large, including many parents or other adults who may serve as volunteer leaders or officials.

5. To assist in coordinating the total community sports program, so that overlap is avoided, and major events or similar activities are not scheduled against each other; to provide facilities for other community agencies, such as churches, "Y's," and industrial leagues, and to assist them with problems of leagues and public relations

In general, it is important to stress that while individuals with high levels of ability and interest should be served, wherever possible, it is the chief concern of the community recreation department to serve the bulk of the population—including many with only mediocre skills or less. This is equally true of the other agencies that may sponsor sports programs, such as the armed forces, industrial leagues, and unions. Although there is glamor and excitement in a top-flight competitive program, far more people are meaningfully served at the lower levels of ability.

PROFILES OF COMMUNITY SPORTS PROGRAMS

Clearly, there are many different patterns of sports sponsorship in different communities, and no single program would be typical of all. However, here are some illustrative examples. First, it is revealing to see how a single activity—swimming—may be presented in many different forms, within a single community recreation program.

Aquatic Recreation. In Bloomington, Indiana, population about 32,000, swimming is an extremely popular sport. The local recreation-sponsored team, numbering well over 100 boys and girls, has gained state-wide recognition in swimming competition. In addition, during the summers, the Indiana University varsity swimming team is permitted to use the Bryan Park pool (an outdoor 50-meter facility) for early morning practices. Beyond these competition-oriented elements of the aquatic program, however, the following activities are sponsored:

1. Public swimming in two outdoor pools from May through September, with over 100,000 participants recorded in a single season
2. Basic swimming instruction classes, with 1,100 children served during the season
3. Life-saving classes
4. Water safety training
5. Special swimming class for retarded children
6. Annual water show, involving over 100 participants and 2,500 spectators
7. Adult "learn to swim" class
8. Special class for the physically handicapped
9. Low-cost rental of the smaller pool to community clubs or organizations, industrial concerns, and summer camps, during special hours that do not conflict with other public uses

This is a good example of the diversity that may be achieved in scheduling activities based on a single sport, within a given community. Another example is that of tennis, which has declined in popularity in some areas, possibly because of the cost of building and maintaining facilities. A number of communities have initiated plans to renew public interest in this excellent sport.

Promotion of Tennis. East Detroit, Michigan, feeling that tennis had an important contribution to make to its public recreation program, has done the following: added a number of new courts; acted as host for state recreation association meetings; developed expanded programs of public tennis instruction on all levels of ability; sponsored tennis award nights; developed an Inter-City Tennis Association and a strong Girls Little League Tennis Team; brought in such outstanding stars as Althea Gibson to conduct clinics, and generally promoted the sport so that it has reached new levels of popularity.

On a much larger scale, tennis in the San Francisco Bay area has received a healthy boost through free tennis clinics which have been initiated by a group of private individuals who formed an incorporated Youth Tennis Foundation. Program services were provided first in depressed areas, and then on a city-wide basis. Eventually, the game was brought to over 40,000 children between the ages of 8 and 15—many of whom had never held a racquet before—in San Francisco and other Bay cities. Demonstration clinics were held before as many as 2,000 junior high school children at special rallies, or for as few as 50 or 60 children in regular physical education classes. As a consequence of this effort, many physical education teachers have gained a renewed interest in the sport as a school activity, and tennis in general has climbed back to popularity in the San Francisco Bay area.

Each of these are examples of how a concerted effort may be put on to promote a single sport as part of a community recreation program. On a broader level, a good illustration of the total scope of sports within a community recreation department may be found in Fresno, California, a city of 140,000 population.

Sports and Athletics in a Single Community. In terms of staff and facilities, the Fresno Parks and Recreation Department places sports and athletics under the direction of a Recreation Supervisor (who is in turn responsible to the Superintendent of Recreation). The Supervisor is in overall charge of 14 baseball fields, 28 softball fields, 1 soccer field, 17 gymnasiums, 8 running tracks, and sports programs in 14 secondary schools. It is the Supervisor's task to direct and organize sports leagues, do detailed planning and make operational decisions, and carry out immediate supervision of personnel, facilities, and equipment. In addition, there is a Maintenance Foreman, who maintains, repairs and cleans all city recreation facilities, including 3 recreation centers,

8 playgrounds, 16 tennis courts, 2 dance slabs, 2 swimming pools, 4 learner pools, 5 field houses, and 38 school playgrounds. Other personnel include two golf professionals, each of whom is responsible for an 18-hole golf course, and a swimming pool supervisor, who directs and operates the municipal swimming pools.

To illustrate the variety of sports and athletics in Fresno, the following were program features within a recent year:

Physical fitness activities, including special elementary school and junior high school age classes for boys and girls, stressing both gymnastics and free exercise; also physical education meets and Junior Olympics competition

A scheduled program of soccer for junior high and high school age boys, with three leagues participating

A track and field program (with both district meets and a city-wide championship) in which over 1,000 boys and girls under 14 years of age participated

Night softball, with 71 men's teams and 50 boys' teams taking part in regularly scheduled league play during the spring and summer; also 15 girls' softball teams, involving a total participation of 95,926 men and boys and 8,481 girls

Spring and summer baseball activity in: 48 Spartans League teams for boys 12 and under; 34 Babe Ruth League teams for boys 13 to 15, and 7 American Legion teams for boys 17 and under

Winter basketball scheduling in Fresno that uses every available city and school gymnasium throughout the city in the late fall, winter, and early spring; also, an extensive program of Saturday morning playground basketball for junior high school age boys with the total number of men's and boys' teams, 105; women and girls, 14 teams

An adult soccer league comprising six teams with (because of the popularity of soccer in other lands) many participants of varied nationalities, many of whom take part in no other public recreation activities

Other programs and events: (a) a boating safety program, with a special course given to 175 boys and girls in the proper and safe handling of water craft; (b) an annual city golf championship; an annual San Joaquin Valley Swimming and Diving Championship; (c) varied sports activities for cerebral palsied and mentally retarded children and youth; (d) a swimming program with a heavy emphasis on instruction for children; and, (e) seasonal instruction of folk games on all playgrounds, including such traditional activities as rope-skipping, hopscotch, and jacks for girls, and kites and marbles for boys

In order to operate such a diversified program successfully, there must be a careful preliminary detailing of all responsibilities and functions. These include the development of seasonal and year-long schedules; the assignment of instructors, playfield personnel, coaches and officials;

the purchase, storage, repair, and assignment of equipment; the planning, development, and maintenance of facilities and areas; the thorough and timely carrying out of promotion and public relations; the efficient conduct of tournaments and meets; and, finally, an ongoing process of evaluating outcomes and measuring the success of all program activities and services.

It is not possible for a book, devoted, as this one is, to a broad examination of recreation programs and leadership, to analyze such an operation in complete detail. However, it is helpful to examine the specific responsibilities of a single individual, the playfield director within a large metropolitan school-sponsored recreation department. The following guides illustrate these tasks and functions:

Introduction to Athletic Field

. . . This manual has been prepared to assist the teacher in developing and maintaining a successful athletic field program. The purpose of the Board of Education athletic fields operated by the Bureau of Community Education is to provide a program of planned and supervised recreational activities for all age groups and to make the fields a focal point of community leisure time activity by publicizing, promoting, organizing, and conducting individual, group, and team activities. The activities conducted at a field include all or some of the following: tennis, handball, softball, baseball, "Little Fellas League," dance festivals, track and field meets, dances, volleyball, basketball, shuffleboard, quiet games, tournaments, and other activities. These may be sponsored by the Bureau of Community Education, outside agencies, or both.

The athletic fields operated by the Bureau of Community Education vary in many ways, such as type of community, size, facilities, accommodations for participants, and provisions for spectators. Consequently . . . a program which is successful at one field may be unsuitable for another. The teacher must be alert to the needs and desires of the community and develop his program accordingly. . . .

The manual then proceeds to outline the scheduling system under which the athletic fields are used, including season, time, and hours of operation, and special arrangements for weekends and holidays. It then outlines the duties and responsibilities of field men, including the three major tasks: (a) promotion; (b) administration; and (c) instruction:

. . . the promotion of a field calls for widespread publicity in the press. All community agencies and groups who conduct programs on athletic fields are to be contacted. The position of field teacher calls for many personal and professional contacts made prior to the field assignment. These contacts are a prerequisite to successful field operations. . . .

Promotion—There are three types of organization which should be promoted:

1. In which all activities, including track, basketball, tennis, and baseball, are sponsored by the Bureau of Community Education
2. In which the above activities are sponsored and conducted jointly by the Bureau of Community Education and recognized community organizations
3. In which the teacher provides the facilities for organizations and groups to conduct their own program on the athletic fields

Administrative Duties—These include, generally, making sure that every area available for formal and informal play is activated; that requests from community organizations for the use of recreational facilities are promptly acknowledged and acted on; and that the field and facilities are kept in a clean, safe, and well-maintained condition by the custodian responsible.

Instruction—The following courts or game areas may be found on a given athletic field: baseball, basketball, football, handball, shuffleboard, soccer, softball, tennis, track, volley ball, and badminton. The teacher assigned to the field must stimulate interest in these by teaching, organizing clinics and/or demonstrations, by encouraging the formation of leagues or teams, and by supervising overall play.

Under these general headings, the field teacher has a variety of other responsibilities relating to:

Safety Procedures—He is required to follow a departmental bulletin dealing with handling of accidents and cases of sudden illness, first aid and emergency care, reporting accidents, release of information and records, fire drills and Civil Defense drills.

Facilities, Equipment and Materials—He is required to supervise and work with the custodial staff to maintain, clean, and make available for use all diamonds, fields, courts and grandstands. Sports equipment must be repaired, stored, marked and made available, including indoor recreational games for inclement weather. Check-out systems must permit safe lending of equipment.

Promotion and Publicity—The field teacher must achieve full community understanding of the program, and maximum participation in sports and athletic events. He is responsible for bulletin boards, scheduling of special events for publicity, preparation of fliers and newspaper releases, and direct contacts with community groups such as P.T.A.'s, housing centers, churches, clubs, synagogues, and the like.[7]

Clearly, within such a framework, the direct organization and leadership of sports activities represent only a portion of the playfield leader's concern. However, they represent the key element and must be intelligently and responsibly carried out. It was indicated before that

[7] *Physical Education Handbook, Part II* (New York: Bureau of Community Education, Board of Education, 1964).

the major sports, such as baseball, basketball, swimming, and softball, tend to represent the largest percentage of athletic participation in recreational programs. However, two other types of activities must be identified here as important to the total success of the program:

1. Games which represent lead-up activities, and which prepare children and youth to take part successfully in the more difficult team games
2. Adaptations of most popular games and sports, which make them more generally available or more playable by the bulk of participants in the program

LEAD-UP GAMES

Lead-up games are presented in this chapter, rather than in the preceding one, because they tend to be primarily athletic in nature, leading directly to participation in regular sports activity. They are especially important for young children who have not yet acquired the coordination or physical ability needed to engage in more highly organized or complex sports. By developing specific techniques directly related to ball-handling, throwing, catching, kicking, or other skills, the youngster is given confidence. In addition, he learns to work as part of a team, to cooperate with his fellow players, and to understand the concepts and rules of different sports.

Several examples of lead-up games follow. Each is directed to teaching the skills of a particular sport.

Punch-A-Cat

Baseball lead-up game. Teaches hitting, running, throwing, and fielding skills.

Players and Formation:	May be played by six to ten participants. There is only one base and home plate. One player is at bat; the others are in the field (Fig. 7).
Equipment:	A rubber or tennis ball.
Rules:	The player at bat bounces the ball once and then punches it toward the field. The object is for him to run to first base and back, before the ball can be fielded and returned to a base before him, making him "out." A fly ball caught is also "out."
Scoring:	A player scores one point each time he runs to the base and back to home plate safely. He remains at bat until he is put out. Then he goes to the outfield, and all the other players move up one position. Each player takes his turn at bat.

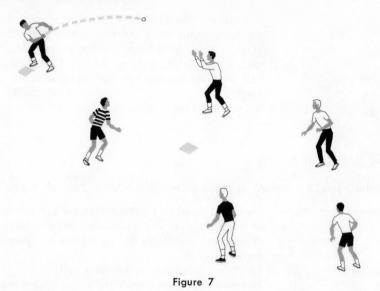

Figure 7

Flies Up

Baseball lead-up game. Teaches hitting and catching.

Players and Formation: May be played by six to ten participants. One player
                           is at bat; the others are in the field. There is no base-
                           running.
Equipment: A bat, and a softball or baseball.
Rules: The player at bat tosses up the ball, and then hits it to
                           the field. If a fielder catches it on the fly, he becomes
                           the new batter. If he catches a grounder, the batter
                           must place the bat flat on the ground, and the fielder
                           "bowls" the ball toward the bat (Fig. 8). If he succeeds

Figure 8

in hitting it (the ball usually bounces up into the air) the batter must catch the ball before it touches the ground again, in order to remain at the plate. If he cannot, the fielder goes up to bat. If the "bowled" ball does not hit the bat, the batter remains at the plate.

Scoring: No score is kept.

Guard Basketball

Basketball lead-up game. Teaches passing, catching, and guarding.

Players and Formation: Six to ten players on a team. One team stands behind an outer circle (with one teammate in the center). The other team stands on the inner circle, spaced out evenly (Fig. 9).

Equipment: Basketball or rubber playground ball.

Rules: Players on the team outside the larger circle must pass the ball to their teammate in the center, while players

Figure 9

on the inner circle try to prevent the pass from being completed. The "guarding" team may hit or kick the ball away, but may not catch it. Each time the ball is caught by the center player, it is passed out to the outer circle without interference, and the play is resumed.

Scoring: Each time a pass is completed to the center player, one point is scored for his team. After about five minutes of play, teams reverse positions. The team with the highest total at the end wins.

Square Soccer

Soccer lead-up game. Teaches kicking and blocking.

Players and Formation: Eight to twelve players on a team. Each team stands along two adjacent sides of a square, with two players behind a center restraining line (Fig. 10).

Equipment: Soccer ball or rubber playground ball.

Rules: The two active players try to kick the ball below shoulder height through the opposing team. Defend-

Figure 10

ing players may use any part of the body to block the ball, but may not catch it with their hands. The ball remains in play until it goes through a team and over the boundary line.

Scoring: One point is scored when the ball is kicked by an active player through the opposing team. After each score, the two active players on each side change places with others on their team, and the team that was scored against is given the ball to begin play.

Flag Run

Football lead-up game. Teaches running and dodging skills.

Players and Formation: Six to twelve players on a team. Teams are on opposite sides of a center line. Total area should be about as large as a basketball court.

Equipment: "Flags" (pieces of cloth, tucked in the belt behind the player; these may be homemade or bought commercially).

Rules: At a signal, one team attempts to cross their opponent's territory and reach the end line, without losing their "flags." The defending team attempts to pull away their "flags" (this is less rough than tackling, and easier to judge than tagging) (Fig. 11).

Scoring: One point is scored for each player who manages to dodge his way through to the end line without losing his "flag." When both teams have had a turn, the team with the highest total wins.

Figure 11

Many other useful lead-up games may be found in the collection by Blake and Volp.[8] Activities of this type, because they can be played by large numbers of children without a high degree of skill, are extremely useful for playground and playfield situations as well as for indoor gymnasium programs.

OTHER MODIFIED SPORTS

For youth at large, and also for adults who are past the age of highly vigorous play, the recreation leader may wish to modify certain major sports. The point of the modification may be to permit larger numbers to enjoy the game, to make it safer, or to encourage less highly skilled players to take part. A good example of this would be "Flag Football"— a modification of the game in which players do not forcibly tackle and and block each other, but in which most of the other elements of football have been retained. Here are other examples of modified sports:

Slow Pitch Softball. This game differs from regular softball in the following ways:

1. The ball is 16 inches in circumference, compared to 12 inches for the regulation softball. Gloves are therefore not needed. The ball is easier to hit and catch and does not travel as far or fast as the regulation ball.

2. The ball, when pitched, must describe an arc (reaching a point above the batter's head) before it reaches the plate. This slows it up, makes it easier to hit, and prevents speedy pitchers from dominating the play. There is more action for both hitters and fielders.

3. An additional player, a "short center-fielder" is added to the team, giving more players a chance to join in.

This version of softball has become a popular recreational sport in the Midwest in recent years, with many older players (including some teams with no one under the age of 60) taking part. Recently it has spread to the West Coast and has caught on there. Other variations of the game (some make use of a 14-inch ball, and are called "Mush-Ball") have become popular elsewhere in the country.[9]

Indoor Hockey. This game was carried on originally in the Recreation Department of Battle Creek, Michigan, and has since spread to a number of other communities. It represented an attempt to develop a variation of hockey that could be played in any community, without having to have a rink, that would be fast and strenuous but safe, that would give smaller and younger children a chance to play, and finally, that would use simple and inexpensive equipment.

[8] O. William Blake and Anne M. Volp, *Lead-Up Games to Team Sports* (Englewood Cliffs, N.J.: Prentice-Hall, 1964).

[9] Thomas A. Peterson, "Slow Pitch Boom," *Recreation,* October, 1963, p. 375.

The game is played with lightweight plastic sticks and pucks that may be commercially purchased. It has simple rules and may be taught in 15 minutes or less. The director of the Battle Creek Recreation Department indicates that the total cost of equipment for a league of 15 to 20 teams need only be about $30, plus plastic face masks for goalies. In Battle Creek, as many as 43 teams have been participating in an organized league, plus many other teams in junior high school indoor hockey programs—including in many cases both boys and girls, and in some cases, handicapped children.[10]

Stake Golf. A form of golf which is particularly appropriate for small grassy areas and which may be used by institutions, rest homes, or nursing clinics, is "stake golf." This is like Miniature Golf, but is based entirely on putting. Stakes are placed around an area, as in croquet; each player competes in putting his own golf ball around a course and then into a cup. The equipment is simple and the game quite enjoyable, particularly for those with limited physical skills.

Four-Square. This game represents a variation of handball. The essential differences are that it is played on a flat hard-surface area without a vertical back wall, and that it makes use of a volleyball. The game is played on four adjacent squares, each one 10 feet square (Fig. 12). Simply

Figure 12

described, the ball is served with an underhand scooping motion by the first player into any square or box not his own. It must be received on one bounce and directed to any other square. A player commits a foul (and receives a penalty point) when he does one of the following: (a) fails to direct the ball into another square; (b) hits the ball downward (known as "spiking"); (c) volleys (ball must bounce in his square before being

[10] Tom Harter, "Indoor Hockey," *Recreation,* March, 1964, p. 101.

played); (d) plays the ball on more than one bounce; (e) hits the ball so it touches a line; (f) hits it into the same square twice in a row; or (g) holds or catches the ball. As the game is played, a player stays in the same square, but the serve rotates from player to player.

Each time a player commits a foul, a point is scored against him. The player with the least number of points after a set time period is the winner.

OTHER SPORTS ACTIVITIES

In addition to the standard team and dual sports, lead-up games, and the type of modified game just described, what other sport and athletic activities are suitable for playground programs? Here are several:

Volleyball. Volleyball, which many have thought of as an extremely simple game lacking any real challenge, can in reality be played with great skill and excitement. True, it may be enjoyed by the aged or handicapped. It has also been played as a form of international competition before huge audiences throughout the world. The Japanese women's championship team has held their spectators and opponents literally spellbound with brilliant acrobatic feats; here in the United States, beach volleyball as played in Southern California attracts thousands of outstanding players, a number of whom have become national tournament stars. It has been estimated that well over 20 million players take part in volleyball—on beaches, in camps, schools, colleges, and the armed forces. It is a game that can be enjoyably played by those from 8 to 80—and yet too few community recreation departments make use of this excellent sport.

Skiing. In recent years, we have seen a winter sports boom. In the northern section of the country particularly, there have been many private commercial skiing developments. These have been extremely expensive ventures, including tows, chair lifts, artificial snow machines and often other elaborate facilities. Can skiing be offered by community recreation departments? As a basic sports activity, a number have already done it.

Some recreation and park departments have set up ski slopes and in some cases installed snow-making machines. They give instruction, offer clinics, and carry on varied skiing activities—close to home. Actually, it is not even necessary to have snow in order to have a skiing program. Vendien points out that it is possible to sponsor an indoor ski school, in which many of the basic techniques, safety procedures, and rules of skiing etiquette may be learned and practiced—before the learner ever goes outdoors. Basic conditioning can be carried on. Rules of safety, information, and ski terminology can be imparted. Skiers may learn both beginning and intermediate techniques. If all this is done knowledgeably, with the help of films, slides, diagrams, and photographs, and using balance beams, ski parallel boards, ramps, and hand-pulley arrangements, learners may go so far that they actually can bypass some of the beginning classes on the actual ski slope later and move more rapidly into intermediate classes.[11]

True, all this requires ingenuity and skilled leadership, but the imaginative recreation administrator should be able to supply, or locate, both!

Bowling. Again, this is an activity which is widely available for youth and adults in commercial bowling centers. However, many young people fail to take part in the activity because of the expense or lack of instruction.

A number of municipal recreation or school-sponsored departments have therefore organized junior bowling programs which include instruction, competition, and the opportunity to engage in a wholesome activity under proper supervision. For example, a Junior Bowling Program was developed in Westbury, New York, and grew from 50 to 200 participants during a three-year period. Making use of both volunteer and professional instructors, special tournaments, free bowling clinics, and an annual awards banquet, this developed into an attractive and successful feature of the total community recreation offering. Recreation administrators have found that, when properly approached, bowling center proprietors have been willing to make their lanes available at reduced rates or, under some circumstances, without charge, for an introductory period. They have also been cooperative in providing bowling shoes and instruction at minimal cost, and in prohibiting the sale of liquor during the hours that children are on the premises.[12] In other communities, recreation departments have organized housewives' leagues during the morning hours or have established special bowling programs for the physically handicapped or mentally retarded.

Skating. For years, this has of course been a popular activity carried on informally on streets or frozen ponds—or in commercial rinks or centers.

In more and more communities, artificial ice skating rinks have been built by public recreation departments, particularly when the climate has permitted a skating season of at least four or five months. The activity has proven to be extremely popular—especially when it has been intensively promoted with effective publicity, and with such features as season tickets, instruction classes, special events, and rental to hockey leagues—as a means of offsetting costs. While it may not be a fully self-supporting enterprise, the well-managed and budgeted artificial ice

11 Lynn Vendien, "Learn to Ski Without Snow or Hill," *Journal of Health, Physical Education and Recreation,* January, 1962, p. 33.
12 N. Arthur Bleau, "Bowling for Everyone," *Recreation,* October, 1961, p. 423.

skating rink should come close to paying for itself. It should even be possible to offer free sessions for youngsters who cannot afford to pay a small entrance fee. In addition, ice skating is one of the few sports activities which lends itself to participation by the total family.

Roller skating, too, has been effectively sponsored by a number of community recreation departments. In some cases, as in New Orleans, this has been traditionally presented on outdoor hard-surface areas or paved tennis courts. In others, as in Los Angeles, it has actually been run as a highly successful indoor program, in recreation centers. The Los Angeles Recreation and Park Department found that skates with wooden or fiber wheels could be modified so that the nuts on the outside of the wheels were countersunk—and did no damage whatsoever to asphalt tile, parquet, or other wood flooring surfaces. In Los Angeles, a traveling unit system of setting up a "portable" roller skating program has been established. Using special units of skates, musical equipment, ticket rolls, and similar materials, the programs are run for two-hour afternoon or evening sessions throughout the city. Skating sessions are patterned after those of the commercially operated rinks, including marches, couple and trio skating, strict rules of behavior—and extremely inexpensive fees for participation.[13] This too has been a successful family sports activity.

Bicycling. How often is bicycling thought of as a community recreation activity? True, more than 55 million Americans own bicycles. But, all too often, they use them only occasionally because of the lack of opportunity or safe roads on which to travel. Today, bicycling has become increasingly recognized by the American Medical Association, the American Heart Association and many individual doctors, as an excellent form of physical conditioning, for young and old alike. The American Association for Health, Physical Education and Recreation has therefore published a booklet outlining the recreation potential of this activity.[14]

What can recreation, or parks and recreation departments do to promote bicycling? First, they can help to establish safe biking routes within a community, in parks, or even along highways which are being built or planned—as in Europe, where hosteling by bicycle is a major pastime. In addition, some communities have sponsored bicycling clubs, which plan trips to picnics or cookouts, bicycle safety programs, map-reading or orienteering contests, and similar events. On summer playgrounds, a Bicycle Rodeo, with races, games, and the like, is always a popular program feature. Fitness, fun, and safety should be the keynote of any recreation department or school that initiates bicycling recreation for youth or adults.

[13] Ralph Borrelli, "Traveling Roller Skating Rinks," *Recreation*, November 1956, p. 436.

[14] *Cycling in the School Fitness Program* (Washington, D.C.: American Association for Health, Physical Education and Recreation, 1963).

Aquatics. Certainly, this is one of the major areas of growth in American recreation programing. Boating and other water sports are dealt with in Chapter 6, under the heading of outdoor recreation and nature activities. Swimming and diving as such should properly be considered sports, when presented within a municipal recreation department's program.

Many park and recreation departments have joined in the trend toward water sports by building swimming pools—along with private families, neighborhood associations, and county park systems. Few are as impressive as the remarkable swimming pavilion in Commerce, California, which is not only a center for aquatic activity but also provides facilities for community meetings, dinners, and a great variety of civic events and functions. The Aquatorium, as it is called, is actually a complex of three buildings, including two pools, meeting rooms, patios with food service facilities, physical conditioning pavilions, and portable bleachers for spectator events.

The Aquatorium is used for 16 hours a day, every day of the year. Among its unique features is an underwater observation room with a sound system that enables instructors to speak directly to swimmers and divers while underwater (important in the training of skin and "scuba" divers). Who uses the center? Swimming classes are offered for babies of just six months to three years of age. "Peewee" beginners between the ages of three and five also have special classes. Beyond that, students go into such classes as "beginners," "advanced beginners," "intermediate," "swimmer," "junior-senior lifesaving," and "diving" instruction. In addition, adults are provided with graded swimming or lifesaving classes, water ballet, skin diving, "scuba," and youth competitive swim programs. Local employees in nearby industries use the pool for a popular noon-time program that includes physical conditioning, a low-calorie lunch, and a quick swim. Small wonder that the pool's attendance passed the hundred thousand mark within eight months after being opened!

It is interesting to note the story of admission costs in the Commerce pool center. In an era when costs of most services have been steadily mounting, the original admissions fees (during the early months of operation) were set at the modest amounts of 40¢ for adults, 20¢ for juniors, and 10¢ for children. Finding, however, that some families were using the pool so much that they were spending up to $4.00 a week for admissions alone, the city officials promptly lowered the admissions fee to 10¢ for all. This quickly increased adult and junior use of the pool— and it still was a financially sound operation.[15]

In general, in planning pool schedules for community-operated pools or aquatic centers, the following guides are helpful:

15 Arnold J. Robles, "New Aquatorium 'On Target,'" *Recreation*, November, 1963, p. 413.

1. Make sure that each potential user of the pool in the community has a chance to swim each day, with instruction being given for each level of ability, age, and sex.
2. Keep class or activity standards or performance levels consistent with other aquatic centers, schools, or camps, by following American Red Cross class outlines.
3. Provide for a logical progression from one class to the next level; there should be clear-cut goals or rewards (in terms of certificates or participation in special programs or competitions) at the end of each swimming season.
4. Provide a social outlet for teen-agers in particular; a special time should be designated for them, and for adults, to swim during the evening or at night.
5. If there are empty or little used periods in the schedule, plan to have special interest groups, small classes, or the handicapped (whose time should be fairly flexible) make use of these time slots.
6. When large classes are scheduled one after another, try to stagger the time arrangements so that overcrowding is prevented (rather than have excessive numbers in the showers, locker room, or pool all at once).
7. Once the schedules for the year have been established, try to make sure that major program features (such as open swimming, instructional classes, or family hours) are kept consistently at the same time, rather than frequently changed. Thus, confusion will be avoided, and attendance maintained.[16]

OTHER SPORTS INTERESTS

Certain other sports activities may appeal to special tastes in the community—particularly to those who seek adventure and thrills. Thus, in some Western states, the public recreation department may sponsor classes or clubs in mountain climbing, or may sponsor special river canoe trips or other forms of hazardous sport. Usually, however, individuals who are interested in this sort of pastime, or in such hobbies as spelunking (cave exploration), do so on their own or in private clubs.

One exception to this has been the sponsorship by a number of recreation departments of drag strip racing—i.e., competitive racing clubs for young "hot-rodders." The intention of such ventures has been to provide exciting activities for youth and to offer the same kinds of thrills that might otherwise be sought under more dangerous and unsupervised circumstances. Such clubs have frequently gone beyond the mere scheduling of drag races under supervision. In a number of cases, they have included talks by well-known individuals in the automotive industry, or by famous racing drivers, and have stressed the promotion of safe driving on highways, courtesy, and aid to motorists in trouble. Some recreation departments which have sponsored "hot-rod" clubs or drag strip racing have insisted on the members living up to codes stressing these positive aspects.

16 Adapted from John M. Klang, "Developing a Pool Schedule," *Recreation,* June, 1961, p. 318.

Nonetheless, drag strips as such have been condemned by the International Association of Chiefs of Police and by the National Safety Council. Each community must decide for itself whether, if the racing aspect of the activity can be minimized, the constructive potential of hot-rodding offers a sufficiently sound basis for public sponsorship.

Equally unusual, but not as controversial, is the unique riding program sponsored by the Parks and Recreation Department of Pompano Beach, Florida. This public agency gradually took over the ownership and operation of what had formerly been a private riding facility. Today, the recreation department is in charge of a facility that houses over 50 horses and ponies, has both an adult Saddle Club and a junior club, the Mavericks, and makes use of over eight miles of bridle paths. The riding program includes instructional classes, moonlight rides, horse shows, barbecues, sponsorship of monthly Western Horsemen's Circuit Shows, as well as training in care of horses and stalls, and in precision riding, spectacular drills, and other equestrian hobbies.

It is important to note that today, technology and improved kinds of machinery and equipment are making it possible to present forms of recreation that never had been available before—particularly within the realm of sport.

Technology and New Sports Opportunities

With respect to water sports, water skiing, or the unique kind of skiing in which the skier is drawn up into the air with a kite-like kind of contraption, illustrate mechanized forms of play.

"Scuba" diving, particularly diving to great depths, or the kind of underwater recreation center that offers an underwater "hike" along a scenic trail (in which the "hiker" does not surface for a long period of time), represents another form of technologically based play that could not have been envisioned years ago.

Winter sports, when dependent on artificial freezing, chair lifts, snow machines, and similar technical advances, clearly have received a great stimulus from recent inventions.

Of greater meaning to most community recreation departments has been the introduction of night-lighting techniques that make it possible to construct great banks of lights for aftersunset participation in tennis, golf, baseball and softball, and other recreational pursuits. Clearly, an increasing number of departments will be exploring the possibilities of night-lighting for expanding their sports programs.[17]

Another interesting innovation has been the development of "mobile" recreation program units. One simple example has been the roller-skating

17 See "More Light on Sports," *Recreation*, September, 1964, p. 352, and Joseph Curtis, "Floodlighting Saves a Problem," *Recreation*, May, 1963.

units that are "portable" in Los Angeles. Another is the development of "portable pools" in Los Angeles, in which a single two-and-a-half-ton truck carries the frame, sides, and liner for a good-sized learners' pool. This is brought to a neighborhood playground and quickly assembled and filled, to serve hundreds of children in a full schedule of classes. These pools, costing slightly more than $2,000 at present, make it possible to provide swimming instruction in many settings where children would not have otherwise learned to swim.

Similarly, in other areas of recreation service, ingenious planning and design have created mobile dramatics presentations ("traveling show wagons"), mobile libraries, and mobile science and outdoor recreation programs.

The alert recreation administrator will continue to seize every opportunity afforded by these new techniques to diversify and enrich his program.

SPORTS COMPETITION

In sports, more than in any other area of the program, the competitive instincts of children, youth, and adults come into play. Within certain limits, this is highly desirable. It stimulates a high level of interest and motivation; "playing to win" is a normal and accepted phenomenon in our culture. What is important is that competition does not become the *sole* focus of the sports program. Scheduled games, meets, tournaments, and awards all make sense—provided that they are not afforded at the cost of eliminating less formal, more relaxed forms of competitive play. The player with poor or mediocre skills must be given a chance to compete on his own level of ability, or not to compete at all, if he does not wish to do so. With these limitations, competition can add much to the sports program in communities, summer camps, and other recreation settings.

The most useful ways of structuring competition are often based on meets and tournaments. Meets usually represent a single day's competition by a large number of individuals affiliated with teams, in such broad areas as gymnastics, or track and field. Individuals compete in varied events, like the sprints, hurdles, long-distance runs, and throwing events, and are given points according to their place in the scoring: first, second, or third. At the conclusion of the meet, each team is given the total number of points scored by its members, and the winning order of the teams is determined.

Tournaments, on the other hand, usually represent organized competition by individuals or teams, in a single type of contest. The effort is to select a winning individual or team, either in a single day's play in which the winner comes to the fore, or in competition spread over a longer period of time. The advantages of such events over informal competitive play are: (a) the place and time of the event are set and publicized; (b) equipment, officials, and supervision are supplied; and (c) play culminates in a championship.

TYPES OF TOURNAMENTS

There are several types of tournaments. The recreation leader should be familiar with each of these and select the one which is most appropriate for his situation, based on the kind of game to be played, the amount of time allotted, the needed equipment, the available facilities, and the number of participants. It should also be possible to promote the most evenly matched competition, and to keep the issue of who the winner will be open until the very end of play. The following are examples of three popular types of tournaments.

Elimination Tournaments

These are based on the idea of eliminating all contestants but one, through successive stages of play, until only the winner remains. Elimination tournaments are suitable when the players are of equal ability, or when their ability is unknown. It is a speedy way of conducting a tournament, and in many sports and games, can be concluded in a single day. Usually, elimination tournaments are based on having numbers of contestants that are multiples of eight: 8, 16, or 32 entries. These players (individuals or teams) are placed on a diagram or chart (Fig. 13) showing when they are to play. If there are more than 32 entries, it may be desirable to run preliminary tournaments, to cut down the total number of contestants.

Some familiar terms in tournament play are:

Brackets: pairings that show which players will compete with each other
Round: a vertical row of brackets showing how contests will be scheduled; i.e.,
    the first round of play, the second, third, and fourth
Drawing: starting positions, to be determined by lots

In some tournaments, the best players may be "seeded" and spaced out through the brackets so that they do not eliminate each other and remain in play until the later rounds. The first round of play is held; each player who is defeated drops out, and the winner moves ahead to the next round of play. This is continued through quarter-finals, semifinals, and finals, until the winner is selected.

One weakness is that the elimination tournament gives an individual only one chance to play. If he is having a momentary off-game, he may be quickly and permanently eliminated. Therefore, this type of tournament may be played as a *double elimination,* in which the losers in the

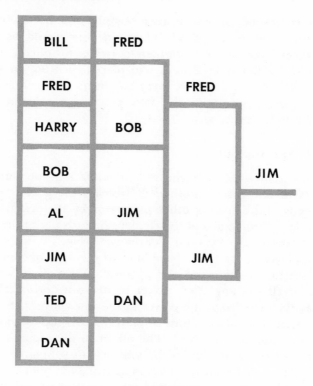

Figure 13

first round of play are placed in brackets to the left of the diagram. They play each other to determine a final winner. He then plays the winner of the regular tournament to determine the final winner.

Round Robin Tournaments

This type of tournament is useful when there is sufficient time and enough facilities available so that every player may meet every other player at least once—thus producing a "true" winner. The ultimate winner is determined on the basis of his games-won-and-lost percentage at the end of the tournament.

No formal diagram is used, since players need not advance against each other. Instead, it is customary in scheduling play to place all contestants or teams in two vertical columns, thus:

Row A	Row B
Jim	Fred
Alex	Bill
Bob	Bert
Sam	Harry

In the first round, or contest, each boy plays the boy in the opposite column with whom he is paired. Then, one row would be kept fixed and the other row rotated counterclockwise, to obtain subsequent matches. After each boy in Row A had played each boy in Row B, he would then be scheduled against every boy in his own column, and vice versa. Then the player with the best percentage of wins would be declared the tournament victor.

Challenge Tournaments

This is a somewhat freer and more flexible kind of tournament in that no player is actually eliminated. Instead, the goal is to advance by challenging and defeating other players or by the default of a challenged player (failure to accept the challenge). Each player seeks to climb to a higher rank in the Pyramid Tournament (Fig. 14), for example, by defeating a player in the rank above him. In this type of contest, players draw for starting positions on the pyramid. When play is begun, any player may challenge any other player in his own horizontal row. The winner may then challenge any player in the row above. If he wins, they must then exchange places; thus a player moves up or down in the Pyramid, according to his record. The player in the topmost position at the end of a set period of time is the tournament winner.

Another type of Challenge Tournament is the Ladder Tournament (Fig. 15), in which players are listed on a vertical row of names (constructed like a ladder) and may challenge either of the two players directly above, in order to move up.

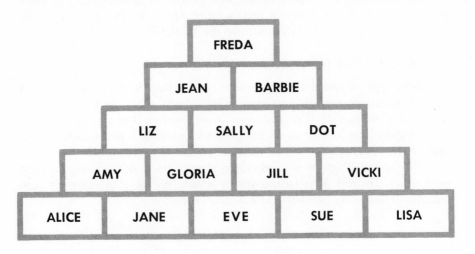

Figure 14

DON	PHIL
PAUL	SAM
BART	BOB
ROD	KEITH
DAN	VAN
WOODY	CARL
ANDY	JOHN

Figure 15

Because Challenge Tournaments can be conducted over a fairly long period of time, and matches are arranged at the convenience of the contestants, it is a very flexible kind of competition and useful for situations when all the players may not be available at a given time. It may also lead to disputes, in that some players may disagree about whether a challenge was fairly given or accepted within the stipulated time period.

SPORTS AND PERSONAL VALUES

We hear very frequently about the amateur ideal, and the positive contributions made by sports in helping children and youth learn to win and lose with self-control, to become effective team members, and to learn to obey rules and play according to the "code." As a consequence, many individuals accept unquestioningly the idea that sports will automatically build character and contribute to sportsmanship. Unfortunately, nothing could be further from the truth. In point of fact, our highly competitive system of sports competition in American colleges has resulted in the fostering of extremely dubious values and practices on the part of the college athletes. In many conferences and regions of the country, a college football or basketball player is a subsidized athlete, a *professional* for whom the amateur ideal or principles of sportsmanship are little more than a mockery. The goal, both for the player and the coach, is to *win,* at almost any cost. Small wonder then that we hear of gambling and point-trimming scandals in college basketball—when the true ideals of sport have been so ignored.

In a sense, this narrow view of the role of sports competition, which places such great emphasis on winning, is not the fault of the athletes or coaches, but simply a reflection of the American society and its ideals. Boyle writes:

> The competitive energy that many Americans have given to business has carried over to sport, and attendance records prove that Americans demand a winner. Frank Merriwell and fair play are passé. "How can you be proud of a losing team?" asked the late Jim Tatum. Another coach, Woody Hayes of Ohio State, has said, "Anyone who tells me, 'Don't worry that you lost, you played a good game anyway,' I just hate. . . ." Branch Rickey, a strict Sabbatarian who refused to attend ball games on Sundays, defined his ideal player as one who "will break both your legs if you happen to be standing in his path to second base." A major league manager tells his team, "Cheat a little bit, especially at first and second when you're going to tag up after a fly ball." American sport has nothing comparable to the English maxim, "That's not cricket." Instead, all too many honor Leo Durocher's wisecrack, "Nice guys finish last." [18]

We know too that varsity athletes in secondary schools and colleges often have lower levels of sportsmanship and other desirable character traits than do nonathletes, contrary to popular belief. This has been a major concern of many physical educators in recent years. Indeed, the American Association for Health, Physical Education and Recreation held a joint conference in 1962 of its Division for Girls and Women's Sports and the Division of Men's Athletics, which dealt with the whole relationship between sports and athletics and the task of ethical values in secondary school and college students.[19]

What can organized recreation service do in this regard?

The answer is—a great deal! Unlike highly competitive college play, where victory is regarded as essential to the prestige of an institution and where coaches are likely to have their contract terminated because

18 Boyle, *op. cit.,* pp. 56–57.

19 "Values in Sports," *Report of the Joint National Conference of the Division for Girls and Women's Sports and the Division of Men's Athletics* (Washington, D.C.: American Association for Health, Physical Education and Recreation, 1963).

of a losing season or two—recreation has an entirely different set of values and goals. It is not just for the highly skilled but for all. It recognizes that the important purposes of sports play are to have fun and to grow as a person through participation, rather than just to win. This means that the recreational sports leader or supervisor is in an ideal position to further constructive values and goals. He need not be hampered by the restraints or pressures that frequently force the school or college coach to stress undesirable goals and attitudes.

What about specifics? Working with children and youth, the recreation leader can constantly stress sound values and sportsmanlike attitudes. He encourages honesty and fair play. He encourages unquestioning acceptance of the referee's decision. He encourages generosity and sympathy toward an opponent. Even working with parents, as in a Little League program that is assisted by the recreation department, the recreation professional may further his point of view. Too often, parents will be more abusive and argumentative than the Little League coaches or players on the field. Too often, a parent will scream to his son, the pitcher in a tight spot, "Hit him in the head! Knock him down!" Thus are values formed. And, in such situations, the recreation leader is the person in a unique position to present sound values and ways of behavior.

In addition, through his total sports program, the recreation leader is careful to provide certain activities that offer only a minimum of competitive drive or interest, as well as many others which are satisfying to participants of all levels of ability. Through these, he encourages participants to recognize and accept their own limitations, which they will have to do in any case as they grow older and less capable. When contrasted to many athletes on a top level of competitive skill (who, once they can no longer play a game at peak performance, often quit and never enjoy it again), the true recreational sportsman wants to continue throughout his life. To satisfy this need, the recreational leader schedules many activities for children and youth that have carry-over value for later life. In addition, he provides many sports and games activities which are suitable for older age levels, as part of his ongoing program through the year.

These are appropriate goals and purposes for organized recreation service. Recreational sports must achieve major psychological, physical, and social outcomes and must provide healthy rewards of enjoyment and pleasure, if this major aspect of the program is to be justified.

SUGGESTED QUESTIONS FOR DISCUSSION

1. What fundamental values and ethical ideals should underlie the promotion of sports activities by recreation departments? Why are they often in a better position to promote these values than athletic directors in other settings?

2. Compare the approach of the U.S.S.R. to that of the United States, as far as sponsorship of sports activities for the public is concerned. What strengths and weaknesses do you see in both positions?
3. Outline a total sports program for a hypothetical community of 25,000, bearing in mind climatic and regional factors, and the needs and interests of various population groups. What facilities and staff would be needed to carry out this program?

Chapter 6

Outdoor Recreation and Nature Activities

One of the areas of organized recreation service which has expanded most dramatically within the past few years has been that of outdoor recreation. As pointed out earlier, many Americans have had a deep concern about the extent to which our precious natural resources have been depleted and misused. On the federal, state, and county levels, heavily financed efforts are being made to develop new outdoor recreation areas, to reclaim and protect potential resources, to open up breathing spaces within the cities themselves, and to develop "green belts" around our urban centers.

In accordance with the recommendations of the Outdoor Recreation Resources Review Commission, a Bureau of Outdoor Recreation has been established within the Department of the Interior. Hundreds of millions of dollars per year are to be expended through the 1964 Land

and Water Conservation Fund Act, much of it by the states, based on carefully thought-out plans for statewide recreation development. Major new regional programs are creating new reservoirs for boating, fishing, and swimming. On local levels throughout the country, the growth of municipal or county park and recreation departments means that outdoor recreation is receiving added scope and emphasis.

MEANING OF OUTDOOR RECREATION

Exactly what *is* outdoor recreation? In the past it has been defined very loosely or not at all. Some refer to it simply as any form of recreation which is carried on in the outdoors. But should a game of checkers on a park bench, or basketball played in a school yard, or a choral performance in a band shell all be considered outdoor recreation?

There must be a more precise and meaningful definition than this.

The essential point is that outdoor recreation should have a meaningful relationship to the world of the outdoors. It should consist of *those recreational activities that can best be carried on out of doors, and which have in some way a direct relationship or dependence on nature, or that place the participant in direct contact with the elements.* Seen in this light, such activities as hunting, fishing, hiking, camping, water skiing, snow skiing, scuba diving, picnicking, pleasure driving, horseback riding, archery in the natural setting, or bicycling along trails—all are clearly perceived as outdoor recreation.

Certain activities may be more difficult to differentiate. Thus, tennis (played on a standardized court and with little relation to the world of nature) probably should not be considered outdoor recreation as such, although it may very well be part of a multiuse outdoor recreation facility. Golf, on the other hand, because it involves tramping over fairways and roughs and, to a degree, combatting nature, may fairly be called outdoor recreation. Swimming in an indoor pool cannot justify the name, but swimming in an outdoor pool or in a mountain lake or ocean beach facility, does.

Perhaps it is not necessary to make too sharp a distinction. What is most important is that this form of recreation be based on, or have significant contact with, the world of nature.

What then is the *rationale* for promoting and expanding outdoor recreation facilities and programs? Why is this so important to the American people today? Underlying this drive are the following key factors:

1. We Americans have a great national tradition of outdoor living. More than any other nation, we have had a history of conquering the wilderness over the past several centuries; our national heroes have been the outdoorsman, the cowboy, the explorer, the overland immigrant. Our literature, our songs, our folklore, and even our movies and television

programs have glorified the pioneer, the Indian, the hunter, and lawman of frontier days. Now that the frontier has disappeared, camping and outdoor recreational pursuits are seen by many as a way of recapturing this early heritage, and as a means of returning to our pioneer origins. For many, the outdoor life represents a simpler, more honest and generous way of life—as contrasted with the complexities and artificiality of city living.

2. A secondary, but allied explanation is that our lives have become so sedentary and so mechanized (we now have automobiles to take us a block or two, television for effortless amusement, electric can-openers, electric carving knives, electric toothbrushes, to cite only a few examples) that we need desperately to do more vigorous physical things ourselves. This means the kind of action, exploration and satisfaction in doing things for one's self that can be found in canoeing, camping, hiking, swimming, biking, hunting, fishing, climbing, and skiing.

3. Closely related to this is that the tenor of modern living has so much tension, noise, competition, and tempo, that there is a great need for all of us to get away from the hubbub of urban living and industrial life, and to come into contact with the world of nature. This means that man can become, even briefly, a tiny entity in the vast world of fields, forests, mountains, streams, and lakes. He is free from the strain, abstractions, and cog-in-the-machine pace of city living. He sees himself in the context of total existence. He sees order and beauty in the world, and perceives vastness, space, silence. He meditates and examines his own values and way of life.

These reasons, as well as the obvious need to preserve our natural resources as a nation, lie behind the expansion of outdoor recreation facilities and opportunities. They tend to take two forms:

1. The first is the provision of facilities that include forest camping areas, ski centers, scenic overlooks, fishing streams, geysers and other unusual natural phenomena, historical monuments, mountain trails, and similar resources. For the most part, these do not involve direct instruction, leadership, or supervision of activities; the participant is generally free to carry on by himself, although in some programs there may be instruction, interpretive lectures, or guided tours.

2. In many programs of outdoor recreation, particularly on the county or local levels, there are a variety of activities that require direct leadership. This may involve continuing instruction, coaching, or organizational assistance to recreational groups. To a much greater extent, then, this requires planning and the provision of staff aid, on the part of the sponsoring agency.

This text will consider briefly the role of state agencies and county park and recreation departments in providing outdoor recreation opportunities. It will then go much more fully into an examination of the program services offered by municipal park and recreation departments in the area of outdoor recreation and nature activities.

STATE OUTDOOR RECREATION SERVICES

Each of the 50 states today provides a host of outdoor recreation activities and services, both for its own residents and to encourage tourist travel for obvious economic benefits.

One of the most active states in this regard is New York, which is blessed by a great wealth of natural resources and highly developed recreational facilities. The Empire State will therefore be described here as a prototype of state services offered throughout the nation.

New York has a wide variety of scenic views, historical sites, build-ings and museums, fishing streams, reservoirs, resort areas, boat basins and marinas, summer colonies, waterfalls, underground caverns, battle-fields, chasms, ski centers, gliding centers, motor racing tracks, arts festivals, canals and fish hatcheries—all of which attract huge numbers of residents and tourists. These are scattered among several different types of recreational regions: the ocean beaches of Long Island, the impressive Hudson Valley, the Adirondack and Catskill mountain ranges, and several lake areas.

Statistically, it offers the following:

State Parks. The New York State Conservation Department operates 85 parks which provide facilities for picnicking, swimming, camping, hiking, golf, and other sports, in many cases on sites of great natural beauty.

Camping. The Adirondack and Catskill forest preserve region alone offers a vacationland of nearly two and a half million acres of state-owned mountain land. Well-developed highways provide access to over 40 large public campsites, including, on Lake George, nearly 50 islands open to camping by boating enthusiasts.

Hiking. New York State has more than a thousand miles of marked trails, several hundred of which provide lean-to's for wilderness camping. Hikers in the north can reach such famed spots as Mount Marcy and Lake Colden; in the overall Adirondack region there are 42 mountains over 4,000 feet in elevation that are of interest to climbers.

Boating. The Empire State offers some 1,600 square miles of water-way, including 800 miles of connecting canals and rivers, and hundreds of lakes and ponds for boating. Canoe trips through wilderness sections of the Adirondacks, including one of over 100 miles, from Old Forge to the Saranacs, provide varied challenges.

Fishing. The State Conservation Department promotes fishing very intensively, with a network of hatcheries and many programs to stimulate and improve fishing practices. They publish a brochure for sportsmen, with such listings as "1,001 Top New York State Fishing Waters" (with a county-by-county listing of lakes, ponds, streams, and rivers), and another called "Hiker's Special—300 Remote Adirondack Trout Ponds Stocked by Airplanes" (which must be hiked into, using U.S. Geological Survey quadrangle maps).

OUTDOOR RECREATION AND CONSERVATION EDUCATION

In addition to these facilities, the state considers an important part of its function to be the education of its citizens—chiefly the young—for the most intelligent, safe, and enjoyable use of outdoor recreation resources. Three aspects of this program, conducted by the New York State Conservation Department, are briefly described here:

Hunter Safety. New York State law requires that all new hunters be instructed in the safe use of firearms and long bows, and in good hunting practices. The State Conservation Department therefore helps organize and promote hunter safety courses, in cooperation with the National Rifle Association. These are conducted by skilled volunteer instructors, and cover all phases of firearm safety, good hunting manners and practices.

Boating Safety. The Conservation Department, through its Division of Motors Boats, gives a New York State Young Boatman's Safety Course, which is mandatory for all young boatsmen between the ages of 10 and 14. This course covers knowledge of the laws, of equipment, rules of waterways, techniques of piloting and handling, safe boating maintenance practices, and knowledge of accidents and first aid.

Conservation Education. The Conservation Department produces many films dealing with fish and wildlife conservation, basic ecology, hunting and shooting, recreation in state parks, and similar subjects, as well as a profusion of pamphlets and guides, which are distributed to interested civic groups, clubs, and individuals. In addition, it sponsors several Conservation Education Camps for teen-age boys throughout the state. These provide week-long sessions for boys who are sponsored by community organizations. The camp curriculum includes the following topics: rifle and shotgun training and shooting practice; small mammal traplines; tree and shrub identification; forest management; forest fire control and ranger work; soil and water conservation; sportsmanship and campfire activities; fisheries management; visit to fish hatchery; fly and bait casting; stream improvement; plus varied recreational experiences geared to the outdoors.

COUNTY OUTDOOR RECREATION PROGRAMS

County park and recreation departments have a unique and growing role. Statistically, their growth is impressive. Not too long ago, the county governmental unit was considered by many to be obsolete. Today, it is

undergoing a remarkable growth of responsibilities, functions, and powers.
To illustrate:

> In 1950, there were 933 county parks. Ten years later, in 1960, there were
> 2,610 county parks averaging 170 acres each. In 1950, there were 5,000 volun-
> teer recreation workers in county parks and recreation programs. By 1960
> there were seven times as many—35,000—a 600 percent increase in one
> decade. In 1957, a total of 62 million dollars was spent on county park and
> recreation programs. In 1962—122 million—nearly a 100 percent increase in
> less than five years.[1]

The State of California has developed an Outdoor Recreation Plan,
based on a three-year study, which sees the role of counties as twofold:
(a) to meet or assist in the provision of services for neighborhood-com-
munity needs, in unincorporated communities (which do not have other
public recreation departments); and (b) to provide day-use regional types
of recreation needed within approximately one hour's travel from urban
centers.

Because county governments often embrace fairly large geographical
areas, including land beyond metropolitan or municipal boundaries, they
are in an advantageous position to develop major outdoor recreation
facilities, sited to meet a variety of different needs. At the same time,
because county recreation and park departments tend to provide services
for cities or large towns that lie within their borders, they are frequently
able to provide outdoor recreation opportunities for families that cannot
travel the longer distances to state or federal parks.

Dade County, Florida. One of the best known parks and recreation
networks established on a county basis is Dade County, Florida. This
system includes several large marinas, 27 neighborhood recreation centers
(with some including swimming pools), a central stadium, a Museum of
Science and Natural History, a zoo, and such special areas as Vizcaya
(a nationally famous home, displayed for its architectural interest), the
Trail Glades Range, and two golf courses. The park division includes
10 wayside areas scattered throughout the county for casual use and
picnicking, and 39 neighborhood parks in unincorporated areas that offer
complete local recreation programs for all residents.

The philosophy of the Dade County Park and Recreation Department regarding outdoor recreation planning is illustrated in a General
Policy Statement adopted in 1958:

> The purpose of this department is to acquire and develop natural land pre-
> serves utilizing natural features or advantages. The recreational facilities
> and activities are to be of a nature and number to serve the public taking

[1] *County Parks and Recreation, A Basis for Action* (New York and Washington,
D.C.: published jointly by the National Association of Counties and the National
Recreation Association, 1964), p. 11.

part in activities normal to that area. The distribution is to be county-wide for easy access.

The family and day-use concepts offering opportunities not possible or in keeping with the neighborhood parks are to be of first concern. Special emphasis is to be placed on beach and water areas of all types. The preservation of the native flora and fauna so unique and desirable in this area shall be paramount. Whenever practical, emphasis is to be placed on the natural—not the artificial—in facility or landscaping. Due to the climate, wildlife and tropical growth of the area, Dade County is a most desirable place in which to live and vacation. It is in the public interest that these features be preserved.

Parks in this category are designated *major* parks and are so listed by name. . . . They are not now, nor should they be, transformed into local use areas or changed in any way which would lessen their county-wide appeal in favor of individuals, neighborhoods or other confined segments of the population. The criterion for designation of a park as a *major* park is that it be of county-wide significance. Size, type of usage, etc., are important too, but are not the sole basis of designation. Areas having county-wide cultural, sociological, historical or topographical significance may be the basis of designation.[2]

Similarly, an increasingly large number of county park and recreation departments throughout the country are developing recreation programs and facilities ranging from local-use playgrounds and centers to the kinds of unique natural parks typified by the passage above.

MUNICIPALLY-SPONSORED OUTDOOR RECREATION PROGRAMS

To fully understand the role of municipal recreation or parks and recreation departments with respect to outdoor recreation services, it will prove helpful to examine several outstanding locally sponsored programs. These will be presented first, in terms of total programing; following this, a number of specific *kinds* of outdoor recreation program activities will be examined, with examples drawn from many communities.

Pasadena, California. The Department of Recreation in Pasadena, California, is set up as a coordinated operation of the school system, city and county; it is administered by the Board of Education. For over 10 years, it has included a Nature and Outing Division, under the leadership of a skilled specialist in this area. The division's purpose is to provide a variety of year-round outdoor services for all age groups, in most cases closely integrated with the school curriculum.

One of the major program features of the Nature and Outing Divi-

2 *General Policy Statement* (Miami, Florida: Dade County Park and Recreation Department, 1958).

sion is an annual Family Camping Course (cosponsored by the Pasadena Casting Club). This consists of six in-town lecture-and-demonstration sessions, plus one weekend practice camping trip to the mountains. Average attendance in this course has been 400 participants. Its topics include: (a) introduction to family camping opportunities in California; (b) guides on equipment and clothing; (c) camp foods and cookery; (d) setting up camp (site selection, tent pitching, camp housekeeping, comfort and sanitation, safety and first aid); (e) camp activities (nature study, photography, fishing, and hiking); and (f) advanced camping (animal and pack camping). Other family recreation activities sponsored by the division include family flashlight hikes and a variety of other family outdoor excursions.

The Pasadena Recreation Department also sponsors an elementary school "Nature-Science Excursion Program." This represents an outdoor education and conservation program for fifth and sixth graders. The nature specialist visits the classroom in advance to prepare the children, and then an all-day trip is made to the primitive Arroyo Seco Park area. There, children engage in a two-hour exploration hike, visiting a flood-control dam, a water channel, a settling basin, a nature trail, a sand and gravel plant, and other facilities of this type. Students build an open fire, cook lunch, collect nature specimens for their classroom, and visit a U.S. Forest Service station. While the program is geared toward conservation learnings, it is clearly an outdoor recreation experience for many youngsters, and prepares them to take part successfully in vacations in the out-of-doors. Special excursions of this type are also provided for physically or mentally handicapped children in the school system.

The division operates a Children's Museum, with varied hobby and nature study displays and project opportunities.

Each playground, throughout the year, schedules large-scale cookouts. As part of the regular program during the summer, many nature study activities are presented, with children exploring natural phenomena, carrying out experiments with soil, making collections of plants and insect life, and playing nature games.

The Nature and Outing Division also sponsors the following: (a) fly-tying classes; (b) introduction to fishing classes (both fresh water and salt); (c) ski shows; (d) dry-land ski schools; (e) hunter safety and gun safety programs; and (f) a Youth Camp site which is made available to many youth groups in the community, who provide their own leadership.

Milwaukee, Wisconsin. The Milwaukee Public Schools Department of Municipal Recreation and Adult Education sponsors many activities relating to outdoor recreation and education. These are intended: (a) to make individuals aware of available outdoor recreation opportunities; and (b) to promote an understanding of conservation.

Typical activities include the following:

On summer playgrounds, large numbers of children take part in "nature jaunts," in which boys and girls travel by bus to "wilderness" areas in the Milwaukee County Park System, accompanied by playleaders and nature guides.

Week-long day camps are held in Kettle Moraine State Forest for children between 8 and 12. They are picked up at neighborhood playgrounds in the morning and returned to them around 5:00 P.M. In these daycamps, nature hikes, cookouts and campfires, woodland crafts, and nature lore comprise the program. Trips to nearby places of interest include a dairy farm, fish hatchery, conservation planting area, and lookout peak.

During the summer playground season, younger children attend four-day Tepee Camps that emphasize Indian lore; among other activities, these 6- to 9-year-olds learn Indian dances and construct tepees.

During the spring, a Green Thumb program for 8- to 11-year-olds is presented on Saturdays. Playground groups travel to a nearby recreation department facility, for a day of gardening and conservation activities, along with nature fun. Exploration hikes in the state forest for 8- to 14-year-olds are also held on Saturdays.

Other activities include junior and senior conservation clubs; astronomy and 4-H clubs; a Junior Audubon program; gun, boating, and water-safety clinics; fishing trips and hiking programs.

Adults are served in the following ways. The "Muni-Hikers" club for men and women facilitates group exploration of the out-of-doors throughout the year. Members also enjoy occasional social programs, issue a monthly bulletin, and help promote public interest in conservation. Finally, a Family Camping Association is sponsored, in which over 1,000 families share their camping interests and experiences. A bulletin service provides information about new campsites and helpful hints about successful camping practices. Emphasis is placed on the strengthening of family living through camping. Camping demonstrations are arranged from time to time, and occasional "camp-outs" are held.

Phoenix, Arizona. The bulk of outdoor recreation services provided by local recreation departments tend to be for youth, as evidenced in the preceding examples. The Parks and Recreation Department of Phoenix, Arizona, offers an impressive selection of leisure activities for *adults,* many of which include outdoor recreation services. Examples follow:

Archery. Lighted archery ranges are located at Encanto Park. . . . Archery equipment is available for checkout from Recreation Leaders. Clubs affiliated with the Parks and Recreation Department are: Black Feather Archers, Encanto Archers, and the Chaparral Bowmen. The latter group frequently gives archery demonstrations to promote the activity and provide entertainment.

Bird Walks. Bird walks are held from November through April.

Everyone interested in knowing Arizona birds is invited free of charge. Visitors from all over the United States and many foreign countries have taken part in these walks through the years. Free illustrated bird lectures are also presented by the Maricopa Audubon Society in cooperation with the Phoenix Public Library.

Bicycling. Bicycle rides are scheduled weekly with a predesignated meeting place to start each trip. Rides to spots of interest for both beginners and experienced riders are planned from October through May under the Arizona State Council of the American Youth Hostels. Breakfast rides, steaks fries, and cookouts are enjoyed by the bicycle buffs. Bicycles may be rented, and visitors are welcomed.

Bridle Paths. A shaded bridle path leading to the Arizona canal and over 40 miles of riding trails in South Mountain Park are maintained by the Phoenix Parks and Recreation Department. In addition, a circle ride of 150 miles is being marked by the Arizona Horseman's Association and the Maricopa County Parks and Recreation Department; this may be used for riding, hiking, or biking.

Canoeing. Canoes, electric and pedal boats may be rented at the Encanto Boat Dock; individual or group rides may be arranged on the Encanto Queen Paddleboat.

Camping. Shelters for camping are available at the city's park in the pines, known as Horsethief Basin, 92 miles from Phoenix in the Bradshaw Mountains. Cabins may be rented at a nominal fee, from the end of May through November. Also, a camping clinic is given each spring, cosponsored by the Phoenix Parks and Recreation Department, the Maricopa County Parks and Recreation Department, and the Maricopa Family Campers, a club which meets in the city park each month.

Fishing. A fishing and casting clinic, sponsored by the Arizona Flycasters' Association, is held each spring in the Encanto Park Lagoon.

Hiking. The Arizona State Council of the American Youth Hostels sponsors scheduled hikes and bicycle rides from October through May. Nonmembers are invited. Hikes are planned to points of interest, including the Superstition Mountains and Camelback Mountain.

Horseshoes. This sport may be played at eight different parks in the city.

Museums. The ancient Indian ruins and a museum of artifacts and Indian lore at Pueblo Grande are among the city's main tourist attractions; group tours may be arranged.

Nature Study. Nature trail walks in Encanto Park are scheduled throughout the year; these are keyed to a Nature Trail Guide that identifies trees and shrubs in the park, and that is available free of charge at the Parks and Recreation Office. It includes an introduction to the rocks and minerals of Arizona, a visit to cactus gardens, and a glimpse at bird life, as well as the identification of exotic trees and shrubs.

Picnics. Three mountain parks operated by the Phoenix Parks and Recreation Department offer picnic sites in untouched desert terrain. Picnic facilities are also made available for use by family groups or large organizations, and at other fireplaces scattered in parks throughout the city.

Rockhounding. A variety of Arizona gems may be found during trips, generally scheduled from November through May. Lapidary equipment to cut and polish stones is available at the Phoenix Arts and Crafts Center, where instruction in techniques is also available. A Rockhound Primer printed by the Arizona Development Board pinpoints areas for hunting gems and minerals.

Safaris. The Phoenix Visitors Safari Club travels to points of interest in the state. Tour members take their own cars and meet at designated points for a picnic lunch or cookout. Each person provides his own food and drink; trips are planned by a volunteer committee of visitors to the state, and provide an opportunity to get acquainted with others and enjoy Phoenix out-of-doors.

Shaded Areas. Benches and tables, flowers and grass, and drinking fountains are provided for Phoenicians and visitors at four "close in" parks.

Skiing. "Dry land" ski instruction is given in October at the Encanto Park Band Shell. Equipment and instruction for the four-lesson series is generally furnished by the Arizona Snow Bowl in Flagstaff.

Zoo. The Phoenix Zoo is operated by the Arizona Zoological Society; it features a variety of wild animals, a children's zoo, and a safari tour train.

Phoenix thus offers a good illustration of the various types of recreational activities that may be offered to adults by a single recreation department. In other areas of the country, different patterns of services may be found, based on climate or geographical factors.

At this point, a number of specific kinds of program features relating to outdoor recreation are described in detail, showing how they may be organized on a local level. These include the following: (a) boating and boating safety; (b) sailing classes and clubs; (c) hunter safety and community shooting programs; (d) family camping clubs and courses; (e) day camping programs; (f) outdoor recreation for handicapped children; and (g) nature activities, projects, and games.

BOATING AND BOATING SAFETY

One of the most important contributions a community recreation department can make, in the area of outdoor education, is to educate local residents in boating safety. In 1904 there were 15,000 pleasure boats. Today the figure approximates 7.5 million. In a recent article titled "Perils of the Surface," *Time* magazine describes the current scene:

> . . . Their skippers commit all manner of insanities—overloading outboards to the swamping point, buzzing each other for fun, cutting across bows, swooshing through swimmers with never a thought for their whirling propellor blades, examining the scenery instead of the sea before them as if there were no tomorrow. Frequently there is none.[3]

As a consequence, each year there are thousands of unnecessary fatalities from accidents caused by power boats. While a number of states have licensing requirements for powered pleasure craft, none have them for their pilots. All too many amateur pilots zoom away from the dock in their powerful new cruisers without even having a chart of the waters they are approaching—or the knowledge of how to read a chart, if they had it. Therefore, many recreation departments make an important contribution to life and limb by sponsoring boating safety courses like the one mentioned earlier which is offered by the New York State Conservation Department, or the classes given by the Power Squadrons.

Often a recreation department will design and offer its own course. For example, the following eight-session class in outboarding was offered by the Superintendent of the Park and Recreation Department in Brookfield, Illinois, and staffed on a volunteer basis by a local boating sales-and-service shop owner. With the help of the Outboard Boating Club of America, a class was designed for boys and girls in the 12-to-16 age bracket. It included the basic fundamentals of outboarding and actual experience on the water, with the following sequence of lessons:

1. History of outboard boating (lecture plus film)
2. Types of boat construction and analysis of advantages, as to weight, durability, cost, and maintenance
3. Analysis of selecting appropriate boat for personal or family needs and water-skiing demonstration
4. Nautical nomenclature and safety rules
5. Matching motors and boats; safety factors (with on-the-water experience)
6. Safety rules and equipment (with on-the-water experience)
7. How to select, use, and maintain a boat trailer
8. General review of maintenance and care of boats and motors

This course is somewhat geared to the particular interests of the instructor and to those of the children as potential purchasers of boats. The New York State Boating Safety Course has a somewhat broader approach. First, it stresses a thorough learning of the "Safe Boating Code":

1. I will learn to swim well enough to care for myself and help others in difficulty.

[3] "Modern Living," *Time*, July 5, 1963, p. 56.

2. I will have all my safety equipment on board before I leave shore.
3. I will keep my boat in good repair.
4. I will ventilate closed areas in my boat before I start my motor.
5. I will not leave shore in a leaky boat.
6. I will check my fuel supply before starting to be sure that it is ample for my boating needs.
7. I will keep bilges and decks clean.
8. I will obey the rules of the road.
9. I will learn to use navigation aids to guide me.
10. I will not hurry or be careless.
11. I will not allow horseplay on my boat.
12. I will see that all passengers who cannot swim wear life preservers.
13. I will heed weather warnings.
14. I will not use my boat in dangerous or off-limit waters at any time.
15. I will use caution when boating in areas that are not familiar to me.
16. I will not operate my boat near swimmers.
17. I will respect the rights of others.
18. I will keep my wake down.
19. I will not misuse my boat and its power.
20. I will inform others of where I plan to go and when I expect to return each time I take my boat out on the water.

In detail, each of these points is spelled out in the course. Attention is given to the following aspects of boating safety: registration, safety certificates, and safety patrols; required safety equipment on all motor boats; meaning of signals on boats; safe fueling procedures; boarding; loading; safety checks; rules of the road; knots and lines; piloting; buoys and lights; use of compass; speed, winds and currents and charts; docking and mooring; trash disposal; weather; water skiing; fishing; meaning of skin diver's flag; swimming away from boat; cruising; procedures for accidents; rescue breathing; drowning, shock, and sunburn; first-aid courses; rescue procedures; use of trailers; and glossary of useful terms.

An increasing number of community recreation and park departments now offer courses of this type. Even when boating waterways may not be immediately accessible, so widespread is the interest in this sport that it has become an important and highly valued program feature.

SAILING CLASSES AND CLUBS

Another popular aquatic sport is sailing. Far from being the exclusive toy of a wealthy few that it was years ago, sailing today appeals to hundreds of thousands of all ages and social classes. An example of how sailing may be developed as a community recreation activity is found in Quincy, Massachusetts.[4]

Quincy, a city with 27 miles of shoreline and 90,000 inhabitants, has

[4] Lawrence P. Creedon, "Sailing in Quincy Bay," *Recreation,* June, 1962, p. 309.

always had an active interest in sailing as a livelihood and a sport; for a number of years its Recreation Department staff has included a Supervisor of Boating and Sailing. His major purpose is to introduce Quincy youngsters to boating, familiarizing them with safety principles and procedures and helping them learn basic sailing skills. His program involves a fleet of 28 boats, a staff of 7, and over 400 young participants.

How is the instructional program organized? It is divided into four levels: Basic Seaman, Beginner Sailor, Intermediate Sailor, and Junior Leader. Normally it takes three summers for completion, with a Red Cross certificate of satisfactory performance awarded at the end of each level. To illustrate:

Basic Seaman. Children must pass a qualifying swimming test to enter. This phase is designed to familiarize children with no prior boating experience with safety precautions on the water, rowboat handling, and knot-tying skills. Class size is limited to 25 and meets three times a week for 90-minute periods, including both lectures and demonstrations on the beach and practical application afloat.

Beginner Sailor. A 14-boat fleet of 10-foot Turnabout sailboats is used for three two-hour sessions each week. Children become familiar with boating nomenclature, equipment maintenance, and rules of the nautical road as well as sailing skills which include tacking, running, and reaching, along with mooring and docking procedures.

There is a similar progression in skills through the *Intermediate Sailor* and *Junior Leader* programs. The latter includes a small group of highly responsible teen-agers who participate daily in the program, engage in competitive swimming, and assist adult leaders with instruction of beginners. As a result of the growing popular interest in sailing, a parents' class has been formed; frequently parents find themselves taking lessons from their teen-age son or daughter in the Junior Leader group.

An annual feature of the sailing program in Quincy is Nautical Day —held each year just before Labor Day. All summer participants take part in a variety of events and demonstrations—rowing and sailing races, parent-child races, knot-tying exhibitions, rigging drills, mooring exercises, and formation sailing—with certificates being awarded to all who have passed requirements. Sailing thus becomes, in the hands of capable instructors in a sea-minded town, a varied and attractive recreation program activity.

HUNTER SAFETY AND COMMUNITY SHOOTING PROGRAMS

Hunting is generally viewed as an activity with a high danger potential; gun accidents annually provide a highly publicized number of tragic accidents and deaths.

What is not realized is that the actual total is remarkably low, in comparison with other recreational pursuits. In a five-year study, recently carried out by a major insurance company, of claims paid for accidents suffered during sports participation, hunting and shooting rated 16th from the top, far below such sports as baseball, football, golf, and fishing. Fewer claims, it was stated, were recorded by men carrying guns than by those indulging in recreation at church socials. Specifically in New York State, there has been a steady decline of fatal hunting accidents. In 1964, the impressive total of 975,000 hunting licenses and tags were sold in the state—double the number that were sold in 1949. During that 15-year period, however, the actual number of fatal accidents has declined. Why? One good reason has been the state's requirement that a first-time hunter must pass a hunter-safety course [5] of training in the use of firearms, and a qualifying test. Over 636,000 New Yorkers have already taken this test, which is given by 6,000 volunteer National Rifle Association instructors.

The course ranges from teaching the following Safety Commandments: (a) Treat every gun as if it were loaded; (b) Keep the muzzle always pointed in a safe direction; (c) Be sure of your target; (d) Keep your finger off the trigger until ready to shoot; to a detailed program of instruction covering the following points:

A Hunter's Code: What It Means to You to Be a Licensed Hunter in New
    York . . . as a Hunter, Sportsman, and Conservationist
The Facts about Hunting Accidents
Conservation Laws for Safety
How to Reduce Hunting Accidents
Safety Precautions before You Hunt . . . during, and after Hunting
Landowner-Sportsman's Relations
Conservation Law Enforcement

In a considerable number of communities, schools or recreation departments have sponsored gun safety courses to promote safe hunting and shooting recreation. In Little Rock, Arkansas, for example, every junior high school boy and girl receives instruction in gun-handling and firing in a two-week physical education class unit. The need for this program was based on findings that the majority of boys and girls were already hunting or target shooting, and that most student gun accidents were statistically shown to occur at the junior high school age level.

The course stresses knowledge of the mechanics of gun handling and safe practices in target shooting and while hunting. The police department, which cooperates in the sponsorship and the staffing of the instructional sequence, takes the position that it not only helps to reduce ac-

[5] See: "Hunter's Guide for Safer Hunting and Better Sportsmanship," *Hunter Training Program Manual* (Albany, New York: State Conservation Department).

cidents, but that it creates a more responsible attitude generally about the use of firearms.[6]

In other communities, shooting has become a popular recreation activity, making use of a variety of facilities. Shooting ranges, both indoor and outdoor, may range from the very simple and functional to highly elaborate and expensive areas. Their objectives may be purely social or may include hunter safety and competitive shooting.

One of the newest and most modern public shooting facilities is the Blue Mountain Reservation, operated by the Westchester County, New York, Department of Parks, Conservation and Recreation. Costing $250,000 to construct, it features outdoor rifle and pistol ranges from 15 to 300 yards, plus archery ranges, fly and bait casting pools, and trap and skeet fields for shotgunners. Open seven days a week, admission is 25¢ for Westchester County residents, and 50¢ for nonresident guests. Hourly fees for use of the ranges extend from 50¢ an hour for pistol shooters, to $1.50 for high-powered riflemen. Ranges are constructed to eliminate the possibility of bullets leaving the area accidentally, and spectators are confined to safe areas by fences and other barriers.

Another outstanding public shooting facility is located at San Mateo, California, near San Francisco, where an unusual range was built by the county in the center of an area which includes a college, yacht harbor, golf course, and bathing beach. A 100-yard layout was constructed with a series of steel baffles across the 46-point firing line which prevents any shot from going over the targets and provides complete safety for handguns, small-bore and high-powered rifles. The range has fluorescent lighting which permits night firing. A heavy classroom program is provided for National Rifle Association junior hunter safety classes, adult pistol classes, and junior rifle club programs.

Davis writes:

> Where municipal funds are not available for initial range construction, wildlife clubs, rifle and pistol clubs, and trap and skeet clubs can organize and conduct special fund-raising campaigns; then, when the individual clubs have raised enough funds to finance building costs, the project can be turned over to city or county recreation or parks departments to be operated as a public facility. This is just one way to get a county or municipal club started. There are other equally successful methods, according to the National Rifle Association . . . which has more than 11,000 affiliated clubs. . . .

> Some communities have potential club sites on tracts of wasteland, abandoned air fields, or other suitable areas where housing encroachments will not force them to cease operations within a few years. . . . It . . . appears that the sports park idea is the best solution for most heavily populated

[6] Gus Albright and Cecile Hudson, "Community Action for Safety," *Journal of Health, Physical Education and Recreation,* November–December, 1964, p. 30.

areas. The principal advantages of public ownership of a sports park where rifle, pistol, trap, skeet, archery, boating and fishing can be combined are:

1. A place where the public can shoot under competent supervision.
2. A place where shooters can bring their families to enjoy suitable recreational facilities, while the shooting members fire at targets.
3. Reduce range fees, less than those charged by privately operated clubs, and no requirement to belong to an expensive gun club.
4. Better equipment and facilities than most private clubs can afford.
5. Provision for expansion as the interest in shooting mounts and the population of the community increases.
6. The ranges can become self-supporting; thus they will eventually cost the taxpayers nothing for an excellent community facility.[7]

All in all, hunting and shooting programs appear to be one of the most appropriate areas for local recreation and park department activity sponsorship, in the broad field of outdoor recreation.

FAMILY CAMPING CLUBS AND COURSES

Family camping has been growing steadily in participation, as an enjoyable and inexpensive form of family fun; more and more county, state, and federal parks have been expanding their facilities for tent and trailer camping. Equipment ranges widely from simple pup or mountaineer tents, or just plain sleeping bags and ponchos (for the hardy), to elaborate and expensive convertible trailer outfits. Some camping families go to primitive areas and live on dehydrated foods, which they must pack in over mountain trails, or carry through rough water by canoe. Others live as luxuriously as if they were at home. But, whatever the details, this is certainly one of the most popular forms of outdoor recreation for millions of Americans.

The very idea of camping implies that one goes to a wilderness or forest site away from home. How then can most community recreation departments realistically offer camping programs? Few of them actually operate campsites, either locally or at a distance—as Phoenix does.

The answer is that local recreation and park departments may stimulate interest in this activity, may offer courses in family camping, and may sponsor clubs or organizations based on it. The following are some examples.

Moline, Illinois. The Recreation Department in Moline, Illinois, sponsors a family camping club which rapidly expanded from an original eight families to over 140 families with 560 members, within the course of a few months. The club holds monthly meetings, including panel discussions, displays of equipment, and special programs. They have club

[7] Leonard L. Davis, Jr., "Community Recreation Shooting Programs," *American Recreation Journal*, July–August, 1964, p. 101.

identification patches and auto stickers, and plan weekend club camping trips to a state park 100 miles away, in addition to other mutually enjoyed recreation activities.[8]

Linden, New Jersey. Under the auspices of the Linden, New Jersey, Recreation Department, a family camping club has been in operation for a number of years. Its name, "The Hitch-um and Pitch-um Travelers," betrays its special interest; club members include both travel-trailers (the mobile type easily attached to the rear of cars, not the larger house-trailer types) and tent campers. The group members hold club rallies at state parks and private campsites on six scheduled weekend campouts during the spring, summer, and fall. At each rally, they enjoy mass cook-outs (with the men taking over at the barbecue), softball, swimming, horseshoes, and other sports. While New Jersey boasts many trailer clubs, the Linden group is the only one sponsored by a recreation department. Its members are therefore extremely active on advisory committees to secure additional and improved campsites in the state, and are affiliated with a number of recreation and conservation departments in the effort to promote family camping.[9]

West Allis, Wisconsin. The West Allis Joint City-School Recreation Department sponsors a Family Camping club. This group publishes an extensive brochure, giving guides for those investigating the activity—with recommendations about clothing, equipment, food, and other details. They also carry out detailed investigations of private and public campsites in Wisconsin county parks, state and federal forests, privately owned grounds, and other areas. In addition to publishing much of this material, and a useful bibliography of camping books and magazines, they sponsor a variety of other special events and meetings.

Recreation departments that seek to promote family camping can get much help from states that are usually quite willing to send detailed brochures and other information about their camping areas, public and private. The National Park Service (Department of the Interior) and National Forest Service (Department of Agriculture) will also send maps and booklets telling details of camping opportunities. The National Campers and Hikers Association has made a practice of contributing copies of "Tent and Trail" to such ventures, and local manufacturers or distributors who handle camping equipment or food are usually quite willing to set up demonstrations, contribute pamphlets or possible samples of dehydrated food, as prizes. The recreation department may wish to set up a Family Camping Night, with demonstrations of camp skills, games and contests, skits, and displays of equipment, slides, films,

---

[8] Jack Fogel, "Families Plan Now, Camp Later," *Recreation*, December, 1960, p. 480.
[9] Frank M. Krysiak, "Hitch-um and Pitch-um Camping," *Recreation*, March, 1964, p. 130.

and speakers. If sufficient interest is shown, it may then lead directly into the formation of a family camping club.

DAY CAMPING PROGRAMS

An important aspect of outdoor recreation for many municipal park and recreation departments has been the establishment of day camping programs. This usually differs from a regular playground program in that children are signed up for regular participation over a period of time. This may be the entire summer, or may involve only a week or two, with the membership being rotated to give as many as possible a chance to participate. Day camping should involve transportation to a wooded or natural site away from the regular neighborhood playground and should also include the serving of at least one meal to the children.

Customarily a full schedule of activities is planned, with a strong emphasis on nature activities, games, and crafts. Children are usually divided into small groups under competent leadership, in a decentralized type of program operation. Two good examples of recreation-sponsored camps follow.

Bristol, New Hampshire. The "Slim Baker Day Camp," sponsored by the Bristol, New Hampshire, Recreation Department, was designed to be more than just a displaced playground moved to a wooded lot. Meeting three times a week, 60 boys and girls from 9 to 15 hike to the mountainside site each day. There they raise the flag, and divide into small groups to work on a prescribed program of activities involving nature skills, under the supervision of adult leaders and junior assistants. The groups are given Indian names, and work together on such activities as learning and practicing the Conservation Pledge, safely handling jackknives and hatchet, knot-tying and lashing, marking trails, knowing what to do when lost in the woods, and building and cooking over open fires. They are visited and taught by county foresters, U.S. soil conservation specialists, fish and game department wardens, school outdoor educators, and mountain climbers.

Each child works toward four proficiency classifications, under the titles of "Pioneer," "Frontiersman," "Sourdough," and "Voyageur." Each one usually takes a summer to pass. Day campers also strive to qualify for the season ending "Camporee" which is held in one of the state or national parks in New England. The expense of the program has been minimal, and an interesting outcome has been that a number of Bristol families have taken up family camping after their children have been introduced to the activity in this way.[10]

10 Robert P. Ledger, "Day Camping—An Answer to Summer Needs," *Recreation*, March, 1964, p. 116.

Hawthorne, California. Because of crowded conditions in their area of Southern California, and the lack of appropriate sites for camping and other outdoor activities, the citizens of Hawthorne, California, joined together to purchase and develop a 20-acre all-year mountain camp, 100 miles northeast of their city. Located in the San Gabriel Mountains, near the 6,000 foot level of the Angeles National Forest, the camp provides a varied program for children in eight-day sessions from June through August, and a school outdoor education experience for classes from the elementary school district, during the winter. Winter weekends are scheduled for family visits, at the modest cost of a dollar per camper per weekend. Cost for the summer campers are little more—$15 per child to cover food, transportation, supervision, lodging, and insurance.

How can this program be provided so cheaply? This is partly illustrated by the way the large centrally located lodge of the camp was built—by volunteered money, material, and labor. Similarly, nine separate 16-bunk cabins were built at minimal expense. Believing strongly in the need for this type of outdoor recreation experience for all ages, the residents of Hawthorne have cooperated fully to make the experience possible for all, providing financial aid for youngsters, when needed. The summer eight-day session includes such activities as: fishing, horseback riding, wildlife study, forest lore, geology, panning for gold, weather forecasting, and astronomy.[11]

An increasing number of communities have built camping sites of this type, some close by for day camping programs, as in Bristol, and some at a greater distance for more extended periods, as in Hawthorne. In a number of cases, the same camp may be used both for day camping and overnight programs as well; the Croton Point Camp operated by the Westchester County, New York, Department of Parks, Recreation and Conservation, is an example of this.

OUTDOOR RECREATION AND CAMPING FOR HANDICAPPED CHILDREN

A later chapter will deal in full detail with the planning and development of recreation programs for handicapped children and adults. It is appropriate, however, at this point, to examine several examples of outdoor recreation and camping programs that have been designed specifically for handicapped children and youth.

Cerebral Palsy Day Camp. In Nassau County, New York, there is the unusual example of a playground specifically designed to meet the needs of physically handicapped children. On the grounds of the Nassau County Cerebral Palsy Association, in Roosevelt, Long Island, New

11 Cossie L. Smith, "Mountain Youth Camp," *Recreation*, March, 1962, p. 145.

York, the area is composed of several large (50 feet in diameter) circular sections, connected with each other by wide, semipaved paths.

Each area is equipped with slides with graduated approach ramps, wide bicycle paths, a maze that can be explored by youngsters in wheelchairs, and with a water-and-sand play area designed to be used by children in wheelchairs or on crutches. The whole purpose of the playground is to modify activities and facilities so that they can be used successfully by children with cerebral palsy—and so that the youngsters can be encouraged to dare new adventures and learn new skills. There is a "mountain climber," with rails and heavy rope supports which children may climb, and a "magic forest," which they may explore in several different ways.

In addition, a day campsite, placed in the woods next to the playground, offers large tents placed on wood platforms flush with the ground, a crafts area and storage house, a swimming pool, and a fishing hole (made from an old concrete foundation) where children may sit in their wheelchairs and fish through a screened opening for safety. There are also paved paths throughout the woods, used by the children for hiking and for group nature activities.[12]

In all, the camp is an unusual example of ingenuity and the determination of parents and interested professionals to see that these handicapped children are not deprived of their right to enjoy nature and explore their own creative abilities in an outdoor setting. A similar motivation was responsible for the development of the Daniel Boone Camp, in St. Louis, Missouri.

Daniel Boone Camp. The St. Louis Society for Crippled Children has been active for many years in helping to sponsor and arrange the admission of handicapped children in regular residential summer camps in its area. A number of private or agency camps have cooperated quite effectively in this effort. However, it was found that a number of children were so severely handicapped that they could not function adequately in regular camp programs. Therefore the Society built a special camp in St. Charles County, called the Daniel Boone Camp, which is used by the most severely disabled youngsters—including children with such varied diagnoses as cerebral palsy, hydrocephalus, spinal bifida, epilepsy, post brain-tumor operations, postencephalitis, and blindness.

The program is much like that of any summer camp, except that children do not stay overnight, because of the excessive complications this would entail. Activities include nature lore, swimming, hikes, rifle shooting, archery, singing, story telling, arts and crafts, skits, and similar projects. Children are treated basically as normal children, without any emphasis on their handicap—although they have been admitted under

[12] Morton Thompson, "Cerebral Palsy Day Camp," *Recreation*, March, 1961, p. 141.

careful medical clearance and guidance, and a trained social worker supervises the camp activities. It has been found possible to integrate children with many different types of disabilities, providing that the groups are kept small, the program flexible, and the staff capable and well-oriented.

One of Daniel Boone Camp's main concerns has been to motivate children to try *new* skills and experiences. Many of them, with severe disabilities, have been so overprotected that they have failed to live up to their full potential in terms of physical performance. As they have gained confidence, a number of severely handicapped youngsters have moved from a summer at Daniel Boone to the point where they were capable of being admitted to a regular camp, for an integrated experience with nonhandicapped children.[13]

Canoeing for the Blind. A most unusual example of the potential abilities of handicapped children and youth may be found in the program of Camp Lighthouse—a summer center for the blind—on Barnegat Bay, New Jersey.

Because of the location of the camp, many activities for the campers (all of whom are legally blind, although some may have up to one-fifth residual vision) take place on and near the beach. They swim and dive, row, fish, clam, crab, do synchronized swimming, skin and "scuba" diving, water skiing, and canoeing. Gordon T. Howes, director of the camp, describes one venture:

> Last summer we tried a Basic Red Cross Canoeing Course with an all-day canoe trip as a windup. The course had as its objectives: to teach the campers to be safe canoeists; to give the campers a very real and exciting experience to be remembered and talked about; to give the camper a sense of accomplishment equal to a sighted person; to give the camper a recreation outlet that could be used with sighted or blind companions; to develop the independence of the camper. The campers were in for a four-week stay, and felt that in this time they could accomplish all the necessary skills.[14]

The campers—all of whom had to be capable swimmers before they could enter the canoe course—learned a wide variety of canoeing skills. They learned basic balance, learned to get in and out of craft safely, took paddling practice in various forms, learned to paddle in a straight line (which many sighted individuals find difficult), and to paddle through heavy water. They practiced in a canal in the salt marshes and on the open water, and finally successfully accomplished their all-day trip, a tiring and difficult feat, without any sort of untoward incident.

The point they illustrated clearly is that, under capable leadership

---

13 Dorothy Spear, "Daniel Boone Roams Again," *Recreation*, March, 1960, p. 116.
14 Gordon T. Howes, "Canoe Course for the Blind," *Recreation*, March, 1962, p. 131.

and given the opportunity, even the most severely handicapped are able to do far more things than they have been given the opportunity to try.

NATURE ACTIVITIES, PROJECTS, AND GAMES

In addition to the kinds of outdoor recreation programs described earlier in this chapter, there are many activities which may be used on summer playgrounds, or in neighborhood parks or wooded areas, by groups of children or adults who are particularly interested in nature. These include games which are based on the natural environment, nature arts and crafts, the learning of camping skills, and nature-study projects. A number of examples of each type of activity will be presented here. In addition, several books are listed in the bibliography which give much fuller examples of each form of nature recreation.

Nature Games

Some of these games are played best when on a hike through natural terrain. Others may be played anywhere. They involve certain specific kinds of skills: identification and knowledge of natural objects, trailing skills, alertness and awareness of the natural world.

Sniff. Players are blindfolded and, one by one, are allowed to smell certain common objects which have been gathered in advance. These should have strong and recognizable odors, like: cedar, apple, cucumber, mold, tomato, skunk cabbage, balsam, mint, black birch, onion, fish, and similar choices. The player who can correctly identify the largest number of objects is the winner.

Feel. The same game may be played by having each child in turn feel certain objects, like shells, stones of various types, flowers, leaves, bark, and whatever can be gathered in the vicinity. Each object should have a very distinctive texture or shape, and must be exactly identified. The player with the highest score of correct answers is the winner.

Nature Sounds. The group sits quietly in a clearing in the woods. Each person listens, writing down all of the nature sounds he hears—the wind, birds, insects, leaves rustling, etc. (each sound must be specifically identified). After a 5- or 10-minute time limit, each player reads his list. The longest correct list wins the game.

Nature Relay. Children divide into several equal teams. Each team is given a list containing in order the names of several natural objects that are to be found in the vicinity: acorns, nuts, pebbles, bird feathers, pine cones, grasses, leaves, etc. At a signal, the first child must run to obtain the first object on the list. When he returns, the second child must find and bring back the next object. This continues until one group—the winning team—has completed the relay. The game may also be played under the title "Nature Scavenger Hunt." In this version the entire team goes to work at once to collect the listed objects.

Nature Treasure Hunt. The players are divided into several teams. Each team is given a map which leads them, by a different route, to the same "treasure." On the map are directions and clues, which make use of natural objects, rocks, trees, flowers, etc.; at each clue, directions to the next clue are found. The first team to reach the "treasure" is the winner.

Retrieving. This game is somewhat similar to "Nature Relay." Players are divided into several teams. One player from each team is active. The leader holds up some object or nature specimen—a leaf, twig, flower, or feather. At the signal, "Go!" the active player on each team must run to find and bring back a similar object. The first player to do so wins one point for his team. Each player is active in turn, and the first team to total a given number of points is the winner.

Nature Artists. Players divide into teams. Each team sends an "artist" to the leader. When they are all together, the leader shows them the name of a natural object (bird, animal, tree, or plant) he has written down. They run back to their groups and draw the object, until it is correctly named by a member of the group. The team to guess correctly first wins one point. So the game goes until each child has had a chance to be the "artist."

Prove It. Players sit in a circle, in a woodland setting. The first child says, "From where I am, I can see a small pond." The next one says, "From where I am, I can see a small pond and a black crow." The game goes on, with each player repeating what has been said before—in the same order—and adding something else that he sees. If anyone doubts the previous statement, he may say "Prove it!" and the previous speaker must defend what he has said by pointing it out. The game goes on until only one person has been able to repeat all that has gone before, and add a new object. He is the winner.

Nature Alphabet. This game is played with two teams facing each other in lines. The leader names a category, such as birds, flowers, trees, or animals. Then he names a letter of the alphabet. In turn, the first player in Team A and then the first player in Team B must name something in the correct category starting with that letter—within 5 or 10 seconds. If he cannot, the other team wins a point. The game is repeated with the next player in the line and with a new letter each time. If the same letter is used again, players may not name the same object as before. The team with the highest total of points at the end is the winner.

Trailing Games. There are many different types of "trailing" games. In the simplest kind, the leader, or one of the players, goes cross-country into the woods, marking his trail by bending twigs or deliberately leaving footprints. After an interval of time, the group tries to find him; the first player to do so is the winner.

A so-called "Whiffenpoof Trail" is made by driving long nails into a log about two feet long and five inches thick. A rope is attached to this, and the leader drags it along the ground to create a trail. The others follow this, as in the previous game, and the first player to find the leader is the winner.

Any such game must be played within well-designated boundaries and with children who are old enough so that there is no risk of their becoming lost in the woods.

Hunt the Animals. Before the group gets together, the leader places a large number of small pictures of animals (or other nature objects) around the playground area. At a signal, the game is explained, and each child must walk around, mentally making a note of each animal he sees —but not touching it. After a time limit, there is a signal, and all the players return and write down the names of each animal they saw and the place it was located. One point is given for each correct listing, and one point is deducted for each inaccurate item. The child with the highest score is the winner.

Guess the Name. This game is best played with a small group of youngsters, sitting close together. The leader holds up a sheet of cardboard, with a hole in the middle. He shows a leaf, so the edge may barely be seen through the hole. Gradually, he moves it over so a little more can be seen. The first child to correctly identify it is given the leaf (if a child calls out the wrong name, he may not guess again on this leaf). The game is played several times, and the child who amasses the largest collection is the winner. Bird or animal pictures may also be shown in the same way.

Firefly Tag. This game is played around a campsite when the sun has gone down and it is quite dark. One child has a flashlight. He is given a count of 20 to get away, and the others pursue him. He must shine his flashlight briefly every few moments as they chase him. The first child to touch him takes the flashlight and becomes the new "firefly."

NATURE STUDY ACTIVITIES

It is important to recognize that nature study is not just a matter of listing a number of practical projects and activities to carry out. Instead, it is necessary to have an outlook toward nature that sees it as something exciting and meaningful, even in its tiniest or least significant aspects. Children are usually eager for adventure and exploration, and recreation leaders and camp counselors must join them in this spirit, as they approach nature involvement.

It is not necessary to be rich in nature lore or science information, although the nature specialist in a camp or recreation department should be well versed in his field. What is more important is that the counselor should be resourceful in exploring each situation on the playground, in the park, the pond, or the forest—to uncover the many possibilities for nature discovery that lie close by. This means viewing each plant, each insect, each water creature, leaf, bird, or twig as a source of wonder and interest. The leader who brings along a magnifying glass, or a pocket book to help in identifying nature objects is on his way!

What are some specific activities that children enjoy in a camp or recreation setting? They include the following:

Collections. Recognizing that it is important not to pick growing things unless they are in abundance, children may make collections of flowers, leaves, twigs, seeds, insects, bird nests, seaweed, sea shells, rocks, minerals, and similar objects. These may then be displayed on easily constructed "nature shelves" that may be suspended by rope from trees, or in cabins or play centers.

Bird Houses. Children may be helped to make bird houses, feeding trays or baths, for wooded areas near their homes or near the playground. The National Audubon Society and the U.S. Fish and Wildlife Service publish inexpensive bulletins which give details of the types of homes which should be built for different bird species, how to space them out, what sorts of food should be put out to attract and properly nourish birds, and similar information.

Gardening. This is a particularly useful hobby, even for comparatively limited areas, and it is one that sustains interest through an entire playground season, as different flowers and vegetables are planted and grow. Children may cultivate their own small plots, may do landscaping, may do transplanting, and even—with adult direction—carry out more ambitious projects, such as developing rock gardens, growing miniature or dwarf plants, and propagating plants and shrubs. In many communities there are garden clubs with interested adults who will be glad to volunteer as instructors in gardening programs on summer playgrounds.

Weather Study. Again, under competent guidance, children may carry out a variety of activities related to weather study. They may learn basic facts about climate, to make and read barometers, to use weather forecasting instruments, and to record, chart, and interpret data. A study of astronomy may be closely linked to such projects.

Soil Experimentation. Children will enjoy experimenting with different types of soil that may be found around the camp or playground: clay, sandy, forest soil, open field soil. Using glass collecting jars, they may carry out water penetration tests, to see how fast the water runs through each type, and how much of it is retained. They may test each type for acidity, using Hydrion paper. They may practice growing beans or seeds in each type, or may construct jar displays showing how earthworms live in the soil, tunnel through, and aerate it.

Terrariums. Children may construct simple, miniature terrariums, using mosses, small plants, bright stones, and berries to make colorful displays. These may be used to house salamanders or small turtles, although care must be taken to provide sufficient food for these small pets, since the terrarium itself does not provide natural food for them.

Hiking. Hiking, of course, is an ideal nature activity. It can be far more than a simple tramp through the woods. In the winter time, children may look for tracks in the snow, or may build snow sculptures where the snow is deep enough. They may take photographs on a special "Photo Hike," and later have a display of the pictures that were taken. They may pause from time to time, just to listen to sounds of nature, or from the distant town. Trailing games may be played, or special hikes taken in which children discover clues which lead them to new clues and then to the final destination. They may follow a brook or stream, and observe the forms of life in it or along its banks. The possibilities for variety in hiking are great.

Nature Crafts. Among the many craft activities based on nature are: photography, making plaster molds of prints or other nature objects, whittling or wood-carving, or making prints of leaves (using a spattering or ink-rolling method). Other activities may involve fly-tying, weaving or making displays with cattails, constructing models using "lashing" techniques, and making decorations, book-ends, centerpieces, or lamp bases with driftwood. Children may do block printing using cut potatoes or apples, may make tiny decorative trees, using pods and cones, and may construct nature jewelry.

Nature Clubs. In camps or on playgrounds, the following types of clubs may be formed: "junior naturalist" club, "astronomy" club, "dog trainer" or other "pet-care" clubs, "nature photography" club, "hiking" or "bicycling" club, "youth hosteling" club, and many others.

CAMPCRAFT ACTIVITIES

Closely allied to these activities are the skills that are needed for survival in the woods, or simply for the most comfortable and enjoyable living in the outdoor setting. They include the following:

Knotcraft. Either as part of a sailing program, or simply as an aid to pitching tents and shelters and making camp in the woods, it is essential to be able to make a number of useful knots that can be tied easily, will hold fast, and can be untied without difficulty. Several of these include the square knot (or reef knot), the close hitch, the bowline knot, the sheet bend, and the half-hitch knot.

Compass. Children enjoy learning to read, understand, and use the compass. They may undertake special problems, involving finding their way to certain spots by compass, or may play the Swedish game, "Orienteering," which tests several kinds of compass skills.[15] Similarly, they may learn to read maps, to understand contour lines, and gain practice in making their own maps.

Measurements. Part of outdoor living involves learning to measure distances or dimensions. Children may learn to measure distance, first by estimating it roughly and then (having determined the length of their individual pace) by pacing it off. They may also learn to quickly measure things by using their own personal dimensions (hand span, length of index finger, length of foot, height, eye level, or upward stretch).

Morse Code. Children are always fascinated by the universal language of dots and dashes. Once they have learned to send it and to receive it, however slowly, they may experiment with different ways of signaling. These may include the use of flags, smoke, arms, whistles, buzzers, or, at night, fire, lantern, or flashlight.

Lashing. This technique, used by woodsmen to construct tables, stands, tripods, or other camp articles of convenience, involves the use of sturdy doweling (saplings may be used, if it is permitted to cut them) and binder twine. There are several basic types of bindings used, and ingenious models making use of lashing may also be approached as a hobby activity, or to make useful camp equipment.

Fire-Making. Children may safely be introduced to fire-making skills. They learn how to make various types of fires: a basic "A" fire, a tepee fire, and a "crisscross" fire. This may be done as preparation for a hike, cookout, or overnight trip.

Skills Tournament. At the end of a summer season, children may participate in a tournament where they compete in performing the various campcraft skills they have learned. They should be divided into teams, with each youngster having a chance to compete in one or more events, while his teammates "root" for him. Activities include the following: (a) pitching a tent; (b) making a tripod basin rack or other lashed construction; (c) building a fire (sometimes done so the first child who has a pot of water boiling is the winner); (d) driving nails into a log; (e) making a pile of shavings with a jackknife; (f) making knots; (g) giving signal messages, and similar types of tests. Each event is scored for speed, with the first to complete it given three points, the next two, and the next one, so that players are encouraged to keep going, even if they are not the first.

COMMUNITY APPROACHES TO NATURE ACTIVITIES

In addition to the kinds of examples cited earlier, many communities sponsor interesting types of nature activities, services, and demonstrations. A number of illustrations follow.

[15] Bjorn Kjellstrom, "The Sport of Orienteering," *Recreation,* March, 1954, p. 170.

Austin, Texas, Nature Center. The Austin Recreation Department sponsors a city-wide Nature Center, which includes clubs and classes that meet weekly, in such areas of interest as astronomy, archaeology, plant and animal life, earth sciences and meteorology. Participants meet with advisors and teachers from such organizations as the Travis Audubon Society, the Austin Gem and Mineral Society, the Forty Acres Astronomy Club, and various science departments of the University of Texas. They carry out field trips, develop science and nature projects, and have received considerable assistance from the national organization, Nature Centers for Young America.

Milwaukee "Starwagon." Another example of science interests being promoted by a municipal recreation department may be found in the traveling observatory and planetarium operated on playgrounds in Milwaukee, Wisconsin. Most of the funds required for the "Starwagon's" construction were raised from private sources, although the Milwaukee Astronomical Society assisted in designing it, and it was actually built by the recreation divisions service and maintenance department. The mobile unit itself is 21 feet in length and has a 15-foot diameter collapsible dome with a colorful rainbow steel arch. Its equipment includes a $3\frac{1}{2}$-inch refractor telescope and a 6-inch reflector telescope, a planetarium projector, charts, space-interpretation globes, satellite-tracking telescopes, and similar devices necessary for a space program. The entire unit is attached to a department truck or jeep and can readily be taken to any section of the city.

Playground programs using the "Starwagon" are usually conducted in the evening. The specialist in charge covers such subjects as recognition of constellations, daily and seasonal course of the stars, planetary positions, and man's present attempts to explore space. The formal lecture usually lasts about three-quarters of an hour, and viewing by children and adults through the telescopes may go on long after that.[16]

Gardening Projects. In Washington, D.C., the Recreation Department has sponsored a summertime gardening program, in which as many as 65 playgrounds and 800 children participated regularly. Activities include: planting, cultivating, and fertilizing flowers and vegetables in garden plots; flower-pot and window-box plantings; weed and insect identification; the care of tools; and related craft activities. In one Washington center, handicapped children from a special school, using modified techniques and projects, were given their first experience in gardening. For them, and for children generally in a large metropolis, this kind of experience provides important new learnings and possibilities for growth.

Nature Trails. As indicated earlier, a number of municipal park

16 Donald B. Dyer, "The Starwagon," *Recreation*, April, 1963, p. 165.

and recreation departments maintain nature trails, which are used both for outdoor recreation and outdoor education purposes. One of the most interesting of these is the Nature Trail operated in Encanto Park by the city of Phoenix, Arizona. The Parks and Recreation Department provides a "do-it-yourself" guide, designed to add to the visitor's enjoyment and understanding of the trail. It identifies trees and shrubs, step by step, and gives their interesting background. It describes the birds which are likely to be seen, explores the rocks and minerals of Arizona in a special section of the trail, and explains the wide variety of cacti to be seen in the Cactus Garden.

The booklet gives directions on how to follow the trail throughout the park, and also provides assistance to leaders of youth groups (especially those of Brownie, Bluebird, and Cub Scout age) who may be working toward nature badge requirements, and who are visiting it for that reason.

Animal and Pet Activities. A popular form of nature activity in community recreation involves the sponsorship of pet owner's clubs and of other hobbies or activities dealing with animals. This may include workshops on the proper care and training of animals, in which veterinarians are brought in to discuss such topics as animal nutrition, diseases, and medicine, and kits or other materials from dog food companies are displayed.

It may include dog obedience classes meeting over a period of 10 or 15 sessions, at several levels of training. Often the final sessions of such courses involve demonstrations, contests, and the judging of special events and performances. One such club, in Reading, Pennsylvania, the Berks County Dog Training Club, has compiled an enviable record of public service through entertainment given to hospitals, and through cooperation with city police in solving problems caused by unruly pets.

Probably the most unusual pet club of all is to be found in the "Loyal Order of the Serpent," a snake club founded by members of the recreation department in Fayetteville, North Carolina. Club members catch and contribute snakes to the city zoo, give lectures to interested organizations, develop display charts of poisonous and nonpoisonous snakes, and, in general, pursue an interesting nature hobby and provide community service as well.

On summer playgrounds, pet shows may include a wide variety of events and categories—some of them humorous. All, however, should be aimed at developing sound attitudes regarding pet-owner responsibilities, plus effective skills in actually caring for pets.

Nature Festivals. Finally, a number of recreation departments have sponsored nature festivals on a community-wide basis as important special events. In Richmond, Virginia, for example, the Department of Recreation and Parks has presented a large outdoor nature show, including two elements: (a) a cross section of the city playgrounds' organized nature programs; and (b) displays by organized groups, including astronomy, mineralogy, and garden clubs. The festival was housed under a large tent, and had such features as: playground collections of rocks, reptiles, butterflies, arts and crafts displays, birdhouses and gardens; an azalea exhibit; a Boy Scout exhibit on erosion control; private collection of South American iguanas, lizards, turtles, and quail; Indian dances; and displays by the Virginia State Commission of Game and Fisheries and State Park Service. In all, an estimated 12,000 persons attended the two-day event, and plans have been made to continue it as an annual program.[17]

This chapter has described a variety of examples of municipally sponsored outdoor recreation activities and services. Without question, as the life of Americans becomes increasingly urban-centered, there will be an increasing need for such nature and outdoor-oriented programs.

SUGGESTED QUESTIONS FOR DISCUSSION

1. What accounts for the unusual recent growth of interest in outdoor recreation in the United States? How is this related to important trends in modern industrial society?
2. Define and illustrate the roles of several levels of government (federal, state, county, and local) in promoting outdoor recreation facilities and programs. What might the roles of schools and colleges be, to supplement the efforts of governmental agencies?
3. Outline a number of ways in which the physically handicapped may be served in outdoor recreation programs. What factors exist in present-day programing that may discourage or prevent the handicapped from taking part freely?

[17] Xenophon Morris, "Nature Festival," *Recreation*, April, 1963, p. 164.

Chapter 7

The Performing Arts:
Music, Drama, and Dance

One of the most exciting aspects of the present-day recreational scene in the United States is the growth of cultural programs in communities large and small. As described in Chapter 1, there has been, since World War II, an unprecedented increase in the amount of artistic involvement and performance. Orchestras, choral groups, bands, modern dance and ballet companies and instructional programs, little theater groups, drama workshops, and a host of similar enterprises are to be found springing up like mushrooms.

Within this total scene, community recreation departments and agencies have been extremely active in promoting the arts. As of 1964, 20 community recreation programs had established cultural divisions, with the promise of more to come. Prendergast suggests that it is the role of community recreation to provide facilities, leadership, and encourage-

160

ment to all forms and levels of artistic involvement. He offers a 10-point program for the development of the cultural phases of recreation:

1. Cultivate the broadest possible concepts for the role of organized recreation in the arts.

2. Create and strengthen cultural planning advisory bodies within the administrative structure of organized recreation and establish liaison with appropriate organizations and institutions.

3. Develop policies and practices for the arts as recreation in accordance with general policy that do not restrict but rather encourage expansion and flexibility.

4. Encourage the use of specialized leadership of quality in building the cultural recreation program.

5. Arrange for more workshops in the various arts for exploratory purposes as well as training purposes.

6. Develop better techniques for educating authorities, the staff, and the public in the use and benefits of a cultural recreation program.

7. Undertake the formation of new groups and special events. Cultivate the indigenous.

8. Make freer, fuller, more frequent use of talented groups and individuals in reaching the public, using them for civic purposes and for interpreting recreation.

9. Accumulate a supply of basic and useful equipment for the various arts. Plan for an increase of the availability of basic facilities for the arts.

10. Strive constantly for quality in this phase of organized recreation programs.[1]

CATEGORIES OF ARTISTIC EXPERIENCE IN RECREATION

Specifically, what kinds of artistic experiences may be found in community recreational programs? Essentially, they may be divided into two categories:

The Performing Arts. This term implies the kind of artistic involvement in which the participant uses himself as the medium of expression. He acts, he sings, he dances, but no tangible evidence of his performance remains, unless it is recorded or filmed. The *doing* is the important thing, whether or not an audience is involved.

The Applied Arts. This suggests the kind of involvement that results in the creation of a tangible product. Thus, the participant in arts and crafts may create a pot, a block print, or a rug; the sculptor creates a statue; the writer creates a short story or a poem. It is the product that

[1] Joseph Prendergast, "Cultural Growth in Capital Letters," *Recreation*, November, 1964, p. 440.

is then perceived as the outcome of the experience rather than the participant and what happens to him.

This chapter deals in detail with the performing arts; Chapter 8 is concerned with the applied arts—primarily arts and crafts.

It should be understood that people tend to classify artistic involvement as being "serious" or "nonserious." To illustrate, with respect to recreation activities:

Dance may be approached as a serious art form, as in ballet, modern dance, or ethnic dance, which places emphasis on stage performance at a high artistic level. On the other hand, dance may simply be a form of casual, social fun, as in a teen-age dance party, with little artistic significance. Similarly, music programs may include the serious performance of classical or contemporary works by symphony orchestras or chamber music groups, or may consist of barber-shop quartets or informal community singing or rhythm band activities.

Between the two extremes, of course, certain activities may have elements both serious and nonserious. Thus, in dance, some individuals may take part in modern dance simply as a "fun" or "conditioning" activity. By contrast, many participants in such recreational forms of dance as square or folk dancing take their hobby very seriously and reach an extremely high level of skilled performance. In any case, the community recreation director would be making a mistake to accept too seriously a distinction between "highbrow" and "lowbrow" forms of artistic experience, or to assign a higher status to the former. The "highbrow" individual is likely to enjoy so-called popular art forms, and the so-called "lowbrow" always has a potential for learning to understand and enjoy the more elite forms. All forms of artistic and expressive activity add to the cultural richness of a community, and all should be encouraged.

VALUES OF ARTISTIC EXPERIENCE IN RECREATION

What are the unique values or goals of artistic experience in programs of community or agency recreation?

1. The individual learns to discover himself as a person. In a world of conformity and mass expression, he is creatively involved in learning new skills, exploring latent talents, and giving voice to ideas, sounds, shapes, or movements that are his alone.

2. In a world marked by nonparticipation, in which more and more work is done by machines and entertainment offered to us by other machines, the participant in artistic forms of recreation is making his *own* fun. He is a "doer," and not just a passive recipient.

3. An important value of artistic involvement is that it serves to

enrich the overall level of cultural taste in the community or nation at large. While some may scoff at the quality or significance of "amateur" performance or imply that it has little aesthetic worth—the fact is that, through mass participation in the arts, we are building a huge audience for professional performance. This is not a matter of numbers alone; the Sunday painter is likely to be a more intelligent, sensitive, or discriminating audience than the individual who has never held a brush in his hand.

4. Finally, through artistic experience, we reach a new dimension of living. We become more aware of life about us, more sensitive to beauty; the whole quality of our national culture is enhanced.

In addition to the foregoing points, which justify the inclusion of creative and artistic activities in community or agency recreation departments, the arts have certain important administrative advantages.

1. They appeal to many individuals who, by temperament and personality, may not be at all interested in programs of sports or games. Unlike the latter forms of activity, they stress cooperation rather than competition, the intellectual rather than the physical, and thus diversify the attraction of the recreation program for different groups.

2. They extend and continue school learnings. Too often, individuals who have learned to play a musical instrument, to sing as part of a chorus, or to enjoy a certain form of craft activity, would have no encouragement or opportunity to continue this hobby, if it were not for an organized recreation program.

3. The arts may be enjoyed on a wide variety of levels of skill and are equally appropriate for little children and aged persons. They can be carried on indoors and in all seasons. Thus, in regions where the climate limits outdoor play through a good part of the year, the arts are particularly useful.

4. The arts have a unique capacity for enhancing desirable social relationships. In them, the friendly camaraderie of the barber-shop quartet or Little Theater group, the intense cooperation and discipline required by the orchestra or performing dance group, invariably result in a level of friendly cooperation and responsible citizenship that does much to improve social interaction within a community or neighborhood.

INTERRELATIONSHIP OF THE ARTS

Although each of the performing arts is dealt with separately in this chapter, it should be pointed out that they all have strong links with each other. Not only do they share certain common elements such as rhythm, balance, color, contrast, or design, but they are often closely related in actual performance. Thus, dance is usually performed to musical accompaniment. The theater involves building stage sets, certainly a form of design and the craftsman's art. Opera involves music, drama, literature, and dance. Literature is closely linked to the theater. All are interwoven and are often drawn together in performances and stage presentations. Many successful recreation programs of children's activities stress this integration of the arts.

In the three sections that follow, the major kinds of music, drama, and dance that appear in community recreation programs are described and analyzed. The special aspects, values, and forms of each activity are described. A number of illustrations of how the particular activity may be presented in a given community or agency are offered, and, in each case, several specific examples—dramatic activities, songs, and dances—are described in detail. These will be useful for those who are using this book as a source for program ideas, or as a course text in recreation leadership or program planning.

MUSIC IN COMMUNITY RECREATION

As pointed out earlier, music is an extremely attractive and appealing form of recreation activity. It is extremely adaptable, and can suit any age, sex, taste, mood, or level of ability. It may be used with other activities, and frequently is an accompanying feature of civic celebrations, pageants, therapeutic programs, sports events, and ceremonials of every kind. It has been pointed out that "people singing and playing instruments and making music for their own enjoyment is a great American tradition. The *Bay Psalm Book* (Cambridge, Massachusetts, 1641) was the first book ever printed in America. The singing of these hymns by the early settlers has served as a precedent for the performance of religious music for the past three centuries." [2]

Participation in musical activities in American schools and colleges has grown to an all-time high. By the early 1960's, it was estimated that there were 35,000 orchestras, 50,000 bands, and 100,000 choruses in public secondary schools in the United States. At that time, the National Recreation Association sent out a questionnaire exploring the nature of community music participation. They found that music is today a major factor in public recreation programs—with services ranging from "kazoo bands to symphony orchestras, from musical games to opera."

Specifically, what forms of musical activity are offered by recreation departments? A partial listing follows:

[2] "Music is Recreation," *Recreation*, May, 1961, p. 243.

Accordion Lessons and Band
Band Instruction and Concerts
Boys' Band or Choir
Choral Clinics or Groups
Classic Guitar Instruction
Concert Bands and Concerts
Fife and Drum, or Drum Corps
Glee Clubs
Harmony and Counterpoint Classes
Jam Sessions
Mandolin Orchestras
Music Camps and Summer Schools
Music Conferences and Festivals
Percussion Bands
Record Concerts
Talent or Variety Shows
Attendance at Musical Events

Barbershop Quartets and Groups
Chamber Music Group
Christmas Caroling
Combos for Dance Accompaniment
Creative Music for Children
Folk Singing or Folk Guitar Lessons
Group Instruction in Instruments
Instrumental Brass Workshops
Jazz Clubs and Concerts
Military Bands
Music Appreciation Classes or Listen-
ing groups
Orchestral Concerts
Playground Music and Festivals
Recorder Groups and Instruction
Trips to Concerts

In general, community recreation departments promote musical participation in the following ways:

1. They offer instruction, primarily to children's groups, throughout the year but most intensively in the summertime. In this, they often relate their activities closely to those provided by the school system; frequently the school music specialist is given an opportunity to work more intensively with children through the recreation program.

2. They provide facilities, in the form of auditoriums, outdoor theaters or bandshells, rehearsal or practice rooms, and storage areas. Some recreation departments with highly developed music programs may also provide equipment, such as instruments, music libraries, costumes, recordings, tape recorders, and similar needed materials.

3. They cooperate with other agencies in helping to organize and promote community-wide musical events, such as festivals, clinics, concert series, children's programs, and the like.

4. In collaboration with musical organizations, or with the schools, recreation departments may help the training of leaders in this field by sponsoring institutes, workshops, courses, and similar sessions.

5. They may actually sponsor musical groups themselves, such as dance bands which play at events in local communities, "pop" bands, accordion bands, choral groups, symphony orchestras, and smaller units. These may serve both as a means of entertaining the public and as a direct form of recreation for those who participate as musicians.

To illustrate these recreational uses of music, it is helpful to look at several outstanding examples of community music programs, each of a different type.

Community Music Center—Portland, Oregon

For a number of years, the Parks and Recreation Department of Portland, Oregon, has operated a highly successful Community Music Center. This program has the dual purpose of helping many participants become high caliber performers, while others become "discriminating amateurs who attend concerts and strive to create an ever growing cultural climate in their community." [3]

The program began in 1956, when an adult amateur orchestra was founded in Portland. Shortly after, a Children's Conservatory was begun, offering a program of private lessons, sòlfege, theory, chamber music, chorus, and orchestra. This is available to young people over a 12-year span (from the age of 6 to 18), at the minimal cost of $10 per semester. Since there is known to be a shortage of capable string players in the symphony orchestras which have increased well over 50 percent in recent years, the Conservatory concentrates on developing string players.

The Parks and Recreation Department finds that this is one of their most successful and respected activities. The Community Music Center, as the entire program is known, has two string orchestras, advanced and intermediate; these perform frequently at art festivals, museums, and other civic or cultural events. Monthly recitals are also held, at which children may perform their original works.

Summer Music Camp—San Mateo, California

In many American communities, the recreation department sponsors special summer music schools or workshops, usually in close collaboration with the schools. Often school facilities are used, and those in charge of instruction are the regular school music specialists, although other talented teachers may be used, since certification is not required in such settings. These summer schools have certain advantages as far as intensive enrichment of the child's musical education is concerned: (a) there is no competition from academic subjects; therefore children have more time for practicing and make greater progress; (b) because the music program usually takes the entire morning, five days a week, there is sufficient time to give each child solo instruction two or three days a week, if not daily; (c) with large groups of youngsters participating, it is possible to group them according to ability; and (d) because each child is present because of his ability and interest, on a voluntary basis, morale is high.

Usually, these summer music schools cover the entire range of strings,

[3] Marion Egbert, "The Case for Community Music Instruction," *American Recreation Journal,* March–April, 1965, p. 39.

brass, woodwind, and percussion accompaniment. When the community or school district is large enough, there may be several schools acting as music centers, spaced throughout the area. Some teachers may be assigned to a regular center, while others who are more specialized may travel on a regular schedule from center to center, giving instruction.

A unique form of summer music school is sponsored by the Recreation Department in San Mateo, California. For a number of years, it was felt that the community's cultural program needed variety and a new spark of interest. The idea of combining camping, recreation, and music was advanced. After careful preliminary planning, the recreation superintendent and the music coordinator of the high school district initiated a music camp program during the summer of 1960. Initially, it was offered to high school students, for a one-week session at minimal cost.

The camp was held at the mountain site owned by the San Francisco YMCA at La Honda in the Santa Cruz Mountains, just 35 miles from San Francisco; the use of the camp was offered for a very reasonable charge. Obtaining professional staff proved easy; support was so enthusiastic that eight high school music teachers offered to serve for a minimum fee or, if necessary, without fee in order to get the program started. The board of trustees of the high school district provided music, instruments, and other needed equipment without charge, and the use of school buses at cost.

The program got under way with an initial enrollment of 111 high school students, a professional music staff of eight, and three professional recreation leaders. The camp day was divided in two. Music education (including band, orchestra, chorus, harmony, conducting, dance band, and individual instrument study) filled the mornings. Recreation (including swimming, volleyball, softball, table tennis, arts and crafts, and social recreation) filled the afternoons. Evening programs included forms of recreation built about music—such as performances, singing, musical games and contests—and dancing.[4]

So successful was the first year's venture that in 1961, a second week was added to the music camp, to serve the seventh and eighth grades. In all, over 270 campers attended, with many of them sponsored by patrons' groups offering scholarships. Thus, whether in summer music schools or in special camps, as in San Mateo, the music instruction program can be a vital part of the recreation department's total cultural program.

Music Programs for Special Groups

Within the total range of organized recreation service, many groups and organizations provide musical activities for their members. Often, it is found that music is an extremely popular activity for older par-

[4] Matt C. Thiltgen, "Music Under the Redwoods," *Recreation,* June, 1962, p. 312.

ticipants—the so-called "Golden Age" group. In many senior centers or
community music centers, senior citizens are taking up instruments, forming orchestras, dance bands, and choral groups.

Two examples may be found in New York City. The Sirovich Day
Center is a social agency serving the needs of older, retired persons in the
metropolitan area. During the late 1950's, they discovered that there
were a number of retired musicians attending the center. Quickly, an
extremely capable orchestra was formed, with the age membership limited
to those over 60. Since then, this orchestra has rehearsed regularly and
has performed on radio and television, and in many civic events or programs. The "Singing Seniors," a New York City glee club composed of
older persons, was also organized during the 1950's. It is cosponsored by
the Federation of Protestant Welfare Agencies, in cooperation with the
Musician's Emergency Fund. The club meets weekly for rehearsals; there
is a regular attendance of about 80 percent, which is remarkable, considering the ages of many of the members and the distances they must
travel. This group, too, has given frequent concerts at various homes and
day centers, and on radio and television.

Many other examples of musical programs for the aged or for other
special groups in the community might be cited.

Opera as Recreation—Arlington, Virginia

Opera, as a form of musical art, has been spreading rapidly throughout the United States. Recent estimates indicate that it is today offered
in over 600 communities, chiefly on an amateur performance basis. The
term "opera" should not be understood to mean only "grand opera."
Instead, it may be defined as any musical drama that is performed almost
entirely in song, including the collaboration of singers, dancers, and
instrumentalists. Thus, all ballad operas, folk operas, musical comedies
or operettas, lyric dramas, and puppet operas are included. In many cases,
these are sponsored by public recreation departments.

For example, the Philadelphia Recreation Department assists two
opera companies and produces opera in its summer program. Houston
has for many years prepared and produced light and serious opera as part
of its music program. In Cleveland, opera workshop activities and performances are sponsored in several recreation centers.

Perhaps the best example is sponsored by the Arlington, Virginia,
Department of Recreation and Parks. Since 1961, that department has
assisted the Arlington Opera Theatre in presenting such classics as "The
Barber of Seville" and "Cosi Fan Tutte," performed by skilled local
musicians and vocalists. The Opera Theatre is formally governed by a
board of 17 to 20 directors, at least three-fifths of whom must be residents
of Arlington. This board completely manages the opera program, through
six standing committees: fund-raising, publicity, ticket, business, artistic

(which recommends works for performance), and a women's committee which assists in many important ways.

As in any large scale artistic production, there are financial problems which must be solved. The Arlington Opera Theatre offers three major performances each year. Through the Department of Recreation and Parks, the county pays approximately half of the production expense of these performances. The remainder must come through contributions and ticket sales. Fees are paid to the stage director, the costume designer, pattern maker, and set designer. Occasionally too, expenses are paid to principal singers in the cast or leading orchestra members. However, most performers or technicians work on a completely volunteer basis; their motivation is both artistic and recreational.

Ticket prices are scaled to fit community ability to pay, and it is worthy of note that with each successful year of performances, larger advanced ticket sales and larger audiences have been achieved. The directors of the Arlington Opera Theatre are confident that within a few years their program will be completely self-supporting.

Music as a Playground Activity

Of course, all recreational music is not as ambitious, financially or artistically, as the programs which have just been described. Music is in many ways a continuing activity of the regular recreation program—particularly for young children—on playgrounds and in community centers throughout the year. Usually, in this context, it does not involve formal music instruction, in the sense of learning to read music, to play an instrument, or to understand the structure of music. Instead, the emphasis is on the informal enjoyment of music through singing, rhythmic movement, or the playing of rhythm instruments. Rosenberg summarizes the essential purpose of recreational music for younger children:

> While note reading, theory and harmony are an essential aspect of a child's music training *later on,* we believe it is far more important to instill . . . that vital spark—a genuine love of melody, rhythm, the moods of music, dance, lyrics, etc.—before we ask them to apply themselves to the *hard work* of learning the skills of music. . . .[5]

Singing on the Playground. When songs are introduced in the recreational setting for children, the emphasis is on a creative and enjoyable, rather than a formal or drill-like approach. It is important to select songs that will be attractive to children, placed in a comfortable key, with easy-to-remember melodies and choruses. Folk songs are among the most suitable kinds of materials, particularly songs of other lands which give children a sense of experiencing foreign cultures and even singing in

[5] Martha Rosenberg, *It's Fun to Teach Creative Music* (New York: Play Schools Association, 1963), p. 6.

foreign languages. Rather than a line-by-line learning of words and melody, as songs have traditionally been taught, it is wise to teach the song by singing it through several times. Gradually it will become familiar, and, when repeated, it will be performed with increasing confidence and success. The leader may help children explore certain phases and explain the meaning and highlights of the song, so that it becomes a living experience.

Children themselves may be encouraged to suggest or ask for songs they know or have heard. Sometimes it is a good idea to have a song-listening session, by playing records of folk songs. All children should be encouraged to take part; even if a child cannot sing on pitch to begin with, he should not be left out. By the same token, no child should be forced to sing. Instead, although he may lack confidence to begin with, being part of the group and with the gentle encouragement of the leader, it is likely that he will join in before too long.

With young children, arrangements of songs should be extremely simple, without part singing or the attempt to introduce harmony in singing. By the age of 7 or 8, however, they should be ready to explore the following ways of singing:

Rounds. Here, children are divided into groups, usually three or four, according to the construction of the song. One group begins to sing. When it has reached the end of the first phrase or line, the second group starts the song from the beginning. Then the next group comes in in turn. Usually, the entire song is sung through three times, with each group stopping in turn the final time through.

Harmony. This is a form of part singing, in which one set of voices sings the set melody, while another group of children sing a melody that blends harmonically with the first group. To do an expert job of song leadership making use of formal arrangements with harmony, the music leader should be able to read music and teach the different parts clearly. Sometimes, however, particularly if he has sung a good deal himself and has a good "musical ear," the leader can teach harmonies without a formal music background.

Part Songs. Other songs may be sung contrapuntally, in that different sets of words or melodies are sung against each other simultaneously by groups of children. Or there may be arrangements in which children sing only portions of the song, as in a "question and answer" type of folk song, in which one group may sing a verse answering a question, and another group may respond in alternate verses.

In singing, it is important to cultivate sensitivity to the sound of the words and music. Children should have a sense of being part of something lovely and creative, and should listen to the others as they sing, rather than just shouting or drowning each other out. For this reason, it is important to select songs with a wide variety of moods. In addition to songs which are spirited, gay, and loud, or forceful and strongly rhythmic, some songs should be sad, slow, and moving. Often, it helps to use the "crescendo-diminuendo" approach, in which children begin by singing very softly, build up gradually to a strong volume, and gradually back to a low volume again, almost whispering by the end of the song.

The leader will also wish to select songs from a wide variety of sources, and to include patriotic songs, camp songs, fun or novelty songs, "add-on" songs in which phrases or words are repeated each time through, and action songs in which physical gestures accompany the singing. But always, the emphasis must be on enjoyable participation, and on inculcating a love for music.

Creative Movement as Part of the Music Program

Particularly for younger children, it is wise to capitalize on the innate rhythm that most youngsters share and on their ability to express melody and rhythm through creative movement. This may take the form of *free expression,* in the sense of rolling, galloping, jumping, leaping, turning, or other forms of twisting, swinging, bending, swaying, or shaking. It may also involve *pantomimic action,* in that children consciously respond to music by imitating (often in an abstract or nonliteral way) the movement of trains, planes, animals, birds, or similar stimuli. Sometimes the emphasis may be on *mood response,* in which the music that is played suggests a sad feeling, or a gay, joyous sound, or a martial and stirring spirit.

To encourage this sort of participation, the playground leader may play a piano or other melody instrument—either setting the pattern himself, or picking up the tempo and spirit of the children as *they* dance. The singing of children themselves, or the playing of a record may provide background for creative rhythmic movement. Or, the leader or children may experiment with rhythm instruments to provide the basis for movement:

. . . light taps on a drum or woodblock can suggest rain pattering on a roof or windowpane, Santa's reindeer, leaves falling and so many other things. Heavy, slow beats might suggest giants, rumbling trucks on a city street, lions or ocean waves. . . .[6]

Always, as Rosenberg points out, it is important that children try to *invent,* and not to *imitate,* movement.

Gradually, the creative movement aspect of the music program may draw on other "props" and devices. Children may experiment with bouncing balls in different rhythm combinations or groupings, to musical accompaniment. They may use colored scarves of nylon or silk (these may be made with dyed sections from army surplus parachutes) which children

[6] *Ibid.,* p. 10.

twirl, swing, and toss lightly through the air as they dance. They may use plastic hoops to invent forms of movement, walking with hoops held high over their heads to suggest "giants," twirling or swinging them back and forth, using them as tunnels to crawl through, or setting them on the floor and using them as "rocks in the water," to skip or hop around from one to the next. The possibilities for creative rhythmic movement are endless, and children themselves, if encouraged, will constantly suggest new ideas to the alert leader.

Rhythm Instruments as Playground Activity

The well-equipped playground or community center should have a good supply of rhythm instruments: drums and tom-toms large and small, shaking instruments like rattles and maraccas, tambourines, woodblocks, finger-bells, triangles, clappers, scrapers, and others. Often, as an arts and crafts activity that is linked with music, children may be helped to make their own instruments, using juice cans, nail kegs, gourds, and cereal containers with pebbles or beans in them. Usually the most successful "home-made" projects are percussive or rattling instruments; the kind that require playing of notes on a scale or the tuning of strings are not generally feasible.

How are rhythm instruments used in informal musical activity?

Children may improvise with them, after experimenting to find out the different kinds of sounds they make. They may be used to accompany recorded music, or the playing of a live melody instrument, or group singing. Different arrangements may be developed, so that certain instruments are played during the verse of a song, and others during the chorus. Some children may play rhythm instruments, while others dance. Rhythm instruments may be used during storytelling, to create effects or accompany descriptive action.

Song Leadership in Social Recreation

Another important aspect of music as recreation is informal song leadership in social recreation programs. Community singing is one of the most popular activities of teen-agers, young and middle-aged adults, family groups, and older citizens. It is often the ideal choice to get everyone swinging along in rhythm on a hiking trail, or to liven up a boring bus trip. It is a spirited "waker-upper" as a break in a club meeting or business meeting of a PTA or civic association. In social clubs, on picnics and outings, at church parties and barbecues, singing appeals to all!

What kinds of songs are best for community singing? They are the ones that people know best—the old familiar songs: patriotic and religious and old love songs, popular songs of other lands, folk songs and ballads of our nation's past, popular show-tunes that have lasted, favorites of camping or Scouting days. In any group, there will be a core of songs that come spontaneously to mind, as well as many others that members of the group will suggest at a moment's notice.

How much leadership is actually required for singing in social recreation? This depends on the circumstances. If the group is a small, friendly one, with the members knowing each other well, it is likely that not too much actual leadership will be required. If one or two individuals happen to have guitars for informal accompaniment, the singing will flourish spontaneously—almost with a life of its own. On the other hand, if the group is large, if the intention is for them to learn a number of new songs, or if they are new to each other and have not sung together before, a song leader is necessary.

Some guides for group singing might include:

1. Get the singing under way quickly, by introducing a very familiar song or two. This creates confidence and a spirit of participation. Gradually, other new or unfamiliar songs may be taught, although at the beginning and end of the session, the songs chosen should all be well known.

2. There should be variety in the songs that are chosen—including some fun songs, action songs, or other novelty numbers—but with the main emphasis on doing songs that are just plain good singing. This should also include variety in the mood, tempo, and musical quality of songs.

3. The leader may, if he is capable of doing this, rely on the traditional hand gestures to indicate the meter (see Fig. 16). If not, he may simply move his hand in a small arc to indicate the rhythm as he feels it. In any case, he should feel relaxed and natural. With a large group, his gestures should be rather large and dramatic, to be visible and unmistakable. In a small group, no gestures at all may be necessary, except to indicate the beginning tempo, or when a note is held or cut off.

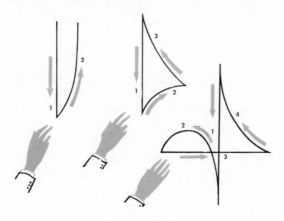

Figure 16

4. Song leadership should be enthusiastic, although not artificially so. It is important to begin a song in the correct pitch and to keep the tempo at a comfortable level. An accompanist is helpful in both respects; with a large group, this should be someone playing an instrument like a piano or accordion. In a smaller group, a guitarist or banjoist is excellent.

While it is helpful to have a good voice and a knowledge of music structure, it is just as important to have a warm personality and sound judgment about the songs to be presented. The author has observed some song leaders who knew very little music technically, and, in fact had rather poor voices, but who nonetheless had the gift of getting groups to sing with deep feeling and great pleasure. They hardly used their own voices, but they drew out the best that was around them.

The following examples illustrate the type of songs that may be used to enliven social gatherings. They represent only a tiny portion of the diversified materials available to the recreational song leader; several excellent collections of melodies for community singing are listed at the end of this text.

Tell Me Why

This traditional song is popular with all ages. It should be sung slowly and with feeling.

Source Unknown

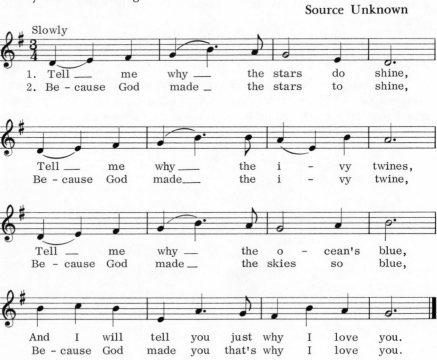

The More We Get Together

A lively song of good fellowship, fitted to an old German folk tune.

English verse:

English Anonymous   German Folk Tune

The more we get to-geth-er, to-geth-er, to-geth-er,

The more we get to-geth-er, the hap-pier we'll be.

For your friends are my friends and my friends are your friends,

The more we get to-geth-er, the hap-pier we'll be.

German verse:

    Ach, du lieber Augustin, Augustin, Augustin,
    Ach, du lieber Augustin,   Alles ist hin.
    Stock ist weg, Hut ist weg,   August selbst liegt im Dreck,
    Ach, du lieber Augustin, Alles ist hin.

Actions to be performed while singing: During first two lines of song, do rhythmic action in 3/4 time. *Clap* own hands once, then *pat* knees twice. Beginning on the first "more," do this action seven times, ending with a *clap* on the "be" at the end of the second line. Then extend arms along neighbors' arms and sway in rhythm to the *left* and *right* two full times during the next line. On the last line, do *clap-pat-pat* action again, starting with the word "more," three times and end with a *clap* on the word "be."

Pick a Bale o' Cotton

Here's a spirited and rhythmic Negro work song, to be sung at a fast tempo.

Very fast

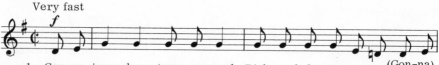

1. Gon-na jump down turn a-round, Pick a bale o' cot-ton (Gon-na)

jump down turn a-round, Pick a bale a day.   Oh, Law-dy,

Pick a bale o' cot-ton, Oh, Law-dy, Pick a bale a day.

2. Me and my wife can pick a bale o' cotton.
   Me and my wife can pick a bale a day, etc.
3. Me and my brother can pick a bale o' cotton, etc.
4. Picka, picka, picka, pick-a pick a bale o' cotton, etc.

Keep Moving

This lively action song adds a word or phrase each time it is repeated.

1. One   fin - ger, one thumb, one hand   keep

mov - ing,____   One   fin - ger, one thumb, one hand   keep

mov - ing,____   One   fin - ger, one thumb, one hand   keep

mov - ing, And we'll all be hap - py and gay.____

2. One finger, one thumb, one hand, two hands keep moving, etc.
3. One finger, one thumb, one hand, two hands, one arm keep moving, etc.
4. *Add:* two arms
5. *Add:* one leg
6. *Add:* two legs
7. *Add:* stand up, sit down

As the words are sung, singers move the part(s) of the body mentioned in rapid succession. Each time a new word or phrase is added in the bracketed measures of music.

Sweetly Sings the Donkey

This rousing three-part round may also be used as an action song, to enliven a drowsy group.

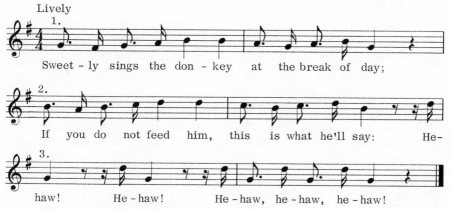

After the words have been learned, practice this action: place thumbs at the ears and flap hands forward in rhythm like a donkey's ears. Then do the song as a round, with each section in turn standing up and doing the hand-flapping routine on the last line: "Hee-haw! Hee-haw! Hee-haw, hee-haw, hee-haw!"

White Coral Bells

A traditional old song with a lovely melody, is this two-part round.

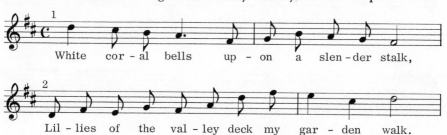

O, don't you wish that you could hear them ring?

That will hap-pen on-ly when the fair-ies sing.

The Orchestra Song

The part song will take some time to learn, but has a striking effect when finally mastered.

Violins

The vi-o-lins ring-ing like love — ly— sing-ing,

The vi-o-lins ring-ing like love — ly— song.

Clarinets

The clar-i-net, the clar-i-net makes

doo-dle, doo-dle, doo-dle, doo-dle det, The clar-i-net, the

clar-i-net makes doo-dle, doo-dle, doo-dle det.

Trumpets

The trum-pet is bray-ing ta-ta-ta-ta,

ta - ta - ta -ta - ta - ta - ta,   ta - ta - ta -ta - ta - ta - ta,

The   trum - pet   is   bray - ing,   ta - ta - ta - ta,

ta - ta - ta - ta - ta - ta - ta - ta.

Horns

The   horn,   the   horn,   a - wakes me   at   morn,

The   horn,   the   horn,   a - wakes me   at   morn.

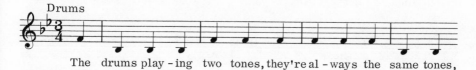

Drums

The drums play - ing   two   tones, they're al - ways the same tones,

The   drums play - ing   two   tones, they're al - ways the same.

Violins

The vi-o-lins ring-ing like love — ly sing-ing,
The vi-o-lins ring-ing like love — ly song.

Clarinets

The clar-i-net, the clar-i-net makes doo-dle, doo-dle, doo-dle, doo-dle det,
The clar-i-net, the clar-i-net makes do — dle, doo-dle, doo-dle det.

Trumpets

The trum-pet is bray-ing, ta-ta-ta-ta,   ta-ta-ta-ta-ta-ta-ta, ta-ta-ta-ta-ta-ta-ta,
The trum-pet is bray-ing, ta-ta-ta-ta,   ta-ta-ta-ta-ta-ta-ta.

Horns

The horn,   the horn,   a-wakes me at morn,
The horn,   the horn,   a-wakes me at morn.

Drums

> The drums play-ing two tones, they're al-ways the same tones,
> The drums play-ing two tones, they're al-ways the same.

The group divides into five sections. Each section learns a verse. The song may then be done with all five melodies being sung simultaneously, or with the "violins" beginning and each of the other instruments coming in in turn. Singers may also imitate with gestures the instruments they are portraying.

The Tree in the Wood

Another favorite "add-on" song—a real test of memory!

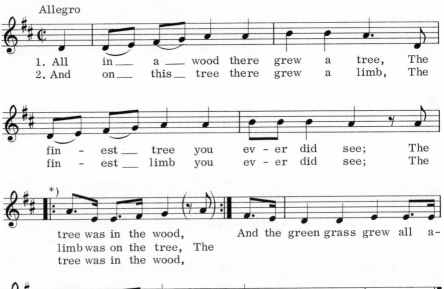

Allegro

1. All in ___ a ___ wood there grew a tree, The
2. And on ___ this ___ tree there grew a limb, The

fin - est ___ tree you ev - er did see; The
fin - est ___ limb you ev - er did see; The

tree was in the wood,   And the green grass grew all a-
limb was on the tree, The
tree was in the wood,

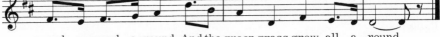

round, a-round, a-round, And the green grass grew all a-round._

3. And on this limb, there was a branch,
   The finest branch you ever did see,
   The branch was on the limb,
   The limb was on the tree,
   The tree was in the wood, etc.
4. And on this branch, there was a nest, etc.
5. And in this nest, there was an egg, etc.
6. And in this egg, there was a bird, etc.
7. And on this bird, there was a wing, etc.
8. And on this wing, there was a feather, etc.

NOTE: Repeat bracketed measure as often as needed, as verses are added.

DRAMA IN COMMUNITY RECREATION

The National Recreation Association, in its publication, "Drama is Recreation," reveals that there are today approximately 3,000 amateur theater groups in existence. Many of these are associated with public recreation departments; indeed, most organized recreation agencies in the country include some form of dramatic activity in their programs. In all, it has been estimated that some 120,000 nonprofessional stage productions are presented annually. Specifically, community recreation dramatic activities include the following:

Arena Productions	Camp Dramatics Activities
Children's Theater Productions	Choral Speaking
Charades and Dramatic Games	Drama Leadership Training Workshops
Community Theaters	
Dramatic Readings	Theater Workshops
Mobile Theaters and Show Wagons	Play Festivals
	Pantomime
Pageants	Puppets and Marionettes
Radio and Television Broadcasts	Shadow Plays
Skits	Sociodramas
Story Plays for Children	Storytelling
Talent or Variety Shows	

Basically, however, there are three major types of dramatic involvement:

1. The sponsorship of *adult community theater programs* which put on performances, often with indoor or outdoor theaters, or drama centers. Often these have a somewhat independent status in the community, with the recreation department offering certain specific kinds of assistance.
2. The sponsorship of *children's theater programs,* which place emphasis on instruction in dramatic techniques as well as the development of stage performances. This may also involve the sponsorship of adult groups which put on performances for audiences of children throughout a community, as part of a children's theater program.
3. The use of dramatic activities as a *tool in regular recreation programs.* This is usually in the form of creative drama, chiefly for children. It includes improvisation, pantomime, storytelling, charades, dramatic games, and acting combined with other art forms. Informal dramatics of this type may also be found in social recreation programs as well.

The Values of Drama in Recreation

1. Perhaps the most significant value of drama in community recreation is that it is an important part of cultural life. As no other artistic medium does, it expresses man's hopes and dreams, his view of life, his

tragic or humorous episodes or experiences. Thus, it reflects, interprets, and enriches life.

2. Like music, dramatic activity can be enjoyed by people of all age levels and a variety of backgrounds. Acting seems to appeal to a basic urge in many people to project their own personality or to assume the role of another, to both escape and come to grips with themselves. Because drama runs a wide gamut of forms and moods and degrees of complexity, it has this varied appeal.

3. In addition to acting, recreational drama offers many other forms of potential involvement: dancing, singing, stage lighting, carpentry, ushering, costume design and making, staging, make-up, publicity, music and ticket sales. Like the other performing arts, it places a heavy premium on cooperation, and, providing a goal of production and performance, usually manages to sustain a high level of interest over a period of time.

To illustrate some of the forms which community drama assumes, several examples are presented here.

Children's Theater—Washington, D.C.

The Children's Theater of Washington, D.C., operates as a non-profit, self-sustaining organization under the sponsorship of the District of Columbia Recreation Department. The directors of its executive board are skilled volunteers interested in the promotion of the Children's Theater as a community project. They include representatives from the District Congress of Parents and Teachers, the Junior League of Washington, and the Recreation Department. Advice of an artistic and technical nature is given by a Professional Advisory Board of the Capitol area's outstanding theater professionals and university professors. An Associate Council, made up of volunteers with a special interest in children's theater, also assists with projects.

The Children's Theater of Washington has received a number of awards and special grants to support its activities, which include the following:

Producing. It promotes the theater arts by producing plays with and for Washington children and by presenting important dramatic productions from other cities.

Touring. It brings these productions to widely separated areas of the city and to audiences of hospitalized children.

Training. It trains recreation leaders and public school teachers in creative dramatics workshops.

Sponsoring. It sponsors summertime story-telling programs for children of all ages on neighborhood playgrounds; an annual One-Act Play Festival, in which neighborhood center leaders direct plays put on by children in neighborhood playgrounds; a Children's Theatre Club, made up of performers in local productions, which serves to promote an over-all interest and involvement in the theater.

Children's Theater—Downey, California

Over 2,000 children a year have taken part in a children's theater program in Downey, California, a city of only 85,000 population. Having begun in 1955, within three years it performed for paying audiences totalling about 10,000. In the 1959–60 season, it produced 44 full-length performances of such plays as "Beauty and the Beast," "Heidi," and "Aladdin."

How does such a program get under way?

It was begun by three individuals—the superintendent of the Downey Recreation and Park District, a senior recreation director, and a trained specialist in theater production. When announcements were made in local newspapers and elementary schools of tryouts for children's parts in the first production, "Hansel and Gretel," 250 youngsters volunteered. A double-casting policy for all children's roles was begun, to give twice as many children a chance to participate, and to protect the production if one child could not take part. In addition, many adults quickly volunteered to help as instructors in workshop classes, scenery designers and builders, program printers and publicity workers. A nonprofit civic organization was founded, to support the program, with a budget of approximately $10,000 annually.

As it developed, the program had two major goals: (a) to offer recreation and dramatic instruction to as many children as wished it; and (b) to produce interesting, well-acted plays for the community at large.

Thus, the Children's Theater has included, in addition to its major schedule of productions, a workshop program of weekly sessions in creative dramatic activities. By 1960, there were as many as 18 workshops meeting concurrently during the school year. These are geared chiefly for 9- to 12-year-olds, with 16 the maximum age of participants. In the performances themselves, it is the practice for child actors to have no more than one major role per season but to take minor roles in other productions. The drama program has had interesting and constructive outcomes as far as adult participation is concerned:

> The volunteer work done by adults, so necessary in holding down expenses, has required a staggering amount of cooperation and organization. You cannot tell someone who has had no experience to make billboards and distribute them, do advertising and publicity, print tickets, make costumes, construct sets—and let it go at that. Because of the high degree of integrated effort necessary, people of different races, religions, and backgrounds must cooperate actively with each other. Director Hume has said, "There's something about a program of this sort, requiring unselfish effort on the part of

everyone, that causes people to submerge differences that might otherwise make amicable relationships difficult.[7]

OTHER COMMUNITY THEATER PROGRAMS

In Oak Park, Illinois, a successful teen-age drama program, the Stevenson Players, has been operating since 1940. The club meets weekly, to study dramatic acting, makeup, speech, and other phases of theater —including costume and scenic design, lighting, and properties. The adolescent members of the Stevenson Players work with a trained theater director, to learn stage technique, and to study voice, diction, projection and body movement as part of a program of one-act play production. The group's membership usually numbers between 50 and 60, with a constant turnover each year as older members leave for college, while new ones come in.

The Players' repertoire has included such traditional favorites as "The Little Princess" and "The Christmas Carol," as well as many light comedies and stage mysteries. In 1953, the club initiated a Children's Theater venture, putting on a number of plays like "Winnie the Pooh," and "Jack and the Beanstalk," for juvenile audiences. In all, the young performers have made many appearances at service clubs, churches, servicemen's centers, playgrounds, and VA hospitals. The adult sponsors and advisors are convinced that dramatic activity of this kind pays rich rewards not only in terms of encouraging talent, or improving speech, but also in terms of building well-rounded personalities, good character, and effective citizenship.

Similarly, one of the most active portions of the drama program operated by the Bureau of Recreation, of the Division of Parks and Recreation, in Dayton, Ohio, is a group of four different teen-age drama companies called the Day-Teen Players. Each group, meeting in its home recreation center weekly, is part of a total community theater program which includes an adult production company, a junior dramatic theater, summer variety shows, T.V. programs of children's plays during the summer, storytelling, festivals, and creative dramatics for children.

Numerous other community-wide recreation programs might be cited, such as the highly successful Palo Alto Community Players, sponsored by the city's recreation department. The unique feature of this program, which has been in operation since 1931, is that it is fortunate enough to have an excellent theater building, donated by a public-spirited resident, and that it makes use of an efficiently structured committee system and advisory board to plan and carry out its production schedule each season.

[7] Edward R. Lucas, "The Youngsters Take the Stage," *Recreation*, November, 1960, p. 421.

One of the most unique examples of drama in a recreation program can be found in the theater activities that have been carried on at the Menorah Home and Hospital for the Aged and Infirm, a Jewish non-profit agency in Brooklyn, New York. This center has many extremely aged men and women residents; in addition, it offers a nonsectarian day center for older people in the community. One of its most popular activities has been a drama group, which has concentrated on performing Biblical stories of the Old Testament. These stories, already familiar to most of the participants, are approached using a "no-script" method. Members of the drama club (most of whom are over 70, including some who play in wheelchairs) begin by discussing a specific story which they intend to act out. They "break it down," discussing characters and their motivations. Gradually, they block out scenes and cast the parts. In rehearsals, they simply improvise and update their dialogue as they go along. The "no-script" method is particularly suited for the aged because of their memory lapses; it frees them from the strain of having to remember lines and permits them to act fully and freely.

In addition to the actors, other participants (about one-fourth of all the residents of the home) make props, sets, costumes, and assist in other ways, under the supervision of occupational therapists and other staff members. The value of the program for these aged people has been summarized:

> The Menorah Players program proves that neither age nor physical disability is a deterrent to living a full life, replete with well-planned recreation. Drama is a particularly good activity for many reasons. Planning and staging a play requires many hands and many talents, consumes much time and thought. There are tickets and programs to be printed; costumes, props, and sets to be designed and made; and, then, any number of rehearsals. Once the play is over, its production provides a topic of conversation for everyone, for weeks afterwards, until the next play is under way. And, during the years left to these people, they will have the warm memories of the day they participated in a play, either behind the footlights or as a spectator.[8]

APPROACHES TO COMMUNITY DRAMA

The municipal recreation department which wishes to initiate a sound program of community drama should realize that this needs to be supported by certain basic steps. Briefly stated, the following are required:

1. The community must become interested; meetings and surveys should be held, and those who have special skills, knowledge, or support of any type to offer, should be enlisted in an advisory committee or theater council.

[8] Jean Wachtel, "Drama Is Ageless," *Recreation*, May, 1960, p. 220.

2. The director of the recreation department must have a real conviction about the value of cultural programing in community life and a special awareness of the potential of dramatic activities. If he has these, and if his community is large enough, he should take steps to form a special program division for the arts, or cultural activities, of which drama would be a subdivision.

3. Specifically in charge of the program should be a trained drama specialist. He offers general leadership to all dramatic activities in the community and formulates a plan for developing program experiences in this area.

4. Under the drama specialist's direction, many community groups and individuals may be brought together to contribute their services and coordinate their activities.

5. Within the program itself, three elements should be stressed: *variety, progression,* and *standards. Variety* implies that a wide diversity of interests and levels of performing ability should be served, as well as the general cultural purpose of presenting effective community theater events. *Progression* implies that it should be possible for children or adults to move through the program and become increasingly challenged by more complex or demanding dramatic activities, so that their interest does not wane and they continue to grow. *Standards* suggests that, no matter what the activity, whether it be informal dramatics, a puppet show, or an adult theater program, it should be of the highest quality possible.

6. Finally, in a really comprehensive program of community theater, the following goals should be striven for: (a) a center for the performing arts, with a good auditorium, stage, lighting and sound equipment, and storage rooms; (b) a drama library and collection of costumes which may be used for all sorts of productions; and (d) the use of mobile units or "show wagons," which will serve to reach audiences young and old throughout a metropolitan area, with theatrical experiences.

It is important to remember that many communities will not be large enough, or will not have sufficient resources, to go into a full-scale program of dramatic activities. However, simply because this is so, a municipal recreation director should not hesitate to initiate certain dramatic programs. These may include creative activities on playgrounds, informal dramatic games or stunts in teen-age groups or senior citizens clubs, or the assistance of theater clubs or amateur dramatic groups in the community at large. Even in a limited way, such programs can contribute much to the cultural and recreation life of each city or town.

GUIDES FOR LEADING CHILDREN'S THEATER

Children's Theater, as described earlier, consists of programs carried on for children and youth in the community that involve classes or workshops in acting and associated stage skills, and that may or may not lead to performance. Usually, motivation and interest are greater when production becomes a definite goal. Two general approaches may be described: (a) a *formal,* or traditional, approach to children's theater, and (b) an *informal,* or less-structured, approach.

Formal Approach

In the formal approach, the teacher or play director assumes a fairly authoritarian role. He is the key to the enterprise, and the creative contributions of the children themselves are minimized. Usually, this means that he selects the play himself, that he schedules tryouts and selects children for specific roles, or assigns them to other duties, and that he operates much as a professional director in adult theater programs would. While he is sensitive to the children's feelings, and does not unrealistically expect them to perform beyond their potential, he does not really work with them creatively, in terms of evoking individual expression. Usually, in this type of theater program, a formal script is used and memorized. Stage directions are worked out carefully and the director himself is the source of most suggestions for staging or changes made to improve visibility or audibility.

Informal Approach

Much more widely used today is the informal, or creative approach, as developed years ago by Winifred Ward, an outstanding pioneer in the field of children's dramatics. Briefly stated, this consists of taking a story from the wealth of classic or modern children's literature and having the children themselves evolve their own creative stage presentation, based on the tale. An illustration of how this process is carried on may be found in the following guide, developed by the children's theater specialist in the Culver City, California, Recreation Department: [9]

Initiating the Program

1. Gather the children into a group. Be prepared with a story at the first meeting.
2. Some of the children might not be too familiar with the program, so take time to discuss for a few minutes what they will be doing during the classes, e.g., "Stories are so much fun to hear, and they're even better when we can be the people in the story."
3. Discover the children's interests. Ask them what kind of stories

[9] *Children's Playground Theatre* (Culver City, Calif.: Recreation Department Staff Manual, n.d.).

they like. (Make a list of the stories written down on the children's registration blanks.)

4. Tell the children that you've brought them a surprise story, and would they like to hear it now?

5. Read the story (choosing one that has action or is easily dramatized).

6. There should be a spontaneous response from the children when the story is ended. From this, lead them into a discussion of it. What did the characters look like? Who was the hero? What were his qualities? Where does the story take place? Questions like this should help the children get a more complete picture of the story, familiarizing them with the characters and setting, making dramatization possible.

7. If this initial story is liked by the children, it could be used for the summer play. If not, find the stories they like and read another at the next meeting. Let the children feel they've chosen their own play, but guide them so that they don't take on more than they can accomplish.

8. Most stories for this age level involve a central character. In the discussion of the story let the children make up characters, e.g., the townspeople, the hero's family, etc. In this way, more children will be able to participate and the play will become their own.

Conducting the Rehearsals

1. Schedule the rehearsals for a regular time and place, letting the children realize that this is not free play time, but that they are accomplishing an important project.

2. After deciding on a story discuss with the children the characters, setting, action, properties, and special effects they are going to need.

3. Cast the play as the need arises for the characters in a scene. Don't try to cast everything at once. Encourage those children not chosen or those who seem interested, but shy, to remain with the group. A good play will need a good crew: (a) craftsmen; (b) publicity men for posters and tickets; (c) costumers; and (d) various jobs that come up during rehearsal.

4. Strive for a professional attitude with the group. They will feel more grown-up and more will be accomplished by learning to: (a) be courteous to the other actors; (b) remain off-stage when not performing; (c) let everyone contribute ideas; (d) follow stage directions. These standards, in order to be maintained, should be developed by the children.

5. In directing the children, use the terms designating stage areas correctly, and have the children do likewise (see Fig. 17). This will help to avoid confusion.

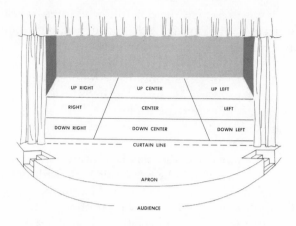

Figure 17

6. In the beginning phases, do not stress perfection of dialogue; let the children create the scenes as they feel them. Through repetition of rehearsals the lines will pretty much cement themselves in play form.

7. As the scenes and dialogue develop, a new character may be created or an episode added. Keep the rehearsals flexible, using this creativity of the children. The play will be dead without it.

8. Integrate the rehearsals with the construction of backdrops and properties. The children remain enthusiastic when they see progress. Following rehearsal, a craft period of construction may be held, or while the actors are rehearsing in one area the stage crew might be painting, etc., in another. This would be the leader's decision.

9. Have the children gather properties and accessories immediately after beginning play rehearsals. Have them be thinking about their costumes and know what they will wear and where they will get it. Small "props," e.g., canes, hats, etc., may be worn to help the actors get into character during rehearsals.

10. As the play develops and the children have organized the action into scenes, with a climax and an ending, work may be done on polishing the performance. See that the children pick up their cues, project their voices, and in general keep the dialogue flowing.

11. Stage scenery should be completed at about the same time as the play. A full dress rehearsal may then be scheduled, using sets, props, and costumes. Make-up should be saved for the day of the performance.

12. Publicity people should have posters made to advertise the play, and tickets or programs to hand out to the audience. Develop a good response from the park and neighborhood, so that the children will have a representative audience. This is part of their achievement, having people present to applaud their efforts.

13. The play is presented the day following dress rehearsal. Following the play, have a big curtain call, and depending upon the group, arrangements might be made for refreshments for the cast and crew or audience.

14. Have a Master of Ceremonies to introduce the play and the cast members and crew afterward. Be sure that he practices his part carefully, in order to avoid last minute stage fright.

15. Arrange to have a clean-up crew to strike sets and put everything in order following the production.

Above all, remember that the play is a means to an end, not an end in itself. The experience should be a fun-filled one with opportunities for all those who are interested to participate. The finished product will not be perfect by professional standards, but if the children have enjoyed themselves and developed an appreciation of the theater, then the program will have been more than successful.

GUIDES FOR INFORMAL DRAMATIC ACTIVITIES

Many kinds of dramatic activities may be enjoyed on the playground or in community centers, even if there is no intention of putting on a formal play. These may include the following: (a) pantomime and improvisation; (b) dramatic games, charades, stunts, and skits; (c) puppet shows or shadow plays; and (d) performances which are put on for children, often with the use of mobile theaters or show wagons.

Pantomime and Improvisation

These are particularly useful in leading up to more advanced dramatic activities and provide great enjoyment in themselves. They help children become aware of their own expressive potential and make them more sensitive to sensory perception. Several categories of pantomimes follow:

1. "Acting out" activities, which other children may guess at. Such humorous ideas may be presented as:

   a lady trying on a new hat
   a man stifling a sneeze in a movie theater
   a boy taking castor oil
   stepping into an ice-cold bath or pool
   having your arms full of packages while a dog is snapping at your ankles
   coming up to bat in the big game with two out in the ninth

2. Pantomimes involving the senses:

   touch: picking up a soft kitten; sewing and sticking yourself with a needle; pulling taffy and getting your fingers stuck *smell:* smelling a delicious hot pie on a window sill and finding your way to it; trying to decide which perfume to buy as a gift; smelling a skunk

hearing: listening to an alarm clock waking you up early in the morning; hearing a call for help while exploring in the woods; hearing an auto crash

taste: taking castor oil; finishing the chocolate icing in a bowl

3. Expressing emotion, based on different settings or happenings:

fear: going past a graveyard late at night

anger: someone has taken your model airplane and carelessly broken it

pity: a baby robin falls from a nest and dies

surprise: you spy a house on fire, and rush to bring help

Pantomime may be taught almost as an art form, with a high degree of discipline and specialized training to increase suppleness, body control, and flexibility. Each portion of the body may be disciplined, with the use of hands, elbows, shoulders, feet, knees, head, and facial expressions analyzed for the fullest and most precise expressiveness. However, particularly in working with children, it is most important to stress the idea of "moving as people feel *inside.*" Effective pantomime is more than simply copying movement accurately. It must involve gathering the *essence* of a movement and showing it with a real sense of what the person performing it is like.

Dramatic Games, Charades, Stunts, and Skits

Many games are based on pantomimic action; a number of these may be found in game collections. The most useful ones are basically *charades,* which involve acting out a famous name, play, movie or book title, saying or proverb—so that others may guess it. Charades are usually done without speaking, although in some cases sounds may be permitted. Several types of charades follow:

1. *Individual charades.* One person acts out a name, title, or saying, while others try to guess what he has in mind. He usually begins by showing the category of the charade (if it is a title of a book, he pretends to read a book; if it is a television show, he describes with his hands the shape of the television screen; if it is a saying, he holds up two fingers of both hands, indicating "quotes," etc.). He then proceeds to act out word by word, or syllable by syllable, what he is doing. Thus, he holds up one finger and the others say, "First word." He holds up two fingers, and they say, "Second syllable." As he continues to act, the others guess the words or syllables, and he nods affirmatively when they are correct. When one player guesses it correctly, that player will be the next to act out a charade.

2. *Individual "pass" charades.* This is a variation of the first form.

One player thinks of a title or phrase. He passes it to another, by whispering it, or passing it on a slip of paper. That person must then act it out, for the others to guess.

3. *Team charades.* Each group of about six or eight players selects a title or phrase. They prepare a group charade, either giving the whole title at once, or showing it word by word in several short scenes. Then they act it out, for the others to guess. Each team in turn acts its charade out for the other.

4. *Team "pass" charades.* A variation of the preceding is for each team to select a title or phrase, write it on a slip, and pass it to the team on its right, to act out. Or the leader may prepare a number of titles on slips, and each team acts out the title it is given.

5. *Relay charades.* The overall group divides into several teams, which must be spaced at a distance from each other. The leader has a list of several titles. Each team sends a player up; he is given the first title and must run back to his team and act it out as rapidly as possible. When his team guesses it satisfactorily, a second player runs up; he is given the second title, which he must act out quickly. This is continued, until the first team to complete the entire list is the winner.

Groups that play a great deal of charades learn to use specific gestures to speed up the guessing process. For instance, holding up the thumb and forefinger close together indicates "small word." The other players quickly call out "the," "it," "and," or similar words, until the "actor" indicates by nodding which is correct. If the other players are calling out a word which sounds like the one being acted, the "actor" indicates this by pointing at his ear—to guide them in their guessing. He may indicate that the word being sought is a longer form of a word they are guessing (by "stretching" his hands apart) or that it is a shorter form (by making a "chopping" gesture). Thus, charades may become a fairly skilled activity, or they may be approached on a very simple basis and still provide much enjoyment.

Skits and *stunts* are extremely popular, particularly with older groups of participants (teen-agers or adults).

Basically, they take two forms: (a) those which are made up in advance and acted out, either through memorization or being read from scripts; and (b) those which are created by the group, possibly based on a common idea or suggestion given by the leader.

Examples of the former type include group gags, monologues, short poems, "blackouts," and other humorous skits, which may frequently be found in collections. "The Handbook of Skits and Stunts," and other books by Helen and Larry Eisenberg are excellent sources for this type of material.[10] Although many other collections may be found, it is im-

---

[10] Helen Eisenberg and Larry Eisenberg, *The Handbook of Skits and Stunts* (New York: Association Press, 1953).

portant to scrutinize them carefully before using skits or stunts with groups. This is so for two reasons. First, many tend to be extremely old-fashioned and "corny," rather than topical and modern in their humor. Second, many of the older skits are offensive or in bad taste, in that they use dialect that ridicules those of racial or religious minorities.

Improvised skits or stunts are often more genuinely amusing in that they express the real ideas and interests of the group members, and give those who have a flair for humor or improvised acting a real opportunity to express themselves. The best such skit the author has witnessed was when he was recreation director on a ship traveling to Europe. Large numbers of American students were aboard, as well as many European students returning to their homes. A group of Italian students prepared a skit for a talent night, in which they satirized the American way of life. Their costumes, use of slang, and exaggerated comments on American customs had the international audience in a convulsed uproar. Without being unkind, they struck home! While one talented member of the group may write such skits, it is often better if all the players join together in preparing the script, letting their ideas stimulate other ideas, just as professional gag-writers do.

There are also a number of devices that group leaders may use, in informal dramatics, as a basis for making up skits.

The leader may give each group several "props" (varied objects like toys, knives, pens, ties, books, feathers, etc.) in a paper bag; each group must build a skit based on its set of props.

The leader may assign a one-sentence plot outline to each group; the players then develop their own skits, based on the outline. It is interesting to see the many variations that may be evolved from as simple a line as, "You are rushing to get somewhere, and there is an unexpected interruption."

Puppet Shows and Shadow Plays

One of the most popular forms of playground or community dramatic activity is the puppet show. Children and teen-agers may enjoy making their own puppets, of various types: sock puppets, which may be designed so fingers actually work the mouth and give expression to the face; puppets with papier-mâché or clay-model heads, with the fingers of the performer tucked into felt or cardboard hands and arms; paper-bag puppets, with the face designed with paint or crayon; tin-can puppets; and vegetable puppets, in which a large potato, apple, turnip, or carrot may serve as the head. Designing and making puppets for a playground performance provides an enjoyable arts and crafts activity (Figs. 18, 19, and 20).

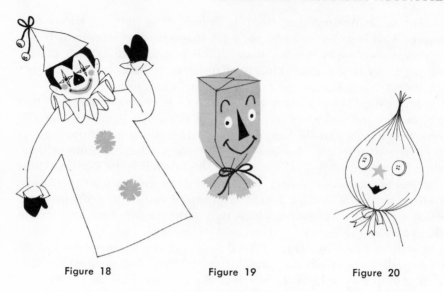

Figure 18   Figure 19   Figure 20

Many simple hand puppet stages may be built or improvised. These include a small cardboard carton with a stage opening cut out, which is placed on a table or desk, behind which the players crouch; a "doorway stage," with a broomstick stretched across a doorway or between chairs, with "curtains" hung from it; or a more formally constructed stage involving a mattress or bicycle carton standing on end, or even a real stage constructed from two-by-fours and plywood panels (Figs. 21, 22, and 23).

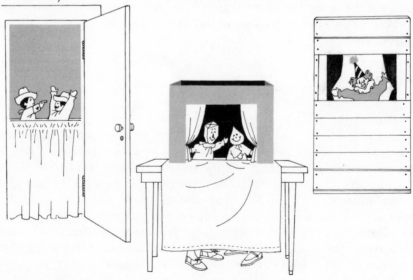

Figure 21   Figure 22   Figure 23

Children may use these to put on plays that they have made up themselves, or to present plays based on famous stories drawn from children's literature, just as in children's theatre programs. They may be presented with a minimum of props or may involve real miniature stage sets and lighting.

In some communities, puppetry becomes a major portion of the summer playground program. In Phoenix, Arizona, for example, there is a Puppetry Guild, which meets monthly during the school year, presenting plays in many settings and conducting workshops on puppetry. It is assisted by the Phoenix Parks and Recreation Department, which makes puppet kits (consisting of boxed samples of hand puppets and directions for making and using them) available to parks and playground leaders year-round, and to community groups during the school year, on a "loan" basis. The advantage of puppetry is that it may be approached as an extremely casual activity by small groups who entertain themselves in informal settings, or it may represent a long-term and highly skilled creative effort. Marionettes, of course, demand much more careful construction and operating "know-how" than puppets, as a rule, and often are presented as a form of professional entertainment, by skilled performers.

Shadow plays are usually done by having a large sheet hung between two posts, or in a doorway, with a strong light shining from behind. The players may then, by using puppets or appearing themselves, put on a performance (from behind the scene) in which the figures appear sharply outlined as silhouettes, on the sheet. They may speak themselves as the action goes on, or they may perform to a prerecorded, taped sound track of voices and sound effects.

Mobile Drama Programs

Increasingly, many community recreation departments are using "stage wagons," or "stagemobiles," which are cleverly designed so that they can be transported by trucks that then open up to form compact stage sets. They can be quickly set up, to permit traveling acting troupes to give performances on playgrounds throughout a city or in centers throughout a large county area. Although the construction of such mobile units is rather technical, and must, as a rule, be handled by professional staff, they can be used to give young drama participants an opportunity to act or be part of performances in many settings. As such, they are an important part of the up-to-date cultural arts program in many communities.

DANCE IN COMMUNITY RECREATION

Since the beginning of recorded history, dance has been one of mankind's primary forms of artistic and social expression. For both

primitive and civilized man, it has met certain basic needs of society, including the need to worship, to educate in communal customs, to express tribal or national loyalties, to engage in courtship, to assist in the
therapeutic process, to become creatively involved in artistic expression,
and, finally, as a social or recreational form.

Years ago, Havelock Ellis wrote:

> Dancing as an art, we may be sure cannot die out, but will always be under-
> going rebirth. Not merely as an art, but also as a social custom, it perpetually
> emerges afresh from the soul of the people. . . . Dancing is the loftiest, the
> most moving, the most beautiful of the arts, because it is no mere translation
> or abstraction from life, it is life itself. . . . For the artist life is always a
> discipline and no discipline can be without pain. That is so even of dancing,
> which of all arts is most associated with pleasure. To learn to dance is the
> most austere of disciplines. . . .[11]

The unique duality of dance is well illustrated here. It represents
both pleasure and pain for, as Agnes de Mille has pointed out, the training of a concert dancer is a long, rigorous, and physically demanding
ordeal. Yet, dancing is a joyous and stimulating experience. Dance may
be a tightly woven group experience, or a highly individual art form. In
the history of mankind, dance has frequently been used as a form of
religious worship—as when King David danced before the Ark. Yet, in
the Puritan society of our colonial period, it was sternly prohibited as
irreligious.

Today, of course, dance is widely accepted, both as a respected art
form and as a means of social recreation. During the period of the late
1950's, for example, the National Recreation Association has pointed out
that the number of public recreation departments reporting participation in various forms of dance activity more than doubled. In many large
municipal recreation departments, many forms of dance have been an
important part of the program; in small departments, only a few types
are stressed.

Which forms of dance are most frequently found in community
recreation programs? A partial list includes:

Ballet	Ballroom (Social) Dancing
Block Dances	Creative Dance for Children
Clog or Tap Dance	Latin American Dancing
Modern Dance	Dance Film Showings
Folk Dancing	Hawaiian Dance Instruction
Pageants and Festivals	Playground Dance Programs
Record Hops	Round Dancing
Square Dancing	Talent Shows

[11] Havelock Ellis, *The Dance of Life* (Boston: Houghton Mifflin, 1923), pp. 60, 65,
277.

Of these, the most common types would be divided basically into two categories: (a) the creative, or concert forms of dance: modern dance, ballet, modern jazz, and primitive dance; and (b) the social forms, including ballroom dance, folk, square, and round dancing. In addition to sponsoring instructional classes, performing groups, regularly meeting dance clubs and recitals or concerts, many recreation departments also assist in providing clinics, workshops, and leadership training in dance instruction.

Principles Underlying Dance Activities Sponsorship

The recreation department that undertakes the sponsorship of dance activities for the community at large should subscribe to certain basic principles:

1. The conviction that dance is worthy of acceptance as one of the performing arts (along with music and drama), and should be an integral part of the cultural arts program.
2. The recognition that dance takes many different forms and is approached on several skill levels; it therefore has broad appeal for different age groups and types of participants.
3. That successful dance programing is based on competent leadership; without this, standards of excellence and consistent public support and involvement cannot be achieved.
4. The role of the community recreation department takes two forms: (a) to provide actual instruction or leadership for various kinds of dance on playgrounds, or in community centers controlled by the department itself; and (b) to assist other community groups interested in dance by coordinating their efforts, helping with public relations, sponsoring workshops and demonstrations which interpret this activity to the community at large. Thus, both direct skill and public appreciation and understanding are achieved.

Types of Sponsorship Activities

The community recreation department should, therefore, become involved in whichever of the following functions are appropriate for the public it serves and for its own staff and facilities resources:

Scheduling dance activities as an ongoing part of the year-round program, including: *free creative dance* for younger children (aged 4 to 7); *singing games, simple folk and square dances* for children in a middle range (8 to 12); *beginning ballet and modern dance* instruction for preteens; *social dance programs* for teen-agers, along with *folk and square dancing, ballet and modern dance;* a wide variety of *recreational dance and concert dance forms* for the adult age group; and, finally, *social and square dancing* for senior citizens

Providing assistance in the form of *facilities, leadership* (when available), *publicity, leadership training,* and *coordination* to community groups interested in sponsoring dance activities themselves

Acting, when there are a number of such groups, as the moving force in bringing them together in a *dance council* or *association,* or in publishing a *dance newsletter* or *bulletin*

Throughout, it is important that the recreation department avoid competition with private studios or organizations that are already successfully meeting community dance needs. Instead, it should seek to fill gaps in service rather than overlap or duplicate what is already being offered. Usually, by conferring with recreational or creative dance leaders in the community, a program can be developed which does this successfully, and which succeeds in raising the whole level of dance appreciation in the community. Private dance instructors or studio owners in a community may sometimes resent the public recreation department's involvement in this area. When they are called upon to assist in planning and leadership, this concern will be lessened. In addition, when public interest in dance activities grows as a result of programs and events sponsored by the recreation department, this benefits all who provide services in this area.

EXAMPLES OF COMMUNITY DANCE ACTIVITIES

Civic Ballet—San Diego

The first civic-sponsored ballet program for young people in the United States was founded in San Diego, California, in 1947. Approximately 300 students ranging in age from 8 to 18 enroll in three semesters during the year: fall, spring, and summer. They are divided into eight groupings, based on ability. While no tryout or proficiency test is required to enroll in the beginning classes, advancement through the more skilled levels is based on ability. All those in the more advanced classes must have had at least four years of experience on the beginning and intermediate levels. The San Diego civic youth ballet program has produced many ballet performances, including annual operetta and Christmas programs, and a recently instituted spring ballet concert.

Teacher Training—White Plains

A good example of teacher-training in dance is found in the White Plains, New York, 1965 series of modern dance leadership workshops, sponsored by the city's Parks and Recreation Commission. The purpose of this program has been to prepare individuals interested in teaching modern dance to children of elementary school age in recreational situations. The workshops have included the planning and presentation of classes, as well as specific materials to be taught. Movement techniques, creative approaches and problems of dance accompaniment are covered in detail. The classes, taught by outstanding professional instructors, are open to anyone 16 years of age or older, who has had previous experience in dance, music, or physical education.

Broad Approach to Dance Instruction—Montgomery County

The Montgomery County, Maryland, Department of Recreation has for a number of years offered an extremely varied program of dance classes in the following areas: *ballroom dance* for teen-agers and adults; *modern dance* for children, teen-agers, and adults; *round dancing* (American set-pattern couple dances) for adults; *"slimnastics"* for adults; *"character" dance* (Spanish, Russian, etc.) for adults; *ballet* for children, teen-agers, and adults; *body rhythmics* for adults; *square dancing* for adults; *tap* and *ballet* combined for children and teen-agers. Included also are special square dance workshops and young peoples' ballet workshops and a ballet theater production program.

In this county recreation program, no fewer than 25 different instructional classes on various levels of ballet were offered during the 1964–65 season, in various school and recreation centers. As many as 14 different ballroom dance classes for teen-agers and adults were offered at the same time, throughout the county.

Folk Dance Specialization—San Antonio, Texas

One of the values of community dance activity is that it gives members of different ethnic or national groups an opportunity to continue to practice, and to take pride in, their precious folk heritage. No better example can be found than in San Antonio, Texas, where the Recreation Division offers two unique services: classes in Mexican and Spanish dancing free to all who are interested, regardless of age or national background, and programs of these dances presented as a form of public entertainment. Because San Antonio is a major gateway to Mexico, with many Mexican-American citizens and with Mexican and Spanish influences seen on all sides, there is a natural interest in this form of folk activity.

> Classes . . . are taught on the playgrounds over the city. Babies, as soon as they can walk, begin learning to move to the Latin rhythm; the girls learn to swirl their skirts. As they develop, they are taught heel work, castanet playing, and all of the techniques needed for both Mexican and Spanish

dancing. They then progress to the authentic dances of old Mexico and flashing flamenco of Spain.[12]

The classes are taught by two outstanding teachers, Bertha and Yolanda Almaguer, widely experienced in Mexican and Spanish dance forms. Each year, Yolanda Almaguer choreographs one of the classics in Spanish music, such as "Capriccio Espanol" or "The Three-Cornered Hat," for performance with the symphony orchestra of San Antonio, in the municipal auditorium. These are performed by skilled dancers who have been trained in the classes. She also directs a "Fiesta Noche Del Rio" which is presented three times weekly throughout the summer for thousands of visitors to the city. These performing services are offered by the Recreation Division to conventions, service organizations, hospitals, armed forces, Red Cross, and similar groups. So popular are the Latin dancers that their bookings are frequently made a year or two in advance —always, however, free, except for expenses.

The Dance in Voluntary Community Agencies

In addition to dance programs that are sponsored by public recreation departments, many voluntary agencies offer dance instruction and activities as part of their total social or cultural program. In many YWCA's, for example, it is customary to have courses for adults in ballroom dancing and Latin-American dancing, as well as regularly meeting ballroom dance events for "Y" members and their guests. Often, too, the "Y's" sponsor folk and square dance clubs, and modern and ballet courses and workshops. The McBurney YMCA in New York City, for example, acts as a center for a number of national folk dance groups which meet regularly and rehearse in its facilities. Another unusual example is the Clark Center for the Performing Arts, of the West Side Branch YWCA in New York City. This cultural program places great stress on the dance, offering concerts by leading performers and companies each year and sponsoring classes in such varied forms as: African dance, American mime, ballet, fundamentals of modern dance, jazz forms, Lester Horton modern dance technique, intermediate and advanced modern dance, and movement for singers and actors.

Settlement houses too, with their strong emphasis on cultural programing, frequently offer excellent dance programs. The Karamu Center dance workshop and company in Cleveland, Ohio, is an excellent example. Perhaps the most unusual performing arts program of all is found in the Henry Street Playhouse, on the Lower East Side of New York City. Here, an extensive variety of courses in music, drama, and

[12] Lou Hamilton, "Mexican and Spanish Dancing in Recreation," *Recreation,* January, 1962, p. 39.

dance are offered for children and adults who come not only from the immediate neighborhood but from all over the New York Metropolitan area. In addition, the Henry Street Playhouse serves as the home base of Alwin Nikolais, who is today recognized as one of the leading chore-ographers of contemporary dance. Using the small but well-equipped stage owned by the Henry Street Settlement, Nikolais has created entire new forms of movement, and stage effects of costuming, lighting, and properties that have taken the artistic world by storm. For years, too, the Henry Street Settlement has offered popular programs of folk and square dance participation for the public at large.

Dance in Social Recreation

Social, square, and folk dancing are widely used as an important part of social recreation for teen-age and adult groups in the community. They may be approached on two levels.

Regularly Meeting Clubs. There are today thousands of clubs devoted to square, folk, and round dancing. These are found throughout the country, but particularly in suburban areas in the Far West and Mid-western states, where they cater chiefly to adults in the middle-age bracket. They tend to place a great stress on a high level of performing skill. Often they are attended only by couples, who must first take a 10-to-20-week course in dance fundamentals before they are offered membership. Participants in these groups, particularly the more ad-vanced square and round dance groups, take their hobby very seriously. They may actually dance several nights a week, visiting different clubs or traveling long distances to hear outstanding callers, or attending special dance camps and workshops during the summer. Since new dances are constantly being evolved, it is necessary for them to do this to keep pace. While a small percentage of square, round, and folk dance groups are "open" clubs which place little stress on expert performance, the majority of them do not welcome unskilled participants.

Occasional Use of Recreational Dance. A much larger number of individuals of all ages throughout the country take part occasionally in square and folk dancing as part of general social recreation activities. Thus, a church, Parent-Teachers Association, 4-H Club, YM or YWCA, hotel, teen club, or similar organization may plan a special social or party which introduces simple square and folk dance activities. Usually, when presented in such settings—if the instruction is brief but effective— participation is relaxed and enthusiastic. Square and folk dancing can be one of the most successful ways of getting participants to mingle informally, to "let their hair down," and to join in friendly groupings. Similarly, in many therapeutic recreation situations, in working with psychiatric or even physically handicapped patients, square and folk dancing provide useful tools for socialization and healthy physical activity.

There would be little point to providing descriptions of the more advanced square or folk dances in this book, although a number of sources are included in the bibliography. Instead, guides are offered for the successful leadership of these forms of dance in social recreation situations. In addition, several illustrative dances are given, which may be used for teaching assignments in recreation leadership courses.

Guides for Recreational Dance Leadership

1. *Selection.* Dances should be chosen to suit the musical and rhythmic tastes of the participants, their physical status, and social needs and interests. Thus, in a senior citizens center, emphasis should be placed on older, more traditional forms of ballroom or round dancing, on relaxed mixers and rather simple, slow square dances. Among teen-agers, it is important to provide spirited dances with catchy melodies. Dances chosen should build on previously learned skills and should always include some new materials to maintain interest at a high level.

2. *Programing.* In any given dance session, dances presented should have variety, and should involve a gradual progression of skills. They should be blocked in groups: two or three folk dances or mixers, two or three square dances, and, if social dancing is part of the program, a period of time for general dancing. It is usually a good idea (if the group has not done this kind of dancing before and resistance may be anticipated), to begin with social dance icebreakers or circle dances without partners. When the majority of participants have become involved, and are enjoying the activity, the most difficult or challenging dances should be presented. Toward the end of the session, the pace "tapers off," and it should end with fairly simple, familiar dances.

3. *Instruction.* This should be clear, enthusiastic, and as brief as possible, so that people do not become bored with repetitious, drill-like teaching. The following steps are involved:

a. The appropriate formation should be taken and the dance introduced.
b. The dance should be demonstrated by having the group walk through the action. In a folk dance, this is usually done in "teachable units," i.e., sections of the dance that form recognizable blocks of action, fitted to sections of the music. Usually, in a square dance, the specific "figure" of the dance is explained and walked through all at once. If the activity is a social dance icebreaker or mixer, it may only be necessary to explain it briefly, and then begin.
c. If the dance is at all complicated, the separate parts should then be assembled and reviewed. If it is simple, this is not necessary.

d. The group then does the dance. If they have learned it correctly and the bulk are doing it satisfactorily (in any group, a few individuals may always have some difficulty), it should continue. If there is much confusion, it may be necessary to stop it, re-teach the part that is causing difficulty, and then start over.

In terms of square dancing, a large group or a club that wishes to do the more advanced dances will need an expert caller, or is likely to use records with calls on them. In a beginning group, or a general social occasion where some square dancing is being done, the caller need not be very expert, although he should be a good teacher. He has the choice, always, of calling the dance himself, or of using records with calls that are suitable for the ability range of the group.

The following section includes a number of simple folk dances, traditional dance mixers, and social dance icebreakers that are useful for informal recreational situations. More advanced dances and a variety of square dances (which are not included here) may be found in the sources listed at the end of this text.

Shoo Fly   American Play Party Mixer

This lively partner-changing dance is a good lead-up to square dancing.

Formation: A circle of partners with hands joined, all facing the center. Each girl is on her partner's right.

Words to be Sung	*Action*
Verse	
Shoo fly, don't bother me,	Keeping hands joined, all take four walking steps forward to the center, and four steps backward to place. Repeat entire action.
Shoo fly, don't bother me,	
Shoo fly, don't bother me,	
'Cause I belong to somebody.	
Chorus	
I do, I do, I do,	All swing partners. Children may use a two-hand skipping swing, or an elbow swing. Adults use a "buzz swing" (Fig. 24). At end of verse, each boy faces the center and passes his partner across in front of him to his left side. Hands are joined in the circle again.
I ain't goin' to tell you who,	
I belong to somebody,	
Yes, indeed, I do.	

NOTE: The girl now on the boy's right is his new partner. The dance is repeated from the beginning, as many times as desired.

Phonograph record: RCA Victor, LE-3000 (words are sung on record).
          Folk Dancer, MH-1108 (without words on record).

Figure 24

Oh, Susannah   American Play Party Mixer

This circle dance introduces the grand-right-and-left and promenade, and so might be done as one of the first numbers of a recreational dance program.

Formation: A circle of partners with hands joined, all facing the center. Each girl is on her partner's right.

Words to be Sung	*Action*
Verse	
Oh, I come from Alabama with My banjo on my knee, And I'm going to Louisiana My true love for to see.	All the girls walk four steps to the center, clapping hands on the fourth step, and four steps back to place. All the boys do the same.
It rained all night, the day I left, The weather, it was dry, The sun so hot I froze to death, Susannah, don't you cry.	Facing partners, all do a grand-right-and-left. Give right hands to partners, pass, left hands to next person, pass, and continue for remainder of verse (Fig. 25).

Figure 25

Figure 26

Chorus

Oh, Susannah,
Don't you cry for me,
For I'm going to Louisiana
With my banjo on my knee.

Oh, Susannah,
Don't you cry for me,
For I'm going to Louisiana
With my banjo on my knee.

Each person meets a new partner and swings this person with sixteen "buzz" steps (see Fig. 24).

In promenade position (Fig. 26) new partners promenade 16 steps counterclockwise around circle. At end of chorus, all face center, with girls on partner's right, ready to begin dance again.

Phonograph record: RCA Victor 45-6178 (without words on record). Educational Recordings of America S.G. 2, (with words on record).

Savila Se Bela Loza   Yugoslav Folk Dance

This is a lively, simple circle folk dance, an example of the popular Yugoslav "kolo."

Formation: Dancers join hands in a single circle, facing the center. No partners are needed.

Action

Part 1   With hands joined and beginning with right foot, run 18 steps to right (counterclockwise). Then step again on right foot, hop lightly on it, and swing left foot across in front.

              Turning to left, run 18 steps to left (clockwise), beginning with left foot. Then step again on left foot, hop lightly on it, and swing right foot across in front.

Part 2   "Basic kolo step." Facing the center, with hands still joined, step
              on right foot, traveling to right side, cross the left foot in back,
              step on right foot again, and hop on it, swinging the left foot
              across in front.

              The same action is done to the left: step on left to side, cross right
              in back, step left, and hop on it, swinging the right foot across in
              front.

              The entire action is done three full times, with small steps, close
              to the floor. Then the dance is repeated from the beginning.

Phonograph record: Folkraft 1496X45-B (recorded in Yugoslavia by Dennis Boxell).

Jibidi Jibida   French Folk Dance

       Another easy circle folk dance without partners, with an infectious
melody. Both children and adults may enjoy this one.

Formation: Dancers join hands in a single circle, facing the center. No partners
               are needed.

Action

Part 1   All step to the left side with the left foot, and bring the right foot
               to it, taking the weight. Repeat this action. Then swing the left foot
               forward and back, brushing the floor lightly and bending the right
               knee. Stamp in place with the left foot, and pause for one count.

               This entire action is repeated.

Part 2   Spring lightly in place on the left foot, putting the right foot for-
               ward, heel on the floor and toe pointing up. Spring lightly in place
               on right foot, placing left foot forward, toe pointing up. Then do
               the same action quickly three times: spring with right forward, left,
               and right again. Pause for one count.

               Do the same action starting with left foot forward: left, and right,
               and left-right-left.

               The dance is then repeated from the beginning, as many times as
               desired. Hands are kept joined throughout.

Phonograph record: Folk Dancer MH-1044.

Seven Steps   German Folk Dance Mixer

       A lively European folk dance which makes use of the schottische, a
fundamental folk dance step.

Formation: A double circle of couples facing to the right (counterclockwise) in
               open position (Fig. 27).

Figure 27

Action

Part 1   Starting with the outside foot (boy's left and girl's right), take seven running steps forward. Pause on the eighth count, lifting inside foot (boy's right and girl's left).

Starting with the inside foot, take seven running steps backward. Pause on the eighth count, lifting outside foot.

Part 2   Releasing partner's hand, and with both hands on own waist, each person does a schottische step away from his partner, to the side. Boy goes to left, stepping left, right, left, and hop, while girl does reverse footwork. Each person does a schottische step back to partner. Boy goes to right, stepping right, left, right, and hop, while girl does reverse footwork.

In shoulder-waist position (Fig. 28) each couple does four step-hops, turning once clockwise. Boy begins with left foot and girl with right foot.

Figure 28

Part 3   The action of Part 2 is repeated. The boy, however, instead of re-
            turning to his partner with a schottische, moves *ahead* to the *next*
            girl, while his partner moves *back* to the next boy. In shoulder-
            waist position, they turn with this *new* partner, with four step-hops.

NOTE: The dance is repeated as many times as desired, each time with a new partner.

Phonograph record: Folk Dancer MH-1048.

Doudlebska Polka   Czech Folk Dance Mixer

    This couple dance mixer, making use of the polka step, has become
a favorite of many American folk dancers.

Formation: Couples scattered around the dance floor, in closed dance position.

Action

Part 1   All couples do 16 polka steps, traveling counterclockwise around
            the hall and turning clockwise as couples.

Part 2   Forming small circles with 6 to 10 couples in a circle, couples march
            counterclockwise. Each boy has his right arm around his partner's
            waist, and his left hand on the left shoulder of the boy in front of
            him (Fig. 29). They take 16 steps forward.

Figure 29

Part 3   Boys release partners and face the center. In the polka rhythm,
            they clap their own hands twice and then clap hands once with
            their neighbors (Fig. 30). This clapping action is done 16 times.

Figure 30

Meanwhile, the girls polka individually, without turning, 16 steps clockwise around the outside of the circle.

NOTE: At the end of Part 3, boys turn to the outside to find a new partner. They form couples again and start the dance from the beginning. It is repeated as many times as desired.

Phonograph record: Folk Dancer MH-3016.

Virginia Reel   American Country Dance

This is probably the best known and liked of all the traditional recreational dances.

Formation: A line of boys, facing a line of girls. There should be between four and eight couples to a set, with six being the best number. The couple nearest the "caller" or source of music is the first, or "head" couple. If dancers turn to face the music, each girl should be on her partner's right.

Action

Part 1   Taking hands in lines (girls holding hands in their line, and boys in theirs), all take four walking steps forward toward opposite line, and four steps backward. Repeat this.

All walk forward, join right hands with partner's right hand, and walk clockwise around partner, returning to place with eight steps.

Repeat this action with left hands joined, turning counterclockwise.

Repeat this action with both hands joined, turning clockwise.

All walk forward and "do-si-do," passing around partner back-to-back (beginning with right sides passing) and returning to place.

Part 2   The first couple joins both hands and slides eight steps down the
set (between the lines) and eight steps back up to their starting
position (Fig. 31).

Figure 31

The "reel." The first couple does a right elbow-swing once, turning clockwise. The first boy then turns the next girl in the girl's line
with a left elbow, turning counterclockwise. At the same time, the
first girl does the same with the next boy in the boy's line. This
action is repeated several times, with the first couple working their
way down the set, first turning each other with a right elbow, and
then the *next* person on the side with a left elbow.

"Cast off!" When they reach the "foot" of the set, the first couple
joins both hands, and slides up to the "head" of the set. They face
forward (toward the music) and "cast off." The first boy marches
to the left and down to the foot of the set (with the other boys
following him) while the first girl does the same to the right (Fig.
32). When they reach the foot, the first couple joins both hands and
makes an arch. The others go under the arch and back up to place,
keeping the same order, but leaving the first couple at the foot.

Note: The dance is repeated as many times as there are couples, each time with a new
first couple.

Phonograph record: RCA Victor 45-6180 (without calls). RCA Victor LE-3002 (with
calls).

SOCIAL DANCE ICEBREAKERS AND STUNTS

The most commonly found form of recreational dance is couple
social dancing. While fads may come and go—with new dances constantly
being invented—this age-old social activity continues to have great

Figure 32

appeal for all ages. Particularly with young people at informal high school or college-age dances, there may be a need for special icebreakers, mixers, and stunts to break down shyness and reserve. Here are several examples of useful mixers of this type.

Invitation Dances

When participants enter the hall, they draw slips from a bowl (separate bowls for boys and girls). Later, for a special dance number, each boy must find the girl whose slip matches his. She becomes his partner for that dance.

1. "Matching Slips." "Adam" must find "Eve," or "Salt" must find "Pepper."
2. "Matching Pictures." Pictures may be taken from magazines and cut in half. Each boy then tries to find the girl whose half-picture matches his.
3. "Matching Numbers." Each boy tries to find the girl whose number is the same as his.
4. "Matching Songs." Each slip contains a song title. At a signal, each person must move about the hall, singing his song and trying to find the person with the same song.

Conversation Mixer

Two circles are formed, with girls on the inside and boys on the outside. As march music is played, the girls walk clockwise and the boys counterclockwise. When the music stops, each person is facing a new partner. The master of ceremonies announces a topic of conversation, which should be rather light and humorous, and suited to the interests of the group. They are given about a minute to chat on this topic. Then social dance music is played, and they dance together for a minute or two. The mixer is repeated several times, each time with a new topic of conversation, and with dancers meeting new partners.

Cinderella Dance

Girls are asked to take off their right shoe and to place it in a pile in the center of the floor. At a signal, each boy takes a shoe, and looks for the girl it belongs to. He puts it on her foot, and they dance the next number together.

ELIMINATION DANCES

There are many novelty elimination dances which serve to break up a session of social dancing, by providing humorous contests, usually with inexpensive prizes being awarded to the winning couple.

Hat-Passing Contest. As couples dance, boys must pass a battered old hat around the room, from couple to couple. When the hat is placed on a boy's head, he must wear it for a moment, before he can pass it. The couple possessing the hat when the music is suddenly stopped, is eliminated. This continues until only one couple—the winner—remains. If there is a large crowd of dancers, several old hats may be used.

Limbo Contest. A bamboo pole or broomstick is stretched between two uprights, or held by two volunteers. The dancers move around the room in a circle, with each couple dancing under the pole in turn. It is gradually lowered. When couples touch it, they are eliminated. The last couple to go safely under the pole is the winner.

Many other useful icebreakers and mixers may be found in *Party Games for All*, by Mason and Mitchell.[13]

SUGGESTED QUESTIONS FOR DISCUSSION

1. What are the unique values and advantages of the performing arts as recreational activities in today's society? Contrast the approach to one of the performing arts as a *professional* activity with its approach as an *amateur* activity.
2. Discuss the role of organized recreation services in providing leadership and program activities in one of the performing arts areas: music, drama, or dance.
3. Based on the examples cited in this chapter, how would you initiate and develop support for a beginning program on the community level for one of the performing arts? Describe a hypothetical community, and the specific steps that might be taken.

13 Bernard Mason and Elmer Mitchell, *Party Games for All* (New York: Barnes & Noble, 1935).

Chapter 8

Recreational Arts and Crafts

The second major aspect of creative participation in organized recreation programs concerns those activities in which there is a physical product or outcome, commonly referred to as "arts and crafts." As in the performing arts, a distinction is usually drawn between two kinds of activities: those which are clearly of an artistic and creative nature, requiring a high degree of technical skill, and those which are somewhat more mechanical, simpler, or lacking in expressive content.

In a pamphlet on the arts published by the North Carolina Recreation Commission, the distinction is made in this way:

> . . . a craft has some functional application. For example, a craft product may be used as a place mat or as a vase or for some utilitarian purpose. Using this definition, examples of crafts would be woodworking, pottery, ceramics, weaving, and jewelry making. . . .

> On the other hand, an art object is enjoyed primarily for itself and for the emotional response it elicits from the viewer. It does not necessarily have

any utilitarian purpose; it is simply there to be enjoyed because it is beautiful or because it expresses the intellectual and emotional being of its creator.[1]

It should be made clear that this division is somewhat arbitrary.
Thus, an oil painting, which is commonly viewed as an "art" form, may
be crude, unimaginative, and quite lacking in aesthetic worth. On the
other hand, a woven tapestry or ceramic object (both considered "craft"
forms) may have great artistic merit and style. Perhaps, in this light, it
would be best to designate *three* major categories of activities under the
general heading of "arts and crafts."

1. The first consists of those graphic and plastic forms which are
commonly referred to *as* art, including painting (oil, watercolor, or
tempera), drawing, print-making (wood block, etching, or lithography),
and sculpture. These are generally nonutilitarian in nature, other than
having the function of serving as decoration. They place a heavy stress
on personal expressiveness.

2. The second category includes those activities which place a heavy
stress on mastery of a given craft or technical skill, and which produce
objects that are customarily seen as having functional value: carving,
leatherwork, woodworking, ceramics, weaving, jewelry making, and
similar crafts. Again, in the hands of an imaginative and gifted performer,
these "crafts" have high aesthetic value.

3. Lastly are those forms of activity which have no pretension to
being original or creative in a true sense, which may represent either
art or craft. These represent a mechanical approach to drawing or painting, including "painting by the numbers" (filling in designated areas with
numbered colors), assembling mosaic pictures in the same fashion, using
molds to make ceramics, or carrying out any of hundreds of mechanical
manipulative processes using "kits" or prestructured materials.

All of these activities provide certain forms of enjoyment and personal satisfaction, as part of recreational participation. Obviously, however, the greatest values come from those activities in which the performer
is *himself* developed as a creative being most fully, and in which the
product is most fully expressive of his personality. Thus, a creative, non-
stereotyped approach to the teaching of arts and crafts should be emphasized.

THE CREATIVE APPROACH TO RECREATIONAL
ARTS AND CRAFTS

What are the significant values of artistic involvement by individuals
of any age or background? They lie in two areas: personal and administrative.

---

[1] *Recreation and the Arts,* Bulletin No. 33 (Raleigh, North Carolina: North
Carolina Recreation Commission, 1964).

Personal Values. Arts and crafts activities fill the important need of all human beings to explore their own resources, to manipulate the environment, and to create something that is beautiful, personally expressive, decorative, or useful. While every individual certainly does not have the capacity to become an *artist* in the sense of becoming a highly professional and technically skilled creator of outstanding art products, he certainly can make a personal expression that is valid for himself and can uncover heretofore untapped talents and abilities. In addition, he can and should begin to develop his own aesthetic judgment, and heighten his own interest in the arts and his sensitivity to them—an important component of the fully rounded individual in our culture.

Administrative Values. In terms of the advantages of arts and crafts activities for the administrator of organized recreation programs, there are several significant factors. As in the performing arts, they fill another dimension of human need and appeal to many persons who are not interested in sports and games, outdoor recreation, or similar physically or competitively oriented programs. They may be carried on indoors or out, at all seasons of the year, and by persons of all ages or physical condition. In addition, they may be carried out in all sorts of groupings, with people working on common projects, or within similar media (each person working on his own task or product), or even by individuals working completely on their own. Thus, they are extremely flexible, as far as program organization is concerned.

Exactly what is the creative approach to arts and crafts leadership?

Conant points out that many people have fallacious ideas about art, and that it is a mistake to assume that every person can become an artist —just as it is a mistake to assume that every leader who has had some personal experience within an art medium (or who has read a "how-to-do-it" book on art instruction) can lead it successfully. He suggests that creative art teaching is more than just letting participants do what they please. It is a special kind of highly skilled teaching that requires extensive professional preparation and experience—far more difficult and arduous than teaching in a cut-and-dried or mechanical fashion.[2] Undoubtedly, it is this fact that prompts many leaders to rely on "shortcut," "pseudoart" projects, such as assemble-your-own, precut belt kits, predesigned painting or mosaic sets, or copyist approaches.

Specifically, the creative teacher of art activities does the following:

1. He introduces the medium to the participants, initially selecting it on the basis of what he knows to be appropriate for their age level or stage of artistic development. Thus, in working with younger children, he might begin with finger-painting or the use of tempera, or drawing with chalk or similar media. With teen-agers or adults, oil or watercolor painting might be more suitable ventures.

[2] Howard Conant, "Creative Arts Teaching in Recreation Programs," *Recreation,* January, 1960, p. 16.

2. He gives initial instruction in the use of the medium—how paper or canvas surfaces should be prepared, how pigments are to be applied, or how brushes may be used, for example. This does not imply a rigid, set method which must be followed, but rather a helpful introduction to the technique. In the case of crafts activities, obviously, a more detailed presentation of the technical process is needed, before participants can become involved creatively.

3. The teacher may help participants get under way in their exploration of the medium by providing a certain amount of structure, in terms of projects. Thus, he may take them on a sketching walk, he may set up a model or still-life, or he may, in discussion, help them decide on subjects they wish to draw or paint. They should be free to work on their own problems, either of a literal or nonliteral nature, although sometimes it is valuable for all of the members of a drawing class or group to work on the same problem. He may also introduce certain ideas of design, composition, use of line, masses of color, textures, or rhythms, which members of the group may explore in their drawings or paintings.

4. Without imposing his own critical judgment (and thus giving participants the idea that they must satisfy *his* standards), the teacher helps the members of the group know *how* to look at or think about a drawing or painting. In other words, they begin to develop their own critical judgment, both in examining their own work and that of other members of the group. At this stage, the teacher may skillfully draw out in discussion certain principles that will guide this process—such as an awareness of strength in composition, variety, balance, or contrast. The effective use of color, the different ways of using pigment or brush strokes, all are analyzed, and group members grow more secure in their own knowledge of technique.

5. He may introduce certain concepts of drawing, dealing with the structure and proportions of the human body, physical forces underlying movement, the use of geometric forms in blocking out figures, or even the rudiments of perspective drawing. The purpose of this is not to turn out individuals who can draw accurately in a photographic sense, but rather to help them understand the basis of valid draughtsmanship that underlies even highly abstract work.

6. Throughout, the teacher should stress the growing ability of the participant to judge what is genuine, creative, and expressive in his own work—as well as what is superficial or artificial. Thus, he helps them begin to understand the value of art as a form of personal expressiveness, and to look in a sophisticated way at other drawings, paintings or forms of art.

7. Finally, he promotes a general interest in the arts. Paintings and drawings are exhibited, children and adults are encouraged to bring in reproductions for display, and trips to museums, exhibitions, and other art events are arranged.

All this is to be done with the honest conviction that what the child or adult produces is important, whatever the level of participation, provided that it represents creative growth for him and an enhancement of his general understanding of the artistic process.

OVERALL RECREATION PROGRAMS IN THE ARTS

What should the overall role of an organized recreation program be, with respect to the graphic and plastic arts, and to craft activity? Five functions may be defined:

1. These activities should represent an important part of the ongoing recreation program for children throughout the year, on playgrounds and in indoor centers. This suggests that all recreation participants should have a minimal exposure to satisfying activities in arts and crafts, whether or not they have a special interest in the field.

2. They should also be presented to adults, in the form of special recreation or adult education classes which are scheduled, usually on a weekly basis, along with many other recreational choices.

3. In recreation programs that are designed to meet the needs of certain special groups, such as the physically handicapped, the mentally ill, or the aged, in institutions or in the community at large, arts and crafts are extremely useful. They are highly adaptable both to limited physical functioning, and to providing emotional outlets for persons who need them or cannot express themselves effectively in other ways.

4. On a somewhat more advanced level, a recreation agency or department may develop an intensive program in the arts, which stresses variety and depth—serving children and adults with *many* types of arts and crafts experiences in a special setting. Often, in such programs, teachers who are themselves outstanding artists may be employed, and students with special talents are given the opportunity to develop to a high level of proficiency.

5. Finally, the recreation department within a community may serve to assist and promote the work of other organizations (schools, clubs, civic art associations, etc.) by arranging or coordinating shows, art festivals, workshops, and exhibits—thus acting as a strong force for community culture.

EXAMPLES OF RECREATION DEPARTMENT FUNCTIONS

Arts and Crafts as Part of the Ongoing Program for Children

An excellent example of the place of arts and crafts activity in summertime recreation programing for children may be found in the Summer Staff Manual of the Division of Recreation of the Department of Parks and Recreation, in Louisville, Kentucky. Its rationale is presented in this passage:

> The object of the Arts and Crafts program is to satisfy every participant's creative instinct, to enrich his daily life, to develop a sense of beauty and to satisfy the desire to use his hands. The program is not intended solely to develop special talent, but rather to meet the needs and interests of the group, and to provide for the steady growth of art awareness in our every-day world. . . .
>
> Since (creative) expression comes from within, there must be something to bring it out. Hence the need of various outside experiences. Discussions, stories, pictures, suggestions, excursions, all aid enrichment which is important as the first step in a creative program. There should be some emphasis on proper handling, care of and responsibility for materials and tools used, and cleaning up afterward in order to establish desired attitudes and habits. Work skills and habits usually need to be taught to most children; they do not just happen. Projects and materials (should be offered) in such a way as to provide a creative and stimulating experience. Playground Crafts are so much more than busy work, or a "keep-them-off-the-street" project. Give the participants a chance to explore, touch, finger, experiment, create, and achieve.[3]

Specific arts-and-crafts projects for three groupings on the Louisville playgrounds include the following:

Younger Children	Boys	Girls
Painting	Wood Work	Weaving
Paper Mosaics	Space Rocket	Plaster Jewelry
Paper Toys	Painting	Decorated Boxes
Fancy Paper Hats	Treasure Chest	Autograph Books
Doll Houses	Masks	Painting
Pull Toys	Papier-Mâché	Dolls
Scrap Books	Puppets	Papier-Mâché
Story Hour Sit-Upons	Toy Boats	Sock Puppets
Yarn Pictures	Wire Sculpture	Sewing and Embroidery
Rhythm Band Instruments	Pebble Pictures	Wire and Bead Bracelet
Tissue Paper Pictures	Plaster Castings	Spoon Jewelry

Other activities, for older boys and girls and adults, include the following crafts:

Woodcarving	Whittling	Posters
Model-Making	Prints	Textile Painting
Basket Weaving	Nature Crafts	Shell Jewelry
Colored Burlap	Sand (Plaster) Casting	

In the Louisville Manual, the following guides suggest approaches

---

[3] *Summer Staff Manual,* Louisville, Kentucky, Department of Parks and Recreation, 1964, p. 75.

to leading painting and drawing activities. Here, recognizing that many leaders will be in charge of playground activities who are not themselves artists or trained art teachers, the point is to encourage the children, to free them to express themselves creatively, and to give them a sense of confidence:

Suggestions

1. Take a group on a "sketching" tour around the park or the neighborhood. Tell the children to draw what they see. They can make sketches of the activities in the park, the trees, the nearby houses, cars, other children, or whatever else can be seen. Some of these sketches can be used in larger paintings.
2. Use "Suggestion Cards." For example: A Rainy Day—A Trip to the Store—The Circus—My Pets—A Trip to the Moon—Sea Creatures—A Dream—What Scared Me Most—Cowboys—On the Farm—Fighting Animals—Strange Birds—My Favorite Sport.
3. Have different children pose for the group. Drawing from a model is the best way for children to learn to draw people. Change the pose about every 10 minutes in order that they may learn to draw people in many different positions. These sketches can be done in a few quick lines with a soft pencil or crayon.
4. Suggest that each one in the class draw a picture about the thing he likes to do best. Have a discussion before beginning.
5. Read an imaginative story to the class. Let the children illustrate the story the way they visualize it, or draw the part of the story that was most interesting to them. Songs and poems can be illustrated in the same way.
6. Have an art exhibit on your playground. A child feels proud and encouraged to see his paintings displayed; an exhibit will help to arouse interest in art for others.
7. Have the children make "scribble drawings," and from these obtain ideas for shapes and forms to be developed further as drawings or paintings.

Brief descriptions of other arts and crafts projects, and nature craft activities, as presented in the Louisville playground program, follow. Obviously, all of these might not be feasible for presentation with a given group of children. The basis for selection might be: (a) the interest of the children; (b) the availability of materials; and, (c) the feeling of competence on the part of the leader in certain areas.

Arts and Crafts Projects, Briefly Detailed

Cardboard Carton Crafts—making waste baskets, treasure chests, floats, decorative headdresses or masks, puppet theaters, and pull toys
Sawdust Modeling—use of an inexpensive modeling material made of mixed fine sawdust and wallpaper paste, to create simple sculpture objects
Feltcraft Novelties—making dress accessories, hats, lapel dangles, purses, headbands, etc.; decorating with colored sequins or beads

Marbleizing—a decorative process which can be used on paper, cardboard, wood, etc., especially useful for scrapbook covers and fancy papers

Woodworking Activities—making toy and model airplanes, birdhouses and feeders, wall shelves, tool or garden boxes, game boards, and boat models

Simple Bookbinding—making scrapbooks, notebooks, and other book-type articles

Papier-Mâché—making animals, birds, story-book characters, puppets, masks, toys, float decorations, and similar objects, using papier-mâché (torn newspaper strips and wallpaper paste process, built onto skeleton frame made of wire, rolled newspaper cylinders, wood strips, or similar constructions)

Nature Crafts—activities include pebble-painting; the use of nuts, seeds, cones, shells, gourds, or reeds to make decorative objects, jewelry, dress accessories, etc.; making of "sculpture," using weathered driftwood (both natural and carved); wildlife whittling; sandcasting, and similar projects

Many recreation departments have developed detailed and illustrated manuals showing how each of these activities may be developed and presented to children. While they are somewhat more structured and less creative than drawing or painting would be, they have much appeal for children and make use of readily accessible nature materials. In addition, of course, they yield attractive and interesting products which children may then take home, or which may be displayed.

Arts and Crafts Activities for Adults

Similarly, a wide variety of arts and crafts activities may be found within the ongoing recreation program for adults. Frequently, these are presented as adult courses extending over a period of 10 or 15 weeks, or even through the winter seasons. A typical example may be found in the William Cullen Bryant Adult Center, an adult recreation and education center sponsored by the New York City Bureau of Community Education. The following courses are offered on weekday evenings; some of the most popular ones may be given with two or three different instructors, on different nights of the week:

Woodworking and Cabinet Making	Elementary and Advanced Ceramics
	Painting and Sketching
Oil Painting	Dressmaking
Sculpture	Sewing
Millinery	Drawing and Painting for Beginners
Tailoring	Color Photography
Watercolor Painting	Enameling on Copper
Portrait Painting	Arts and Crafts for Counselors and Leaders
Life Painting and Sketching	

Usually, such classes are offered with a minimal fee being charged each participant, and with the understanding that, if there is an insufficient enrollment (between 10 and 15 students are usually required to justify giving a course), the class will be canceled. Usually, however, courses of this type maintain consistently good enrollments, particularly of middle-aged and older participants in adult-center activities.

Arts and Crafts for Special Groups

As indicated earlier, one of the special advantages of creative activities of this type is that they have strong appeal and value for older persons. Max Kaplan has written:

> The aging person needs guidance to encourage, not to limit and stifle, him. Traditional standards are important to art, but as a leisure activity for the old person, the approach is social, as well as aesthetic: what art does to me as well as what I do with art. The pressure to be avoided here is that of the pedantic teacher. The rewards to be sought through the arts are personal expression; insights into the use of materials and symbols; the response of others; the integration of personality; a concern with the concepts of beauty, form, balance, style, symbolic meanings. These are not experiences reserved for the young. . . .[4]

Because of physical handicaps or possible inhibitions or fears which older persons may have, if they have not engaged in arts-and-crafts pursuits at an earlier age, it is necessary to be extremely careful in introducing them to creative activities of this type. Their fear of possible failure or ridicule needs to be reduced by warmth and understanding on the part of the instructor. If their first projects are extremely simple, they will be encouraged and ready to try more difficult tasks. Gross describes the use of art with senior citizens in the Baltimore, Maryland, Bureau of Recreation:

> Motivating older people in the field of art may be accomplished in many ways. To see a display of work by others of their age group hanging in an attractive location will do wonders in stimulating them to join an art class. Suggesting that the finished painting or craft may be given to a grandchild or a friend will also add to their interest. Most older people are anxious to keep active and they respond readily to the opportunity to receive instruction in the field of art. To stress the opportunity to be of service to others as well as the entertainment and pleasure they will receive will serve as a strong motivating force.[5]

Gross suggests that, in setting up an art program for the aged, the following guides will be helpful:

Know the activity well yourself and choose one that you enjoy. Be aware of any pitfalls and try to anticipate and avoid them.

---

[4] Max Kaplan, quoted in: Selma W. Gross, "Creative Magic for the Senior Citizen," *Recreation,* May, 1964, p. 235.
[5] *Ibid.*

Consider the desired goals. Offer pleasurable, creative activities that will give numerous hours of relaxation and satisfaction, giving everyone the thrill and satisfaction that comes in the act of expressing oneself.

Make explanations simple and concise. Use illustrations wherever possible. Repeat directions frequently. Remember that some students may be hard of hearing and make a special effort (to insure) that they understand.

Adapt the activity to the group. Put the main emphasis on trying and not on competition or success. Praise often. In explaining the activity use an enthusiastic approach. Be positive.

Plan frequent displays of the finished work. Hang the work attractively and give it the look of importance it deserves. . . .[6]

Many other types of special groups in the community may be served through arts-and-crafts activities. Often the most severely disabled child or adult, who is unable to take part in other forms of play, will find or adapt a way to paint, draw, or carry out crafts projects. Janet Pomeroy describes in detail the use of pottery, papier-mâché, and other graphic arts experiences with physically handicapped children and adults at the Recreation Center for the Handicapped, Inc., in San Francisco. One excellent illustration tells the story of 12 children with cerebral palsy, whose ages ranged from 10 to 21, who formed a pottery club:

> With the guidance of the recreation leader, they elected officers, chose a club project, and selected the club name of "The Jolly Mudslingers." They decided to make ashtrays, bowls, and tiles which were to be offered for sale at a Hallowe'en bazaar. Those who had only slight hand coordination were taught to work with a potter's wheel, an activity which, incidentally, was effective therapy as well as fun. One girl who could not use her hands at all was taught to use a potter's wheel with her toes. She made several ashtrays and eventually designed and made the club's pins, using only her toes. The group often utilized the assembly line process. Those who were seriously handicapped and had only slight use of a hand, for example, contributed to the group effort by sanding the objects in order to make them ready for firing. Others were able to roll coils of clay to be used in making coil vases, bowls, and ashtrays. Still others learned to make decorative slab pieces by flattening clay with a rolling pin and cutting out objects with blunt-edged instruments or cooky cutters. Several members of the group learned to coordinate their hands well enough to use glazing brushes; others, whose hands were unsteady, were encouraged to drip glaze on the objects to be fired. . . . "The Jolly Mudslingers," who had learned to work together for the benefit of the club project, became a closely knit group.[7]

Similarly, in psychiatric hospitals, arts-and-crafts activities form an extremely important part of the total activity therapy program. At Hill-

    6 *Ibid.*
    7 Janet Pomeroy, *Recreation for the Physically Handicapped* (New York: Macmillan, 1964), p. 263.

side Hospital, in Queens, New York, a leading center for the treatment of mentally ill patients, such crafts as weaving, jewelry making, ceramics, metal working, and carpentry are provided under individual supervision. A close working relationship is maintained between the therapist and psychiatrist to determine which areas of art involvement will be most helpful to each patient. In addition, a specialized form of art therapy uses art as a therapeutic and psychodiagnostic tool. In this process, patients' artistic productions are analyzed to reveal visual expression of their attitudes toward current life situations.

The rationale for the therapeutic use of graphic arts includes six advantages of art therapy over the usual free-association method used in psychotherapy. These may be briefly summarized in the following manner:

1. It is more difficult for the patient to be evasive graphically than verbally. His attitudes toward the object depicted are revealed, intentionally or not, in the manner of his drawing, his application of color, his style, and his focus on detail.

2. Personality traits are more readily and more clearly displayed in creative work than in unchallenging, routine work.

3. Anxiety is much less likely to be aroused during painting than during conversation, because the patient may not be aware of the symbols used by him to the same extent that he is conscious of them in his speech.

4. The need for consistency, objectivity, and rationality is much less obvious in free art work than in speech, because nonverbal symbols, being less frequently employed for social communication, are less standardized.

5. There is greater freedom for the free flow of the patient's imagination in painting than in conversation. During the creative process, the patient works uninterruptedly, without any interference from the therapist.

6. In painting, the patient is involved neuromuscularly and physiologically more than in talking. For literate and highly educated adults this fact indicates that eye-hand-motor coordination seen in graphic imagery might be nearer the unconscious than is the producing of words.[8]

While these advantages apply to the *art therapy* situation, they also suggest some of the value of arts-and-crafts activity as recreation for the mental patient in the institution, or the discharged mental patient in a community-based treatment center or halfway house. It is a further illustration of the use of arts-and-crafts activities to meet the needs of special groups.

8 Zygmunt Piatrowski, statement summarized in: Elizabeth Rosen, *Dance in Psychotherapy* (New York: Teachers College, Columbia University, Bureau of Publication, 1957), pp. 32–33.

Art Centers

A number of municipal or county recreation departments have taken the lead in establishing special buildings where intensive programs of arts and crafts are provided. An excellent example is the Adult Arts and Crafts Center established in 1952, by the St. Petersburg, Florida, Recreation Department. Serving many hundreds of men and women, including large numbers of retired residents of the city, this center has been housed in recent years in the Maritime Base, formerly a Marine training station in Tampa Bay. The scenic surroundings (boats, docks, and colorful waterfront activities) provide interesting subjects for painting, oils, watercolor, and pastel classes. Other activities include sculpture, and such crafts classes as loom weaving, woodworking, basketry, ceramics and pottery, metal art, enamel on copper, leather work, puppets and marionettes, and doll making. The Weavers Guild, consisting of a large group of elderly ladies, takes up a huge room with 40 looms; many of the weavers have reached a professional level of skill. In the ceramics shop, as many as 9,500 pieces have been completed and fired within a single year—indicative of the high level of interest and participation in the St. Petersburg Adult Arts and Crafts Center.

One of the most successful county-sponsored programs of arts and crafts is to be found in Westchester County, New York, where the County Department of Parks, Conservation and Recreation operates the Westchester Workshop. This offers classes in arts and crafts on three levels: a junior workshop, a teen-age workshop, and an adult instruction group. In a recent year, over 2,400 students were served, coming from 42 communities in the county. There were 76 classes in 34 different subjects. Nineteen exhibits were held during the year in a small gallery, with one major week-long exhibit of student work in a main hall that was attended by several thousands of viewers. In addition, the County Department offers field services in arts and crafts to 27 communities, and offers recreational crafts leadership-training courses to many individuals or communities, for use locally, on playgrounds, in camps, or recreation centers. More important than the impressive statistics, however, is the extremely high level of performance of students in the Westchester program. Many individuals of all ages participate year after year in the well-equipped ceramics, sculpture, jewelry making, and metal working shops. They are taught by leading specialists and artists, and many of them go on to build personal reputations as artists and craftsmen themselves.

It is important to recognize that, in some communities, arts and crafts may not be presented as a separate area of activity, but may be linked to the performing arts within a total program of cultural and creative involvement. For example, in Rocky Mount, North Carolina, there is a unique Arts and Crafts Center. This began in 1957 as a community arts center, supported heavily by small, voluntary contributions of interested citizens. A large house was rented, and classes were offered in drawing, painting, ballet, music and art appreciation, taught by qualified instructors from neighboring colleges. Activities also included lectures, exhibits, sidewalk art shows, concerts, ballets, and theater performances.

The public response was outstanding, and, after three years the Rocky Mount Recreation Department head proposed a joint-sponsorship between his agency and the Arts Center. An old railroad "pumping-station" was purchased and renovated, to house the Center's expanded activities. The building, including a massive "steel-barrel" tank, was converted to a three-floor structure with a circular gallery, workshop rooms, an auditorium suitable for film showings, lectures, and the performing arts. Several painting studios and photography facilities were also included in the new Arts Center. In recent years, the city of Rocky Mount, through the Recreation Department, has assumed full financial support of the regular program, with supplemental funds that are gathered by the Center's governing board being used to support new or experimental ventures, as the need arises.

Promotion of Community-Wide Arts Programs

A final function of the municipal or county recreation department is to assist and promote the work of other organizations in the cultural field, through community-wide efforts. To illustrate, the Ottawa, Canada, Department of Recreation and Parks has sponsored, since 1958, a summertime community arts festival. In so doing, it has worked closely with the Ottawa Municipal Art Center, and has promoted a number of exhibits prepared by the Art Institute of Ontario. With the assistance of the Ottawa Community Players, a drama group was formed which has given as many as six different plays during a summer festival, some in both English and French. In the 1960 festival, 42 different events were planned in the areas of music, drama, films, and art. Through the use of a trust fund available to the Musician's Union and provided by the recording industry, a considerable number of musical events, orchestral and jazz concerts and recitals have been offered without charge to the public.

The emphasis in Ottawa has been on presenting the work of local or regional artists, and on gradually raising the artistic standards and tastes of the community at large. Gradually, through these festivals, the Department of Recreation and Parks has developed strong relationships with many cultural groups in the community and surrounding area, and has succeeded in bringing the artist and his public closer to a common level of understanding and appreciation. Such coordinating and promotional efforts in the arts (in addition to the direct sponsorship of recreational arts and crafts, or arts centers) are becoming increasingly a function of today's municipal and county recreation departments.

This chapter has demonstrated a number of ways in which municipal recreation departments may serve the needs of children, youth and adults, as well as special groups, in the area of arts and crafts. Various examples of programing are described, and a number of activities and leadership guides are briefly cited. More detailed descriptions of arts-and-crafts projects and instructional techniques may be found in the handbooks and texts listed in the bibliography.

QUESTIONS FOR DISCUSSION

1. Distinguish between arts and crafts, based on the discussion early in this chapter. What are the special roles of recreational arts and crafts in today's society?
2. React to the statement "Only a gifted few are really talented as artists; there-fore the mass of people should not engage in this form of activity."
3. Outline a program of arts-and-crafts activities suited for participants of a specific age level, within a community or agency recreation center. How would you provide for leadership in this program, and in what way would you at-tempt to build motivation and interest?

Chapter 9

Special Events, Parties, and Outings

In addition to ongoing program activities, almost all recreation departments or agencies feature special events, parties, and outings from time to time. These serve to liven up the program, giving it added sparkle and maintaining interest at a high level. Several types of special events are described in this chapter, under the following headings:

1. *Community-Wide Events and Celebrations.* This refers to the type of large-scale program which is sponsored by a municipal recreation department for the community at large, usually to celebrate a holiday or some other special occasion. Often it involves the cooperative sponsorship of many civic groups. It may be carried out simultaneously in several locations, or in one central spot.

2. *Special Local Program Features.* It is customary to sponsor a number of playdays, tournaments, festivals, or pageants as part of the

summer playground program. They may be given two or three times during the season in each neighborhood, or much more frequently. Examples of such activities include Art Shows, Pet Fairs, Bicycle Rodeos, Fishing Contests, Hobby Shows, Aquatic Meets, Stunt Nights, and many other novel or amusing programs.

3. *Parties.* Most organizations or clubs that meet regularly for social or other purposes plan special parties as a means of keeping morale and attendance high and promoting interesting and enjoyable social recreation. This may be done by Scout groups, 4-H Clubs, Senior Citizens, adult couples' clubs in churches, Parent-Teacher Associations, Hi-Y clubs, and similar groups. The activities presented usually embody a wide range, including dancing, dramatics, games, music, stunts, and refreshments. Usually, they are most enjoyable when the party's program is based on a special theme.

4. *Outings and Trips.* Another attractive form of "one-shot" activity that is becoming more and more popular as part of organized recreation is the sponsorship of trips and outings. Many hospitals plan outings to sports and cultural events for their chronic or long-term patients. Often, summer playground programs sponsor trips to major league baseball games, or day outings to camping sites. Girls clubs in YWCA's frequently plan trips to New York or Washington, as senior projects. Golden Age clubs often plan boat rides or similar excursions.

The purpose of each of these forms of special occasions or events is to provide variety in the regular program. Often, in planning a community-wide celebration, much work must be done in planning the program, preparing skits, tableaux, decorations, or costumes. There is a heightened camaraderie, a sense of anticipation as the event draws near, and then, when it is over, a feeling of accomplishment and satisfaction. Thus, whether it is a fairly casual party or a much more elaborate festival, the special event is an important ingredient in overall recreation program planning. Each type of occasion is analyzed and illustrated in the section that follows.

COMMUNITY-WIDE EVENTS AND CELEBRATIONS

The most common program of this type is the patriotic celebration or holiday festival, sponsored by the municipal recreation department but involving the collaboration of many individuals and groups in the community. Three examples of such celebrations are: Independence Day, United Nations' Day, and Founder's Day (or similar programs based on local tradition and history).

Independence Day. Assisted by such groups as the American Legion, VFW, Elks, Kiwanis, or Rotary Club, the recreation department frequently arranges a day-long or evening program, including any or all of the following kinds of activities: (a) an afternoon program of games and races (awards may be given during the evening ceremonies); (b) an outdoor picnic, if picnic grounds are available; (c) a band concert; (d) a parade by uniformed youth or adult clubs or organizations; (e) patriotic tableaux of historical scenes; the reading of the Declaration of Independence; (f) singing of patriotic anthems, such as "America," "Columbia, The Gem of the Ocean," and "The Star Spangled Banner"; (g) and speeches by local officials. In the evening, it is traditional to have a fireworks display. Overall, the dual purpose of such Fourth of July celebrations is to lessen the risk of accidents from uncontrolled fireworks by providing a large, controlled, and legal display and to promote patriotic understanding and respect.

United Nations' Day. When viewed properly as an affirmation of our desire as a nation to promote the cause of peace and the cooperation of the free, democratic nations of the world, United Nations' Day represents a significant form of community celebration. Often, it will receive the full cooperation of public schools, churches, and many civic organizations. It should include such program features as: (a) speeches by representatives of the United Nations or local government; (b) displays of folk art, folk songs of different nationalities, or folk dance demonstrations; (c) pageants showing how people of many lands originally settled the United States; (d) educational displays of the work of such organizations as UNESCO or the World Health Organization; (e) films showing the overall work of the United Nations in promoting peace, education, and health practices in the underdeveloped nations of the world. Groups of children from different playgrounds, community centers, or schools may participate by presenting songs, dances, or dramatic presentations—all of which may be held together by a unified script and narration.

Founder's Day. Many communities throughout the nation have certain days which they celebrate as being significant to their history—either the date they were first settled, or possibly a tribute to the heroes of a particular battle, or an outstanding citizen of the past. Such annual programs serve to strengthen community spirit, and to give children and youth in particular a sense of history and patriotic obligation. Like the other kinds of programs that were cited, they may include pageants, community singing, band or orchestral concerts, dramatic displays, speeches and similar activities. An excellent example of such a local historical program was sponsored in 1963 by the Recreation Department of the City of Janesville, Wisconsin.[1] This involved groups of boys and girls, representing 16 playgrounds, each of which was responsible for developing a dramatic presentation about an important person from Janesville's past. In addition, another large group took part in a music and dance

[1] Don N. Anderson, "Making History on the Playground," *Recreation,* April, 1964, p. 172.

festival entitled, "Those Who Settled Wisconsin." The drama specialist of the recreation department wrote the script for the overall pageant, but the children themselves did much research, made field trips to historical sites, dug out old picture albums and costumes, built scenery and had a highly creative and educational experience. The program, which was presented at the Lincoln-Tallman Museum, ended with many of the boys and girls becoming members of the "Janesville Playgrounds Chapter of the State Historical Society of Wisconsin."

Other community-wide celebrations may be based on such traditional holidays as Halloween, Christmas, or Thanksgiving. Each of these days suggests a special theme, certain customary kinds of activities, and a unique set of purposes. A Halloween program, for example, usually has the purpose of giving children and youth in the community an organized and entertaining program that absorbs their energies and tends to prevent mischievous pranks and vandalism which might otherwise occur. Thus, the recreation department and the local businessmen's association or Chamber of Commerce may cosponsor a large costume parade, or costume judging contest, a Halloween talent show, or a Halloween store window painting contest. Such a program often tends to be one of the most successful annual events in communities that have established it as a continuing tradition.

A partial list of other traditional holidays which may be observed by the scheduling of community programs includes:

January 1	New Year's Day
January 1, 1863	Negro Emancipation Day
January 24, 1848	Gold Discovered in California
February 2	Groundhog Day
February 12, 1809	Birth of Abraham Lincoln
February 14	St. Valentine's Day
February 22, 1732	Birth of George Washington
February 29	Leap Year Day
March 17	St. Patrick's Day
March 21	First Day of Spring
April 1	All Fool's Day
April 9, 1865	Lee's Surrender to Grant at Appomattox
April 18, 1775	Paul Revere's Ride
April 19, 1775	Patriot's Day (Battle of Lexington and Concord)
April 24, 1564	Birth of William Shakespeare
May 1	May Day
May 21, 1927	Charles A. Lindbergh flew the Atlantic
May 30	Memorial Day (Decoration Day)
Second Sunday of May	Mother's Day
June 14, 1777	Flag Day
June 17, 1775	Battle of Bunker Hill

June 25, 1876	General Custer's Defeat by Sitting Bull
Third Sunday of June	Father's Day
July 1	Dominion Day in Canada
July 4, 1776	Independence Day
July 14	France, Bastille Day
August 11, 1807	Fulton's Steamboat
September 14, 1814	Star Spangled Banner, Written by Francis Scott Key
September 17	Constitution Day
September 23	First Day of Autumn
October 12, 1492	Columbus Day (America Discovered)
October 31	Halloween
November 11, 1918	Armistice Day
Last Thursday of November	Thanksgiving Day
December 17, 1903	Wright Brothers' First Airplane Flight
December 21	First Day of Winter, Shortest Day of Year
December 21	Mayflower Landed at Plymouth Rock
December 25	Christmas

Certain days, such as Arbor Day, vary from state to state. Other holidays of a religious nature may be celebrated in one locality but not in another, depending on whether there is a predominant population group of one religious denomination or ethnic strain.

SPECIAL LOCAL PROGRAM FEATURES

Any or all of the holidays that have been listed may also provide the basis for planning pageants, festivals, or other special events on local playgrounds or in community centers. In addition, there are many other kinds of special events which may be scheduled on a community-wide *or* local basis. In White Plains, New York, for example, the annual report lists the following special events which were sponsored by the Park and Recreation Commission during a given year:

Halloween Festival	Easter Egg Hunt
Christmas Toy Program	Award Nights
Talent Shows	Ping Pong Tournament
Christmas Week Activities	July 4th Track Meet
Outdoor Arts Show	Gymnastic Clinic
Playground Olympics	Playground Leadership Institute
Summer Teen Dances	Fishing Rodeo
Twilight Track Meets	Horseshoe Tournament
Punt, Pass, and Kick Contest	

In White Plains, special events of this type are viewed as the "spice" which makes the year-round programs sparkle. Every effort is made to involve local organizations and large numbers of people in these events, thus stimulating local interest and community pride.

Similarly, in Louisville, Kentucky, the Recreation Department schedules a large number of varied special events on the playground, to be carried on by the local director, with the assistance of his departmental supervisor. These include such ideas as:

For Children Under 12

Bubble Blowing Contest	Toy Show
Doll Show	Doll Buggy Parade
Picnic Events	Spacemen Party
Sandcraft Contest	Rope Jumping Contests
Songfest	Singing Game Festival
Marble Tournament	Swap Day
Pull Toy Parade	Hobby Exhibit
Pet Show	Freckle Contest

For Any Age Group

Treasure Hunt	Scavenger Hunt
Shadow Play	Stunt Night
Fair	Carnival
Wading Pool Carnival	Lantern Parade
Puppet Show	Circus
Family Night	Square Dance
Pie-Eating Contest	Barber Show Quartet Contest
Music Festival	Hobby Show
Mock Track Meet	Newspaper Fashion Show
Spelling Bee	Flower Show
White Elephant Exchange	Hobo Day Picnic
Hat Show	Mother and Daughter Afternoon

In the playground activities manual in Louisville, many of these are described in detail. For example, the "White Elephant Exchange," when conducted as a special program feature on the playground, is handled in this way:

What is one person's discard or reject may be another heart's desire. Ask each person to bring a "white elephant" (object for which he has no use) in a brown paper bag fastened with a rubber band. Place them in a pile, unopened, and, after marching around them, at a given signal everyone picks up a bag. If satisfied with his prize, the player gets out of the circle. Others replace their bags and try again. The last six must keep their bags, as the game ends.

Or—"Family Night":

Those Friendly Fun Nights when grown-ups show up for rest and relaxation, after a hard day's work. Exercise after sitting all day in the office. Entertainment to break the daily routine. Sociability to visit with friends and neighbors. Game areas all freshly marked? Equipment ready to set out? Tables and benches ready? Stage or open area set up for later? Plan games and sports—mix the teams—father-son, parents-children, mother-daughter, sister-brother, family vs. family,

Or—"Pet Show":

Dogs—cats—rabbits—birds—fish—guinea pigs—hamsters—turtles—crickets—etc. Awards may be made in this list of classifications: most talented, biggest, best-looking, best-behaved, most unusual, or add your own.

When the program is an elaborate, formal, or complicated one— as in the case of a large scale play-day, sports competition, or dance or music festival involving many groups—it will require careful planning and organization. Thus, even when it is sponsored by a single playground or center, it is necessary to do the following:

1. Set up committees of children and playground leaders to help plan, organize, publicize, and conduct the special event.

2. Seek out parent volunteers and workers, if special skills are needed, or extra help required.

3. Develop plans which take into account the limitations of the facility, and the age, interest span, and abilities of the children involved.

4. Prepare a tentative schedule of the program, allowing time for transportation (if necessary) and forming of groups, preparation, the event itself, awards, refreshments, cleanup, and orderly dismissal.

5. Necessary materials and equipment should be prepared in advance: lists, score cards, posters, directions, floor markings, loudspeaker system, costumes, stage, properties, or other needed items.

6. If it is a game or contest program, more activities than needed should be planned, so that last minute substitutions can be made if some activities do not "work out," or if there is considerable time available at the end. If it is an entertainment program, with singing, dancing, or dramatic activities, each program number should be timed in separate rehearsals and, if possible, in a dress rehearsal all together, prior to the actual event.

7. Effort should be made to keep the special event from being a completely separate program feature. As much as possible, it should be integrated with, and drawn from, ongoing program activities.

8. Maintain control of participants and audience through careful supervision, ropes marking off areas, simply and clearly stated (and enforced) directions.

9. Finally, after the event, evaluate it both with the participants and with members of the staff, to determine whether or not it met its objectives—and how it might be improved.

Among the committees which may be needed, depending on the nature of the special event, are the following: program planning; publicity; construction; decoration; equipment and facilities; prizes and awards; judge and officials; and hosts and hostesses.

PARTIES

In addition to the kinds of events just described, which are useful for large numbers of children, many recreation organizations or clubs sponsor parties of a social nature for their membership. These usually tend to be groups of teen-agers, adults, or senior citizens. As indicated before, parties of this type are most successful when they are based on an interesting or topical theme. An interesting example of how a YMCA Hi-Y Club of ninth to twelfth graders has enriched and strengthened its social program through a series of imaginative and enjoyable parties may be found in Seattle, Washington. At a local YMCA branch, a small and struggling Hi-Y club, under its new advisor, decided to attempt to make its dances, held three or four times a year, as outstanding as possible. Operating on a low budget, this group employed ingenuity and a talent for making something from nothing, to turn the "Y's" game room into a Hawaiian beach, a spook house, a waterfront (complete with a tramp steamer docked at one end of the room), a lost city, a South Sea island, and, last but not least, a Roman orgy. . . .

> From the viewpoint of chaperones, the spook house was an endurance test. Eerie shrieks, rattling chains, and the constant pounding and groaning of ghosts in torment made the night an ear-splitting, nerve-wracking affair. . . . The chaperones also complained a bit when the lost-city dance took place. Entering the remarkable ruins through a small tunnel on their hands and knees was hard on middle-aged joints and muscles.
>
> The Roman orgy proved an outstanding example of decorating, the effect being a cross between an early catacomb and Pompeii after its highly regrettable demise. Shattered columns lined the walls; a fountain splashed in one corner in a bank of trees and flowers; dry ice was tossed into the lighted, glass punchbowl, creating a pink, frothy ambrosia; and platters of grapes were served for refreshments.
>
> The "Romans" were there in full dress—black togas with gold braid, pink fluorescent capes, purple caps, gold capes, and plenty of white togas and gowns. Every household found its sheet supply unaccountably depleted that week. Boys and girls alike sewed, stitched, dyed, and called upon mothers for assistance.
>
> In accordance with long-standing Y policy, no one was fed to the lions, no Christians were tortured, dancing girls were not in evidence, the wine was missing, and slaves went unwhipped. It might be assumed that such restrictions would make for a pretty dull orgy. Nonetheless, in their own modest fashion, the teen-agers had fun . . . proving it does not take expensive entertainment to insure a good party.[2]

[2] Betty Parks, "Return to Paradise," *Recreation,* September 1964, p. 363.

How were these elaborate decorations developed? Every member of the club pitched in. The boys managed to borrow bamboo for backdrops, fishnets, driftwood, floodlights, beach umbrellas, and logs. In building the fountain for the Roman orgy, they constructed tiered basins from papier-mâché, painted them with leftover blue enamel, placed them in a child's wading pool, and borrowed a small pump to circulate the water. The tramp steamer used in the waterfront party was painted on paper 18 feet long and 8 feet high, and moored against a "dock" made of old hawsers, tree stumps, and packing boxes. A huge fishnet stretched from floor to ceiling and wall to wall, serving as a barrier to inquisitive dancers; the whole was lighted with floods from beneath. . . .

Interestingly, as this Hi-Y Club gained success and reputation through its series of parties, it grew in size and stability. Its members became extremely active as "junior leaders" in the "Y," assisting in the day-camp program, teaching swimming classes, helping with grade-school athletics, and also participating in the "Y" youth and government program.

In carrying through specific party themes, the activities that are carried on should be specially chosen or adapted. Three popular party themes for the mid-winter season are: Patriotic Party (held in February, at the time of Washington's and Lincoln's Birthday), Valentine's Day Party (February 14), and St. Patrick's Day Party (March 17). Examples of suitable games and mixers for each of these parties follow:

Patriotic Party. The theme of patriotism would be carried through by decorations, flags, red-white-and-blue bunting, cherry tree and log cabin decorations, etc. Patriotic music would be played, and games would include:

1. *Cherry Tree Relay.* Players line up in equal teams. With cardboard hatchets, each first player runs up to a "cherry tree" (which may be improvised by placing cranberries or other small canned fruit on a cut sapling). He takes a "cherry" and, holding it on his hatchet, runs back to his team. The action is continued until one team, the winner, is finished.
2. *Scrambled Presidents.* The leader holds up placards on which the names of presidents have been painted, with the letters "scrambled." Thus—NNLIOCL (Lincoln) or EGIDOLOC (Coolidge). The guests are divided into teams, and must either guess the correct name as in a spelling bee, with the first player of each team taking a turn, or with the first player who guesses it ringing a bell and then identifying the name. Each correct answer is a point scored for the player's team.
3. *Log Cabin Building.* Guests divide into small teams. Each team is given a milk bottle and a box of wooden matches. Players take turns in placing the matches, one at a time, on the bottles, trying to build a "log cabin" that is as high as possible. After 10 minutes, a whistle is blown, and the team that has the highest structure wins.
4. *"Honest Abe" Quiz.* In this contest, the guests divide into teams. The leader

asks a series of questions, each of which must be answered by a word containing the syllable that *sounds like* "Abe" (although it need not be spelt this way). Examples:

"What Abe sends a message?"	Cable
"What Abe do you find at the race track?"	Stable
"What Abe is the littlest of all?"	Baby
"What Abe do you find on a tin can?"	Label
"What Abe is a lady's name?"	Mabel

Valentine's Day Party. Here, of course, the theme is romance. Decorations and refreshments include pink streamers, hearts, proverbs about love, red jello or ice cream in heart-shaped molds, pink lemonade, etc. Favorite songs like "Let Me Call You Sweetheart" or other old-time love songs would be played or sung. Games and mixers include:

1. *Matching Partners Mixer.* To take partners for social dancing or other activities each guest is given a red heart with a name on it. The names represent "famous couples." The boy with "Julius Caesar" must find the girl with "Cleopatra"; the boy with "Napoleon" must find "Josephine," etc.
2. *Heart Hunt.* Before guests arrive, hide numbered hearts throughout room or hall where party is to be held—under chairs, behind curtains, in flower pots, etc. There should be at least five hearts for each number, and as many numbers as there will be guests. At a signal, they are asked to hunt for hearts, the object being to see which player can first collect five hearts bearing the same number. To do this, they will also have to circulate around and "swap" hearts with each other. The first player to have five hearts with the same number is the winner. This may also be done by couples.
3. *Famous Proposals.* Guests divide into couples. Each is given the name of a famous historical personage on a slip of paper. One couple then performs; the boy must propose to the girl in the style of *his* character and she must reply in the same vein. Thus, he might propose as "Genghis Khan" or "King Henry the Eighth," and she might reply as "Joan of Arc," or "Florence Nightingale." After the dialogue has gone on for a few minutes, the others try to guess who they are.

Many other games can easily be adapted to the theme of romance, including charades and quizzes.

St. Patrick's Day Party. Here, of course, decorations and food reflect typical Irish customs; the shamrock is widely displayed and the color green appears wherever possible. Irish songs like "McNamara's Band" or "Did Your Mother Come From Ireland?" may be sung. Irish jigs may be played—and if anyone can teach the step, others may enjoy trying it. Games and mixers include:

1. *Shillalegh Duel.* Three boys stand in a circle. Brown paper bags are put on their heads, and they are given shillaleghs (rolled up newspapers, in this case). They are then blindfolded and, at a signal, try to knock the brown paper bags off each other's heads. To help them locate each other, each one

must keep calling out his own name: "Pat," "Mike," and "Kevin." This slap-stick stunt provides informal fun and no one will be hurt.

2. *Irish Potato Race.* Just like a regular potato race, but with popular Irish tunes playing in the background, and with players scooping up potatoes using green cardboard shamrocks, instead of large spoons. This is played as a relay.

3. *Drawing the Pig.* Otherwise known as "Blind Pig." Each player is given a large sheet of drawing paper and green crayon. The lights are turned out (or several players at a time are blindfolded), and while unable to see, they must draw a pig smoking a little clay pipe and trying to scramble over a stile. When everyone has had a chance, the drawings are exhibited, and the one that gets the most applause wins.

4. *"Pat" Who?* Like the "Honest Abe" Quiz, this consists of a contest in which the correct word containing the name "Pat" must be given in reply to each phrase:

"Pat in the army"	Patriotic
"Pat in the nobility"	Patrician
"Pat sewing a tear in his coat"	Patching
"Pat on the police force"	Patrolman

Other ideas may readily be found in the dictionary, to add to these. Other obvious theme ideas for parties include:

Halloween	Harvest Dance
Christmas Party	Gay Nineties Party
Ocean Cruise Party	Hobo Party
Spaceman Party	July Fourth Party

Specific suggestions for refreshments, games, songs, and dances for parties with a folk theme may be found in "Folk Party Fun," by Dorothy Spicer.[3] This includes detailed descriptions of programs for the following themes, among others: "Latin-American Fiesta," "Hawaiian Beach Supper," "Cornhusking Supper," "One World for Peace Banquet," "Chinese Moon Festival," "Swedish Lucia Fest," "African Game Party," "Mexican Piñata Birthday Party," and "Pennsylvania Dutch Party."

An excellent set of guides for party planning has been developed by the Dayton, Ohio, Bureau of Recreation.[4] Briefly summarized, these indicate that four basic tasks need to be done, and a subcommittee of the overall party committee should be formed for each one:

"Build Up." This subcommittee "builds up" anticipation and curiosity about the coming event—through word of mouth, impromptu skits given prior to the actual event, through unusual posters, bulletins and clever invitations, and other forms of publicity.

"Atmosphere." This group sets the stage for the party through costuming and decorations, and gives the first arrivals something specific

[3] Dorothy Spicer, *Folk Party Fun* (New York: Association Press, 1954).
[4] John Mahan, "Party Planning," *Recreation,* September, 1964, p. 360.

to do which puts them at ease and gets them into the "party spirit."
Thus, part of the costuming or decorating job is left undone, and they
may work on it when they arrive.

"*Program.*" This subcommittee's job is to see that "the most people
have the best time possible, and everyone goes home a little better person
for having participated in your party." Specific hints include:

1. Remember the size of the group, the age, and the space you have to work
   in when selecting activities.
2. Balance your program so that it will appeal to a wider group than just those
   people who have enough nerve to request activities they like especially.
3. Balance the leadership so that no one person is too outstanding—help new
   leaders emerge at each session.
4. Plan simple activities early in the evening and more demanding stunts after
   the group has warmed up.
5. Strive to have smooth transitions from one activity to the next, so that time
   is not wasted in taking different formations, teams, partners, etc.
6. Gradually "taper off" the party, ending with a mellow and pleasant feeling,
   after its climax.

"*Refreshments.*" Keep refreshments simple but make sure they fit
into the party theme. Instead of having people "line up" to be served,
try a method of serving that will be unusual; also try variations in chair
arrangments, such as little "conversation circles" that will bring people
together in friendly groups.

Finally, the Dayton party planning guides offer the following suggestions for the direct leadership of activities in social recreation:

1. In teaching, demonstrate more and talk less. Stand where everyone can see
   you. Be a part of and not apart from the group.
2. Your attitude will be contagious, so make it enthusiastic and friendly.
3. Maintain control of the group by: (a) having a hand signal or musical signal
   to get quiet and attention (particularly with younger groups); (b) using
   members of a committee to quiet people in different parts of the room; (c)
   speaking in a slow, controlled voice, and varying the range and tempo of your
   voice for emphasis; (d) being continually alert to how participants are getting
   along; mentally "standing in their shoes."

OUTINGS AND TRIPS

One type of special event which is particularly useful in adding
variety to the recreation program is the scheduling of outings and trips.
This may include simple picnics to nearby wooded areas, or brief excursions to nearby places of interest. It may involve more extended trips,
over a weekend or more, to more distant places; the recreation department of Long Beach, California, sponsors an excursion club for senior
citizens, for example (see page 351). Some industrial recreation depart-

ments have actually developed trip programs to the point of chartering air flights to Europe or the Caribbean for the employees they serve. Travel has become an increasingly important part of the total American recreation picture, and in one form or another, is a useful and adaptable kind of project.

The Parks and Recreation Department in Phoenix, Arizona, plans many excursions for Phoenix residents, young and old. They have developed an "Adventure Trips" handbook, which provides the following rationale for this service:

> Adventure Trips are expeditions of exploration and discovery. They may lead to far places . . . or take place within the community and its outlying areas. Far away places are beyond the reach of most of us, but there is much to explore close at hand that is exciting and fun, as well as leading to discoveries about the community in which we live.
>
> The trips suggested here are adventures of interest to children, youth and adults, including Senior Citizens. Age is no limit to interest . . .
>
> Trips may be taken any time of the year. For children and youth in school, late afternoons, Saturdays and school vacations (summer and winter) are times for planning excursions. For the retired, any time is right.
>
> Values in adventure trips lie in the fun and excitement of going to a new place (or re-visiting a favorite), growth in knowledge and understanding, awareness of the variety and complexity of community enterprises, and the socializing factors in planning and sharing experiences in a group. For young people, adventure trips can have vocational overtones, with glimpses into different kinds of work. Trips can emphasize and stimulate interest in volunteering, through visits to hospitals, Civil Defense, etc.
>
> Emphasis on exploring and discovery, coupled with enthusiastic leadership, make trips "adventures" for participants. There is something in everyone that responds to adventure—to going places, doing something new, finding out.[5]

Adventure Trip Program Plans

There are several ways a trip program can be organized:

1. A single trip (or several) for fun, to visit a place of interest as a highlight or change of pace in program, or to fulfill rank, badge, or honor requirement of a group, such as Boy Scouts, or Camp Fire Girls
2. A series of trips for an Adventure Club with registered membership
3. "Lead-in" or "follow-up" trips for participants in special interest activities to enrich the program, as an art museum trip for members of an arts-and-crafts class, or a trip to a Big League ball team practice for the ball team

---

[5] *Adventure Trips,* Leader's Manual, Phoenix, Arizona, Parks and Recreation Department, 1964.

4. "Know Your Community" trips to major categories of community activity: communication, manufacturing, cultural centers, parks, etc., or to several places in a single category for exploration in depth
5. Trips to point up vocations or opportunities for volunteering
6. Trips for all the family; for boys only; for girls only

Tips for Leaders

Successful adventure trips don't just "happen"; they require thoughtful planning for "before, during, and after."

Before the Trip
1. Let the group help plan and make arrangements as far as possible.
2. Decide on place, date, time, meeting place.
3. Contact place to make reservations, if necessary.
4. Secure volunteer transportation.
5. Secure an adequate number of volunteer adult leaders and teen aides, if appropriate. Explain their responsibilities.
6. Publicize—by word of mouth, posters, press, invitation.
7. Secure parental permission slips for children and youth.
8. Register participants.
9. Discuss the trip: where going, what to look for, how it is related to us.
10. Discuss what to wear, trip manners, what to bring (picnic lunch, entrance fee, pocket money).

During the Trip
1. Keep group together. Having a leader at front and back of group helps.
2. Be alert to safety practices, especially crossing streets and going to and from cars.
3. Good manners will make your group welcome and pave the way for other groups. Thank those who serve your group.

After the Trip
1. Send "thank you" letter to the management of the place visited. Let a participant write the letter.
2. Thank volunteer leaders and aides.
3. Reinforce the experience through group discussion (or talking with individuals) about the trip and its special points of interest.
4. Follow up with some related activity in program, as a pet show or animal drawings after a zoo visit.
5. Plan another trip to the same place or to a related place for experience in depth, if interest warrants.

Among the types of trips scheduled or organized by the Phoenix Parks and Recreation Department are the following: art museums; children's theater; public library; communications centers (newspaper, radio and television stations); government buildings (county hospital, fire department, state capitol building, civil defense office, Air National Guard, U.S. post office); historical museums; manufacturing and processing plants; outdoor and nature science centers (botanical gardens, mineralogical museums, planetarium, bird sanctuary); service centers and transportation centers (railroad terminals and roundhouses, bus terminals and airports).

Picnics. Picnics represent a time-honored and always enjoyable form of outing for families or organized recreation groups. The City Division of Recreation in Louisville, Kentucky, offers a number of "picnic planning pointers":

1. In choosing a location, be sure to have some shade available, a level, open space for games and other activities, good drinking water, a shelter in case of rain, toilet facilities, tables, and a cooking fireplace.
2. Appoint committees or persons for specific duties: such as transportation, equipment, program events, food, etc.
3. Arrange games, contests, and stunts in which everyone can participate on a team or group basis.
4. Be sure to take along a first aid kit.
5. Inexpensive and humorous prizes add to the fun and enjoyment.
6. Direction signs are always helpful, especially near the picnic spot.
7. Be sure to clean up after the picnic; put out cooking fires, dispose of all waste paper, scraps, etc., and leave the picnic area ready for the next user.
8. Novel invitations always add a touch and may be prepared in the form of maps on brown wrapping paper, picnic basket folders, nature materials pasted on card folder, clever rhymes, etc.
9. Provide something to do for the "early birds." Guessing contests (items in a jar . . . identification of nature objects, etc.), puzzles, horseshoes, and beanbag or board games.[6]

To help stimulate and encourage picnics, the City Recreation Division in Louisville offers community groups a planning and picnic equipment lending service without charge. They also provide personnel to conduct picnic programs at a nominal charge, the cost dependent upon the size of the group, the length of the picnic, and the time required. The equipment that they make available to organized and responsible groups includes such sports and game items as: badminton; beanbags; burlap sacks; croquet; dart boards; horseshoes; softballs, bats, bases, and gloves; tug-of-war rope; and volleyballs and volleyball nets.

This chapter has described several different types of special events, celebrations, parties, and outing programs that may be sponsored by organized recreation groups. In addition, examples of programs and guides for successful leadership are included.

[6] *Picnic Booklet,* Leader's Manual, Louisville, Kentucky, Department of Parks and Recreation, n.d.

SUGGESTED QUESTIONS FOR DISCUSSION

1. What are the values of the type of event or special program described in this chapter, for an ongoing recreation program?
2. Select a popular holiday (not one of those described in this chapter) and plan a party program based as imaginatively and fully as possible on it. Show how such elements as refreshments, decorations, program activities, and publicity may all carry out the theme of the holiday.
3. Formulate a set of guides appropriate for: (a) organizing a large-scale festival or playday in a specific community; or (b) planning a trip for a group of scouts or Senior Citizen's club. Do not describe the activity itself; instead, concentrate on stating the guides precisely, in logical order, and fully.

PART *III*

RECREATION PROGRAM DEVELOPMENT
IN VARIED SETTINGS

Chapter *10*

Program Planning Guides

The final section of this text considers the process of recreation program development, both within public, tax-supported recreation departments, and in such other types of agencies as hospitals, armed forces centers, and industrial recreation programs. In this chapter, emphasis is given to formulating a set of guides for recreation service sponsored by a community agency, such as a municipal recreation, or parks and recreation department. In later chapters, the focus is on the needs of major age groupings, the provision of recreation for special groups in the community, and other types of program settings and sponsors.

THE MEANING OF "PROGRAM"

When the word "program" is used with respect to recreation, what does it mean? Traditionally, it has connoted the different activities which are offered. Today, however, it is accepted that the modern recreation department should also provide a number of other kinds of program services. To illustrate:

1. The first and most important service is to plan, organize, and provide leadership for direct program participation in a variety of forms: playground programs, sports and games, arts and crafts, teen-age social programs, Golden Age clubs, trips, nature study, etc.

2. Secondly, the municipal recreation, or parks and recreation department is increasingly involved in the development of facilities for self-directed, or largely self-directed, use by the public. Particularly with the linking of recreation and park functions, many departments today offer playgrounds and playfields, picnic areas, ice rinks, beaches and pools, and similar outdoor recreation facilities. In these, instead of having fairly stable group participation on a given age level, with direct leadership by a qualified professional, which has been the traditional pattern of recreation program service, the recreation department's function is largely to: (a) design, build, and maintain the facility; (b) to provide supervision, maintain health and safety standards, control behavior, clean up, etc.; (c) in some instances provide some instruction or leadership; and (d) to schedule the use of facilities by organized groups, and to establish and charge fees, when this is part of departmental policy and appropriate for the given facility.

3. A third important function of many recreation departments today is to provide assistance to other agencies in the community, or to families or individuals, which does not involve direct activity sponsorship. Examples would include: (a) giving technical help in program planning and development, in the form of consultation; (b) cosponsoring certain program activities with civic groups or organizations; (c) making facilities or in some cases leadership available on a contractual basis to such organizations, in the conduct of their recreation programs; (d) coordinating services with those of other agencies, in the sense of scheduling, making referrals, using roving social workers, in cooperation with Youth Boards, etc.

Each of these types of services contributes to the major goal, which is serving and promoting the total recreational life of the community. Thus, the word "program" must be viewed as being far broader than "activities" alone.

THE BASIS FOR DEVELOPING RECREATION PROGRAMS

Howard Danford has pointed out that in the past many recreation administrators have operated, in effect, "by the seat of their pants," in planning recreation program services. He describes several widely used methods:

The Traditional Approach. Here program is built chiefly on the basis of what has been done in the past—being accepted on the notion that it has been successful and therefore should be continued.

The Current Practice Approach. Some recreation administrators rely heavily on copying what is done, or provided, in other communities, without attempting to determine whether it is successful in those settings, or would be successful, if transplanted.

The Expressed Desires Approach. This method relies on surveys and checklists to have members of the public indicate what they would like to have offered in the program.

The Authoritarian Approach. Here, the administrator or his assistants simply make all decisions with respect to activities and formulate a program which must be provided in a completely uniform fashion throughout a recreation department.[1]

Danford suggests that, while each of these methods may have a certain amount of value, it also has potential flaws. Thus, what is appropriate in one community may not be when transplanted to another. When one relies on the suggestions of participants (who often may be extremely limited in their interests or past recreational experience) to justify program activity choices, diversification may be lacking. Even when these approaches are combined, an important ingredient is lacking. This is a total sense of purpose. If a recreation program is to be most effective, and if it is to justify itself as an important form of public service, it must be carried on within a philosophical framework.

Essentially, this is done by establishing four major steps: *philosophy, principles, policies,* and *procedures.* These four "P's" offer a means of moving from the abstract to the direct and specific. They are illustrated in the following sequence, in which each step is described and then briefly illustrated, using a hypothetical community, Elmtown, as the setting.

1. *Philosophy.* This word implies a broad but interrelated system of thinking, having to do with fundamental beliefs about the nature of man, the role of government in human affairs, and the meaning of recreation and leisure in human experience.

Illustration of Philosophy. In Elmtown, the recreation director might confidently expect that the community would support him in the following views: (a) human life and personality are precious; (b) each person has a right to lead as full and satisfying a life as possible; (c) government has an obligation to assist the individual by creating conditions or providing services that make this possible.

---

[1] Howard G. Danford, *Creative Leadership in Recreation* (Boston: Allyn and Bacon, 1964), pp. 107–109.

2. *Principles.* These represent somewhat more sharply focused and specific statements of belief, or fundamental convictions which provide the basis for more direct action. Taken together, they may comprise a total philosophy, but as viewed here, they represent an intermediate step between philosophy and the establishment of policies.

Illustration of Principle. In Elmtown, the belief is accepted that one important means of enriching total life experience and providing the opportunity for self-discovery is participation in creative and aesthetic experiences. Thus, the recreation department views as one of its responsibilities (based on the philosophy summarized earlier) the development of participant and spectator opportunities in the arts.

3. *Policies.* These might best be described as major operational guides, which define areas of professional or departmental performance. In effect, in Elmtown, they represent a way of translating principles into performance.

Illustration of Policy. Within Elmtown, the recreation department has adopted the policy that classes and courses will be offered for a number of age groups and in different neighborhoods, in such creative and aesthetic activities as music, drama, dance, and arts and crafts. While this will necessarily be based on the degree of community support and interest that can be developed, the effect of the policy is to say that the department commits itself to a strong program effort in this area.

4. *Procedures.* These are program practices—direct administrative actions which result in services and activities coming into being.

Illustration of Procedure. In Elmtown, the recreation superintendent, in consultation with members of his staff and community representatives, decides to: (a) offer classes in creative activities (music, dance, drama, arts and crafts) in several indoor centers, during the late afternoon for children, and during the evening and on weekends for teen-agers and adults; (b) establish certain other special classes or arts sessions at appropriate times for senior citizens, housewives, handicapped children, and other special groups; and (c) form a civic committee to explore other cultural needs in the community, and tentatively plan an arts festival. Specific steps, in terms of scheduling, public relations, assignment of staff and facilities, are then taken to translate these decisions into reality.

Thus, moving through the stages of philosophy, principles, policies, and procedures, the basis for a community recreation program may be established. Based on such an analysis, the following guides for the organization of community recreation have been developed. They reflect the views of leading authorities in the field, as well as outstanding practices in municipal recreation departments today.

GUIDES FOR RECREATION SERVICE TODAY

1. *Recreation programs must be geared to meet important community needs and to promote the values of a democratic society.* By providing constructive, morally sound, and physically healthful leisure activities and opportunities for group involvement, recreation programs make a significant contribution to the communities in which they are carried on. Thus, they must be viewed as part of the social service field (including education, health, family and vocational counseling, law enforcement and similar services).

2. *Recreation programs must be realistically planned to meet the individual and group needs of participants.* The primary focus, both in the selection of activities and in their presentation, must be on satisfying the important personal needs of participants. These include the universal drive toward relating to others, toward recognition, a sense of belonging and being accepted, of expressing oneself, and of achievement. In meeting these needs, the program should place emphasis on those activities and group experiences which are of the highest quality—in the sense of interpersonal experience, creative involvement, and self-fulfillment. At the same time, the program must stress *enjoyment* and must yield pleasure and satisfaction to participants.

3. *Recreation programs should serve all individuals in the community, regardless of age, sex, religion, socioeconomic class, or other factors.* This guide suggests that the community recreation department must serve the *entire* community, without discrimination, and without ignoring or slighting the needs of any group or class. While this position is valid, it is not valid to say that it must serve them all *equally*—as some authorities have held. Realistically, certain age levels (such as children and youth) are much more likely to participate fully and eagerly in the program than those of other ages. It is also true that in many communities, wealthier residents who belong to country clubs, send their children to summer camps, and in many other ways are capable of meeting their recreational needs independently, are less likely to avail themselves of public services than lower socioeconomic groups. Thus, while the recreation department, as a matter of principle, stands ready to serve all groups, and *seeks* to do so, it may find that its most important contribution is in meeting the needs of those who are socially disadvantaged, or who cannot help themselves.

4. *In planning recreation programs, administrators should survey needs and interests, existing services and potential resources, and should enlist the cooperation and assistance of other agencies and individuals in the community.* In providing program services, the recreation depart-

ment should seek to promote recreation generally throughout the community, filling in gaps, providing an overall, coordinated service, and supplementing the offerings of other agencies, public and private. It should not seek to compete with existing programs, but should work *with* them, and where appropriate, assist them in a cooperative effort. In the planning stage, and throughout its existence, the recreation department should avail itself of an advisory council of interested citizens and representatives of other groups.

5. *Recreation program activities should have diversity and balance.* In order to appeal to all age groups, people of both sexes, and a variety of interests, the recreation program must cover a wide range of opportunities. This includes basic offerings in such familiar areas as sports and games, music, dance, drama, arts and crafts, social recreation, nature activities and outdoor recreation, hobbies and club activities. It should also include more specialized or "offbeat" activities, when these can be sufficiently supported. Balance must be achieved between the following extremes: quiet activities and those which are physically demanding; individual and group activities; those which are culturally on a high plane and those which are less "elite" in nature; activities which appeal to one age group, or sex, or social class. No one type of activity must be permitted to dominate the program, nor should any group of potential participants be ignored in selecting program activities.

6. *The recreation program should involve challenge, continuity, and depth. Challenge* implies that the program must provide activities that are new to people, that challenge their skills and heighten their motivation. Whereas it is often desirable to start with *known* and *accepted* activities, new skills and interests should constantly be introduced, thus expanding the recreation horizons of participants. *Continuity* means that the program provides activities that continue leisure skills and interests that were first developed in the schools or youth groups and makes it possible to carry them on as adolescents or adults. It also means that a person may continue with a hobby or recreational interest year after year, experiencing it in greater *depth* and gaining greater rewards and satisfactions. Thus, there is the necessity to offer certain activities both on a "beginner" or elementary level, and also on "intermediate" and "advanced" skill levels.

7. *Recreation program activities should be carefully geared to meet the interests and abilities of the group participating.* To be most successful, activities must be thoughtfully selected, adapted, and presented to insure fullest participation and accomplishment, on the part of whatever group is participating (in terms of age, sex, numbers, background, setting, etc.). The needs and interests of age groupings are described in Chapter 11.

8. *Recreation programs must also be designed to meet the needs of*

*special groups in the community, such as the aged, or the physically or
mentally handicapped.* This may be done by providing special group
activities for such groups, modifying or adapting activities and facilities
when necessary. It may also involve integrating handicapped individuals
into groups of "normal" participants, when this is feasible, *or* giving
assistance to other community agencies that serve the disabled. Large
recreation departments should have specialists in the area of recreation
for the handicapped; others may rely on help from special consultants.

9. *Whenever possible, recreation activities should be meaningfully
related to each other.* Rather than have each activity operate within a
vacuum, it is possible and desirable to achieve unity and integration
within recreation programs. The nature and outdoor program may also
involve experiences in science learnings, arts and crafts, trip scheduling,
and games. Dramatic activities may also involve music, dance, language
arts, and arts and crafts. Thus, each experience involves richer and more
meaningful outcomes than if it were narrowly approached, and the entire
program is strengthened. Often, culminating events such as festivals, fairs,
circuses, displays, exhibitions, and similar programs, offer a means of
bringing together different portions of the recreation program.

10. *The recreation program must be scheduled at appropriate times
to insure maximum participation.* In serving different groups, it is necessary to "block out" activities so they fit into "time slots" that are convenient for participation. Thus, young children may be served during
the day; school-age children during the afternoon or early evening; older
persons during the morning or early afternoon; housewives during the
day; working individuals on weekday evenings or weekends. Similarly,
it is necessary to develop a year-long seasonal schedule, on the basis of
weather, seasonal interests, and the availability of participants at different times, based on vacations and other involvements. The recreation
program *should* have opportunities for each person to participate *when*
he is able to do so.

11. *Recreation programs must make the most efficient and imaginative use of all community resources and facilities.* Whenever possible, the
recreation department should seek to develop its own indoor or outdoor
facilities, over which it has full control; these should be designed and
built according to professional standards in terms of quality and quantity.
The concept of multiple-use facilities should be explored, so that certain
areas may be useful for different activities at different hours of the day
or seasons of the year. When necessary, the facilities of other agencies
(such as schools, park departments, churches, or "Y's") may be obtained
by mutual agreement; often this is a reciprocal relationship. Even such
private or commercial facilities as bowling alleys or similar recreation
centers may sometimes be used on favorable terms. Thus, the entire
resources of the community are involved.

12. *Qualified professional leadership must be used to fill key positions in recreation departments and must carefully supervise and direct other, subprofessional employees.* It is not realistic to say, as some authorities have done, that all positions in community recreation should be filled by qualified professional leaders. In terms of the number of qualified personnel available and the fact that many positions are part-time, seasonal, or at too low a level to attract a well-qualified individual, this is not practicable. However, if the recreation program is to meet its important goals and objectives, those who hold the key positions in administration and supervision must be professionally trained and have adequate high-level experience in this field. They must also carefully guide, supervise, and provide in-service training for part-time personnel, those who are highly specialized in certain skill areas, or those who come in as seasonal employees.

13. *The recreation program should be meaningfully interpreted to the community at large, through effective public relations.* Sound public relations involve more than just "publicity"—i.e., getting announcements and articles in newspapers, or on radio and television. They require also that recreation leaders and administrators appear before civic groups and organizations, and, in effect, fill a responsible role in community life. They suggest that all elements of the community are drawn into *planning* the recreation program, or making suggestions for its improvement. They are carried out through the establishment of advisory councils, neighborhood associations, and other means of reaching the public. They are based on effective brochures, printed announcements, and annual reports. Finally, and most important, they are dependent on having "satisfied users"—that is, the *best* public relations come about through children or adults who have been successfully involved in the program and who praise and promote it.

14. *The recreation program must have adequate financial support.* A crucial factor in the success of any recreation program is adequate financial support for leadership, facilities, materials and equipment, administrative and other overhead expenses. This implies that each administrator must do an effective job of planning his annual budget so that every item is concisely explained, per capita costs of various program activities made clear, ongoing activities separated from capital expenses —and then, that he work aggressively to have it accepted by the city manager or municipal board responsible for allocation of funds. There is an increasing trend today toward charging special fees for the use of facilities, or for enrollment in specific activities. While this provides a means of financial support, and makes it possible for recreation departments to extend their offerings, it should not be the basis for deciding whether or not a new activity or service is to be offered. Nor should it be permitted to exclude large groups of participants from services that

should be available to all. The fundamental principle is that as many activities as possible should be made freely and easily accessible to all. When a fee system means that deprived children cannot enroll in a day camp, enter a swimming pool, attend an arts and crafts class, or visit a children's zoo, then public recreation has lost its meaning and justification.[2]

15. *The recreation program should be thoughtfully and systematically evaluated.* This final guide tends to be a platitude. All recreation administrators accept it, but few carry it out meaningfully. What it suggests is that every recreation department needs to have a clear statement of goals and objectives, and that it then must carefully examine all program activities, experiences and techniques to determine how successfully goals are being met. How is this to be done? Too often, the only basis for determining success has been through counting "attendance." This must be only one of the means of determining outcomes. There needs to be careful supervision, and the planned use of personal observations, periodic written reports or program forms, interviews with personnel and participants, anecdotal records, and staff conferences—in order to determine how effective the program has been. Evaluation may be carried out on a short-term basis, with respect to specific practices or projects. It may also come as a total program analysis at the end of each fiscal year and may involve the use of outsiders (consultants, other professionals, or recreation educators) who carry out a thorough evaluation of program, costs, facilities, staff, and similar areas as a major assignment.

It must be recognized that when a community recreation program is conducted by a particular *type* of agency, it is likely to have a predominant emphasis on one type of programing. Thus, a municipal park department is likely to offer activities that place stress on the outdoors, and are resource-oriented. In such a situation, fewer opportunities and services will be geared to indoor participation of an instructional or social nature than would be the case in a separate recreation department.

Similarly, a school-sponsored community recreation department is likely to offer fewer activities utilizing outdoor facilities and natural resources, but to place greater stress on programs of an instructional nature indoors. These may include the performing arts, indoor sports and games, youth groups and clubs, hobby programs, and other activities designed to promote effective education for leisure. In addition, the school recreation director may also have responsibility for conducting adult education courses as an allied function, or of organizing a student club or intramural program.

Recognizing, then, that each agency may have a specialized focus

[2] For a fuller discussion of this point, see: Lynn S. Rodney, *Administration of Public Recreation* (New York: Ronald, 1964), pp. 270–283.

and area of concern, it is nonetheless necessary to insure that *total* community-wide needs are met, in the manner suggested by the foregoing guides. If this is not done, the operation must be considered less than adequate. Finally, it must be stated that in many large urban centers, it is the practice for two or three separate public agencies to share the responsibility for community recreation service. When this is the case, it is essential that their operations be fully coordinated, and that cooperative program planning eliminate possible gaps or overlapping in service.

OPERATIONAL GUIDES FOR PROGRAM SERVICE— TEEN CENTERS

It is obviously not possible for this text to provide detailed policy statements or guides which would apply to all forms of program service. However, the example of Teen Centers illustrates how specific operational guides may be developed to meet the needs of a particular area of service. The Department of Recreation and Parks in White Plains, New York, has developed the following policy statement and set of operating standards. Approved by the Common Council and Mayor, they are now in effect.

POLICY

> The Department of Recreation and Parks shall be directed to assist local organizations which operate their own teen centers or youth centers (part-time) if and when such assistance is invited. This assistance may be in the form of leadership, loan of equipment, professional advice or other element essential to successful operation. No direct financial assistance is to be provided.

Intent:

The intent here is to assist local organizations in their efforts to meet the social and recreational needs of White Plains teen aged youth without the duplication or competition of separate teen or youth centers established and operated by the city.

Procedure:

Any local agency, club or organization desiring help in establishing or improving a teen center or youth center (part-time) should write to the Department of Recreation and Parks so stating. The following questions must be answered to the satisfaction of the Commissioner of Recreation and Parks:

1. What specific need for active assistance has been clearly established?
2. Why cannot the operating agency or teen center meet this need itself without department help?

3. Does the teen center involved (existing or proposed) meet minimum operating standards as established by the department?

If all three questions are answered to the satisfaction of the Commissioner, the teen center or youth center is eligible for such assistance. The standards referred to in No. 3 above, were compiled by the department staff after considerable study. They are listed below.

OPERATING STANDARDS

1. *Purpose.* The general purpose of the teen center or youth center should be to provide a place and opportunity for wholesome social activity for local boys and girls under proper supervision during leisure-time hours.
2. *Membership.*
    a. Specific ages should be established. It is recommended that 7th and 8th grade youth be regarded as Juniors and 10th grade age and above as Seniors. Arrangements should permit 9th graders to choose either Junior or Senior membership. Juniors and Seniors should not be mixed in social activities.
    b. Center must be opened to all city residents just as other public recreation programs. *mandatory.*
    c. Identity—some form of membership card must be used and a specific registering and recording procedure carried out. *mandatory.*
3. *Fees.* A fee or door donation of some kind should be assessed and a regular financial report made of these monies, available to all members.
4. *Guests.* A maximum of one guest may be permitted to each regular card-holding member at each social session or event. Regular member and guest should *both* sign the guest book before entering. The guest should conform to the age group regulations and all other rules of the center.
5. *Smoking.* For junior age groups, no smoking should be permitted in, or about the center. For senior age groups, a specific smoking area slightly away from the main area should be arranged. General smoking throughout the center should be prohibited. *mandatory.*
6. *Alcoholic Beverages.* No person who appears under the influence of alcohol or person carrying alcoholic beverages should be admitted to the center at any time. *mandatory.*
7. *Dress.* Boys should wear suit coats or sport jackets and neckties. Girls should wear either a dress, or skirt and blouse. Only exceptions would be at a session devoted almost entirely to games or active recreation other than dancing, when dress appropriate to the event should be permitted.
8. *Maximum Numbers.* A center will admit only those maximum numbers established by the Fire Department of the City of White Plains for the particular room or building. *mandatory.*
9. *Building.* In general, the building or location of the center must conform to all Building Department and Public Safety Department regulations for the City of White Plains. *mandatory.*
    In particular:
    a. A first aid kit must be available.

    b. Adequate lighting must be present, particularly around the entrance.

    c. Clean, separate and sanitary toilets must be available for boys and girls.

10. *Schedules.* Only Friday or Saturday and holiday evenings should be considered for this type of program during the school year. For Junior age groups 10:00 P.M. should be considered the latest hour for closing. For the Senior age group 11:30 P.M. should be the latest closing hour. A "dead-line" time should be set after which no new arrivals would be admitted. This "dead-line" time might be at the ½ mark for the entire evening session, and should never be later than 10:00 P.M.

    Illustration. A center open from 8:00 P.M. to 11:00 P.M. would have a 9:30 P.M. "dead-line" time after which no new arrivals would be admitted.

    All time schedules should be strictly adhered to and should be well publicized in advance.

11. *Control.* Adequate chaperonage is essential.

    a. Chaperones. Minimum should be 1 male adult for each 15 teenage boys, 1 female adult for each 15 teenage girls.

    b. Leaders. A minimum of 1 male and 1 female adult qualified for this type of work should be on duty.

    c. Door. A tight door control is necessary. Only one main entrance and exit should be used. All other doors should be under supervision or surveillance. No one should be permitted outside except to leave permanently. No returns should be permitted.

    d. Police. If the affair is very small (50 or less), Police Department should be notified in advance and invited to make occasional visits by patrol cars. If the affair is large (more than 50), an off-duty policeman should be present throughout the affair.

12. *Administration.*

    a. A written constitution or operating guide for the club or center should be prepared democratically and made available to all members.

    b. Officers from among member teenagers should be duly elected and given responsible jobs in the center's operation.

    c. Work committees should be arranged from among member teenagers with adult guidance. (e.g., Program, Finance, Membership, Refreshments, etc.)

13. *Refreshments.* Simple refreshments should be available to teenagers.

14. *Publicity.* Regular newspaper announcements regarding events should be published before and after events. A clear, attractive, well-located bulletin board should be at the center, and should be kept up-to-date with current announcements.

15. *Program.* Each evening session should have structure to it even if this structure is simple and unobtrusive. The leader must arrange for suitable beginning and end to evening affairs, and a definite high point to the evening.

16. *Rules.* All rules and regulations should be posted prominently at the center.

    Staff members of this department will be happy to discuss any or all of these standards with interested youth and adults at any time.

Standards followed by the word *mandatory* are, for obvious reasons, exempt from change. All others may be modified slightly to suit local circumstances.[3]

OTHER ASPECTS OF PROGRAM DEVELOPMENT

Since this is not a text on recreation administration, such technical administrative functions as budget preparation, public relations, facilities planning, and personnel practices will not be discussed here. However, certain administrative considerations which relate closely to program development, *are* presented in the following section. These deal with the selection of activities, the scheduling process, joint sponsorship of activities, and other forms of leadership services which may be offered to the public at large.

The Selection of Activities

Several of the previously listed guides relate to the selection of program activities. They stress the need for having diversity and balance in the program, and of meeting the needs and interests of all groups within the community, when possible. Beyond this, how does a recreation department determine specifically what activities it will offer, and on what basis? Several considerations enter in:

Major categories of activity may be quickly established, such as games and sports, arts and crafts, music, drama, dance, social recreation, nature and outdoor activities, hobby groups, aquatics, and similar groupings. Normally, within the comprehensive community recreation program, each of these would be represented, and this should therefore be a convenient starting point.

Based on past experience, interest inventories, examples of effective programing elsewhere, and records of participation determine which of the above types of activities seems to have the greatest amount of appeal— therefore justifying stress within the program.

Determine which types of participants or potential participants within the community need additional encouragement, or the provision of services that will be especially appealing for them. Thus, if there has been comparatively little involvement of girls and women in the program, this might be a basis for adding certain activities which would be attractive in their eyes.

Determine the degree of organization, the amount of expense, and the nature of leadership and facilities, that would be required to provide certain

[3] Teen Centers and Youth Centers (White Plains, New York: Department of Recreation and Parks, 1963).

activities. Obviously, some activities require careful planning in every detail, highly skilled leadership, and special facilities and expensive equipment or materials—whereas others demand a minimum of such organizational support.

Review recreation program offerings elsewhere within the community, in order to avoid overlapping or duplication of already existing services which are effectively meeting needs.

Attacking the problem from another angle, examine the department's facilities (play lots, playgrounds, playfields, parks, tennis courts, indoor centers, marinas, little theaters, etc.) and determine whether the program which is being tentatively formulated makes the fullest and most resourceful use of these areas. Do the same for the department's leadership. Are special skills and talents of leaders being fully used?

On the basis of each of these factors, the recreation superintendent and his staff would decide which forms of program activities would have the *highest priority* (would be included under any circumstances); which would have a *medium priority* (would be included if sufficient support or interest is evidenced, or scheduled to a lesser degree); and which would have a *low priority* (would in all probability not be included). He would also then decide what type of program involvement an activity would be given. Would it be a regular, continuing activity as part of the after-school or summer playground program? Would it be a weekly class for adults? Would it involve a special six- or eight-week workshop? Would it take the form of social recreation in a week-end canteen for teen-agers? Would it appear as a "one-shot"—that is, a special festival, exhibition, or community celebration?

These questions lead directly to the next concern, that of effective program scheduling.

The Scheduling of Activities

Several factors enter into the process of scheduling activities. One might be the seasonal organization of the program, in which certain activities are provided during a given season, based on climate, customary emphasis on a given activity during certain months of the year, availability of participants at a certain time, or whether the program is in an "indoor" or "outdoor" season.

Another element would have to do with the organizational structure of the department. In Milwaukee, Wisconsin, the Department of Municipal Recreation and Adult Education divides its program into two major categories: *neighborhood programs* and *city-wide programs*. The former includes daily playground activities for children from about five years of age through the mid-teens; children's social centers for youngsters of elementary school age, operating during the afternoons; and evening social centers, termed "Lighted Schoolhouses," serving youth and adult needs. All of these are operated on a neighborhood basis. The city-wide program involves a system of adult centers, offering more specialized or highly advanced skills in the arts, nature activities, adult education and Senior Citizens programs, as well as municipal athletic leagues and sports instruction. Based on this breakdown, a given activity might be provided in several forms, as part of the total community recreation program.

A somewhat different structure is found in Pasadena, California, where the program is offered through a number of major divisions within the Department of Recreation. These include the following: Playgrounds and Centers Division, Boy's and Men's Sports Division, Girl's and Women's Activities Division, Nature and Outing Program, Dance Division, Drama and Music Division, and Senior Citizen's Section. Clearly, the process of scheduling in Pasadena is based on administrative decisions within each of these divisions or sections.

In smaller municipal departments, scheduling program activities is less complex, and is usually based on resolving several factors: (a) the group(s) to be served; (b) the time period in which they are to be served; (c) the available facility; (d) the leadership; and (e) the activities that are to be included.

Usually, the process becomes one of dividing the available time period into "time blocks" during the morning, afternoon, and evening, or day by day over a period of time. Then, on the basis of the availability of participants, the nature of each activity and the amount of stress that is to be given to it, and such other factors as climate or degree of interest, activities are assigned to time blocks.

A good illustration of program planning on a daily basis may be found in the departmental handbook of the Parks and Recreation Department of the city of Phoenix, Arizona. It shows how certain forms of activities may be carried on concurrently or in sequence on a summer playground, and also shows how leaders, aides, or volunteers may be involved. Its system of establishing time blocks does not give the actual hours that are involved; these may be flexibly treated on individual playgrounds.

Program Planning
Basic Daily Summer Program

A good program is based on a sound daily plan that includes time for administrative activities, self-directed activities, leader-directed activities, and assignment of leadership to specific responsibilities. The assignment of leadership and the number of time blocks used for directed activity will depend on the number of leaders on an area.

Chart of Basic Daily Program

A.M. Time Block	Activity	Person Responsible (Name)
	Open area; inspection tour for condition of area, safety of equipment	Leader
	Get equipment out and set up (tetherball, bases, table games, etc.)	Leader, Aide, or Volunteer
	Start self-directed activities for early arrivals or those not involved in sports (table games, 4-square, tetherball, various ladder tournaments)	Aide or Volunteer
	Active team sports or tournaments (while it's cool)	Leader or Aide
	Start or check self-directed activities for those not participating in activities below	Aide, Volunteer, or Leader not involved in next activity
	One or more special-interest group activities involving direct leadership (arts and crafts, music, dance, nature-science, games, or "emphasis of the week")	Leader and/or Aide or Volunteer
Prelunch Lunch Hour	Self-directed activities, conversation, general supervision, meetings, lunch	All
P.M. Time Block Afternoon	Indoor Activities (hot part of day)	Person Responsible
	Start self-directed activities (table tennis, teen canteen, table games)	Leader, Aide, or Volunteer
Two or More Time Blocks	Special-interest group activities involving direct leadership (arts and crafts, music, dance, nature-science, clubs, etc.)	Leader, Aide, or Volunteer
Predinner Dinner Hour	Self-directed activities, meetings, preparation of reports, general supervision, dinner	All
P.M. Time Block Evening	Indoor-Outdoor Activities	Person Responsible
	Start or check self-directed activities	Aide, Volunteer, or Leader
Early Evening	Girls' program slanted toward self-directed activities, some equipment may be reserved for them at this time— table tennis, game courts, etc. Corecreational activities	

Teen Clubs	Leader or Aide
Sports—Leader circulating as much as possible on area with one Leader	Leader
Check on supplies, inspect area, lock up	Leader, Aide

Planning check list:

1. Are program activities based on interests of participants and designed to meet their needs?
2. Are boys, girls, adults served? Major age groups? Varied interests?
3. Is the work load evenly distributed?
4. Do Leader and Aide have some time to think, plan, and prepare?

Planning the Weekly Program

In Phoenix, as in all summer playground or year-round programs, it is necessary to structure activities on the basis of weekly plans, as well as daily schedules. While the daily schedule (as outlined on the preceding page) is maintained each day of the week, certain elements are added to the weekly program.

For example, each week a different sports or games tournament would be conducted. This would be introduced on Monday, and carried on at appropriate times on the following days, with the finals being held on Thursday. Also, an "Emphasis of the Week" (a special program theme, activity, or event) would be introduced on Monday, with sessions devoted to it throughout the week. The culminating event, which might consist of a performance, an exhibit, a display, or other special program, would be held on Friday.

Another special feature of the Monday morning time period in Phoenix is a leadership workshop, or in-service training session for Leaders and/or Aides. This serves to improve their professional performance in general, offers a briefing session for events and activities in the city-wide program, and may also give technical assistance for conducting activities scheduled for the week ahead. On Friday afternoon, special tasks include preparation of the playground bulletin board for the week ahead and the making out of attendance and other reports.

Summer Recreation Program—Coral Gables, Florida

While daily and weekly program planning are essential, they must be carried on within the framework of an overall seasonal plan. Coral Gables, Florida, offers an excellent example of such a plan. The 1964 summer recreation schedule includes a detailed breakdown of activities provided for five age groups: 6 to 8 years old, 9 to 12 years old, teen-agers, adults, and Senior Citizens. In addition, major programs are offered in such specialized areas as: sports (baseball, track, basketball and softball), golf, swimming, tennis, a summer day camp, and an extensive series of special events.

To provide a realistic picture of a diversified summer recreation program, several of these major program offerings are described in detail in the following section.

Special classes for boys and girls of all ages are chiefly held in a large War Memorial Youth Center, built by the citizens of Coral Gables after World War II. In addition, certain activities are held in a nearby park, and general playground programs are offered at seven areas throughout the city. One segment of the special class program follows:

Weekly Schedule of Special Activities in Youth Center for 9- to 12-Year-Old Boys and Girls

Monday

9–10 A.M.	Tennis Clinic
9–12 noon	Rollerskating
10–10:30 A.M.	Scrap Crafts—Boys
10:30–11 A.M	Scrap Crafts—Girls
10:30–12 noon	Art Workshop
11–12 noon	Tumbling
12:30–1 P.M.	Physical Fitness
1:30–2 P.M.	Washboard Band
2–3 P.M.	Drama
3–5 P.M.	Model Building
3–4 P.M.	Sprinkler Party
3:30–4 P.M.	Ballet (Beg.)
4–4:30 P.M.	Folk Dance
4–5 P.M.	Judo
4:30–5 P.M.	History
5–5:30 P.M.	Dog Training
5–6 P.M.	Gymnastics (Beg.)
5–6 P.M.	Skin and Scuba Diving
6–7 P.M.	Gymnastics (Int.)

Tuesday

9–12 noon	Rollerskating
10–10:30 A.M.	Scrap Crafts—Boys
10:30–11 A.M.	Scrap Crafts—Girls
11–12 noon	Apparatus—Boys
11–12 noon	Poodlecraft—Girls
12–12:30 P.M.	Modeling
12:30–1 P.M.	Physical Fitness
1:30–2 P.M.	Folk Songs
2–3 P.M.	Gym Open—Boys

Tuesday (continued)

2:30–3 P.M.	Guitar (Beg.)
2:30–3 P.M.	Shakespeare
3–4 P.M.	Sprinkler Party
4–5 P.M.	Ballroom Dancing
4–4:30 P.M.	Piano (Beg.)
4:30–5 P.M.	Piano (Int.)
4:30–5 P.M.	Nature Study
5–5:30 P.M.	Piano (Adv.)

Wednesday

9–10 A.M.	Tennis Clinic
9–12 noon	Rollerskating
9:30–12 noon	Sewing
10–10:30 A.M.	Scrap Crafts—Boys
10:30–11 A.M.	Scrap Crafts—Girls
11–12 noon	Tumbling
12–12:30 P.M.	Good Manners
12:30–1 P.M.	Physical Fitness
1:30–2 P.M.	Washboard Band
2–3 P.M.	Nickel Movie
3–4 P.M.	Newspaper Club
3–4 P.M.	Sprinkler Party
4–5 P.M.	Modern Dance

Thursday

9–12 noon	Rollerskating
9:30–12 noon	Ceramics
10–10:30 A.M.	Scrap Crafts—Boys
10:30–11 A.M.	Scrap Crafts—Girls
11–12 noon	Tumbling

Thursday (continued)

12:30–1 P.M.	Physical Fitness
1:30–2 P.M.	Folk Songs
2–2:30 P.M.	Tap Dance—Girls
2–3 P.M.	Games—Boys
2:30–3 P.M.	Tap Dance—Boys
3–5 P.M.	Crafts
3–4 P.M.	Sprinkler Party
3:30–4 P.M.	Ballet (Beg.)
4:30–5 P.M.	Weather Science
4–5 P.M.	Ballet (Int.)
5–6 P.M.	Judo

Friday

9–10 A.M.	Tennis Clinic
9–12 noon	Rollerskating

Friday (continued)

9–12 noon	Field Trips
10–11 A.M.	Arts and Crafts
11–12 noon	Tumbling
12:30–1 P.M.	Physical Fitness
1:30–2 P.M.	Folk Songs
2–3 P.M.	Special Event
3–4 P.M.	Sprinkler Party
5–6 P.M.	Skin and Scuba Diving

Saturday

9–10 A.M.	Gymnastics (Beg.)
10–11 A.M.	Gymnastics (Int.)
10–12 noon	Softball—Girls
11–12 noon	Gymnastics (Adv.)

It will be noted that during certain time periods two or more activities are offered concurrently, each one in a different location and with a different teacher. Thus, a choice is offered to youngsters attending the Center. Certain activities are for one sex or the other, and certain ones are for both. Some activities are offered on different skill levels, although the majority are for "all comers." Most activities are offered without charge, although a fee is required for such activities as Ballet, Ceramics, Dog Training, Gymnastics, and Piano. The most frequently cited fee is $5.00 for a series of nine lessons; in other cases the only charge is for materials (arts and crafts), or admission (field trips).

The program of activities offered for 6- to 8-year-olds and for teen-agers is similar in terms of variety and scheduling patterns. The teen-age program, however, places greater stress on more advanced arts and crafts and music instruction; it also includes instruction in such sports as fencing, weight-lifting, and golf; it sponsors a dance band and Bongo playing, and has an Open Teen Room throughout the day and evening, for dancing and social recreation.

City-Wide Sports Program in Coral Gables

Complementing the Youth Center program, and the activities offered on neighborhood playgrounds, the Coral Gables Recreation Department offers the following sports activities extending through the summer season:

Baseball: April–August
Five different leagues (based on age ranges) involving approximately 23 teams,

plus instructional groupings and special clinics, offer baseball for boys from 6 to 17 throughout the season.

Softball: March–August

Girls' softball is held through an Inter-City Athletic Conference for 12- to 16-year-olds. Men's Summer Slow Pitch softball is offered two evenings a week during the summer season.

Track

Track activities are coached by the University of Miami track coach twice a week during June, July, and August.

Basketball

Games are held twice a week during July and August, for adults and boys 17 years old and under.

Other sports activities (involving chiefly the use of city facilities, with some instruction or clinics) are sponsored in such areas as tennis, swimming, and golf.

Summer Schedule of Adult Activities

The summer schedule of adult recreational activities and classes includes the following offerings:

Adult Exercise—5:30–6:15 P.M., Mondays and Wednesdays
Art Workshop—7–10 P.M., Fridays
Ballet Exercise—9–10 A.M., Fridays
Beginning Bridge—7:30–10 P.M., Wednesdays (three other classes in Bridge, including Advanced Beginner, Advanced, and Sociable Duplicate, are offered at different times)
Chess Club—6:30–10 P.M., Mondays, and 12 noon–5 P.M., Saturdays
Contest Writing—10–12 noon, Thursdays
Creative Writing—10–12 noon, Tuesdays
Fencing—8–10 P.M., Tuesdays
Beginning Guitar—9–9:45 P.M., Tuesdays (two other classes in Intermediate and Advanced Intermediate Guitar are scheduled)
Mah Jongg—7–10 P.M., Thursdays
Modern Dance—7–8 P.M., Thursdays
Sculpture—7–10 P.M., Thursdays
Slimnastics—10–11 A.M., Wednesdays and Fridays
Beginning Spanish—1–3 P.M., Mondays and Wednesdays (Advanced Spanish is also offered)
Stretch and Flex—7:30–9 P.M., Mondays
Women's Tennis—9:30–10:30 A.M., Thursdays

The majority of these adult classes stipulate a minimum enrollment of 10 to 20 participants that must sign up, if classes are to be held. They operate on a fee basis, with the specific charge ranging from $20.00 for 10 lessons (Sculpture) to $2.00 for 16 weeks (Beginning Spanish).

Senior Citizens Program

The Coral Gables Recreation Department sponsors an "All States Club" for Senior Citizens. This meets six days a week, during the afternoon and evening, with a minimum annual charge for residents and a higher charge for nonresidents. Activities offered include: shuffleboard, bridge, pinochle, canasta, birthday parties, monthly luncheons, and occasional trips and outings.

Special Events Schedule

From June 6 to August 29, 20 different Special Events are scheduled by the Recreation Department. These include such programs as a city-wide archery tournament, a city tour, a special junior high school dance, a crafts display, gymnastic show, hole-in-one golf contest, bubble-gum blowing contest, junior Mr. and Mrs. Universe contest, summer carnival, clothesline art exhibit, and field day. In addition, special nights are held regularly for the following age or family groupings: Young Adult Night, Senior Citizens Night, Father and Son Night, and Mother and Daughter Night. Activities offered at these sessions include games and sports, cards, dancing, and informal social recreation.

Coral Gables thus offers a helpful illustration of how different age groups are served through a variety of recreation activities, and of how these activities are organized, scheduled, and, in some cases, financed on a fee basis. Butler, in "Introduction to Community Recreation," cites a number of additional examples of recreation program scheduling practices.[4]

JOINT SPONSORSHIP OF ACTIVITIES

An important and growing concept in the public recreation field today is that of joint sponsorship—meaning the cooperation of recreation departments and other community organizations in offering certain programs or activities. A useful example may be found in Oceanside, New York, a school district recreation department. The rationale of joint sponsorship is offered in a pamphlet printed by the department, entitled "Recreation, A Community Partnership":

> . . . the Board of Education Policy which calls for the Recreation Department to work with the organizations of the community has developed a community concept which has not only cut down the operational costs

[4] George D. Butler, *Introduction to Community Recreation* (New York: McGraw-Hill, 1959), pp. 292–295, 313–320, 365.

through the generous donations of time and money made available by community groups and individuals, but has increased the service potential of the program manyfold. Some of the examples of this relationship follow . . . for each of the programs described, the Recreation Department handles distribution of public information materials, staff assignments, indoor facility and/or field scheduling as well as additional items specifically noted.

Stallion Football Program. A ten-week football program accommodating 260 boys from 8 to 13 years of age. The Recreation Department conducts two leadership clinics, provides District field maintenance and sound truck.

Rotary Touch Football Program. The Oceanside Rotary Club provides voluntary leadership and funds for the purchase of trophies for this program which is conducted weekly at three locations, involving over 160 participants.

Theatre Guild. This is a self-sustaining community organization which is assisted by the Recreation Department in the manner described above.

Hallowe'en Celebration. This event includes a window-painting contest and ragamuffin parade. It is co-sponsored by such organizations as school PTA's, Kiwanettes, Veterans of Foreign Wars and Auxiliary, Jewish War Veterans and Auxiliary, Knights of Columbus and Auxiliary, Lions Club, Rotary Club, and Board of Trade. These organizations offered both funds (for awards, trophies, photographs, paints, etc.) and volunteer leadership. The Oceanside Recreation Department is responsible for pre-planning, window assignments, purchasing, use of sound truck, and general organization.

Children's Theatre Series. Sponsored in cooperation with the School PTA Recreation Chairmen, and aided by members of the Kappa Eta Gamma youth organization, this series of five weekend theatre programs during the year has been attended by almost 1,600 boys and girls.[5]

Other events or programs operated on a cosponsorship or mutual assistance basis in Oceanside have included: Lions Basketball Program, Santa Visits (a gift package program at Christmastime), the annual Christmas Show, the Little League Baseball Program, the Pony League Baseball Program, Physical Fitness Day, a Carnival of Champions, a Baton Twirling Tournament, a Doll Show, a Memorial Day Track Meet, an Easter Egg Hunt, a Homebound Service Program, a Summer Concert Series, and a Pet Show.

Clearly, the kinds of "community partnership" relations that are developed through this concept not only make it possible to offer a greater variety of program activities and services. Equally important, they serve to develop favorable community understanding and support of the recreation department's work.

[5] "Recreation, A Community Partnership," Report of the Oceanside, New York, School District Recreation Department, 1964, p. 3.

SPECIAL SERVICES OF RECREATION DEPARTMENTS

As indicated earlier, many recreation departments have as an important function in their program the assistance of other community agencies in forms that go beyond the kind of cosponsorship just described. This may represent the formal assignment of responsibility for a major aspect of program, as in the City and County of Denver, where the Division of Recreation administers a major Extension Service program. This consists both of the direction of a large 4-H Club Program and also an Adult Program in the areas of agriculture, horticulture, and home economics.

Similarly, in White Plains, New York, the Department of Recreation and Parks performs the following kinds of assistance for a nonprofit Community Chest Day Camp for families of working mothers: (a) it prints and distributes applications for the camp; (b) it issues news releases and publicity; (c) it screens and interviews staff applicants; (d) it later trains day camp staff members, along with members of the city playground staff; (e) it offers a six-week, five-day-per-week swimming program for all day campers; (f) it provides periodic supervision; (g) it assists in planning and putting on special programs and events; and (h) it provides the loan and transportation of needed equipment.

In addition, the White Plains Department of Recreation and Parks offers the following kinds of recreational assistance to the general public:

1. Lending of recreation equipment and supplies to individuals and organizations carrying out nonprofit recreational events, including sound truck, movie projector, slide projector, phonograph, tools, sports gear, records, games, and books
2. Providing a picnic kit service, with basic bag and items for an active game program for groups of 10 to 500—a service utilized by dozens of groups in the community
3. Arrangement of meetings in the Recreation building, or in other community centers, for recreational purposes
4. Giving directions and instruction to private groups in the community for setting up and conducting their own events and programs
5. Providing travel directions by telephone and in person for County facilities and programs, as well as those of the YMCA, YWCA, public schools, and other local agencies
6. Appearing before and speaking to, local service clubs, PTA's, political clubs, women's groups, and other organizations on matters relating to recreation and parks, thus promoting interest and understanding in this field

Most community recreation administrators, if they are alert to the possibilities for improving organizational relationships and concerned about promoting all forms of recreational participation, offer similar forms of assistance to community groups.

This chapter has outlined the nature of recreation program service and provided a number of guides for program development. In addition, it offers useful suggestions for the selection and scheduling of activities, with illustrations drawn from a number of cities, and describes forms of cosponsorship and special services rendered to the community at large.

SUGGESTED QUESTIONS FOR DISCUSSION

1. Why does the author suggest that the term "program" should be viewed as broader in meaning than simply referring to a set of activities which are offered? What other forms of service should be offered by municipal recreation departments?
2. Outline the major principles developing program services within a public recreation department. Which of these do you feel are most significant? Which are less important in your judgment?
3. Describe several traditional ways in which recreation administrators have selected program activities for sponsorship in the past. What are the strengths and weaknesses of these approaches?
4. Describe the process of developing a weekly program, during the summer months, in a hypothetical recreation department. How would you select and schedule activities? Develop a chart illustrating the plan you have developed.

Chapter *11*

Recreational Needs and Interests
of Four Age Groups

How does one tailor a recreational program to meet the specific needs and interests of a group of potential participants? Obviously, such factors as their socioeconomic background, numbers, physical condition, previous recreational experience and educational level are all important. But the single most significant basis on which to plan program activities must be recognized as the age of the participants. While it would be possible to divide the total age span of the population into many short periods, basically four major groupings may be identified:

Children: often grouped into such levels as preschool (nursery school or kindergarten age), 6- to 8-year-olds, and 9- to 12-year-olds

Teen-Agers: including younger adolescents, 13- to 15-year-olds, and older adolescents of 16 to 18 or 19

Adults: including young, single adults, younger married couples, and the middle-aged group of individuals in their 40's and 50's

Senior Citizens: usually implying a minimum age of 60 or 65, although in some
   communities it is used to describe those who are retired, and may include
   individuals who are considerably younger.

Each of these four major groups is discussed in the pages that follow, in terms of: (a) identifying the characteristic needs and interests of
each group; (b) presenting a number of important issues or problems
relating to recreational programing for each group; and (c) examples of
effective program development for each group.

Three points must be borne in mind:

First, it is important to recognize that certain age groups are more
capable of meeting their own recreation needs independently than
others, and should be permitted to do so. The major effort of organized
recreation service must be aimed at those targets where it is most
needed.

Second, certain kinds of recreational interests or desired services are
simply not appropriate for sponsorship by a public recreation department or voluntary agency. This may be a matter of expense, ethical
standards, or good taste—but, inevitably, a major portion of recreational
involvement will continue to be supplied by private or commercial
interests.

Third, each age group must be viewed as part of a continuous
developmental process. One cannot view teen-agers, for example, as if
they existed in a sealed-off compartment and had no relation to any
other age group. They *were* children and they will *become* adults. Thus,
in planning programs for younger children, one must think in terms
of the kinds of preparation we are offering them for the teen-age period
that is to follow. In working with Senior Citizens, it is helpful to know
what their recreational involvement was when they were young or
middle-aged adults. Thus, programing for each age group must be
meaningfully related to a total process. If any age group is slighted or
inadequately served, the other groups will inevitably suffer as well.

RECREATIONAL NEEDS AND INTERESTS OF CHILDREN

Obviously, the group that is most heavily served by recreation departments and agencies consists of young children—aged 6 to 12. In
large measure, it is to meet their needs that most municipal recreation
departments have been formed, although today the well-rounded department serves all age groups. Why is this so? What are the recreational
needs and interests of 6- to 12-year-olds?

First, it should be recognized that children in the elementary school
years have a tremendous urge to participate in recreational activities. It
is one of the most compelling drives in their lives, and far more than

casual or trivial enjoyment. For this reason, the distinguished authority on child guidance, Ruth Strang, has written:

> The play life of a child is an index of his social maturity and reveals his personality more clearly than any other activity.[1]

Similarly, the child psychologists, Gesell and Ilg, have written:

> Deeply absorbing play seems to be essential for full mental growth. Children who are capable of such intense play are most likely to give a good account of themselves when they grow up.[2]

Play provides an important laboratory for growing up in the life of children. Through varied recreational experiences, youngsters gain physical growth and development, and are afforded the opportunity for emotional release, creative expression, and healthy socialization. They are offered a fruitful means of learning about their environment, and for exploring their own capabilities and potential. Finally, through childhood recreational involvement, they learn a variety of skills that may serve them as recreational and hobby interests in the years ahead.

Thus, childhood must be seen as the time for diverse and widely ranging recreational interests of all types: physical activities (games, sports, and dance), outdoor and nature pursuits, creative pastimes (arts and crafts, music and drama), individual hobbies and club associations, and many other forms of play.

Essentially, these activities are provided within three types of settings:

The home, or immediate neighborhood. Here the child experiences activity as part of an informal and usually unstructured group, which may include members of his family, school mates, or other youngsters living close by.

Youth organizations or other membership clubs. As part of the total program of such organizations as the Boy or Girl Scouts, the Campfire Girls, church or "Y" groups to which the child or his family may belong, certain recreational activities may be provided.

More formally structured recreation programs. In addition, the child will find a variety of play opportunities provided within the overall program of a community center, settlement house, or organized recreation offered by a municipal recreation department, school, or similar public or voluntary leisure agency.

Developing Pattern of Recreational Involvement

What characteristic patterns of involvement are found, as the child grows older? There are several:

[1] Ruth Strang, *An Introduction to Child Study* (New York: Macmillan, 1951), p. 495.
[2] Arnold Gesell and Frances Ilg, *The Child From Five to Ten* (New York: Harper & Row, 1946), p. 360.

Increasing Social Emphasis. The child of nursery school or kindergarten age tends to engage in solo activities or, at best, to play side by side with other children. Gradually, through the primary and middle elementary grades, children become more socialized in their recreation and involved in small play groups with their peers. By the time they reach the junior high school years, most youngsters are intensely involved in group experiences, and they have learned the social skills so necessary to adult living today.

Narrowing of Interests. Younger children of 6 to 8 tend to have an extremely wide variety of recreational interests; sometimes as many as a hundred different kinds of activities may be experienced within a week. Gradually, their interests narrow and deepen, and by the time they are 11 or 12, most children have identified a much smaller group of activities that interest them deeply, and in which they participate more fully.

Moving Away from Home. As indicated earlier, the young child finds many of his recreational involvements in his home or immediate neighborhood. Gradually, with increasing age and confidence, he moves away from this protected environment, taking part in activities in community centers, on playfields, and other more distant sites. This represents an important phase of his growing independence.

Involvement with Opposite Sex. Obviously, certain activities hold more interest for one sex than another, and thus tend to be "segregated" by sex affiliation. Thus, baseball tends to be a boys' activity, although there are occasional "tomboys" who will be permitted to play on boys' teams. Other activities within the crafts or homemaking area may be identified as girls' activities and enjoyed chiefly by them. Younger children usually are not very aware of sexual identification, and will play very freely with each other, choosing friends and engaging in activities without any real concern about being a boy or girl. During the years ranging roughly from 8 to 12 (this so-called "gang age" may vary according to the community or region), the sexes tend to separate themselves sharply, and to avoid friendly participation with each other. Then, in the early teen years, boys and girls begin to make peace with each other and to enjoy recreational activities, particularly social programs, in mixed groups without the friction of the "gang age."

Accepting the principle that a variety of constructive activities should be offered under capable leadership, and that the needs and interests of children should be met in recreational programs, what distinct problems or issues are found in serving this age group? These relate to two areas: (a) the question of *overprovision* of recreation programs and organized activities; and (b) the tendency to stress and encourage the socialization of preteens with too *much* emphasis on dating, going steady, and similar experiences.

Too much recreation? The charge has frequently been leveled in recent years that children are given too *many* things to do—that their time is heavily overorganized and overstructured. The proponents of this view suggest that not only has school work become more difficult and demanding, but that the average child is so committed to Boy or Girl Scouts, dancing classes, swimming lessons, religious instruction or youth clubs, music lessons, and a host of similar involvements, that he has no time to be himself. They urge that he be given time to relax, to be alone, to be freer, more spontaneous, and less regimented. Often, this view is couched in terms of a nostalgic throwback to what life used to be like for a youngster growing up on a tree-shaded street of big houses in a small town, years ago.

How valid is this criticism of overemphasis on organized recreational programs for children today?

Certainly, there is a measure of truth to it. All children need time to spend freely in activities of their own choice, or just doing nothing. And many children *are* overscheduled, in the kinds of activities described above, as well as in Junior Red Cross, Little League, and many other kinds of organized youth groups. But is this a universal problem? Does every child suffer from it? The evidence would suggest that it is largely an upper class concern. Parents in cities or well-to-do suburbs, who are extremely social themselves and heavily involved in community life, wish to give their children "every advantage." It is in this type of setting that children are signed up for endless rounds of clubs, classes, workshops, and similar commitments—and in which the parents become glorified chauffeurs to the ballet class, the trampoline lesson, etc.

But how about the vast majority of middle or lower socioeconomic class youngsters today? Are they burdened by an excess of recreational involvement and opportunity? This would not appear to be the case. In a study of several thousand children carried on in the mid- and late 1940's, Jersild and Tasch discovered that the leisure hours of a high proportion of youngsters represented a vast "wasteland." Their free time was filled with lack of involvement, with boredom, with aimless frittering away of hours that might have been spent constructively or with a higher level of involvement and interest. There was a pitifully small mention of intellectual, artistic, cultural, or constructive hobbies, and almost no incidence of family encouragement or assistance, with respect to the use of leisure.[3]

What changes have taken place since this study was carried out? While there has been no comparable, large-scale recent investigation, certain figures relating to television watching by children would suggest

[3] Arthur Jersild and Ruth Tasch, *Children's Interests and What They Suggest for Education* (New York: Teachers College, Columbia University, Bureau of Publications, 1949).

that vast amounts of time are being devoted to this form of activity. In a recent study carried on by UNESCO, it was found that American school children spent from 12 to 24 hours a week watching television. The peak hours were found between the ages of 12 and 13, when the average daily dose was found to be 3 hours.[4]

Certainly no one would suggest that watching television is necessarily bad or devoid of value. But how desirable is it as a form of leisure involvement in which many children spend as many hours a week as they do in attending classes? The UNESCO study sees television as a possible contributory cause to delinquent behavior for the child who is already "maladjusted and delinquent-prone." In their words, "it may trigger off an act of delinquency" by "implanting an unreal idea of the importance of violent behavior in solving human problems. . . ."

Another negative aspect of this form of entertainment is that it has been demonstrated that excessive television viewing can actually make a child physically ill, with typical anxiety symptoms, such as chronic fatigue, loss of appetite, headache, and vomiting. In a report of a study carried on at two U.S. Air Force Hospitals serving the families of military personnel, which was later reported to the American Academy of Pediatrics,[5] this "tired-child syndrome" was identified and described in detail.

The basic point is that television must be viewed as a passive, noncreative, uninvolving kind of experience, for the most part, and one which would not saturate the leisure hours of so many children to the extent it now does if attractive and interesting recreational opportunities were readily available. For too many children of elementary school age, they are not.

Always, when this sort of argument is advanced, the question is raised, "How can you prove the value of recreational experiences for children? Why should organized group activity in sports or crafts be any better than television?" It is almost impossible to *prove* that recreational experience helps to achieve desirable social, personal, and psychological outcomes, because recreation is only part of the total life experience of the child. Its effects cannot readily be disassociated from those of other experiences or activities. Nonetheless, certain findings suggest that recreational involvement is positively related to constructive social behavior and effective emotional adjustment, whether or not it is a *cause* of these. Sheldon and Eleanor Glueck, for example, in the most thorough study of delinquent youth ever carried on, found that compared to a matched group of law-abiding youngsters, delinquent boys have far less recreational involvement in clubs, sports, games, or creative activities, fewer memberships in organized or supervised recreation centers, and far less con-

4 *The New York Times,* February 28, 1965, Section E, p. 7.
5 *The New York Times,* October 27, 1964, p. 41.

structive recreational activity in their homes.[6] Other studies relating to mental health suggest a similar positive relationship between recreational and hobby pursuits, and emotional and social adjustment.[7]

The recreation department or agency that wishes to meet the needs of children must think in terms of complementing the offerings of other agencies in the community. Thus, if the school sponsors social clubs, or if the majority of children in a community are affiliated with church youth groups, the recreation department may not need to offer this type of program. If the Little League or similar organizations provide adequate baseball opportunities for boys of a certain age, the public recreation department should identify another area in which its efforts are *needed*. By the same token, its specific role with respect to activity should be based on what else is available for children. Thus, if community facilities are freely available for participation, but if many children do not possess the needed skills, the recreation department may view its primary role as offering instruction in the rudiments of activity. On the other hand, if the schools have already taught skills within a given area effectively, the recreation department may simply provide an opportunity to take part in the activity on a noninstructional basis.

All this will vary from community to community, and according to the needs and interests of the children themselves.

Social Emphasis in the Lives of Preteen Children. Another important issue today, with relation to recreational programs for children, has to do with the tendency to encourage premature dating and other forms of social activity at too early an age. In many communities, particularly in the more socially elite suburbs and metropolitan areas, parents have encouraged their 10-, 11-, and 12-year-old children to date, dress up, go steady, couple off at parties, and, in general, act as if they were in the middle of the adolescent period. A national Parent-Teachers Association publication is quoted as saying that ". . . teachers in many communities across the nation report that some 9-year-olds are beginning to date, and 12-year-olds are going steady." It predicts ". . . it seems likely that sooner or later this general trend will hit most communities." [8] In one middle-class district, it was found that 40 percent of the 10- and 11-year-olds reported they had started to date.

What has caused this trend—and what are its implications?

Clearly, several factors have been involved. One is the relative affluence our society has gained in recent years, in which the teen and subteen group have come to represent major buying groups in the

[6] Sheldon Glueck and Eleanor Glueck, *Delinquents in the Making* (New York: Harper & Row, 1952).

[7] William C. Menninger, M.D., "Recreation and Mental Health," *Recreation*, November, 1948, p. 343.

[8] Grace Hechinger, "Slowing Down the Social Pace," *The New York Times Magazine*, April 14, 1963, p. 99.

economy, and in which expensive outlays for clothing, parties, and other forms of social entertainment for young children are possible. But the more important factor seems to be the desire of many parents to see their children popular and successful—and particularly the concern of many mothers to have their daughters demonstrate their feminine appeal at as early an age as possible. Thus, they encourage them to wear make-up at the age of 8 or 9, to date, go steady, and even engage in "necking" (all with parental approval) at the point when they should be spinning tops and playing marbles.

The results? Children grow up too soon. They are introduced to emotions they do not understand and cannot handle, and, all too soon, they become bored with childish behavior and are ready for the next step. Margaret Mead has characterized this trend by saying, "We are robbing both sexes of mankind's most precious possession—childhood." [9] Grace Hechinger points out another outcome of this sort of emphasis:

> Preteen aping of half-understood adult social customs puts excessive emphasis on fashionable appearance and material possessions, and this discriminates cruelly against those not well endowed by nature or society. Instead of learning how to make friends and develop taste and judgment about people, youngsters concentrate on becoming frantically popular, especially among the top crowd. Those who are left out suffer. But even those who are "in" are so busy with their grooming, clothes, telephoning, and hectic activities that they have little time for school work.[10]

What solutions have been found for this problem? It is usually self-defeating and frustrating for individual families or groups of parents to attempt to "buck" a trend in community practices. Instead, the most constructive approach is to air the problem on a broad scale, as in Charlotte, North Carolina, where the Parents' League initiated discussions with parents, school and church representatives, and community leaders. Finding that minor changes would not work in altering the social atmosphere in which preteens were dating and going steady, they developed an entirely new code in 1956, which is still in effect today. Rather than attempt to separate boy and girl activities entirely, they agreed to keep them under intelligent supervision, to discourage pairing-off activities, and provide a number of recreational and social programs that were appropriate for the age levels involved. For example, some of the points of the code were: (a) dances were not considered to be appropriate for sixth-graders, although informal afternoon parties might be held: (b) during the seventh grade, cultural activities such as Little Theater and symphony orchestra were stressed; ballroom dance instruction was appropriate for this level, although dating was still to be dis-

9 Margaret Mead, quoted in Hechinger, *op. cit.,* p. 99.
10 Hechinger, *op. cit.,* p. 99.

couraged; and (c) on the ninth grade level, dating should be restricted to double dates, and group parties.

Although children did not welcome these rules at the outset, in the long run they accepted and obeyed them, as did the majority of parents in the community.

In many other communities, similar plans have been developed by interested parent groups. The role of the recreation department in this area is to provide the kinds of social activities which are suitable for pre-teens, with an emphasis on informality, group programing, and such activities as square and folk dancing and similar unsophisticated offerings. Particularly when the program for girls has been inadequate (which is the case in many cities and towns) it is necessary to provide more services as a means of minimizing what would otherwise be an excessive interest in boys and dating.

Increasing Variety in Activities. A final aspect of recreation programing for children within recent years has been the addition of special summer workshops in areas such as fine arts, music, dance, and science. While these supplement and enrich the regular program that has been carried on by the school during the year, they are presented informally and provide the opportunity for intensive learning. Often, workshop classes may be held every day of the week, for two or more hours, thus affording depth exploration over a six-, or eight-week period.

RECREATION PROGRAMING FOR TEEN-AGE YOUTH

The adolescent age group in our society presents a difficult problem for the recreation program planner. Yet, it is the teen-age group that is in the greatest need of imaginative and effective organized program service; thus, the effort, when it is successful, is a highly rewarding one.

In many ways, the youngster in his teens represents a puzzling and contradictory creature. He is torn between the uncertainties of childhood and a desire to have the freedom and prerogatives of adulthood, often without being ready to demonstrate the mature responsibility demanded of adults. As one sociologist has pointed out, the identification of teen-agers as a class unto themselves is a peculiarly American phenomenon and of recent vintage. It has come about through the progressive lengthening of school attendance, and the postponement of the entrance of young people into the labor force. As a consequence, an increasing number of older adolescents have achieved many of the outward aspects of adulthood, but are not yet in a position where they can vote, obtain and hold a position, marry, or participate in many of the other privileges of adulthood. Berger has ascribed many of the problems of today's teen-agers to this background:

The well-publicized conflicts and tensions of the teen-age "transitional stage" stem from the combination of an acceleration in the individual's physical and cultural growth with the continued refusal by society to grant to adolescents many of the rights and opportunities of adults: when sexual desires are more powerful than they will ever again be, sexual opportunities are fewest; obedience and submission are asked of adolescents at precisely the time when their strength, energy, and desire for autonomy are ascendant; responsible participation in the major social institutions is denied or discouraged at the moment when their interest in the world has been poignantly awakened.[11]

Berger comments that these tensions, aggravated by a decline in parental control, a confusion or weakening of values generally, and a world in a state of continuing crisis, all add to general adolescent problems.

These problems take many dramatic forms: the growth of juvenile delinquency, sex delinquency and a rise in the number of illegitimate pregnancies, an increasing percentage of early marriages (characterized by a high divorce rate), outcroppings of drug addiction and experimentation on a number of college campuses, many riots in vacation centers around the country where older teen agers gather during Easter Week and on other holidays, and disturbing instances of group vandalism and "thrill" crimes. Since 1940, there has been a steady growth of teen-age crime, not only in the depressed areas of our cities, but often in well-to-do suburban communities and among the middle and upper classes. In one such town, a parents' committee investigated the problem and found:

. . . a high school senior told the survey committee that "probably about 85 percent of the kids drink—mostly boys, but the girls are no slouches." On one occasion, the report said, liquor was found being brought to school by students in a . . . junior high school bus. A teen-age girl reported that "accepting a date to the drive-in movie is like accepting a date for sexual relations." The committee also was informed of an "alarming number of pregnancies in high school each year." [12]

Recognizing that such behavior is by no means characteristic of all teen-agers, and that the majority of young people are law-abiding and have remarkably stable values, considering the nature of the adult world —it is still a fact there is enough disturbed, confused, and lawless behavior among adolescents today to cause great concern to parents, teachers, religious leaders, and law-enforcement officials. Curiously, the problem seems to be a world-wide one. The "raggare" of Sweden (comparable to our motorcycle-riding "Hells Angels"), the "zoot-suited" Russian teen-

11 Bennett M. Berger, "Teen Agers Are an American Invention," *The New York Times Magazine,* June 13, 1965, p. 12.
12 *The New York Times,* May 16, 1963, p. 35.

age hoodlum, the British "Mods" and "Rockers" all present a picture much like our own.

Within this total context, what is the place of organized recreation service?

Recreation is not a cure-all. The notion was accepted years ago that recreation could somehow prevent or eliminate juvenile delinquency, either by keeping young people busy and "off the streets," or by molding character in a positive way. Although each of these represents legitimate goals of organized recreation service, it is generally conceded today that, taken by themselves, such services will not cut delinquency rates to any significant degree. Kahn points out that delinquents sometimes come to recreation centers, use them for their own purposes, and shun the supervised portion of the program. In addition, it is certainly possible to engage in organized sports activities without the experience having any real effect on the fundamental causes of antisocial behavior. Kahn writes:

> None of this, however, suggests a basis for decreasing recreational endeavors. A well-planned community program of recreation is in itself an indispensable part of modern community provision for both the young and old. This remains the case even though the strongly antisocial delinquents tend to be kept out of some recreational centers or are not reached and affected by others. In the context of local community provision for young people, rather than as a specific preventative, recreation remains extremely important. Along with education, vocational choices, and health facilities, it is part of the opportunity picture which affects the way in which young people perceive and react to their social environment. Because they aim to serve all youth, most recreation programs, in fact, claim only that whatever their crime prevention potential, it is a by-product, rather than a primary justification.[13]

This point is reinforced by Berger, in his analysis of the modern teen-ager, who points out that a major factor which tends to reduce adolescent rebelliousness is the community youth center, the chaperoned dance, organized sports, extracurricular clubs, and the junior auxiliaries of business, religious, fraternal, and veterans' organizations—to say nothing of the comprehensive high school itself.

> Potential adolescent rebelliousness is controlled by a complex network of adult-sponsored youth organizations and by their promise of a bright future to those adolescents who can learn to live with and tolerate the temporary frustrations and deprivations of adolescence. . . .[14]

He points out that the effectiveness of these organizational weapons varies according to the location of particular youths in the social struc-

13 Alfred J. Kahn, *Planning Community Services for Children in Trouble* (New York: Columbia, 1963), pp. 64–65.
14 Berger, *op. cit.*, p. 83.

ture. Where adult leadership is poor or community facilities limited (as in urban slums or certain new suburban areas), where young people see opportunity closed to them in the sense of academic advancement and social mobility, high rates of adolescent tension and disorder may be expected.

What then does this say about the design of recreation program services for the teen-ager of today? First, it is necessary to sharply define one's purposes and to analyze the population that is being served—which obviously differs according to the particular neighborhood or community. Essentially, three types of young people are to be served: (a) the large mass of adolescents who are reasonably stable, law-abiding, and positive in their social outlook and behavior; (b) those young people who, because of personal disturbance or family tensions, or because they live in depressed areas where the opportunity and drive toward antisocial behavior is strong, are "on the fence"; and (c) the comparatively small group (although growing steadily) that has already become seriously involved in delinquent behavior—in terms of juvenile crime, drinking, sex misbehavior, or drug-taking.

Within any recreation department, then, that serves a diverse community, there needs to be these three foci:

1. There should be service applicable to the overall group—not viewed in any sense as a social-work or antidelinquency program, but simply as attractive, interesting, and constructive activities presented under capable leadership.

2. There should be service to "marginal" youth—which serves as a desirable *alternative* to antisocial behavior. The point here is that youngsters in this category may go either way, and if there is *not* an offering of enjoyable activities open to them and designed to meet their needs, it is all the *more* likely that they will become involved in delinquent activity.

3. For those youngsters who are confirmed delinquents or who are more seriously disturbed in their personalities and behavior, it is necessary to view recreation as a form of social therapy. This implies, of course, skilled and knowledgeable leadership and a close integration with other forms of community services designed to meet the needs of problem youth.

Let us examine each of these areas in turn.

Service to the Overall Group. First, in planning and developing recreation programs for the broad range of adolescents in our society who are law-abiding and do not represent obvious problems, it is important to recognize the pressure of academic concerns in their lives. In 1900, only 13 percent of United States' children of the ages 14 through 17 were students. The ratio had risen to 73 percent by 1943, and today enrollment is close to 95 percent of the high-school-age population. More than half of the graduates today enter college. In spite of this expanding number who finish high school and go on to college, academic standards have not dropped but have climbed sharply over the past 10 years. The University of Iowa Measurement Research Center reveals that although seven times as many students take the College Entrance Board Examinations today than a decade ago—and the texts are more difficult than they were—scores have maintained their level. This is due in part to the educational innovations of recent years—team teaching, language labs, curriculum reform, advanced placement, and honors courses—and also to great pressure that has been placed upon young people by their parents and teachers.

All this has three implications: (a) that teen-agers have much less free time than their younger brothers and sisters, particularly if they are in the college-bound group; (b) that they are placed under such tension, and such high expectations are held for them, that there is always the possibility of antisocial behavior exploding as a reaction, when they are in a position where they are relatively free and uncontrolled; and (c) that it is necessary to be sharply aware of possible problems existing among individuals who *appear* to be operating effectively on the surface. Often such disturbance may be manifested in leisure behavior, in the form of antisocial actions and sometimes in the *lack* of constructive social activities or involvement. It is worth noting that in a study of suicides among New Jersey public school children from 1960 to 1963, the following conclusion was reached: "More serious than the dearth of quality remedial instruction was the lack of participation of these children in extracurricular activities." [15]

Several guides for presenting social and recreational programs for teen-age youth within the "normal" range of behavior and adjustment follow:

1. Social activities must provide an element of freedom, as a counterpart to the rigid pressures and supervision that is given adolescents in their academic experience. If a dance, party, or other event is obviously and blatantly chaperoned, and if it is *overorganized,* many teen-agers will simply not wish to attend. The popularity of hangouts in the community where they can escape adult supervision and control is an evidence of this need. At the same time, teen canteens and youth centers which provide social recreation for adolescents within an overall neighborhood or school district *must* have a degree of adult guidance and must operate under very clear-cut rules, or they will defeat their own purpose. Guides for the conduct of youth centers may be found in Chapter 10.

---

[15] James Jan-Tausch, "Suicide of Children 1960–63, New Jersey Public School Students," (Trenton, New Jersey: State Department of Education, 1963), p. 3.

2. Whenever possible, teen-agers should be meaningfully involved in the planning and organization of their own programs. This insures that they will see the program as "their own," and makes it much more likely that it will effectively meet their needs and interests. As an example, junior high school-age boys and girls have been heavily involved in the advisory council of the Tacoma, Washington, Teen Time program which offers social programs on Friday evenings in several junior high schools for as many as 3,500 on an evening. The most successful youth programs are planned and run in large measure by teen-agers themselves, under adult guidance. Wherever possible, they should formulate and enforce their own rules for conduct themselves, rather than have these arbitrarily imposed upon them.

3. Recreational involvement of adolescents need not be restricted to the more obvious forms of dances, sports, trips and similar programs. Many young people are highly idealistic, and wish to be involved in programs where they can give service, where spiritual ideals can be recognized and expressed, and where they may become a meaningful part of society. Thus, in Boston, Massachusetts, the United Community Services has involved several thousand boys and girls over a three-year period in volunteer projects in 73 Greater Boston health, social service, and youth agencies. For some, the purpose was to explore vocational possibilities in the field of social service; for others the desire was to counteract the impression that all youth are irresponsible. But, over-all, the program was a clear demonstration that teen-agers *can* assume civic responsibility and often wish to do so, as leisure projects.

Service for "Marginal Youth." It has been commented that all of the antisocial teen-age behavior of today does not come from the socially and economically depressed youngster in the urban slum. Indeed, there appears to be an increasing number of adolescents brought up in wealthy surroundings who, for one reason or another (disinterested parents, excessively permissive adult attitudes, an "excess" of advantages, or a confusion in values), may represent just as much of a problem. For these teen-agers, as well as for the youngster in the depressed urban environment who is marginal in the sense that he has not committed himself to a consistent pattern of antisocial behavior but has both the temptation and opportunity to do so, recreation must be viewed in a special light.

First, it *must* provide an alternative to delinquent activities. For a youngster to turn to glue-sniffing, theft, or vandalism simply because there is nothing else for him to do that is interesting or exciting, and because no one has taken an interest in him, is truly criminal. It is criminal on the part of the adults who permitted this situation to exist.

Second, the alternative that is provided *must* appeal to the same drives in the teen-agers that might otherwise be diverted to antisocial outlets. This implies that the activity must be prestigeful and "right" for a teen-ager. It should appeal to existing interests, and should, if possible, have the element of risk, thrill, glamor, or other appeal that will make it attractive to potential participants. Often the very activity that, among suburban youth, may represent an antisocial outlet, may be shaped to take a constructive form. The involvement of youngsters in motorcycling or hot-rodding, which often has tragic outcomes, may be shifted to an automobile club in which boys learn mechanics, a code of proper road behavior, carry on special programs and events, and actually become responsible and helpful drivers rather than dangerous menaces. Surfing, in a number of California towns, has captured the interest of many young people. It has been possible to form surfing clubs, under the auspices of recreation departments, that served as an antidote to the kinds of antisocial behavior on the beaches that plagued some communities. Providing community recognition and prestige, organizing the program, and establishing worthwhile goals and status, have been outcomes of such efforts. In some communities, the potential interest of youth in mechanics, aviation and the Space Age has been capitalized on, to develop activities and clubs with great appeal. A "Technical Recreation Club," in which teen-agers have explored mechanics, aviation, space developments, electronics and chemistry, is typical of such ventures.

Overall, what sorts of activities may be provided to meet the needs of teen-agers within a fairly normal range of behavior? An intensive program is provided by the Culver City, California, Recreation Department, based both on the expressed interests and needs of young people (analyzed in student-sponsored surveys) and on the evaluation of existing programs over a period of time. The following clubs are sponsored, within various settings in the community:

School Organizations

Junior High School
Astronomy Club
Girls' Athletic Club
National Honor Societies
Chalk Dusters (future teachers' club)
Stamp Club
Future Nurses Club

Senior High School
Science Club
Spanish Club
Latin Club
Key Club (international high school service organization sponsored by Kiwanis)
Chess Club
Future Medical Leaders
Crystal Crackers (for boys interested in amateur radio operation)

American Field Service Commission (geared to international student exchange
    and communication)
Masquers (drama club)
Quill and Scroll Club (for those interested in journalism)
Girls' League (plans social events)
Boys' League (sponsors sports tournaments and special events)
Tennis Club
Cadets (assists in flag-raising ceremonies and keeping order at football games)
Girls' Athletic Association

Church Organizations

Eight churches and temples in Culver City, representing the major religious
    denominations, sponsor youth clubs providing religious education, and
    athletic, social, and cultural programs.

Boy Scouts and Girl Scouts

Many different troops, on the various levels of scouting, are organized through-
    out the city.

Other Clubs

Several other youth organizations are sponsored in Culver City, some assisted
    by the Recreation Department and others by adult organizations. These
    include:
El Marino Teen Agers Club (a social group which meets weekly and sponsors
    monthly dances)
Glocus Skin Diving Club
Coin Club (affiliated with an adult Coin Club)
Rock and Mineral Club (affiliated with an adult club)

Services for "Problem" Youth. In working with teen-agers who live
in low socioeconomic areas with a high delinquency rate, or who have
already displayed evidence of serious antisocial behavior, it is necessary to view recreation specifically as a form of social therapy. It must
be recognized as part of a total team approach including intensified and
adapted educational services, vocational training and assistance, group
work programs, family counseling and workshops, improved housing,
an adequate referral system, and similar efforts. A number of public,
voluntary, and religious agencies share in this task.

Recreation workers who provide services for delinquent-prone youth
need specialized training in understanding group processes. They must
recognize the social causes of youth crime, and must have the ability to
handle aggressive behavior and function effectively in potentially dangerous situations. They should have training similar to that of social
workers; indeed, they must consult frequently and work closely with
police, social workers, and neighborhood organizations, if they are to be
successful.

In a number of cases, recreation departments have set up special programs designed to meet the needs of delinquent youth. For example, Providence, Rhode Island, has long provided activities and staff services for youth in the so-called "twilight zone" of delinquency. In 1945, this city established a Junior Police Camp serving youngsters in the poorer sections of the city, many of whom had already been in the courts and were on probation. Since 1954, there has been a field-worker system, in which recreation leaders work in the evenings in areas where indices of juvenile delinquency are highest.

Supported by a federal grant in recent years, the Providence Recreation Department has expanded its program for delinquent youth, concentrating on both education and prevention. Working for the Recreation Department, a specialist in this area has organized many activities, trips, special projects, and consultation services. A close working relationship is maintained with the Rhode Island Family Court and the South Providence Youth Board. Concurrent with this program, the delinquency rate (court adjudications) in the area served has dropped from 21.9 to 13.1 per thousand children.[16] Recognizing the weakness of statistics (which may reflect shifting patterns of law enforcement), this is still an impressive picture.

Many public and voluntary recreation agencies not only make no special effort to serve delinquent-prone youth but actually bar them from their program after minor incidents of misbehavior. Often their position is, "We are not able to work effectively with these aggressive, undisciplined teen-agers. In fact, they disrupt our normal program. Let some other agency serve them." But the question must be asked, "What other agency can—and will?" Recognizing, then, that many "problem" youth are incapable of adjusting to the demands and social structure of the organized recreation program, the recreation department that wishes to work effectively in this area must move *outside* of its own facility. As in Providence, or Washington, D.C., the roving leader system must be used. This individual makes contact with youth gangs or "problem" individuals. He gains their confidence and gradually attempts to reshape their social values, personal goals, and forms of leisure activity. Ultimately, it is his purpose to have them shift their emphasis from antisocial behavior to constructive forms of activity, and to move into organized programs and recreation centers.

RECREATIONAL NEEDS AND INTERESTS OF ADULTS

Clearly, this age range (extending from the age of approximately 20, through the 60's) represents an extremely broad span. It covers many important and distinct phases of life, including young adulthood (single

16 Evelyn D. Baldoni, "Providence Takes a Hand," *Recreation*, October, 1963, p. 364.

individuals in college or the community), younger married couples, parents' groups, middle-age, and finally those approaching retirement. Obviously, the needs and interests of each group may vary widely.

Nonetheless, it is possible to characterize this entire age range by stating that adults, as a group, tend to be provided considerably *less* service by community recreation departments than other age groups. Why is this so? Several factors are involved:

1. Adults are in a busy and productive period of life. Men tend to be involved in the business or professional world and in community affairs; women are heavily wrapped up in raising their families, and in many cases working as well. In spite of the overall growth of leisure, young married couples, for example, tend to have a minimum of real free time when compared to other age groups.

2. Adults may be heavily involved in community organizations, such as churches, clubs, neighborhood associations, lodges, union groups, or service organizations. Often the attraction of these membership groups is that they consist of people of *similar* social class, interests, age levels, professions, or religious affiliation. Through them, adults develop their own circles of friends and leisure involvements, and are less dependent on community programs for recreational participation than they would otherwise be.

3. As a group, adults are often capable of meeting their own recreational needs independently. They tend to be physically capable, mobile, and financially able to purchase equipment, drive to recreation attractions, or in other ways satisfy their leisure interests. Thus, again, they are not as dependent on organized recreation programs as children would be, for example.

A final reason why adults do not tend to be widely involved in many community recreation programs is that their special needs and interests are not recognized and imaginatively met. This is unfortunate, because adults *do* have certain recreational needs that can best be met by public recreation departments, particularly during the winter months when other forms of leisure activity are not readily available. In addition, it is extremely important that adults be involved as fully as possible in organized community recreation programs, if they are to understand and actively support such municipal services.

What are the special needs of adult groups, and how can they be met? Perhaps this can best be answered by describing each age level or special group in turn.

Recreation during the College Years. College students, ranging from the late teen years through the early or middle 20's (in the case of graduate students) must basically be recognized as young adults. Essentially, for them, much recreation should center about the institution they are attending, in the form of college union programs, social clubs, athletic events, fraternity and sorority dances and parties, intramural participation, and membership in many college organizations.

Although academic standards, both in terms of admission and course expectations, have risen steadily during the 1950's and 1960's, it is still a fact that the majority of American college students value very highly the social aspects of college life. This was illustrated in a 1964 report of the Educational Testing Service, which surveyed 13,000 freshmen entering college and over 6,000 students who had spent a year or more in college. Over 50 percent of those who replied to the survey indicated that their major interest in college was social life, extracurricular activities, athletics, forming new friendships, and carrying on "college traditions." Vocational goals were given top priority by 26.5 percent of those replying, and the "pursuit of ideas and the cultivation of the intellect" came third, with only 18.5 percent viewing such activities as the most important.[17]

Without attempting to judge the merit of this position, it suggests clearly that colleges and universities should view much more seriously their role in providing their students with constructive and interesting programs of social activities and recreational involvement. In too many colleges, this function is carried on in a scattered, disorganized way by a number of advisors or college union directors. All too often, the real social and recreational life of the college is a subterranean one, carried on by many students in bars or taverns in the nearby community, or in motels along the state highway. Increasingly, college administrators have come to realize that such problems as sex experimentation, drinking and even drug addiction, are affecting significant numbers of students. Often the traditional values no longer pertain, or are not accepted by students, who openly express their resentment of adult strictures.

Within this framework, it is necessary for colleges to come to grips with the question of their role *"in loco parentis,"* and to provide adequate counseling and guidance services, as well as to involve responsible students in the development and enforcement of behavior standards and practices. Closely complementing this process must be the provision of meaningful and enjoyable campus activities, to serve as attractive alternatives to less desirable leisure outlets for students.

Services for Young Adults. Within the community at large, the young, unmarried adult represents another group which often makes minimal use of organized recreation services. Particularly in large cities where so many of the available recreation opportunities are commercially sponsored and are lacking in standards or moral value, it is essential that these individuals in their early or middle 20's be more adequately served.

17 "Freshmen Rank Social Life First," *The New York Times,* October 29, 1964.

To a degree, this can be done through church activities, or programs sponsored by industrial concerns. In addition, however, the public recreation department should provide a comprehensive offering of clubs, social activities, sports instruction and participation sessions, outings and trips that are designed to meet the needs of young adults. Since so many of them are at the point where they wish and need to be part of a congenial social group, and where they can meet members of the opposite sex in a friendly atmosphere, this type of program should be emphasized.

Often, the community recreation department is able to set up special clubs for single individuals in which they take the major responsibility for developing membership, carrying out financial arrangements, and planning activities. This may be done on several age levels. For example, the Denver, Colorado, Recreation Department offers a Stardusters Club for adults aged 25 to 40, and a Meridian Club for those between 35 and 50. Both groups provide dance classes, socials, picnics, dinner parties, trips, and other events. In a number of California cities, clubs with names like "Bachelors and Bachelorettes" are sponsored by recreation departments. Too often, however, the young adult in his early 20's is almost completely slighted.

Recreation and Adult Education. One form of adult recreational activity which serves all age levels in this group is activity of an instructional type. In many communities, a wide variety of classes are offered, usually on a "semester" basis with 10 or 15 weekly sessions scheduled on a fee basis.

Frequently, these programs are described as "adult education" and are provided by public school systems. Unfortunately, when this is done, an arbitrary distinction is made between such "classes" and other activities that are recognized as recreational. In 1951, for example, a committee of the California Senate criticized the public schools of that state for including activities in their adult education program that the committee considered to be recreation. In 1953, a United States Office of Education bulletin defined adult education as including organized educational programs other than regular elementary, secondary, or college programs, which are directed toward recognizable learning goals. Specifically excluded, however, were activities that were primarily social or recreational in nature.

In certain states, there is the practice of providing financial subsidies to activities or courses that are categorized as educational, but not to those which are described as recreational. Thus, in the New York City school system, evening classes for adults that include the following titles are considered to be adult education and are supported by tax funds: "Athletics and Physical Fitness," "Oil Painting," "Folk Guitar," "Opera Workshop," "Choral Group," and "Food Decoration." However, in the same system, other courses that are regarded as Adult Recreation must be self-supporting and do not receive a subsidy. These include: "Contract Bridge," "Golf," "Social Dancing," and "Tennis."

If one accepts the view of Malcolm S. Knowles, formerly administrative coordinator for the Adult Education Association in Chicago, Illinois, that adult education is ". . . any activity engaged in voluntarily by mature men and women that produces changes in their knowledge, understanding, skills, attitudes, interests, or appreciations," [18] one must ask whether there is a realistic difference between adult education and adult recreation.

True, adult education has certain purposes or objectives that are not recreational as such. These may have to do with: (a) citizenship education; (b) teaching fundamental educational skills; (c) assisting in the development of vocational skills; (d) promoting community organization; or (e) improving family living. Recognizing this, Knowles suggests that, if a distinction is to be made, the primary test should be based on "outcome." If the primary outcome of an activity is enjoyment and satisfaction, the activity should be considered recreational, in his view. On the other hand, if the outcome is learning (in terms of knowledge, skills, understanding, attitudes, or values), the activity should be called educational.

But even this avoids the point that many recreational activities *do* contribute to family living, community development, and the important educational goals cited by Knowles. Similarly, many so-called educational activities may have important recreational outcomes, in terms of enjoyment and satisfaction.

Thus, the distinction *is* often an arbitrary one. This may be illustrated by a report of the Division of Adult Education of the Department of Education of the State of New Jersey, which showed the top 15 courses (in terms of enrollment) during a recent year to include the following: "Dancing," "Bridge," "Sewing," "Golf," "Oil Painting," "Art," and "Small Boat Handling." Within the next 15 most popular courses were "Piano," "Ceramics," "Dog Obedience," "Sketching," and similar leisure activities.

Obviously, certain adult education courses may cater to more intellectually or vocationally oriented interests. Thus, at the Taft Youth and Adult Center in New York City, courses are offered in subjects such as "Negro History and Its African Background," "Theater and Film Script Writing," "Elementary Algebra," "Technique of Dramatic Speech," "Magazine Article Writing," "Briefhand," "Human Physiology," "Television Repair Workshop," "Office Machines," "Radio Repair," and "Typing."

The basic point is that many significant needs of adults are met by both adult education and adult recreation programs, but that when tax

[18] Malcolm S. Knowles, "Recreation and Adult Education," *Recreation,* February, 1955, p. 52.

support is specifically denied courses which are labeled recreational, it tends to inhibit the offering of this type of activity and to assign to it a lesser status. Fortunately, many states do not operate on this basis, and in a number of major cities both adult recreation and adult education are offered by the same department with no distinction being made between the two. Boston and Milwaukee are examples of such communities.

Overall, it must be recognized that adult recreation does not represent only trivial or superficial pursuits, but that it may also involve an intensive and continuing learning experience. Often new areas of skill and knowledge may be opened up by such instructional experiences, and hobbies adopted that may continue for the remainder of the participant's life.

Recreation in Family Life. One of the most important needs in community recreation programs for adults is for more programs of family recreation. As indicated earlier, one of the significant underlying causes of delinquency appears to be a lack of family cohesion and of affectionate involvement between parents and children. The first United Nations' Congress on Prevention of Crime declared:

> Delinquency appears to have had an intimate relationship with the social and cultural changes that have operated through the family. . . . It is vital that prevention efforts be designed to produce closer family ties, to achieve greater affection, emotional security and control through the family. The child needs a sense of belonging.[19]

Clearly, effective programs of family-centered recreation build ties of unity, understanding, and warmth. Thus, all recreation agencies—including municipal departments, industrial concerns, religious programs, and the armed forces—should sponsor family programs wherever possible. How can the community recreation department strengthen such efforts? It should sponsor a number of activities that appeal to the entire family, such as sports, family evenings, workshops, picnics, theater or music programs, cultural events, and hobby centers. It should make sure that facilities are designed to be usable by all age levels and, in setting up the schedule for such facilities as swimming pools or skating rinks, should designate certain appropriate periods as "family sessions." When trip programs or outings are planned, they may be organized and promoted on a family basis. The ingenious recreation director will find many opportunities to promote the family's full participation.

Interestingly, a number of colleges or universities have sponsored family recreation programs for their faculty members or married graduate students. The University of Southern California, for example, offers summer workshops or courses in which appropriate activities are scheduled

19 Charles Bucher, "Family Recreation—Foe of Juvenile Delinquency," *Recreation,* February, 1957, p. 46.

for all age groups, so the entire family may attend and participate. The University of Illinois has broadened the use of its recreational facilities to encourage family participation. Boston University sponsors family camping programs at its outdoor camp, as do many other colleges. Clearly, this trend should be encouraged.

Increasingly, the need of rural families for diversified recreation programs has become recognized. While we tend to have a picture of rural families as living happy, stable, productive lives, with strong bonds of affection and family unity, this is not always the case. Often farm life is lonely, characterized by drudgery, and lacking in the amenities of a full and interesting life. One of the important needs is for more recreational opportunity for all members of the farm family. The federal government, through its agricultural extension services and the programs of 4-H Clubs, has focused on recreation as an important aspect of rural living. In addition, a series of National Rural Family Recreation Seminars have been held at the Thor Center for Better Farm Living in Huntley, Illinois, to explore this need. Since local communities tend to be small and isolated, the most effective functioning often is carried on on the county level. Through churches and farmers' organizations, program possibilities may also be developed successfully. In addition, the concern of rural families with recreation may include the development of land and water areas to meet growing outdoor recreation needs. Thus, the farm family may have a direct economic benefit derived from recreation.

Adult Recreation as Preparation for Retirement. An important aspect of adult recreation is that it includes the period of middle age in which patterns of leisure living may be established that will prepare individuals for retirement. Obviously, an important concern in the period of later middle age has to do with the degree to which physical activities formerly enjoyed may still be appropriate. Dr. Paul Dudley White, among other eminent cardiologists, stresses the wisdom of maintaining a program of moderate exercise, to accomplish the following major benefits: (a) maintaining muscle tone throughout the body, including the heart; (b) providing relaxation by relieving nervous tension and anxiety; (c) aiding digestion; (d) helping to control obesity; and (e) improving lung function.

Such activities as formal calisthenics, deep breathing periods at intervals, bicycling and walking, gardening, adapted sports, fishing, swimming, golf and tennis, are all useful in this regard. Too often, however, our youth-centered culture fails to provide encouragement, leadership, or opportunity for older adults to engage in appropriate physical activities—except in those communities that are viewed specifically as "retirement" centers.

In addition to physical recreation, the older middle aged person should be engaging in a range of social, creative, aesthetic, hobby, and service activities. All of these represent an intelligent transition to the period of retirement in which the amount of leisure time available to the participant will dramatically increase.

As the work load diminishes, and as family responsibilities diminish in the years preceding retirement, more time should gradually be spent in enjoyable leisure activities. A desirable plan for the individual who is capable of making this kind of adjustment is to take lengthened vacations or operate on a lightened work schedule in the years immediately before retirement. Too often, the older person works at a full schedule right until the last moment—and is suddenly cut loose from job responsibilities, from a feeling of importance, and from a life and a circle of acquaintances that have been built about the job. For him, the life that lies ahead will be empty indeed, if he cannot fill it with enjoyable recreational involvement.

During the years of later maturity, therefore, the intelligent individual should be planning toward effective retirement, and should be building a solid foundation for this goal. Harry Edgren poses a number of questions which the person in later middle age should ask himself:

1. Do you have a hobby which you enjoy doing alone?
2. Do you have a hobby in which you participate with a group?
3. Do you have a special recreation interest for indoors (winter) and outdoors (summer)?
4. Are you related in any way with some civic organization?
5. Are you a member of a social group of your age?
6. Are you involved in some organization within the church?
7. Are you undertaking some new adventure which you can continue for many years?
8. Do you have some interest in which you and your spouse can participate together?
9. Are you supporting (with time, money, or energy) some cause that is greater than yourself?
10. Do you enjoy participating in activities or experiences with your children and grandchildren?
11. Do you have a definite plan of savings for future use?
12. Do you have a yearly medical check-up? [20]

An important element touched on in this series of questions is that of *service to others* as a rewarding leisure outlet. Many middle-aged and retired persons get great satisfaction out of volunteer service in hospitals, nursing homes or other forms of treatment centers, in religious service work, community organization or political groups. While these activities may not fit the traditional view of what recreation is, they yield great

[20] Harry Edgren, "Effective Living in Middle Age," *American Recreation Journal*, January–February, 1964, p. 16.

satisfaction because they are meaningful, unselfish, and involve a real *giving* of the individual involved. Such efforts are described more fully in the following pages.

It is interesting to note that service involvement of older persons often may make possible recreational participation by *others*. Thus, many hospital recreation programs, or experimental programs with home-bound persons, could not be carried on if volunteers were not available to do the on-the-spot leadership.

RECREATION FOR THE AGING

Having proceeded through childhood, adolescence, and adulthood, we now come to the category of the aging. This group in our population is generally considered to include all those beyond the age of 65, the widely accepted time for retirement. However, in many communities or organizations, the individual in his late 50's or early 60's may be considered a "Senior Citizen," and sometimes the age "cut-off" is even lower.

What are the characteristics and special needs of older persons that make them a group of vital concern to the recreation profession?

Increasing Numbers. First, they are rapidly growing in numbers, as a consequence of birth trends in the past and declining mortality rates in recent years. To illustrate, between 1900 and 1950, life expectancy increased by 17.6 years for men and 20.3 years for women. In the early 1960's, there were 18 million persons in our population who were 65 or older, and it is estimated that this category will number 25 million in 1970.

Other facts known about the aged include: (a) women considerably outnumber men; (b) there is a greater proportion of foreign-born persons and a lesser proportion of nonwhites than in younger age groups; (c) about 50 percent of persons 65 years of age are married, with the remainder single (divorced, widowed, bachelors) and the number of single persons steadily increases through the following years; (d) most older persons live in private households rather than with relatives; and (e) predominately they are persons with less than a high school education.

Other Characteristics of the Aging. Certain basic concepts about the aging have been developed by the National Council on the Aging:

1. Aging is universal, and a normal development process, although it is frequently regarded with fear and aversion.

2. Aging is variable, and no two persons react physically, socially, or emotionally in the same way to this process. The degree to which individuals maintain healthy functioning is heavily based on personal life patterns of activity and interpersonal involvement.

3. Aging and illness are not necessarily coincidental; while there is

obviously a greater degree of specific disabilities with increasing age, many of these can be averted or minimized through intelligent preparation for aging or continuing healthy living habits.

4. Older people represent three generations in that they range from the early sixties to well past 100; it is necessary to identify the variable factors among these three stages of aging.

5. Older people can and do learn. While learning patterns may differ from those of younger people, the capacity is still there.

6. Older people can and do change, and are capable of readjustment to new circumstances.

7. Older people wish to remain self-directing, rather than be governed by the decisions of others.

8. Older people are vital human beings. Although limitations may appear, existing capacities should be used to the fullest extent possible, and stress should be placed on living in the present, rather than in the past.[21]

Accepting these points, it is important to recognize certain negative characteristics of many older persons. In addition to physical disability, they often tend to: (a) refuse to accept new experiences in ideas, foods, or habits; (b) suffer from failing memory, especially for recent happenings; (c) worry or complain excessively; and (d) evidence increasing sensitivity, suspicion of others, and withdrawal from meaningful human relationships. Nonetheless, and this is the most important point that must be stressed, deterioration in intellectual power or emotional adjustment is not inevitable. Irving Lorge, a distinguished psychological researcher, found that:

> . . . fortunately . . . physiological changes are not paralleled by corresponding losses either in intellectual power or in emotional adjustment. People in the sixties have intellectual power equivalent to that they displayed in the twenties. The shift is in performance speed or adapted tempo. . . .[22]

Recreation Needs of the Independent Aging Person. In general, individuals past 65 may be divided into two basic categories: (a) those who have deteriorated to the degree that they can no longer function independently, and are homebound, in nursing homes, or other types of institutions; and (b) those who are capable of taking care of themselves in the community, and of traveling about independently. The first group is discussed in the chapters that follow. But what about the more capable individual? How is he to be assisted in meeting his needs?

First, for the older person with an impressive retirement income or other financial resources, the practice has developed of having so-called

21 "Ten Basic Concepts of Aging," adapted from *Centers for Older People*, Report of the National Council on the Aging, 1962.

22 Irving Lorge, quoted in Arthur Williams, *Recreation in the Senior Years* (New York, Association Press, 1962), p. 17.

"leisure villages," or retirement homes, for the aged in specially planned communities. These villages, which are usually planned and built by commercial developers (often with expert medical and social consultants) are intended for retired or semiretired individuals who either purchase a small home or apartment, or who live on a rental basis. Usually, they are designed to be most suitable to the varied physical limitations of the aged (as far as convenience and safety are concerned) and they may also provide a cluster of medical, housekeeping, shopping, and other services as part of the total community plan.

In addition, these communities typically provide an extensive recreation program of clubs, interest groups, modified sports, hobbies, and cultural activities. Often these programs are under professional direction, and bring in highly skilled specialists to conduct classes. Sometimes older residents who have special leadership skills themselves may be responsible for leadership. An important element of the program is likely to be service activities provided by the aging residents to those in need, in the nearby community. As a single example, in a retirement community in Westchester County, New York, called Springdale, the women have formed a Needlework Guild, which has turned out hundreds of articles of clothing for needy children. Men residents have organized a Santa Workshop, which restores discarded and broken toys for underprivileged children at Christmas time. Holiday programs are presented to children at a nearby orphanage, and some members of the community provide voluntary services at a veterans' hospital in the area.

Thus, even in retirement communities where many enjoyable recreation activities may be provided, it is wise to bolster the older person's sense of self-respect and importance by providing opportunities to serve others and be needed by them.

This emphasis is found also in Senior Citizen or Golden Age groups attended by persons in the community at large. For example, the Committee on Recreation for Older People of the Health and Welfare Council of Philadelphia, Pennsylvania, cites many service projects engaged in by members of 91 groups for the aging in Philadelphia. Typical activities include:

Helping Own Members

Sent Sunshine boxes; visited them when ill or shut-in; sent flowers; organized get-well card showers; wrote to those mourning a loss in their family; assisted families of deceased members

Cheering Other Older People

Visited nearby old-age homes; made place mats and quilts for residents at homes; decorated Easter eggs for aged sick and shut-ins; wrote letters to lonely residents in homes for the indigent

Working for the Hospitalized

> Made surgical dressings, swabs, scrapbooks, afghans; packed baskets of
> candy, books, cards, games, etc.; hemmed towels, sheets, nurses' caps, etc.,
> for various hospitals [23]

In addition, they carried out numerous projects providing service
for little children in hospitals, nurseries, orphanages, and settlement
houses; they gave money for worthy causes and participated in fund-
raising events, and found many other ways to help.

Many other similar programs exist around the country. In Flint,
Michigan, for example, the McKinley Senior Citizens' Center, sponsored
by the Greater Flint AFL-CIO Council and the Flint Recreation and
Park Board, provides many programs, activities, remade toys, and thousands of man hours helping handicapped children in the area.

Wherever possible, aging persons should be involved in constructively organizing, planning, and carrying out their own programs.
Simply to have them served by professional or volunteer club leaders
does not meet their fullest needs. Recognizing that they will have varying degrees of ability and responsibility, those who are most capable
should be given key roles and meaningful tasks. This should apply not
only to the involvement of aging persons in their own centers but also
to drawing them into planning for the aging in the community-wide
setting. To deal most adequately with the needs of this age group, all
interested citizens and agencies should cooperate in developing coordinated services and programs. Inevitably, while professional social
workers, recreation administrators, and other municipal personnel will
take the lead in this process, older persons themselves will have much
to contribute, and should be well-represented on such planning councils.

It is interesting to note that in a number of states, such as North
Carolina and Kentucky, there has been a state-wide effort to analyze the
needs of the aging and to promote effective local services. Each of these
states has published useful brochures on recreation for older citizens,
and assists local programs in many ways.

This chapter has analyzed the four major age groupings of childhood, adolescence, adulthood, and the aging, placing stress both on meeting the needs of the normal population and indicating certain areas of
special need. The following two chapters deal in greater detail with the
needs of special groups, both in institutional settings and in the community at large.

SUGGESTED QUESTIONS FOR DISCUSSION

1. React to the following statement, "Children today are far too regimented in
   their free time, and do not need organized recreation programs or leadership."

[23] "Service Projects for Older People," *Recreation,* February, 1955, p. 90.

2. In what ways can organized recreation service aid in the team approach to preventing or treating juvenile delinquency? Is there any evidence that this form of service is effective?

3. Analyze the community where you live. What organized recreation services are provided for adults, either by public or voluntary agencies (other than commercial)? How does this compare with services and activities provided for other age groupings?

4. Identify and discuss several characteristics of the aging person (recognizing that there are wide variations among those in this group) that must be taken into account, in planning leisure activities for them.

Chapter 12

Recreation in Treatment Centers

One of the most rapidly expanding forms of organized recreation service today is found in hospitals or other treatment centers that provide rehabilitation for the ill and handicapped. Although our concern is chiefly with modern practices in this field, it is worthy of note that the use of recreation as a therapeutic agent has an ancient and honorable history. Frye writes:

As early as 2000 B.C. temples in Egypt were dedicated to the relief of "melancholias" through the provision of opportunities for participation in games and "pleasurable occupations." Priests are said to have been aware that the dispelling of morbid moods was aided by the temple atmosphere, the beauty of lotus gardens, and the ritual songs and dances of the temple maidens. . . . By 420 B.C., diverting amusements and recreation were being offered as treatment in the Aesculapian temples . . . a ritual developed which included rest, followed by purifying baths and ceremonies designed to gain entrance for the supplicant, via dreams, to the presence of the

298

healing god. Some of the more elaborate shrines, such as the one at Epidauros, include not only beautiful temples and baths, but gymnasiums, theaters, and libraries. It seems not unlikely that many who were able to take advantage of the temples' restful regimen and recreational facilities may have felt better even before being admitted to the mysteries. . . .[1]

Many centuries later, at the end of the eighteenth century, those suffering from nervous disorders were frequently encouraged to take part in a combination of moderate work and recreational activities. Patients at Aversa, in Italy, for example, took part in "printing, translating, music, husbandry, and in manufacturing woolen cloth. . . ." In the 1820's, mental patients at the McLean Hospital in Waverly, Massachusetts, enjoyed "draughts, chess, backgammon, ninepins, swinging, sawing wood, gardening, reading, writing, and music." It was believed that these activities provided a healthy diversion from "unpleasant subjects of thought," offered needed physical exercise, and had a tranquilizing effect on the mind.

Several pioneers in nursing and hospital care, including Florence Nightingale, introduced various forms of recreation in hospitals, and this practice became increasingly widespread in the late 1800's, in State Hospitals. In World War II, the Red Cross began to provide a number of recreational activities in military hospitals and convalescent centers. During the 1920's and 1930's, recreation leaders were assigned to military and veterans' hospitals, and to a number of state schools for retarded children. Private psychiatric hospitals increasingly provided recreation services for their patients.

ACCEPTANCE OF HOSPITAL RECREATION

During World War II and in the decades that followed, the hospital recreation movement accelerated greatly. By the end of the war, Red Cross hospital recreation personnel alone increased to over 1,800. In 1945, the Veterans' Administration established a Hospital Special Services Division which included Recreation Service along with Canteen, Library, Chaplaincy, and Voluntary Services; later, recreation was to be administered through the Physical Medicine and Rehabilitation Service in VA hospitals, along with occupational and physical therapy.

During the late 1940's and 1950's, the following developments took place. The American Psychiatric Association formed a Commission on Cooperation with Leisure Time Agencies in 1948, as evidence of its recognition of the importance of leisure and recreation in mental health. The American Recreation Society developed a Hospital Recreation

[1] Virginia Frye, "Historical Sketch of Recreation in the Medical Setting," *Recreation in Treatment Centers* (Washington, D.C.: American Recreation Society, September, 1962), p. 40.

Section in 1949, and the American Association for Health, Physical Education and Recreation established a Recreation Therapy Section in the early 1950's. The National Association of Recreation Therapists joined forces with these other bodies to form the Council for the Advancement of Hospital Recreation, in 1953.

A number of conferences, workshops, and institutes were held in the years that followed, exploring needs in this field. Comeback, Inc., a national, nonprofit service agency concerned with the social rehabilitation of the ill, disabled, and aged through therapeutic recreation service, was founded in 1961. Several colleges and universities established specialized graduate programs in therapeutic recreation service and were supported, beginning in 1963, by training grants offered by the Vocational Rehabilitation Administration of the Federal Department of Health, Education and Welfare. A further indication of growth in this field has been the Registry of Hospital Recreation Personnel, maintained by the Council for the Advancement of Hospital Recreation. This agency has established standards of professional qualifications on three levels: Hospital Recreation Director, Hospital Recreation Leader, and Hospital Recreation Aide.

The initial focus on the hospital as the unique setting in which recreation services are provided for the ill and handicapped has now broadened, however. Today, such services are considered an essential part of the total process of rehabilitation in a number of different kinds of treatment centers. Settings for therapeutic recreation service now include:

Hospitals under varied sponsorship (Veterans' Administration, Military, Public Health, State, County, Municipal, and Voluntary) and dealing with a variety of patient populations (general, chronic disease, mental illness, tuberculosis, and psychiatric, among others)

Schools or residential centers for those with specific physical handicaps (the blind, deaf, orthopedically handicapped, or neurologically involved) or those with mental deficiencies or retardation

Penal institutions for adult criminals, or custodial centers for delinquent youth; reformatories, work camps, and other centers for those who are socially maladjusted

Aftercare centers for discharged mental patients, for former drug addicts, or those who require continuing special services in the form of counseling, psychotherapy, and sheltered or guided social experiences

There are several factors which have given rise to the expansion of recreation services that are specifically designed to meet the needs of the ill and handicapped in our society. The first of these is the striking growth in the number of those who require such services.

THE ILL AND HANDICAPPED IN OUR SOCIETY

The term "handicapped" is used to describe persons who differ from their fellows to a marked degree, with a consequent limitation of ability, performance, or living functions. There is a growing conviction held by many professionals today that the term "disabled" is preferable to "handicapped," because it places the stress on the disability, rather than on the handicap, which may be prevented. However, since the term most widely in use at present is still "handicap" in the literature, in popular usage, and in the titles of organizations in this field, this text will continue to employ it, rather than "disability."

A statement formulated by the 1960 White House Conference on Children and Youth defines the handicapped child as one who ". . . cannot play, learn, work or do the things other children of his age can do; or is hindered in achieving his full physical, mental and social potentialities; whether by a disability which is initially small but potentially handicapping, or by a serious impairment involving several areas of functions with the probability of life-long impairment." [2]

Pomeroy points out that within the category of "physically handicapped" alone, there are a number of separate and distinct groups. These include: persons with impaired vision, impaired hearing, speech handicaps; those with orthopedic and neurological impairments, including crippling conditions which stem from such factors as congenital abnormalities like cerebral palsy, infections like poliomyelitis or tuberculosis, metabolic disturbances like muscular dystrophy, or traumatic conditions like accidents, burns, or fractures. Such conditions may result in mild or total disability, may be single or multiple, and may affect persons of every age, socioeconomic background, race, religion, or region.

While exact figures of the number of ill and handicapped in the United States today cannot be determined, Pomeroy indicates that approximately 10 percent of the children in our society are believed to have an appreciable physical or mental disability. It has been estimated that there are now about 30 million men, women, and children in the United States suffering from some form of incapacitating or chronic disease and disability; more than half of these with mental illness. Specifically, the Children's Bureau of the Department of Health, Education and Welfare has published national estimates for 1970 of certain specific physical handicaps for children and youth in our society:

2 *Conference Proceedings* (Washington, D.C.: White House Conference on Children and Youth, 1960), p. 381.

		Estimated Number
Type of Handicap	*Age Group*	*in 1970*
Epilepsy	under 21	450,000
Cerebral Palsy	under 21	465,000
Eye Conditions Needing Specialist Care	5–17	12,500,000
Hearing Loss	under 21	450,000–900,000
Speech Handicaps	5–20	3,270,000
Cleft Palate and/or Harelip	not specified	120,000
Orthopedic	under 21	2,425,000
Rheumatic Fever	under 21	1,100,000 [3]

In addition to such physical handicaps, it is known that over one half of the beds in American hospitals today are occupied by mentally ill patients, and the prediction has been made that one out of every three people may require psychiatric assistance within the next fifteen years. Whether this is because the stress, tension, and uncertainty of modern living have actually increased the proportion of those who are mentally ill, or because we are more alert today to signs of mental illness and have more resources for dealing with it, is not certain. Nonetheless, the point is clear. A vast and increasing number of individuals in our society have physical or emotional handicaps which require special treatment, either in institutional or community settings. In addition, there is a growing number of retired, older persons who require special services, although they may not be classified technically as ill or handicapped. Modern science has resulted in prolonging or saving many lives. The question is—what can be done to make the life that has been saved as full, productive, and happy as possible?

CHANGED ATTITUDES TOWARD THE HANDICAPPED

Over the past several decades, there has been a radical shift in our thinking, with respect to society's obligation toward its less fortunate members. The entire field of social welfare has expanded greatly. Whereas the aged, the indigent, the hopelessly ill or crippled, were previously treated with a minimum of humane concern and intelligent effort to improve their situation, today this is not the case. Government has established systems of Social Security and unemployment insurance. Social work agencies provide a variety of welfare services for the groups in the community that have special needs. In orphanages, mental hospitals, and residential centers for the handicapped there is a much more enlightened view of the needs and potentialities of those who are being served. In penal institutions and homes for delinquent youth, the accent today has shifted from the punitive to the rehabilitative.

[3] Janet Pomeroy, *Recreation for the Physically Handicapped* (New York: Macmillan, 1964), pp. 3–5.

On every level then, the conviction has grown that in a great and wealthy society, there needs to be a heightened concern with those who require special assistance because of certain limiting handicaps.

To a great degree, we have matured too in our feelings about the handicapped. Centuries ago, the physically or mentally handicapped were often seen with morbid curiosity and viewed as persons who had been cursed by the gods. An obvious physical deformity might be viewed as evidence of such a punishment—sometimes seen as the outcome of parental transgression, in which the stigma was placed on the child. Not too long ago, cripples or mentally ill persons were cruelly treated or disposed of, or treated as objects of ridicule. People feared to come in contact with them. Often, in shame, a family would hide the "queer one" in an attic or back room, screened from society. It was simply not recognized that many such individuals had the capacity for leading full and productive lives and that the very way in which they were treated made their handicap overwhelming.

Today, the public has gradually come to realize that a crippling or otherwise handicapping condition should be viewed rationally and should not imply a social stigma. We have established special schools and classes for "exceptional children," and we have recognized, particularly during and after World War II, that many seriously disabled individuals can hold down jobs in industry and be as productive and responsible as their coworkers. Such organizations as the National Association for Retarded Children and the United Cerebral Palsy Association have helped to promote a considerable body of medical and psychological research, teacher education, legislation, and community services for the handicapped.

Certainly, public attitudes have not yet become fully mature with respect to the handicapped. Many people still have feelings that range from excessive and therefore undesirable pity (which overprotects the handicapped person and makes him less likely to help himself), to dislike, outright rejection, or even fear. However, by and large, the view is becoming accepted that the handicapped are much like everybody else, with important physical, social, and emotional needs that must be met, if they are to reach their fullest potential as human beings.

This recognition is particularly important, both with respect to the rehabilitative process in treatment centers, and the provision of recreation services for the handicapped in community settings.

RECREATION AS A TOOL IN THE THERAPEUTIC PROCESS

As indicated earlier, there has been a steady growth in the use of recreation in treatment centers, particularly in hospitals of all types. What is the underlying rationale for this development? Specifically, what does recreation contribute in the therapeutic setting? How does it relate to the prevention of illness or disability, or the restoration of function?

Basically, the aim of therapeutic recreation, like that of overall rehabilitation, is to help the ill, handicapped, aged, or retarded person *help himself* to live the fullest physical, mental, social, psychological, and economic life possible within the limits of his illness or disability. The goal within a treatment center is to return a happier, more productive, and better adjusted human being to community living or, short of this, to help him live as fully as possible in some type of sheltered environment.

Within Veterans' Administration hospitals, for example, recreation has been seen as having the following objectives:

To facilitate the patient's adjustment to hospital life and to make him more receptive to treatment

To facilitate the patient's early physical, mental, and social rehabilitation, recovery, and discharge

To assist in minimzing the risk of unnecessary readmission, by aiding in the patient's transition to his community, following discharge

The extent to which these objectives are reached is dependent upon the degree to which the patient is provided with recreation program services that:

Improve his morale and sustain it at a high level

Encourage the formation of habits and attitudes which will permit his confident . . . participation in normal activities

Compensate for his disabilities and limitations while inspiring him to fulfill his potentialities

Channel his aggressive drives into appropriate outlets

Encourage his desire to remove or overcome the physical or mental barriers that stand between him and a normal life

Stimulate new or dormant interests and talents, as well as to reestablish old ones [4]

It is important to recognize that hospital routine usually includes long periods of free time (particularly for the long-term or chronic patient) in which no form of medical or other therapeutic service is being provided. Just as in outside life, if stimulating and interesting activity is not provided for the patient who is confined to a bed, wheelchair, or day room, boredom, lethargy, and low morale will inevitably result. When it *is* provided, the ensuing high morale may be definitely reflected in overall treatment outcomes. Dr. Joseph B. Wolffe, Medical Director of the Valley Forge Heart and Medical Center, has commented:

[4] C. C. Bream, Jr., "Rehabilitative Recreation in V.A. Hospitals," *Recreation,* May, 1964, pp. 224–225.

A survey of 1,000 patients has shown that carefully selected recreation to suit the patient's problem and personality resulted in reduction both in drug requirements as well as length of hospital stay, when compared to the control group in the institution without the program.[5]

Another important fact is that hospital patients, particularly those who have had a serious operation, or who have undergone a major break-down, are in great need of reassurance and support. Often, they may feel incomplete, unworthy, or have serious doubts about their ability to return to their families or communities, and assume previously held patterns of responsibility or relationships. The impersonality of the hospital setting, and the fact that too often patients are treated as a "case," (to be prodded, fed, turned over, and applied with medication, almost as a baby is treated) do little to assuage these very normal feel-ings of concern and insecurity. Recreation has the capacity for providing the very kinds of personal experience that can begin to restore awareness of one's continuing capabilities, and feelings of worthiness as a human being.

Other specific purposes of recreation, as carrried on in the treat-ment center, include the following: (a) to help the patient maintain a healthy level of physical fitness, within the possible limitations of his handicap or disability; (b) to provide specific carryover skills which may be useful when the patient returns to community life; (c) to meet certain direct needs of the patient as an individual, based on a thorough examination of his abilities, interests, limitations, and psychosocial characteristics.

Obviously, the specific kinds of activities that are offered must vary according to the type of patient who is being served. Thus, psychiatric patients may be provided recreation experiences that are specially geared to promote social involvement or acceptable outlets for certain emotions or drives. The emphasis in programs of rehabilitation for the physically handicapped may include the adaptation of equipment and facilities to permit paraplegics to play basketball or other active sports, or unilateral amputees to play golf or billiards, or Stryker patients to bowl. Each such activity has a very special purpose in terms of the needs of the patients involved in it.

Overall, however, the fundamental rationale for providing recrea-tion for the ill and handicapped lies in the fact that the basic, universal needs of man do not change simply because an individual differs in terms of mental or physical efficiency from the norm. As Carlson, Deppe, and MacLean put it:

The ill and the handicapped still have the same need to belong, to create,

[5] Joseph B. Wolffe, M.D., *The Doctors and Recreation in the Hospital Setting* (Raleigh, North Carolina: North Carolina Recreation Commission, n.d.), p. 19.

to feel secure, to love and be loved, to feel significant and to experience new adventure. The needs are the same, but they are accentuated through privation. The cerebral-palsied youngster with convulsive motor patterns needs acceptance as much as his pretty, well-coordinated sister. Though the afflicted child may not get recognition for beauty or for motor ability, he must have substitute experiences in which he can feel successful and accepted. The prejudices and fears of society often deny to the handicapped the opportunity for finding their maximum usefulness and happiness.[6]

This principle, as applied to treatment centers, is firmly expressed by Dr. Alexander Reid Martin, in these words: "We cannot relegate recreation to a position of secondary importance in the lives of individuals, and in hospitals we cannot relegate recreation to a position of secondary importance."[7]

In the past, a number of descriptive terms have been applied to this area of professional practice. It has been called "hospital recreation," "rehabilitative recreation," "recreation therapy," "activity therapy," and "recreation for the ill and handicapped." Today the term that is becoming most widely accepted is "therapeutic recreation service."

There has been some controversy as to whether recreation should be considered a "therapy" as such. Partly this is so because its outcomes are more difficult to measure than the results of such techniques as "occupational therapy," or "physical therapy." The position is also expressed that when recreation is viewed as a therapy (rather than as an "allied health field," as it is termed by the American Medical Association) it may lose some of its value. This view has been stated by Dr. Paul Haun:

The hospital recreation worker performs many services essential, in my opinion, to the welfare of the patient. I cannot, however, regard any of them as therapeutic, first because I have never been convinced that recreation in any of its forms is a specific instrument for the modification of a disease process comparable say to penicillin in the treatment of syphilis; second, because I am so fully persuaded of the psychiatric patient's need for recreation *as recreation* that I grudge any dilution of its potency through adulteration with alternative purposes. . . . It is because I believe that recreation is an essential human need that I want it for my patients. . . .[8]

On the other hand, the distinguished Dr. Howard A. Rusk, Director of the Institute of Physical Medicine and Rehabilitation in New York, has stated, "I firmly believe that both individual and group recreation

[6] Reynold E. Carlson, Theodore R. Deppe, and Janet R. MacLean, *Recreation in American Life* (Belmont, California: Wadsworth, 1963), p. 494.

[7] Alexander Reid Martin, M.D., in *The Doctors and Recreation in the Hospital Setting, op. cit.,* p. 7.

[8] Paul Haun, M.D., "Hospital Recreation—A Medical Viewpoint," in *Recreation for the Mentally Ill* (Washington, D.C.: American Association for Health, Physical Education and Recreation, 1958), pp. 57–58.

for patients have a direct relationship upon their recovery—these, in my opinion, are definitely adjunctive therapy." [9] Similarly, the statement by Dr. William C. Menninger that "It has been the privilege of many of us practicing medicine in psychiatry to have some very rewarding experiences in the use of recreation as an adjunctive method of treatment . . . along with direct psychological help, hydrotherapy, shock and insulin therapy . . ." [10] supports the view that recreation *can* be therapy.

Perhaps a distinction should be made to this effect. Recreation can be offered as an informal, completely voluntary form of activity in the hospital program, often on a mass or large-group basis, without any close relationship to other adjunctive therapies or medical guidance and direction. In such situations, it clearly should not be designated as therapeutic. On the other hand, when it is medically oriented, guided and approved, related to pathology, modified or adapted to meet individual patients' needs, interests, and capabilities, and when it has certain specific goals of rehabilitation in mind, it deserves the title.

What is important is that, even when it is "prescribed" for a given patient, the activity should not be approached in a compulsory fashion. A patient may be introduced to the activity, encouraged to participate, and given help—but cannot be forced to take part—or it is no longer recreation. Thus, the recreation worker will need to be ingenious in his effort to motivate patients and (particularly with psychiatric patients, who often are extremely withdrawn and reluctant to take part in recreation) fairly strong in his efforts to persuade. In the final analysis, however, unless the patient comes to the point of selecting activities for participation voluntarily, because he finds them enjoyable and satisfying, the program will not have been successful.

One approach to this problem is to have essentially two kinds of program structures:

1. Required activities of a class-like nature in which a patient *must* participate (although he may have a choice, in a large psychiatric hospital, of several different activities) that would involve the *learning* of specific recreational skills, in the area of music, dance, sports, hobbies, arts and crafts, or similar categories
2. Other activities of a social or recreational nature, to which the patient is invited, or which he must attend (along with his building or ward group), but in which actual participation is not required or even urged

The effect of this dual arrangement is that the patient *must* learn certain skills and *must* take in certain group activities, but that his

[9] Howard A. Rusk, M.D., *Basic Concepts of Hospital Recreation* (Washington, D.C.: American Recreation Society, 1953), p. 7.
[10] William C. Menninger, M.D., "Recreation and Mental Health," *Recreation,* November, 1948, p. 343.

actual recreational involvement in them on a voluntary basis will depend on his own degree of recovery and readiness to participate. This point is discussed at greater length on page 311.

THE SCOPE OF THERAPEUTIC RECREATION SERVICE IN HOSPITALS

It has been pointed out that therapeutic recreation is offered in a variety of settings which serve the ill or handicapped: hospitals, special schools or residential centers, prisons or youth camps, to name but a few. Obviously, the most commonly found institutional setting is the hospital, and it is here that the greatest number of professional recreation workers are employed.

An extensive study of recreation programs in hospitals of all types throughout the United States was carried out by the National Recreation Association.[11] Its report, issued in 1959, revealed that, of the total number of hospitals that responded (3,507), 1,486 (42.4 percent) indicated that they had an organized recreation program. Outstanding in this group were the federal institutions, with Veterans' Administration hospitals (98.0 percent), military hospitals (81.7 percent) and public health hospitals (49.0 percent) operating recreation programs. Similarly, in state hospitals, particularly those devoted largely to the treatment of mental illness and tuberculosis, 89.3 percent had recreation programs.

On the other hand, municipal, proprietary, and sectarian hospitals tended to have a low proportion of recreation programs. This was due largely to the fact that most of these institutions treat patients with acute illnesses who remain in the hospital for relatively short periods of time, and who therefore have a lesser need for organized recreation service.

Another important factor was the size of the hospital. For example, in those responding institutions which had between 100 and 499 beds, only 48.7 percent had organized recreation programs. In contrast, in hospitals with over 1,000 beds, 96.8 percent had programs. The National Recreation Association report points out that since those hospitals offering organized recreation services tended to have the largest patient populations, it appeared statistically that approximately three-quarters of the patients in hospitals in the United States are served by recreation programs.

In terms of activities, the following types of program services were offered by responding hospitals, in the order of frequency of mention:

11 John E. Silson, Elliott M. Cohen, and Beatrice H. Hill, *Recreation in Hospitals, Report of a Study of Organized Recreation Programs in Hospitals and of the Personnel Conducting Them* (New York: National Recreation Association, 1959).

Activity	Percentage
Passive, mental, and linguistic activities (including reading, writing, radio, TV, and movies)	86.4
Arts and crafts	72.5
Social activities	61.0
Musical activities (participative)	47.6
Active games and sports	47.0
Service activities (including work on patient radio station or news-paper, entertainments, and patient-volunteer leadership)	43.4
Nature and outing activities	33.2
Dancing	31.1
Collecting and related hobbies	26.8
Drama activities (participative)	22.3

Many hospitals, particularly mental hospitals, utilized swimming pools, gymnasiums, auditoriums, athletic fields, and special recreation rooms. Wards and other bed areas were the most frequently mentioned site for recreation activities, being mentioned in over three-fifths of the hospitals that had active programs. Solariums and day rooms were used in about one-half of the hospitals, as were special recreation rooms. About two-fifths of the hospitals had auditoriums available and about one-fifth had special recreation buildings available.

Overall, it was estimated that there were 5,236 full-time personnel in charge of recreation services, in responding hospitals, although in many of the smaller institutions there was no single full-time individual charged with this responsibility. In such settings, recreation responsibilities tended to be shared by other hospital personnel, including nurses, occupational and physical therapists, and volunteers. It should be noted that there has been a steady increase of services and numbers of personnel, since this study was carried out.

GEARING SERVICES TO SPECIFIC PATIENT NEEDS

It was pointed out earlier that the nature of the institution and patient population dictates program emphasis, choice of activities, objectives, and leadership methods.

Thus, in the well-known Institute for Physical Medicine and Rehabilitation in New York City, which has pioneered in the rehabilitation of patients who have suffered major losses of physical function due to accidents, strokes, paralysis, or other forms of trauma, the recreation program's emphasis is on relearning the skills of daily living. A particularly important aspect is the trip program. Patients go on many outings: to baseball games at Yankee Stadium or Shea Stadium, to the New York World's Fair, to concerts, to Broadway shows, to Madison Square Garden, and to a wide variety of other amusement centers. The point is that these patients must learn to make use of their existing powers to visit community resources. The trip program develops their confidence and ability to overcome the difficulties inherent in making such outings. Its goal is to prevent them from becoming confined to their homes when they leave the hospital. Thus, the recreation program becomes a bridge to the future.

Similarly, in the 169 hospitals operated by the Veterans' Administration which serve over half a million veterans each year, recreation activities are directly geared to the medical limitations, interests, and needs of patients. C. C. Bream writes:

> As a general principle, emphasis will vary most according to the nature of disabilities and illnesses. For example recreation activities for psychiatric patients are designed to encourage maximum patient participation and to aid in resocialization and reeducation. Recreation activities for pulmonary-disease patients are directed toward programs requiring passive or mildly active participation. Therefore, programs tending to excite, disturb or cause undue exertion are excluded. . . .[12]

Recreation in the Psychiatric Setting

Perhaps the best example of how recreation must be specifically geared to meet the needs of patients is in the psychiatric hospital. Here, it is crucial that recreation participation provide certain kinds of outlets and opportunities for expression. Recreation may be used to strengthen the adaptive equilibrium of the patient and to help him maintain adequate controls. Through such creative activities as painting, sculpture, or dance, the patient may express certain otherwise unacceptable instinctual drives. Such activities as kicking a ball, chopping wood or striking a punching bag may substitute for more dangerous aggressive impulses. Each of these represents a form of defense mechanism which the patient needs to develop, in order to cope adequately with society and function effectively with others. Similarly, through successful experiences and satisfying interpersonal relationships found in the recreation program, the psychiatric patient may compensate for imagined or exaggerated feelings of worthlessness or inferiority.

Martin Meyer, Assistant Commissioner in the Indiana State Department of Mental Health, has developed a rationale for recreation as therapy in the psychiatric setting. He writes at length of the "milieu therapy" approach to the rehabilitation of psychiatric patients, which is particularly useful in large treatment centers where intensive individualized psychotherapy is not always possible. According to this approach, the hospital is viewed as a society or community, in which the staff and patients play real roles, and in which there is an active sharing of re-

---

[12] C. C. Bream, Jr., *op. cit.*, pp. 224–225.

sponsibility. Through communication and meaningful interaction among the staff and patients, the regression of patients (withdrawal from involvement) is combatted. This process is furthered through the establishment of a variety of organized groups for discussion; these groups may focus their attention on such problems as orientation following admission to the hospital, treatment, ward management, recreational activities, and problems anticipated following discharge. Meyer suggests that recreation has particular value in reality-testing and personality development:

> . . . recreation is deeply rooted in community life and may serve as an initial step toward appropriate adaptive behavior, consistent with community standards. Individuality can be blended in with the group and personal identity diffused, until sufficient ego strength is established to risk independent action and responsibility. Interaction within the group is a first step toward more elaborate interpersonal relationships. Recreation can deal with real things. One cannot escape the reality of a ball to be caught or hit, a dance to be performed, or a musical instrument to be played. The way the patient reacts to the activity and relates to the group can be important indicators or reality contact. Social activities such as square dances, parties, and discussion groups, simulate community reality and test readiness to assume a normal and acceptable relationship with one's peers.

The recreator's role as a therapist will vary considerably, depending upon the extent or degree of illness exhibited by the patient. Most psychotic patients will be withdrawn, seclusive and fearful during the early days of hospitalization. Some will be severely regressed, disoriented to time, place and people. They are in fact in hiding, completely withdrawn from reality, living in a private fantasy world. The recreator's rigid insistence on voluntary selection of activity, to keep the "free choice" element of recreation intact, is a fanciful delusion, consistently discredited wherever psychotic patients are treated. For those patients too sick to understand or recognize reality, free choice and voluntary participation is in fact not possible. The selection must be made by the therapist, guided by the prescription, written or verbal, from the attending psychiatrist.

You can lead a horse to water but you can't make him drink. How do you get the patient to drink from the well of recreation? In the treatment oriented hospital, where a therapeutic environment has been established, all personnel direct their attention to this goal. Movement, activity, communication, verbal and non-verbal are constantly encouraged. Consistent attitudes and patterns of behavior, directed toward winning the confidence and trust of the patient, are maintained by all who come in contact with the patient, particularly by the nurse and psychiatric aide. The patient is made to feel safe, trusted, loved, and secure, and to look upon the entire treatment staff as friends. When this feeling of trust and security is established, it is but a short step to encouraging the patient to move toward a recreation program. Some will join quickly and willingly, while others hold back, remain on the fringe, until the contagious atmosphere of the activity finally draws them in.

. . . each new adventure must be successfully experienced and constantly upgraded for new challenges and achievement. Success begets enthusiasm and interest. As confidence is restored or developed, variety and difficulty is added to the program. The simple is replaced by the more (highly) organized . . . an ever increasing variety of activity must be offered to the patient . . . eventually, it will become apparent to both patient and recreator which activities are best suited to personal need, self expression, growth and development, and hold promise for continuing achievement, companionship and release from a world of tension, anxiety and rejection.

If and when this is achieved, recreation becomes the voluntary, free choice part of life, establishing an equilibrium between the extremes of tension and relaxation. This is always the goal, the true fulfillment of the mission of all recreators, regardless of setting and type of clientele.[13]

Examples of Program Service in the Psychiatric Setting

In terms of actual program service, what kinds of activities are most useful in psychiatric hospitals? At the famed Menninger Foundation in Topeka, Kansas, recreation is grouped under the broad heading of Adjunctive Therapies as a major component of the "treatment team." The other four headings are: Doctors, Nursing Service, Social Workers, and Psychologists.

Adjunctive Therapies include a considerable number of activities, some of which are quiet and relaxing, whereas others are extremely vigorous and physically challenging. Activities are scheduled throughout the week, some at a given time or several times each day, and others only once or twice during the week. A few are seasonal, but the majority are offered throughout the year. The total list, as outlined in the hospital manual,[14] includes the following:

Activities Available in the Adjunctive Therapy Department

Creative Arts

A. Ceramics
B. Drawing
C. Painting
D. Sculpturing
E. Minor Crafts
 1. Chip Carving
 2. Copper Tooling

Creative Arts (continued)

 3. Enameling
 4. Leather Work
 5. Looms
 6. Model Making
 7. Radio and Hi-Fi Sets
 8. Sewing
 9. Looms

---

[13] Martin W. Meyer, "The Rationale of Recreation as Therapy," in *Recreation in Treatment Centers* (Washington, D.C.: American Recreation Society, September, 1962), pp. 23–26.

[14] "Scheduled Activities in Adjunctive Therapy Department," unpublished manual of Menninger Foundation, Topeka, Kansas, October, 1964.

Education

A. Adult Classes
  1. Bible Literature
  2. College Correspondence Courses
  3. Commercial Subjects
  4. Cooking
  5. High School Subjects
  6. Languages
  7. Literature
  8. Nature Study
  9. Ores and Minerals
  10. Photography
B. Discussion Groups
C. Documentary Films
D. Forums
E. Library
F. Play Reading
G. Vesper Services

Industrial Activities

A. Auto Mechanics
B. Horticulture ✓
  1. Gardening and Greenhouse ✓
    Groups
  2. Arboretum Group ✓
C. Mechanical Repair
  1. Metal Working
D. Project Groups
  1. Special
  2. Service Groups
E. Woodworking
F. Individual Assignments
G. Volunteer Work

Recreation

A. Social Activities
  1. Amateur Radio Station
  2. Bridge and Other Card Games
  3. COTA (Patient Planning
    Committee)
  4. Dancing
    a. Ballroom
    b. Square
  5. Hobby Clubs
  6. CEA (Committee on Evening
    Activities)

Recreation (continued)

  7. Movies
  8. Parties
  9. Music
    a. Band, Elementary and
      Intermediate
    b. Fundamentals of Music Class
    c. Group Singing
    d. Jazz Combo
    e. Lessons in Piano, Voice, and
      Instruments
    f. Music Appreciation
    g. Chorus
  10. Patient Publications
  11. Dramatics

B. Sports and Athletics
  1. Adult Exercise
  2. Archery
  3. Badminton
  4. Basketball
  5. Billiards and Pool
  6. Boating and Canoeing
  7. Bowling
  8. Calisthenics
  9. Croquet
  10. Fishing
  11. Golf
  12. Gymnastics
  13. Hiking
  14. Ice Skating
  15. Paddle Tennis
  16. Roller Skating
  17. Sailing
  18. Shuffleboard
  19. Softball
  20. Swimming
  21. Table Tennis
  22. Tennis
  23. Touch Football
  24. Track
  25. Volleyball
  26. Weightlifting
  27. Women's Sports
  28. Water Sports

It is important to recognize, however, that effective recreation leadership in the psychiatric hospital setting goes far beyond the mere leading and organizing of activities. These would be pointless if the patient did not develop favorable attitudes toward participation in recreation, both within the institution and after discharge. Fred Humphrey, formerly Director of Activity Therapies at the State Hospital, Jamestown, North Dakota, has described the Recreation Counseling Program in operation at his institution.

The Counseling Process in Recreation Service

Humphrey makes the initial point that recreation must be defined as an attitude or frame of mind, rather than merely participation in activities. He stresses that the following should become integral parts of every hospital recreation program:

1. There should be a procedure instituted to evaluate each patient's recreational interests, coupled with planned efforts to motivate him to expand these interests during the period of hospitalization. An important aspect of this process is to help the patient gain an understanding of the place leisure occupies in the total life pattern, as well as guidance in formulating a positive program for recreational participation on discharge from the hospital.

2. Through unit and hospital recreation councils, patient planning and leadership should be encouraged to the highest degree possible. Such councils must be given real responsibility, with staff members acting as "enablers," rather than "manipulators."

3. There should be an emphasis on hospital-community cooperation, with a continuous exchange of recreation opportunities and facilities. Since social withdrawal is a major problem in mental illness, and since this may be accentuated by hospitalization, it is necessary to minimize the effects of separation from family, friends, and other contacts and relationships in the outside community.

4. A follow-up program must also be developed to assist the discharged patient in making community contacts with groups having recreational interests similar to his own. A positive program must therefore be established within each hospital to relate patients to the opportunities for enjoyable and constructive leisure which exist in their home communities, and to stimulate community recreators to accept their responsibility for cooperation in this effort.

The State Hospital at Jamestown, North Dakota, offers an effective example of the kind of "bridge" to the community that may be developed in a large psychiatric hospital, in its annual Family Recreation Day. The general format of this program follows:

All residents in the hospital are given an opportunity to mail an invitation for Family Recreation Day to as many relatives and friends as they wish. Enclosed with the invitation is a form letter containing a schedule of the day's activities and a questionnaire to be returned, indicating whether the person receiving the invitation plans to attend, and the approximate number to be expected in each visiting group.

Each person receiving an invitation is requested to bring a picnic dinner for those to be in the visiting group, plus the hospital resident or residents to be joining them. The hospital provides pop and coffee for all present. The schedule has been as follows:

8:00 A.M.   Opening of registration tables with the escort service provided by members of the Journalism Club, an organization composed of hospital residents

9:00 A.M.   Catholic Mass for all hospital residents and their visitors

10:15 A.M.   Protestant services for all hospital residents and their visitors

9:30 A.M.–11:30 A.M.   Informal games and visiting in the Family Recreation Day picnic area

11:30 A.M.–1:00 P.M.   Welcome and picnic lunch

1:00 P.M.–2:00 P.M.   Softball games for all interested groups, plus informal games for all others

2:00 P.M.–3:00 P.M.   A series of skits presented by the Hospital Playmakers Club, a group composed of hospital residents

3:00 P.M.–4:00 P.M.   Picnic games and contests for all ages

7:30 P.M.–9:30 P.M.   Family Recreation Day dance open to all hospital residents and all visitors

7:30 P.M.–9:30 P.M.   Movie for all interested hospital residents and visitors with supervision provided by Activity Therapies staff members for the children of all visitors who wish to attend the dance

How successful has this program been? One measure of this has been its attendance; between 500 and 1,000 visitors have come to the hospital each year to participate in a wholesome and fun-filled day with their hospitalized friend or relative. In one case, 75 relatives and friends visited one patient, as they made Family Recreation Day the basis for their annual family reunion. In another case, a family group composed of a grandmother, mother, father, and five-year-old daughter boarded a bus at midnight and rode for eight hours, in order to arrive at the hospital in time for Family Recreation Day.

Clearly, this experience must have great value and significance, for both the patients and the family and friends who come to share it with them.

GUIDES FOR THE CONDUCT OF THERAPEUTIC RECREATION SERVICE IN THE HOSPITAL

Recognizing that there are many different types of hospitals, involving short and long-term care for patients with a wide variety of disabilities and special needs, it is difficult to develop any single set of guides for recreation programs that will apply to all institutions. Nonetheless, the author proposes the following guides:

1. *Statement of Objectives.* The hospital therapeutic recreation program should have a clearly thought out and stated set of objectives and policies, which are in harmony with desirable professional practices as described in the literature and recommended by professional organizations, and which are designed to meet the specific needs and characteristics of the individual institution. These guides and policies should be formulated in a written statement which is fully understood and accepted by the recreation staff, the hospital administrators, and practitioners in medical and other adjunctive services.

2. *Recreation Staff.* Recreation staff members should be hired according to recognized professional standards. They should have regular staff meetings and a continuing program of in-service education. They should participate in professional conferences, should have the opportunity for professional or educational leaves, should be involved in cooperative research and should contribute to the literature. Work schedules should be cooperatively planned and posted, and the levels of pay and personnel benefits should be similar to those of other adjunctive therapists.

3. *Coordination with Other Disciplines.* The recreation program should be fully interpreted to the medical and nursing staff, social workers, psychologists, and other personnel of the hospital, and should be planned and evaluated with their assistance. Recreation workers should operate primarily under medical guidance; this means that they must become familiarized with patients' backgrounds and needs, that they operate as part of the treatment team, that they are consulted regarding the progress of patients, and that recreation is included as a portion of patient case records.

4. *Comprehensive and Varied Program.* The recreation program should be based on the varied interests, needs, and capabilities of patients. At the outset, it should be geared to meet the needs and interests that are shown through patient surveys or interviews; it should then, however, help discover new abilities and develop new interests. The program should cover a broad range of pursuits: active and passive; individual, small group and mass participation; with some activities on a superficial level and others explored in depth; and should provide outlets for physical, social, and creative expression.

5. *Planning for Carry-Over Values.* As much as possible, the program should be planned cooperatively by the staff with patient councils or committees and should make use of patient volunteers in appropriate leadership roles. Emphasis should be placed on program experiences that have carry-over value for discharged patients, and, wherever possible, ac-

tivities and events should be carried on in cooperation with community groups.

6. *Based on Fundamental Needs of Patients.* The program must provide satisfaction for the fundamental needs and desires of patients in these areas: social involvement, security, and sense of acceptance; recognition and achievement; physical and emotional release; discovery of one's capabilities; enjoyment and fun. In attempting to achieve these outcomes, the therapeutic recreation leader must strive to treat the participants as normally as possible, in order to inculcate the same kind of spirit and feeling about recreation that would prevail in a nontherapeutic situation.

RECREATION IN NONHOSPITAL INSTITUTIONAL SETTINGS

As indicated earlier, although the primary type of residential setting in which recreation is offered is the hospital, there are a number of other kinds of institutions which provide recreation for patients or inmates as part of a total program of rehabilitation. These may include the following: (a) homes or schools for the physically handicapped, such as the blind or deaf, orthopedically handicapped, or those with severe, multiple disabilities; (b) homes or schools for mentally retarded children, youth and adults; (c) homes or schools for disturbed or socially maladjusted children and youth; (d) orphanages, homes for unwed mothers, and homes for the indigent; (e) penal institutions, such as prisons, reformatories, and rehabilitation centers for delinquent youth; and (f) treatment centers for those addicted to drugs. The difference between these institutions and hospitals is that they are not usually as concerned with the direct medical treatment of an illness as they are with the long-term rehabilitation and/or education of those they serve, and their successful return to the community. In a few instances, such as old-age homes, there is not this expectation. However, in most cases, the emphasis is on preparing the individual for return to society.

Again, it is not possible to examine in full detail the role of recreation in each of the kinds of institutions that have been listed. Instead, four illustrative categories will be explored here:

1. Recreation programs in institutions for the blind
2. Recreation programs in homes and schools for the mentally retarded
3. Recreation programs in penal institutions
4. Recreation programs in centers for youth rehabilitation

In each case, a number of general guides or principles will be offered, and specific examples of programs or services will be described.

Recreation for the Blind

The term blindness applies to those individuals who have visual acuity no greater than 20/200. Those who fall within the legal definition of blindness may range from an inability to distinguish light from dark, to the ability to get about fairly easily and to read large print with the aid of a magnifying glass. In either case, the loss of sight is likely to cause serious problems of physical, social, and psychological adjustment. This is especially true for those who have had vision and who have then suffered the loss of this function. Blind people tend to become inactive physically and socially. They tend to lack initiative, to show poor physical coordination, to become withdrawn, and to indicate a lack of orientation to their surroundings. All of these tendencies are understandable. They must be overcome, however, if the blind individual is to make a favorable readjustment to life. Within this context, recreation may play an important role in meeting the immediate needs of the blind for social contact and personal expression, as well as helping to reshape the total social readjustment and life pattern of the individual.

What kinds of recreational activities are appropriate for the blind? The basic answer is that almost anything sighted persons can enjoy and do is appropriate for the blind person.

Obviously, certain activities require a degree of modification of adaptation to be played or enjoyed successfully. Still others may be *so* dependent on vision that it simply does not make sense to play them. To illustrate, archery is a sport that occasionally is presented to the blind. However, in "sighting" the arrow toward the target and in knowing whether you have scored, the sport is so visual in nature that the blind person really cannot engage in it with a strong degree of satisfaction. He must be pointed in the right direction, he must be told whether or not he has scored, and, *if* he has, it has probably been luck, rather than his own ability. On the other hand, there are certain sports, such as wrestling, in which the blind can compete on terms of absolute equality. The principle should be that if, through modification of equipment or a degree of assistance, the blind can participate meaningfully or with a reasonable amount of success, the activity may be judged an appropriate one. If, on the other hand, the sport is strongly dependent on visual ability, like archery, skeet shooting, skiing under most circumstances, or bird-watching, it probably just is not worthwhile for the blind to attempt it. The rationale for such an activity may be: "You would think that this activity is impossible for the blind. But, see—we are able to do it. We have overcome even this barrier." The response must be that the barrier has not really been overcome, that they are not realistically engaging in the activity, and that it would be better to seek out recreational experiences in which they really can function effectively.

Appropriate activities fall into the following categories, among others:

Social and Quiet Games. Many forms of group games, icebreakers, quizzes, puzzles, stunts, and contests, are completely appropriate for the blind, either by themselves or in mixed groups with sighted persons. Occasionally, when a visual clue is given, a neighbor may whisper it to them, and, rarely, there may be a game which is not appropriate for them to play.

Table Games. Special checker boards and chess boards have been adapted for use by the blind, with squares either sunken or perforated and with specially contructed pieces which cannot be joggled into the wrong squares. Using cards marked in Braille, the blind are able to play all the common card games and, because of their highly developed sense of memory, may be outstanding in certain games. Dominoes with interlocking ends, and with small tacks used for the dots, have been developed for use by the blind. Recently, a manufacturer developed a crossword puzzle with plastic tiles embossed with Braille letters, which fit into the square recesses of a waffle-like plastic board, and an accompanying book in Braille, which makes it possible for blind persons to enjoy crossword puzzles as a quiet hobby.

Sports and Active Games. These are extremely important for the blind, for several reasons. They give opportunity for better muscle development and physical conditioning, for improved coordination and balance, for the development of a sense of space and direction, and for improved hearing abilities, as well as the obvious recreational benefits to be derived. Among the activities in which blind persons have engaged successfully are the following: camping, skating, horseback riding, swimming, boating, fishing, football, bowling, and adapted forms of baseball and soccer.

To illustrate: the blind are capable of bowling with a degree of satisfaction and success. Indeed, six squads from Brooklyn's Industrial Home for the Blind have been bowling in competition since 1948, and comprise one of the first leagues in the American Blind Bowler's Association, sanctioned by the American Bowling Congress, under ABC rules. A minor concession some blind bowlers may make to their handicap is the use of a portable metal guide rail as an aid in approaching the foul line. Also, team captains who have a degree of vision may assist totally blind players in aiming the ball.

Buell describes adaptations of baseball that are used in various schools for the blind.[15] The game is played on a gravel area. A softball is rolled on the gravel to the batter who must be listening for the rolling

15 Charles E. Buell, *Sports for the Blind* (Ann Arbor, Michigan: Edwards Brothers, 1947), p. 69.

sound, so that he can hit the ball. When he has done this, he runs to a teammate who is calling him from first base. If a totally blind fielder catches the ball while it is still rolling, the batter is out. A large, inflated ball with a bell in it may also be used to play the game. It is usually found that fielding is the most difficult phase of baseball for blind players. Based on the criteria presented earlier, it would seem to be an example of the wrong kind of activity for the blind.

Other sports which would appear to be more suitable are adapted forms of volleyball and soccer, making use of large balls with bells in them so that hearing can, to a degree, replace vision as a means of locating the ball.

Creative and Performing Activities. All forms of creative activity are challenging to the blind, and permit them to operate to their maximum potential. Music, both instrumental and choral, is tremendously satisfying, and the blind can become highly skilled performers. The blind enjoy dancing greatly, particularly recreational forms such as social, folk, and square dancing. Here, it helps to have a few sighted persons dispersed among them and to do dances where people maintain a degree of contact with each other—as in circle folk dances or square dances—rather than those in which they are scattered freely about the floor. Dramatic activities are also extremely successful with blind participants; once they have gotten used to a stage, they can assume roles and move about with uncanny ease and assurance.

Handicrafts. Most craft activities may be carried on successfully without sight. If an individual wishes to continue a craft activity he enjoyed before losing his sight, it may require only a slight alteration in the equipment he used. On the other hand, those who are learning a new craft hobby will require clear, thorough, and precise instruction. Among the handicrafts commonly enjoyed by the blind are the following: sewing, crocheting, needlework, knitting, rug making, raffia work, leather crafts, metal work, stenciling, clay modeling, and sculpture.

Total Programing for the Blind. The range of possible recreational activities for the blind are well illustrated in the program carried on at the Lighthouse in New York City, sponsored by the New York Association for the Blind. Here, in the largest organized recreation program for the blind in the world, almost 800 blind men, women, and children enjoy recreational activities through the year. During the summer, the agency sponsors five camps which serve an additional 600 participants. For some blind people, recreation serves as the first step toward rehabilitation. Activities presented by the Lighthouse include sports and games, arts and crafts, music, dramatics and dancing, social events, lectures, tours, forums, guitar lessons, a college club for students and graduates, and, in a newly built center, bowling and swimming facilities, and a completely equipped exercise room.

While the Lighthouse represents a community facility rather than an institutional program, exactly the same kinds of activities may be offered by the home or school for the blind, both to enrich their lives while they are in residence and to help them make the later transition to community life.

Leadership Guides

In working with the blind, the leader should observe the following guides:

1. It is important to emphasize the fact that the blind individual must do whatever he can to help himself. Sometimes the leader or instructor may fall into the habit of doing things for the blind person because it is easier, rather than force him to learn to do things for himself. This is a mistake, for the major goal must be instilling independence and initiative.

2. As much as possible, normal recreational activities should be used, so that the blind participant becomes able, whenever feasible, to join sighted individuals in recreational activities.

3. The leader must place stress on developing confidence, particularly in the newly blinded person. By placing emphasis on successful accomplishment of reasonable goals at the outset, feelings of inadequacy and insecurity may be reduced.

When recreation is used in this way and made a means of helping the blind individual feel that he is a meaningful part of the world around himself, it becomes a significant part of his total adjustment process.

Recreation for the Mentally Retarded

Another major area of need in programing recreation services for the handicapped lies in the growing concern for the mentally retarded. We are told that there are approximately 6 million children and adults afflicted with mental retardation, with 126,000 retarded children being born each year. Thirty out of every 1,000 children and adults in the United States are retarded—more than the number affected by any physical handicap. Over 1,300,000 of those who are retarded are school-age children. There are 400,000 individuals who are so limited in their abilities that they require constant care and supervision; of these, approximately half live in institutions and training centers.

Exactly what is mental retardation, and why has it become such a great problem?

The modern definition of the American Association on Mental Deficiency considers mental retardation to be significant "sub-average general intellectual functioning which originates during the develop-

mental period and is associated with impairment in adaptive behavior."
Simply stated, the mentally retarded individual is one who experiences
unusual difficulty in learning and is relatively ineffective in adapting to
the problems of ordinary life. Although there have been a number of
technically defined and measured levels of retardation, perhaps the most
meaningful are these: "mild," "moderate," "severe," and "profound."
Among these groups, it is believed that the prevalence of moderate,
severe, and profound retardation among youth and adults will increase
significantly in the next 20 years. Statistics on those with Down's Syndrome (Mongolism), for example, indicate that there is a much higher
life expectancy for this group than was the case years ago.

It is important to note that nearly 3 million adults were once
mildly retarded children. These individuals have managed to achieve an
acceptable level of "adaptive behavior" and in many cases have won
economic and social independence, no longer being recognized as
retarded. However, Kelley points out that an important element in the
education of these young people is in the area of social and recreational
skills:

> It has been confirmed that many young retarded people have not been able
> to adjust in the community and have had to be placed in institutions be-
> cause they have not been able to adjust during leisure, rather than because
> they failed to perform satisfactorily on the job, or . . . in the home. . . .
> As we provide for the education, vocational training, occupational and
> spiritual needs of the retarded, it is equally imperative that we do not
> overlook (his) recreational rehabilitation and social needs. . . . The pres-
> ence of this "plus factor" often makes the difference between a happy life
> in the community or commitment to an institution.[16]

As Superintendent of the Mansfield, Connecticut, State Training
School and Hospital, Kelley places great stress on social training and
recreational opportunity for all children in his institution, on whatever
level of retardation. Thus, with the help of volunteer college students
from the nearby University of Connecticut at Storrs, teen-age girls are
involved in a Good Grooming Project which has a marked effect on their
appearance and manners. Physical activities, including softball, swimming, baseball, basketball, and even football, which is played competitively with other high schools, serve to counteract the common obese
and physically weak appearance of many retarded children. In this
context, it is important to recognize that many of the apparent deficiencies
or limitations of retarded children are a consequence of *disuse*. They are
simply not given a chance to see what they *can* do, or to develop to their
full potential. Thus, an English researcher, Dr. J. N. Oliver, reported

[16] Francis P. Kelley, "Recreational Services for the Retarded—An Urgent Need,"
in *Recreation in Treatment Centers* (Washington, D.C.: American Recreation Society,
September, 1964), p. 12.

dramatic results from a special physical education program for the retarded: all improved in physical ability, physical fitness, and strength, and 25 percent improved intellectually. In addition, they gained significantly in self-esteem, self-confidence, and the ability to get along with others.

At the Mansfield Training School and Hospital, other recreational activities include: weekly dances for the residents every Saturday afternoon and evening, birthday parties, picnics, field trips, a swimming and camping program, and special seasonal activities to celebrate holidays like Christmas, Halloween, and Easter. Children from both the "educable" and "trainable" classifications are admitted to the formal school program at an early age and are trained for eventual return to the community whenever possible. However, some of the most severely handicapped do not have the capacity to leave the school and will spend the remainder of their lives there. For them, as Burghardt comments:

> We must realize the fact that in some instances the recreational skills mastered by the mentally retarded will constitute their major achievements and their most important assets. There is slim hope that their reading, writing, arithmetic and vocational aptitudes will assure them of acceptance by society. Thus, the skills they acquire as a result of the recreational program could mean more to them than they ever would mean to a normal person, insuring a reasonably successful social life.[17]

On every level, then, recreational and social experiences are important to retarded children and adults. Yet, it is a sad commentary that only a small proportion of public recreational agencies in the United States offer program services for the retarded, either in integrated or separate groups. A number of excellent programs of this type are described in the following chapter.

In summing up, it must be recognized that the mentally retarded have the same basic needs as the nonretarded. When properly guided, they can take part in a wide variety of activities, such as swimming, square dancing, skating, bicycling, folk dancing, singing, arts and crafts, and games. Often, their abilities are unknown until they are tested, and at that point, many retardates move well past their so-called assumed limits.

As a single vivid example of what the retarded can do, 65 children and young adults from Letchworth Village for the Mentally Retarded in Thiells, New York, recently put on a full-scale performance of the musical "Oklahoma," before 3,000 guests at the New York City Hilton Hotel. These individuals, with a chronological age of between 8 and 35, and an IQ range between 30 and 79, accepted the assignment for the

17 Edward T. Burghardt, "Recreation for the Retarded, an Aid to Balanced Living," in *Recreation in Treatment Centers, op. cit.* (September, 1964), p. 11.

show as a climax to a fund-raising campaign for the school. They prepared for the performance for six months, rehearsed steadily, and did an almost professional job of remembering their lines and cues.

For many other retarded children and adults throughout the United States today, recreation is opening up new doors to learning and enriched living.

Recreation for the Socially Maladjusted

In quite a different category from the mentally retarded or physically handicapped is the individual who has been placed in a penal or corrective institution because he has broken the law. Yet, he too suffers from a crippling handicap—the inability to adjust to the demands of society or to recognize his own potential as a constructive and law-abiding citizen.

What role does recreation play in the institutional setting for those who are being socially rehabilitated?

First, it is necessary to recognize that, as a group, delinquents and adult criminals have markedly different personality patterns and attitudes about leisure than the population at large.

For example, the Gluecks have shown that delinquents are: more socially assertive and defiant toward adult authority; more resentful of others, hostile, and destructive; more impulsive in behavior; less cooperative and dependent on others; less conventional in their ideas and behavior. In terms of attitudes toward leisure, it is known that the families of young criminals rarely engage in constructive forms of recreation. Instead of hobbies, or active participation in creative or athletic pursuits, the principal form of leisure amusement becomes playing cards, or passive entertainment. Indeed, it is within leisure, and as a form of pathological play, that many adult criminals-to-be begin their careers, carrying on illegal gambling, becoming involved in vice and drug addiction, or engaging in theft or vandalism for sheer excitement.

With this background, what happens when the young criminal is sent to prison or a youth correction institution? Garret Heyns, then a Michigan reformatory warden, has written:

> Among the inmates of correctional institutions there are many who have no knowledge or skills which will enable them to make acceptable use of their leisure. Most of them lack the avocational interests of the well adjusted. They cannot play, they do not read, they have no hobbies. In many instances, improper use of leisure is a factor in their criminality. Others lack the ability to engage in any cooperative activity with their fellows; teamwork is something foreign to their experience. Still others lack self-control or a sense of fair play; they cannot engage in competitive activity without losing their heads. If these men are to leave the institutions as

stable, well-adjusted individuals, these needs must be filled; the missing interests, knowledge, and skills must be provided. They must be brought into contact with opportunities which will eventually lead to their seeking out wholesome recreation interests when they return to society. It is the carry-over of such interests which concerns the institution in its effort at effecting rehabilitation.[18]

This, then, is a primary purpose of prison recreation. Based on the belief that the penal institution's task is not to punish or degrade, but to protect society from the individual who cannot control himself, and to help that individual become fit to return to society, a wide variety of techniques must be used. The modern prison with a sound philosophy today has an extensive education program, provides vocational counseling and rehabilitation, offers both individual and group psychological counseling or psychotherapy, and effective recreation services. The latter may be viewed as having two essential functions:

1. Recreation has certain positive values for the prisoner. It gives him experience in cooperative enterprises, an opportunity to learn self-control and discipline, to build more meaningful and constructive social relationships than in the past, and to learn recreational skills which, after discharge, may replace the less desirable pursuits of the past. There is no claim that these outcomes will automatically occur; however, they represent hoped-for objectives to be achieved.

2. A second major function of recreation in the corrective setting is based on the nature of life in the prison itself. A vivid picture of this is offered by a former convict:

> Prison life provides a set of conditions so unnatural as to constitute a state of existence very remote from living. Under these circumstances, recreation is my only tangible link with normal life. . . . In its simplest meaning to me, recreation is anything that provides escape from the monotonous . . . regimentation and stricture of prison routine. The undeviating monotone of prison life induces in one a deadly, depressive introspection—unless alleviated by mental diversion. . . .[19]

Seen in this light, recreation has the important purpose of acting as a safety valve for the sublimation of aggressive urges and pent-up energies. It helps to make prison bearable.

It is well known that reformatories and prisons frequently fail in their purpose, in terms of the large number of prisoners who return to them after discharge. Whether this is because of the basic inability of the ex-inmate to adjust to society, or society's unwillingness to accept him and give him a fair chance, is not known. However, it is crucial that

[18] Garret Heyns, "Penal Institutions," in *Annals of the American Academy of Political Sciences*, September, 1957, pp. 71–75.
[19] "What Recreation Means to Me," in *Correctional Recreation*, April, 1946, n.a.

the corrective institution make every attempt to really rehabilitate the prisoner—to give him self-respect, new personal and social understandings, skills, and attitudes. If this is to be done, prisons cannot be permitted to remain places where youthful offenders become confirmed recidivists, where hatred of society is enforced, where new criminal skills are learned, and deviant behavior encouraged or winked at.

Thus, the properly run penal institution today provides recreational programing under skilled professional leadership. Activities may include the following: sports, entertainment, movies, individual and group hobbies, arts and crafts, and dramatics. These may be taught or led by inmates who have special skills or, not infrequently, by volunteers who come from outside the institution. Particularly in youth correctional centers, strong efforts have been made to develop such offerings.

Overall, however, far too few prisons today have the facilities, the trained leadership, and the money necessary for fully effective recreation programing. Often administrators fail to press for such resources because of the fear of public criticism and resistance. The old concept that prison is a place basically for punishment and that the prisoner has no real rights as a human being still prevails. Although public attitudes are rapidly improving (as in the case of the physically handicapped), the prison that introduces extensive recreation facilities or services still may be accused of becoming a "country club" in conservative newspaper editorials or on the floors of state legislatures.

That it is not, and that money spent in this way may be far less costly than money spent in apprehending a criminal and returning him to prison again, must be brought to the attention of the public. One state penal administrator states the case well:

> Recreation in correctional institutions, like other ancillary activities, important as they may be, must be operated within the mandate of "and safely keep." The admonition does not negate the possibility of a well-organized program, for when recreation assumes its proper place and balance in the institutional program, it, in and of itself, acts as a custodial device. A minimizing of frustrations in fulfilling normal needs—satisfaction through productive labor, security through uniformity without regimentation, and diversion—tend to prevent the frustrations inherent in incarceration from overflowing into disturbances and to reduce to a minimum the tensions brought about by the intensity of close living. Recreation, therefore, is a distinct part of the correctional process. It must have direction, it must be geared to the resources of the individual institution and be an integral part of the program of that institution. Above all, it must be flexible and many-sided enough to have something valid to offer each inmate, something that is within the range of his physical and mental resources.[20]

[20] Donald H. Goff, "Recreation in Correctional Institutions," *Recreation,* May, 1955, p. 220.

Drama at San Quentin. As a single example of the kind of activity that provides important values for prisoners, the Drama Workshop at San Quentin, California's largest penitentiary, may be examined. This is part of an extensive program of organized recreation involving many interests and forms of activity. The Drama Workshop is completely under the direction of several inmates who are serving life sentences and who alternate in directing and acting responsibilities. All plays selected must be approved by the warden, and all men in prison except those with a "maximum custody" classification may participate in one of several roles—directing, acting, or building sets. Performances, when ready, are presented over a three-day period, for over 2,500 inmates and 300 employees and guests, including specially invited members of the press. Among the plays that have been presented are: "Twelve Angry Men," "The Caine Mutiny Court Martial," "Mister Roberts," "Waiting for Godot," and "Inherit the Wind." After a play has closed, the Drama Workshop keeps active, giving classes in stagecraft, acting, and set construction.

All of the prisoners who participate in the Drama Workshop are also involved in a total rehabilitation program. They attend regular therapy sessions, and many participate in extravocational and educational programs, beyond their required work assignments. The prison administration believes that these combined experiences are of considerable value in helping inmates adjust to the responsibilities and obligations they will face on return to society. Apostol writes:

> Not only does it (the drama group) provide an excellent creative outlet for the men, along with serving as a leisure-time activity, but the group has proved to be a splendid emotional outlet with marked therapeutic values. The men learn to work together and accept a responsibility toward the show they are doing and each other.[21]

Arts and Crafts in a School for Delinquents. Within any given institution, a single form of activity may prove to be of major value in terms of meeting the needs of participants and being feasible, as far as facilities and cost are concerned. For example, at the State Agricultural and Industrial School for Delinquents, in Industry, New York, it was found that youngsters had extremely limited recreational *and* intellectual skills and capacities. One of the areas of activity that they found most interesting and that provided the greatest measure of success and recognition was arts and crafts. Thus, a diversified program of crafts is in effect at the school, including: leather carving and assembling; the making of handbags, wallets, and other salable items; wood projects; aluminum etching; copper and aluminum foil tooling; weaving on hand looms and by hand; basketry; model boat and plane building; wood carving and statuary

21 John N. Apostol, "Drama at San Quentin," *Recreation,* October, 1963, p. 366.

plaster. During the wintertime, a special project is made of snow sculpture.

As a means of motivating participation, annual hobby shows and other crafts contests are held, with large numbers of spectators attending. Awards are given and the products of the youngsters are purchased. In general, the activity serves to promote self-confidence, awareness of creative potential, and, in some cases, to lead to further vocational training or interest.

RECREATION AND TROUBLED YOUTH

The basic issue of whether recreation is a meaningful deterrent or preventative for juvenile delinquency is discussed elsewhere in this text (see pp. 278–285). However, it is generally accepted that it is an important part of the combined "team" approach in community programs of social service. Within institutions that serve troubled young people, it is also a respected element in the treatment process. For example, in hospitals or homes which care for drug addicts, recreation is invariably strongly emphasized.

Hospital for Drug Addicts

The Riverside Hospital for adolescent narcotics users ranging in age from 14 to 21, on North Brother Island, New York City, has included recreation services, along with other therapies, including those provided by psychiatric social workers, occupational therapists, nurses, and chaplains.

The patient population of 128 is divided into six teams, with members of all staffs assigned to each of these teams (each team has a recreational therapist). The recreation program is carried on from 2:45 P.M. to 10 P.M. on weekdays, and from 10 A.M. to 10 P.M. on other days. It includes such activities as: games, movies, music, dancing, discussion groups, dramatics, outings, and field trips. A Recreation Patient Council, consisting of two elected representatives. from each of the six teams, helps to plan recreation programs and events. The close relationship between the recreation therapist and the patient is illustrated in the following passage:

> Doctors and psychiatrists feel that the informal noncompulsive type of relationship which we establish with a patient, in a game or activity, is advantageous because the patient finds it easier to talk when there is not the formal "across-the-desk" type of interview. We very often are in the favorable position of being able to report a great deal about how the patient feels regarding people and life in general. At Riverside, we feel the addic-

tion of the patient is secondary and the mental maladjustment is the main factor to be treated. . . .[22]

In working with patients, it is important to recognize that the addict's feelings of emptiness and isolation need to be met by relaxed, tension-free activities, in an atmosphere of mutual trust and respect. Typically, the addict has a low level of self-esteem, little tolerance for failure or frustration, and a tendency to view the "square-world" (of nonaddicts) with hostility and defensiveness. Thus the program of activities must be flexible and should allow for easy involvement. Specific program sessions should be brief in length (from 30 minutes to an hour), because of the limited attention span of the addict or postaddict.

Although a minimum of pressure is exerted, and the recreation program is comparatively free of rules and regulations (apart from attendance and behavior at sessions), the recreation leader does permit or even encourage a degree of dependency on the part of the patient. Gradually, however, as new interests are discovered and involvement deepens, the therapist strives to become primarily a supportive figure, and to help the patient move to a more independent level of functioning.[23] At this point, the therapist acts as a counselor in preparing postaddicts to attend aftercare or "halfway houses" in the community.

A Youth Camp Program for School Drop-outs

A final illustration deals with young people from lower socioeconomic backgrounds who are undergoing a process of social and vocational rehabilitation which will permit them to become contributing and self-sufficient members of society, rather than members of the permanent army of unemployed. A number of states and major cities have initiated special projects for the training of young men in this category.

In one such program, sponsored by the New York City Youth Board, a job-training center was established at Putnam Valley, New York. Its first group of trainees consisted of youths between the ages of 17 to 20, all of whom were high school drop-outs, culturally deprived, and without job skills or the prospect of obtaining them. Most of them were Negro or Puerto Rican. Although they were not delinquents, clearly their role in society was marginal. The project was financed by the Office of Manpower, Automation and Training, and the Department of Health, Education and Welfare.

Basically, the assignment was to teach these youngsters a specific

[22] Madison Dunn, "Hospital Capsules," *Recreation,* May, 1956, p. 237.
[23] Elliott G. Young and Ira J. Hutchison, "Prescription Recreation: A Bridge to Community Living for the Narcotics Addict," in *Recreation in Treatment Centers, op. cit.* (September, 1964), pp. 59–63.

area of job competence—operating business machines. But, beyond this, as in the case of mentally retarded youths who return to the community, the task was also to help equip them to deal effectively with society on their return.

William Banks, the social worker who acted as project director of the training center, viewed recreation as an intrinsic phase of the program. It was seen as a means of ventilating excess energy in a positive manner, and as a catharsis for emotional problems. Thus the first activities offered—running early in the morning, touch football and basketball— were of a simple, vigorous nature. They also served to promote physical condition and to develop *esprit de corps* among the students. Recognizing the value of these activities, Banks began to explore available community resources. The Commissioner of Recreation in Peekskill, a nearby city, invited the job-training center students to visit one of his recreation centers for informal social recreation. They did so, came into contact with people in the community, and were soon invited to attend Peekskill High School's football games and victory dances. Before long, the students formed a basketball team, competing in the Peekskill Community Senior Basketball League.

Banks writes:

> These experiences provide our students with the opportunity to compete with other young men in their own age group in a positive form of activity. They also tended to eliminate the feeling of being isolated which, I feel, is one of the negative aspects of many residential type settings which are set up to deal with youngsters from socially and economically deprived areas, school dropouts, underachievers and emotionally disturbed youngsters who are not psychotic. . . . The process of rehabilitation is expected to take place in environments quite different from the ones in which the youths encountered their problems.
>
> Our reasons for allowing these youngsters to take an active part in community activities were to encourage them to emulate the constructive values of the youngsters with whom they come into contact. Also, they begin to realize that people are willing to accept them, and this provides them with a feeling of self-worth.[24]

Two other aspects of the Putnam Valley program are worthy of emphasis: (a) an emphasis on dangerous activities and on (b) cultural programing.

Often delinquents and predelinquents deliberately seek out daredevil activities, as a means of proving themselves and demonstrating their courage. Frequently, the activities offered in recreation centers and community agencies are just too tame and unchallenging for them. Recognizing this, Banks comments:

24 William Banks, letter to author, February 25, 1965.

. . . rather than attempt to convince these youngsters that activities of this nature can be perilous, we have attempted to provide them with experiences which can fulfill their needs for excitement, such as sleighing down steep hills, horseback riding along seemingly dangerous trails, mountain climbing, skiing, hiking and overnight camping trips. This afforded them the opportunity to sublimate their aggressive desires into positive channels while being properly supervised.[25]

In terms of cultural activities, the students have also been introduced to a variety of experiences they had never had at home. They went on trips to the ballet, to off-Broadway theater (to see a play dealing with problems of culturally deprived youth) and participated in regular art classes, as part of their total program. Clearly, these activities helped them broaden their perspectives, recognize a new world of leisure opportunity, and become better equipped to deal with the city on their return to their homes and to the new jobs they were able to obtain.

A number of examples of recreation programing in institutional settings for the ill or handicapped, and for the socially maladjusted, have been cited. Throughout, references have been made to recreation opportunities in the community setting for the discharged mental patient or ex-addict, or the physically handicapped or mentally retarded youth or adult. The following chapter analyzes this problem in detail and offers a number of excellent examples of community-wide planning to meet the social and recreational needs of the handicapped.

SUGGESTED QUESTIONS FOR DISCUSSION

1. What is the rationale for the use of recreation in hospital settings? In your judgment, should it be considered a specific form of therapy? Cite the arguments for and against.
2. Give an overview of the specific functions and examples of program service of therapeutic recreation, when offered for: (a) psychiatric patients, (b) the institutionalized blind; or, (c) institutionalized retarded children.
3. "Recreation in prisons or reformatories? We're not running country clubs!" Develop a positive reply to this statement, giving support for the provision of recreation services in penal or correctional institutions.

25 *Ibid.*

Chapter *13*

Recreation for the Ill and Handicapped in the Community Setting

As the recreation movement itself has grown to include participants of all ages and backgrounds and to meet a wide variety of special interests and needs, it now must embrace those who have the greatest needs of all. These are the ill and handicapped who live among us, within the community setting. They include the physically disabled, the discharged mental patient, the mentally retarded child or adult, the chronically ill, homebound older person, as well as many others.

Although therapeutic recreation services in hospitals and other institutional treatment centers have increased greatly, this has not yet become the case in the community setting. Thus far, both the directors of voluntary agencies and public recreation departments have failed to come to grips with this need. Too often, they are characterized by what Elliott Avedon describes as "tunnel vision," an outlook which so focuses on the *limitations* of the individual to be served that either *no* service is provided, or what little is done simply enforces his dependency. Avedon cites a number of examples:

> A middle-aged woman used to do a great deal of swimming before her leg was amputated. When she was back at her job as secretary, she thought she would like to take up swimming again. She went to her local "Y" but was told that the "CP" association conducted "swimming for the handicapped" on Wednesdays from one to three and she would have to see *them*. She explained that she did not need swimming lessons. She was told that the only time she would be allowed to use the pool was Wednesday from one to three because of insurance and "all that."

> An advertising executive was quite a theater-goer before an airplane accident, but now that he's in a wheelchair, he never gets to go. It seems that the fire laws prohibit "standing" in the aisles, and since all theater seats are permanently in place, there is no room for him and his wheelchair. Theater authorities suggested that he move into a theater seat, have someone check his wheelchair, and then he could relax and enjoy the show worry free. However, it occurred to *him,* that if a fire broke out, he might have some difficulty getting his wheelchair back, so he could get out of the theater. . . .

> A file clerk wanted to join the craft group at an adult evening school, but was referred to another agency which serves discharged psychiatric patients. She explained that she was no longer ill and did not want to be with all those sick people who constantly talk about their problems. All she wants is to work with people who are interested in handcrafts.

> The mother knows her blind child is perfectly able to swing on a swing and, for that matter, can play many games with other children at the playground, but the leader keeps telling her about the local association for the blind and the special program it has for blind children. This mother wants to know why the leader does not understand that her child needs a chance to play with children who are not blind. . . .[1]

Each of these cases represents a different type of exclusion or enforced dependency for those who are handicapped, within the community. The basic issue is, what rationale may be found for providing public or voluntary agency-sponsored recreation services for the ill and handicapped at all? The answer is twofold:

1. Like all people, the handicapped have a right to self-expression, social involvement, creative experience, and the other important values of recreation.

2. Unlike other people, many handicapped individuals find most aspects of "normal" life, such as the opportunity to complete their education, to marry and have a family, to enter a profession and earn a liveli-

---

[1] Elliott M. Avedon, "Enable the Disabled," *Recreation,* February, 1965, pp. 70–71.

hood, to travel freely, closed to them. For this reason, recreation represents a particularly crucial need. If it is not provided, their lives are cruelly barren and empty.

As pointed out in the preceding chapter, we have grown considerably in our thinking about those who are retarded, mentally ill, or otherwise crippled or handicapped. The conviction has been accepted that they must be recognized as human beings with inherent dignity, worth, and potential, and that we have an obligation to make their lives as full and happy as possible.

In addition to this healthy shift in public attitudes, the nature of rehabilitative services for such groups as the mentally ill has been changing dramatically. There has been a steady shift away from the custodial approach, in which mental patients are shut up (often without adequate attention or medical services of any type) in large state hospitals. Instead, the trend is toward: (a) having acutely ill psychiatric patients cared for in psychiatric units in general hospitals; (b) reorganizing the larger state hospitals into small, active, custodial care units for chronically disturbed patients, with a "total push" program of work and play in the milieu setting as a primary means of treatment; and (c) establishing special recreation centers for discharged patients to help them adjust to the social and recreational life of their communities.[2] Overall, there are far more voluntary and temporary commitments than formal court commitments today, with fewer patients staying in the hospital and more patients being admitted and discharged after short stays. The importance of family members and of the community itself in the treatment process has become increasingly recognized.[3]

Thus, it becomes impossible to think about the continuing treatment and full recovery of mental patients without providing adequate social and recreational programs for them in the community itself, or without making it possible for those who are capable of the adjustment to enter ongoing activity programs. The same conclusion may be drawn about other major groupings of handicapped individuals within the community.

PAST RELUCTANCE TO SERVE

How many public and voluntary recreation agencies have recognized these needs and moved forthrightly to meet them?

Curiously, the majority of recreation administrators in the past have felt that serving the handicapped was either none of their concern, or

2 Beatrice H. Hill, "The National Scene: Program in Action," in *Therapeutic Recreation in the Community* (Bloomington, Indiana: Indiana University, 1962), p. 23.

3 Donald F. Moore, M.D., "Mental Illness, A Community Problem," in *Therapeutic Recreation in the Community* (Bloomington, Indiana: Indiana University, 1962), pp. 31–44.

that it represented a prohibitively difficult task. A 1958 survey of group work and recreation agencies in New York City, carried on by the Community Council of that metropolis, revealed comparatively few community centers or settlement houses that had instituted programs of this type. The author, in an informal survey in 1962 of public recreation departments and special organizations serving the handicapped in the tristate area of New York, New Jersey, and Connecticut, found little interchange or cooperation between the two. Again, when asked why they did not serve the handicapped in their communities, the public recreation administrators replied: (a) they felt the task would be an expensive and difficult one; (b) no one had brought the need to their attention; and (c) they would not know how to reach the handicapped in their community or to develop a sound program for them.

CURRENT COMMUNITY PRACTICES

The most recent attempt to gather comprehensive information in this field was made in 1964 when the National Recreation Association and the National Association for Retarded Children assisted Ruth Marson in a survey of 2,000 community recreation departments to determine what services were being provided in the community for the mentally or physically handicapped. Of the total number, 427 responded that they provided recreation facilities or programs for either of these groups or both. In response to a follow-up questionnaire which sought fuller details, only 202 communities replied. These, it may be assumed, represented the small core of cities and towns that attempted to provide effective programs for special groups—about 10 percent.

In 139 cases, the mentally retarded were served separately in such facilities as playgrounds, community recreation centers, parks, swimming pools, and day camps.

In 164 cases, the physically handicapped were served separately, in similar facilities.

Overall, it was found that the most common program activities for both groups of handicapped were very much like those enjoyed by non-handicapped in community programs: arts and crafts, games, picnicking, spectator sports, and music performances.

However, Marson points out that even the most popular activity, arts and crafts, is available to the handicapped in just over half of the responding communities, and that the most popular facility was available in less than half of the communities. Only about one third of the responding groups gave transportation assistance to the handicapped, and in many cases these special programs (which tended to be segregated from the regular programs) were supported financially by special fees, charges, and contributions from interested parents or community groups. Marson concludes:

> Despite the tremendous growth of recreation, new developments in medical science and increased leisure time for Americans, there has been a great lag in developing recreation services for the handicapped by community recreation departments. We believe that the next few years will show a marked increase in this service by communities.[4]

EXPANSION OF SPECIAL SERVICES

How valid is this conclusion? Actually, on several levels, community recreation service for the ill and handicapped is being expanded. The federal government, through training grants for graduate students in therapeutic recreation service, is providing important assistance. Similarly, federal agencies in the Department of Health, Education and Welfare have encouraged and supported a number of experimental or demonstration projects involving recreation for special groups in the community.

Statewide Programs

A number of states have taken significant steps to provide needed recreation services for the handicapped. In Massachusetts, for example, a law which had been passed giving financial reimbursement to cities and towns for the education of mentally and physically handicapped children was so successful in increasing special classes and services that, in 1958, a similar law was passed to promote and foster recreation. The legislation assigns responsibility for this function to the Director of Special Education in the Massachusetts State Department of Education, but specifies, "The department is hereby authorized to cooperate with cities and towns which establish recreation programs for the physically handicapped and mentally retarded persons . . ." (General Laws, Chapter 69, Section 39-D of the Resolves of 1958).

In 1959, the first year of the law, the two original public recreation programs that had been in effect expanded to 19. Each succeeding year, recreation services for the handicapped grew rapidly; by 1962, for example, 48 cities and towns were participating.

Program services include day camping, swimming, and various adapted indoor recreation activities. The majority of programs are conducted for mentally handicapped children, and the blind, although programs established for the physically handicapped serve children with nearly every type of disability. Efforts have been expanded to include

---

[4] Morton Thompson, "National Survey of Community Recreation Service to the Mentally Retarded and Physically Handicapped," *Recreation*, April, 1965, pp. 191–192.

the integration of selected children into programs of nonhandicapped youngsters.

Although the administration, supervision, and financing of the program is carried on by the State Department of Education, the actual sponsors are park and recreation departments within the framework of local government. In 1962, almost $40,000 was spent by the state in reimbursing local programs. However, it is a moot point whether the available 50 percent support is the key factor accounting for the growth of these programs, as much as the knowledge that the state as a whole recognized the need for recreation for the handicapped and was *prepared* to support it.[5]

Other states which have carried out surveys of recreation programs for the handicapped, or which have published special directories of such services, include Washington and North Carolina.

MUNICIPAL PROGRAMS SERVING THE HANDICAPPED

Kansas City, Missouri

One of the best known cities to have provided a comprehensive program of services for the handicapped is Kansas City, Missouri.[6] Here, the Recreation Division of the Welfare Department of the city government conducted seasonal programs for crippled, diabetic, cardiac, and cerebral palsied children, as early as 1949. In the early 1950's, it instituted day camp programs for the deaf and hard of hearing, and for the orthopedically handicapped.

In 1955, a Supervisor of Special Recreation was appointed with the purpose of establishing a year-round comprehensive program of recreation service—initially for the orthopedically handicapped, of whom there were about 14,000 within the Kansas City metropolitan area. Wisely, before developing the program, the following agencies were approached for consultation and advice: the United Cerebral Palsy Association, the National Foundation for Infantile Paralysis, the Jackson County Society for Crippled Children, the Kansas City Board of Education, Goodwill Industries, the Muscular Dystrophy Association, the Arthritis and Rheumatism Foundation, the Multiple Sclerosis Association, and others.

It was found that 11 different camping, day camping, Scouting, club and swimming programs were already being sponsored for the handicapped by various organizations. Nonetheless, the preliminary discussions revealed the following important needs:

[5] Frank Robinson, "Pioneering Legislation Provides Recreation for Handicapped," *Recreation,* November, 1963, p. 403.

[6] "Community Organization for Recreation for the Ill and Handicapped: The Kansas City Plan," *American Recreation Journal,* January–February, 1964, p. 19.

1. There was a recognition that the majority of the orthopedically handicapped youth and adults in the city were not being reached by the programs offered.

2. There was a concern for adults who were able to leave their homes but felt they were too handicapped to join regular social groups, and for teenagers who had gone as far as they could in school, but who could not find work, and who therefore had lost contact with all group involvement.

3. There were many homebound children and adults who were completely left to their own inadequate resources in terms of recreational pursuits and hobbies.

4. Existing programs were so handicapped by limitations of budget and staff that they could not satisfactorily meet the needs of those they attempted to serve.

In an effort to meet these needs, a Greater Kansas City Council on Recreation for the Handicapped was formed—to serve not only the physically handicapped but those with emotional and social limitations. Encouragement and support came from a nearby Veterans' Administration hospital which was concerned about the opportunities existing in the community for its discharged patients. Other organizations which joined the first ones to be consulted included the YWCA, American Red Cross, the Junior League, the Boys' Clubs, the Visiting Nurses' Association, and others. This Council worked closely with the Recreation Division in establishing policies and procedures, planning programs, helping to recruit and train volunteers, stimulating interest and participation in the program by the handicapped persons coming in contact with the member organizations, and providing clerical and office assistance. Among the first steps was the establishment of an insurance plan to protect program participants and sponsors.

Through the years that followed, the Greater Kansas City Council on Recreation for the Handicapped developed a program including the following elements:

1. A visiting program for homebound children and adults, to help them discover new interests and abilities in such play areas as games, crafts, puppetry, collections, instrument playing, or other hobbies. This was based heavily on the use of volunteers.

2. A club program for orthopedically handicapped adults, with stress on their taking over leadership responsibility themselves. Activities included weekly meetings, parties for holidays and special occasions, square dancing, group singing, movies, hobbies and hobby groups, dramatics, and games.

3. A similar program for orthopedically handicapped teenagers, with activities suited to their interests.

4. A training program in home recreation activities for orthopedically handicapped children, which was given to parents of such children or other inter-

ested adults. In a series of 10 sessions, workshops and discussions were held, dealing with ways of minimizing disability, modifications of recreational activities, and ways of giving assistance.
5. Television programs which were directed to the orthopedically handicapped. These served both to encourage them by presenting "write-in" tournaments and contests, interviews with handicapped people who had special hobbies, the teaching of crafts projects and games, and also to educate the public in general with respect to the needs and capabilities of the handicapped.

In addition, special outdoor programs were initiated during the summer months, including sleepover camping for children with cardiac conditions, diabetes, cerebral palsy, or blindness, and day camping for children who were deaf or hard of hearing, orthopedically handicapped or mentally retarded. Overall, the Kansas City Council serves a valuable coordinating function by: (a) making surveys as to need, and carrying on research; (b) acting as a referral agency for handicapped individuals; (c) stimulating public interest; (d) enlisting the help of community groups and the public at large; and (e) recruiting and training professional and volunteer workers in this field.

San Francisco, California

San Francisco has, for a number of years, been aware of the recreational needs of the handicapped. Like Kansas City, it has had, over a five-year period, a committee composed of representatives of agencies serving the handicapped and medical and recreational authorities carrying out an extensive investigation of services and opportunities. This committee concluded that the Public Recreation Department should provide the basic floor of recreation services to all persons, including the handicapped. In June, 1964, the Advisory Council submitted a proposal to the Recreation and Parks Commission for the establishment of a varied program of recreation services to the handicapped. The two basic recommendations were approved by the Recreation and Parks Commission, as follows:

1. Creation of a "Special Services for Handicapped Division" within the Recreation and Park Department which would:
   a. provide services to those handicapped who could, with proper information and encouragement, participate in ongoing programs;
   b. provide services to those handicapped who will require special enabling activities leading toward participation in the public ongoing programs;
   c. supervise the services to the severely handicapped (these services to be performed by negotiation of a special contract with individual public or private agencies especially qualified and equipped to provide services to the severely handicapped);
   d. conduct in-service training courses for department personnel and volun-

teers in the skills, philosophy, understanding, and leadership necessary
to conduct and program recreation . . . activities for the handicapped;

e. develop case findings and referrals as a continuing process;

f. develop community orientation and education regarding the availability
of services;

g. work in close cooperation and coordination with the San Francisco Advisory Council on Recreation for the Handicapped, which will continue
to study needs, recommend programs, assist in coordination of services,
and serve as a liaison group with all coordination councils.

2. The negotiation of a contract with a voluntary agency or agencies qualified
and able to provide specialized recreation services for the severely handicapped residents of San Francisco as needed, and on a contractual service
basis.

a. Because there will always be a need for specialized services which are not
being met by any one agency, the San Francisco Recreation and Parks
Commission should contract for special recreation services on a county
and city level for the severely handicapped.[7]

Following this action, a request was submitted for the 1965–66
budget, to support the Special Services for the Handicapped Division,
to the extent of approximately $34,000. In addition, $65,000 was requested as a subsidy grant to the San Francisco Recreation Center for
the Handicapped, to assist that organization in providing a year-round
recreation program for severely handicapped residents who are unable
to participate in other program services sponsored by the Recreation and
Parks Commission. Thus, San Francisco demonstrates a resourceful approach to meeting the recreation needs of the handicapped on a contractual or subsidy basis.

Seattle, Washington

Another city on the West Coast which has provided varied services
for the handicapped through the activities of the Recreation Division
of its Park Department is Seattle, Washington. Here, an extensive program of services is offered under the direction of a full-time specialist in
this area. The Seattle schedule of activities includes the following:

Monthly meetings for handicapped children in various recreation centers
around the city, usually on Friday or Saturday afternoons. These are continued through the year and involve varied club and recreational activities.

Special swimming lessons for handicapped children, in 10-week series during
the fall. These have such special arrangements as: at least one instructor
for every two or three children, with beginners or those who cannot support themselves in the water being taught individually; in one pool the

7 Edward A. McDevitt, "A Big Step Forward," *New Jersey Recreation and Park
Society Annual*, 1965, p. 25.

water temperature is kept from 85 to 90 degrees, and the pool level is lowered below 36 inches. Doctors' certificates and parents' permissions are required, of course, and car pool arrangements are handled by parents to provide transportation.

A summer day camp for handicapped children 6 years of age or older. These are held in three three-week sessions at several camp and park locations in Seattle and King County. Activities include nature crafts, music, games, singing, creative dramatics, sports, cookouts, and hiking for those who are able; again, at least one counselor is provided for every two or three campers.

Other programs in Seattle include special groups organized by the Cerebral Palsy Workshop and the Washington Association for the Retarded. There is a special bowling league for the retarded, and wheelchair basketball for the orthopedically handicapped, as well as a basketball league for adult deaf people. As in other communities of this type, a large portion of the leadership must be obtained through the use of volunteers. Otherwise, costs would be prohibitively high. Through the use of a central volunteer bureau and the assistance of parents and service agencies in the community, it is possible to attract, train, and hold numbers of capable volunteers.

GUIDES FOR MUNICIPALITIES IN PROVIDING SPECIAL SERVICES

Based on a study of recreation services for the ill and handicapped in selected public recreation systems, Miller presents a number of basic recommendations for community organization. While interagency councils may be extremely effective in arousing public awareness of needs or providing certain kinds of advice or technical assistance, it is her view that the public authority must carry the major responsibility in this area. She recommends that:

1. Local public recreation systems recognize and assume responsibility for making recreation opportunities available to the ill and the handicapped in their communities
2. Public recreation administrators assume the initiative and leadership in developing such a program
3. Established principles for community recreation, generally, be used among the guides to establish noninstitutional recreation programs for the ill and handicapped
4. The resources of those agencies familiar with working with the ill and the handicapped be used in planning, cooperating, and evaluating such a program
5. Such programs represent "community efforts," from their initial planning to the developmental phase and then the execution of the program
6. Primary responsibility for administering the program be centered in the local, public recreation managing authority

7. Financial support be established on a continuing basis, through the contributions of both public and private agencies
8. An advisory committee be established, from the community, with definite duties and responsibilities as included in a written charter and consistent with the administrative policies of the local public recreation system
9. Appropriate professional consultation be utilized, especially in the initial stages of planning and development of community recreation services for the ill and handicapped [8]

ANALYZING THOSE TO BE SERVED

Once the emotional commitment has been made to serve the handicapped (and this is extremely useful in arousing support or convincing the public that the job must be done), it does not pay to be emotional beyond this point. Pity for the handicapped is destructive, and a vague sense of "do-goodism" useless, or worse, in carrying out the job. Instead, those who are in charge of organizing recreation services for the handicapped must be professionally competent. They must approach the task with a knowledge of sound recreation principles and with a full awareness of the needs, capabilities, and limitations of those they are to serve. Almost their first task is to recognize that the handicapped (no matter what their specific category of disability) are likely to fall into one of several categories of ability and social independence. Avedon suggests that these may be divided into five: "isolated," "secluded," "limited," "included," and "independent."

Based on these categories, any community or agency serving the handicapped may establish a continuum of five levels of recreation programing. Depending on the individual participant, each program can be regarded either as a step to the next level, or as the optimum level of performance in social and recreational activity that may be reached. Avedon describes the five levels of service:

> *Program for the "Isolated" Person.* Persons needing this level of programing are usually ill or disabled children and adults who have had little or no opportunity to be with others outside their homes. Recreation personnel, trained volunteers or surrogates work together to help the individual—in his own home, explore and experiment with activities that can promote development of psycho-physical skills and a concept of mastery over inanimate objects. Equipment is made available to persons in their homes in much the same way as libraries loan books. When a participant expresses interest in learning some particular activity, personnel with special leadership skills in a specific activity go to the home to teach it to the participant and his family. Activities are encouraged which provide immediate satisfaction for the individual; as well as activities that may pro-

[8] Betty Miller, "Re-Count for Recreators," *American Recreation Journal,* November–December, 1963, p. 19.

mote healthful interaction and participation among all those who are part of his home situation. . . .

Program for the "Secluded" Person. Ill or disabled children and adults who have had some opportunities to acquire recreation knowledge, skill, and experience may be served at an ordinary community center or comparable facility. Recreation personnel on the center staff are professionally prepared to establish special groups for disabled persons with respect to chronological age; physical, emotional, and intellectual limitations; and levels of recreative skills. . . . When an individual shows readiness . . . he is gradually introduced to aggregate activity with some nondisabled persons who attend other recreation programs within the center. . . .

Program for the "Limited" Person. For disabled children and adults who have had successful recreation experiences with a few nondisabled peers, and have been able to use at least one additional neighborhood recreation resource, recreation-counseling may enable them to join ongoing interest groups and clubs available to nondisabled persons within the center and in other neighborhood facilities and gradually increase their range of social interaction experiences. . . . In some instances, participants in this program may need to remain with "secluded" groups for some activities. . . .

Program for the "Included" Person. In programs serving disabled children and adults who are able to use some of the recreation resources in their home neighborhood, recreation personnel arrange with a variety of public, private, commercial, and church recreation programs in that neighborhood to provide opportunities for expanded social interaction with nondisabled peers and increased opportunities for prevocational experiences or for participation in the community's service programs. Consultation with personnel who work in the neighborhood programs is offered to enable them to provide effective leadership with disabled persons. . . .

Program for the "Independent" Person. For disabled children and adults who interact successfully with many nondisabled persons from their own neighborhood, recreation personnel can provide information and referral services to facilitate broader use of community recreation resources through the area, such as beaches, pools, zoos, museums, concerts, camps, and the like. In programs of service for the "independent" person, emphasis is placed on providing public information and education to encourage nondisabled persons to make the community's recreation resources more available to persons with disabilities. Recreation counseling is also offered to the disabled person's family and friends, to indicate to them how they can participate in a wide variety of activities with him. The recreation specialist working in this type of program makes every effort to activate community recreation resources for providing transportation, equipment, and otherwise expanding recreation opportunities for disabled people. He enlists community-wide effort to remove architectural barriers and stimulates development of special directories listing recreation resources available to the disabled.[9]

9 Elliott M. Avedon, *op. cit.,* pp. 71–72.

A key question that must be asked with respect to these categories is —under what circumstances *is* it appropriate to integrate the handicapped child or adult with nondisabled groups? And, by the same token, under what circumstances is this unwise? The programs that follow give illustrations of both types of arrangements, and the basic issue itself is discussed at the conclusion of this chapter.

SPECIFIC EXAMPLES OF SERVICE FOR HANDICAPPED INDIVIDUALS AND GROUPS

Programs for the Physically Handicapped

As indicated earlier, this category usually includes individuals with a wide variety of physical limitations, stemming from various causes. The most common emphasis is on the orthopedically handicapped, not involving mental illness or retardation, or limitation of the senses, such as sight or hearing. Of the many examples that might be cited, two are given here: a community club or organization composed of the physically handicapped, and the overall program of activities for the handicapped at a large Midwestern University.

Metropolitan Activities Club. This is an organization in Detroit, composed of over 100 persons, most of whom have moderate to severe physical limitations. It was formed in 1954 and has operated since that time. The membership ranges from 18 to 72 in age, and there is no restriction on membership based on type of disability. Most MAC's, as they are called, have orthopedic disabilities caused by polio, spinal injuries, birth defects, multiples sclerosis, or muscular dystrophy. Thirty-five members use wheelchairs, and 23 others, crutches.

The members of the Metropolitan Activities Club take full responsibility for their own organization and sponsorship. Although they may accept occasional assistance, they do their own fund-raising and plan their program activities themselves. These include the following: *bowling,* with two groups, each bowling twice a month; *basketball; swimming,* both indoor and outdoor; *square dancing,* with a performing wheelchair exhibition group which has won trophies and appeared on television and at the Michigan State Fair; *singing,* with a choral group that practices weekly and does frequent performances, often at hospitals; and *arts and crafts,* with such activities as copper enameling and picture making, leatherwork and ceramics, sewing and flower-making.

Members of the Metropolitan Activities Club also go by motorcade once a month to such spectator events as the theater, circuses, baseball games, hockey and ice shows. They run their own special parties and gala events at holidays. They do their own fund-raising, through membership dues, an annual yearbook and newsletter, bake sales and craft sales at bazaars, card parties, and an annual refreshment concession at the Michigan State Fair. Much of the money they have raised has been put into the development of a 15-acre campsite north of Detroit, and a camp facility for use by the club.

Recruitment for the MAC's is carried on through their own publications and newspaper articles, addresses over radio and television, professional meetings, community information programs, and from referrals by occupational therapists, social workers, and rehabilitation counselors. Although they are an organization *of* handicapped persons, they do not view the club as a means of withdrawing from the nonhandicapped world. Instead, Spencer and Cantoni write:

> Are the MAC's an ingrown group? Do they take refuge from the world of the nondisabled in their club and in their activities? For the vast majority of the MAC's, the answer to these questions is NO. Their club enables them to engage in the same kinds of activities as the nondisabled. Through it, many have moved from hospitals and rehabilitation centers to a normal life in their own communities. Many have made a transition from self-conscious dependence to confident independence.[10]

Recreation on a College Campus. Of the over 25,000 student residents at the Champaign-Urbana campus of the University of Illinois during the 1963–64 school year, there were 217 severely, permanently physically disabled students attending college on a regular, full-time basis. Of these, 126 were men, 83 confined to wheelchairs all of the time, and 91 were women, 57 confined to wheelchairs all of the time. Many of these students had compound disabilities such as being totally blind with both arms amputated, paraplegia with amputations, paraplegia with epilepsy, quadriplegic cases of spastic and athetoid cerebral palsy, and similar conditions.

These students lived in regular university residence halls and were involved in over 50 different courses of study in 10 colleges and divisions of the University. What was the nature of social and recreational programing available to them? Clearly, if the pattern of normal community life were to be followed, the majority of these students (who, although able to study successfully, had extreme physical disabilities) would find few available activities, groups, or facilities open to them.

This has not been the case at the University of Illinois. Nugent describes the extent of participation of these students:

> They participated in almost every phase of extra-curricular activity, e.g., newspapers, radio, television, bands, or orchestras, choruses, fraternities, sororities, activity clubs, and various campus governing groups, often excelling and assuming leadership. They also participated in swimming,

[10] Shirley R. Spencer and Louis J. Cantoni, "No Limit to Their Activities," *Recreation,* November, 1960, p. 417.

bowling for the blind, wheelchair football, basketball . . . baseball . . . track and field . . . archery . . . dancing, fencing . . . bowling . . . and more.

These students are not accorded any form of attendant help while on campus. Facilities have been designed and constructed for their independent function. Old buildings have been remodeled and modified. For many years, all new buildings have been designed and built so as to be equally accessible to, and usable by, the "able" and "disabled." These include buildings of all types and dedicated to many different uses. Entrances, public telephones, water coolers, residence hall desks and beds, showers, toilets, cafeteria service, dining areas, even library and laboratory facilities (and churches) have been . . . modified and made accessible to, and usable by, the severely physically disabled.[11]

Through their rehabilitation service fraternity, handicapped students manage and finance their own social, recreational, and athletic activities, an annual publication, a biweekly newsletter, and achievement awards. They participate in the National Wheelchair Basketball Association, which has 40 member teams in five conferences throughout the country, and also compete in the National Wheelchair Games, in such events as track and field, swimming, archery, bowling and table tennis, wheelchair bowling, and the like. As a consequence of their full programs of activity, it is believed that both psychological and physical values accrue. Nugent points out that ". . . we have no pressure sores and no significant incidence of kidney, bladder, or bowel problems among our severely disabled, with particular reference to our spinal cord injuries, including cervical level, who are vigorously active, but many of whom may also spend more than eight hours a day in academic laboratories or at an engineering or architectural drawing board." [12] Dramatic examples have been cited of individuals performing far beyond their predicted level of limitation under the stress of game play, or in the recreational setting.

RECREATION FOR THE BLIND ON COMMUNITY PLAYGROUNDS

A considerable number of community agencies today provide organized recreation programs for blind children and youth, either in separate groups, or integrated in regular, ongoing programs. In Vancouver, British Columbia, for example, it was decided to involve blind children in summer activities on supervised playgrounds. They were first placed for one month in a special recreation orientation group and then

11 Timothy J. Nugent, "Let's Look Beyond," *Recreation in Treatment Centers* (Washington, D.C.: American Recreation Society, September, 1964), pp. 33–42.
12 *Ibid.*, p. 39.

integrated into regular playground programs in their own area of the city, for the remainder of the summer. An older, blind girl was designated as the activity leader, and as liaison between the blind children and the administrative staff.

The program got under way at the beginning of July. Swimming was held three times a week, with approximately 25 blind children between the ages of five and 14 attending. A "buddy" system was used, with each blind child being paired with a sighted youngster. Although there was a considerable range of skill and age, all age groups progressed markedly in their swimming ability. The blind followed four major activity themes which were being used on all playgrounds throughout the city: Indian, Circus, Olympic, and the Arts. Activities based on these themes included a story hour, craft sessions, games, and athletics. In addition, many of the blind children took part in trampolining, calisthenics, musical activities, and such self-testing events as tag games, rope swinging and climbing, tug-of-war, and regular apparatus activities on the playground, including the jungle gym, swings, sandbox, teeter-totter, and Maypole. Smith writes:

> The staff soon discovered that at least fifty percent of the deficiency of the child was because of poor physical ability, where weight far exceeded strength, resulting in poor coordination and agility. This was the result, of course, of their sedentary life, and it was felt the children should have more physical fitness programs.[13]

At the end of the summer, it was decided that efforts would be made to integrate the blind children into local community center programs. Staff members were asked to pair off sighted boys and girls with blind children of the same age, sex, and district, so that they might attend local centers together. This was done, and the fall season began with an opening session attended by 43 visually handicapped and 45 sighted children, 20 volunteer adults, and 42 parents, indicating the considerable interest in the activity.

The blind children took part in certain activities separately, such as weight-training for the boys, and "modeling and poise" class for the girls. They also engaged in crafts, low-organized games, and square dancing with the other children. In many activities, recreation leaders observed no difference between the performance of the blind and sighted children. Parents, who were encouraged to attend, were amazed at the activities their children were able to enjoy successfully. In addition, they were overwhelmed by the friendliness of the sighted volunteer "buddies." It is worth emphasizing that such arrangements are important not only for the blind child, who is thus enabled to take part with greater con-

---

[13] Marshal Smith, "Blind Children on the Playground," *Recreation*, March, 1964, pp. 196–197.

fidence, but for the sighted child as well. First, he is able to rid himself of stereotypes he may have held about the "strangeness" or "difference" of those who are handicapped. Second, by engaging in a worthy community service and having contributed meaningfully to the life of another, he is able to gain a sense of altruistic reward and heightened self-esteem.

RECREATION FOR THE AGED IN THE COMMUNITY

In considering services provided for the aged, it is important to recognize that many older persons or retired individuals are by no means to be considered ill or handicapped. They may have mild disabilities but are still quite capable of operating independently—of traveling, engaging in hobbies, and joining social groups that meet their interests. On the other hand, large numbers of aged persons are in nursing homes, are homebound, or can only come to a recreation center with great difficulty. Their range of skills and level of interest and ability may be extremely low. Both groups must be the concern of the community recreation director.

First, it is necessary to consider the special need of the aged for recreation. Dr. William C. Menninger has written:

> Recreation is an extremely important aid to growing old gracefully. People who stay young despite their years do so because of an active interest that provides satisfaction through participation.[14]

This important concept was recognized by panelists at the 1961 White House Conference on Aging, which issued a clear-cut statement of recommendations dealing with the needs of older citizens:

> It Is Recommended That:
>
> Emphasis be placed on the need for greatly extended programs with a broad range of activities sponsored by public agencies, civic organizations, service clubs, churches, men's and women's groups, voluntary welfare organizations, educational institutions, libraries, hospitals, nursing homes, homes for the aged and other institutions with old age residents. Such programs should include day centers, clubs, social and cultural activities, outings, travel, camping, library services, informal education programs, volunteer service by older people to their contemporaries and other age groups, active participation in community affairs, central counseling, referral and information services. They should be available to older persons of all socioeconomic groups.
>
> Opportunities for recreation, voluntary service and citizenship participation now current or that will be established be available to all aging per-

14 William C. Menninger, M.D., "Spotlight on Seniors," *Recreation*, May, 1959, p. 181.

sons through free choice regardless of economic status, race, creed or national origin.

Older persons should be assisted in retaining contacts with younger groups. Some programs are more appropriate when they include several age groups, while in other instances they may best be conducted for the aging alone.

Family-centered projects, in which older persons may help to plan and implement the programs, should be encouraged, and more should be done to seek and assist older persons living in their homes to use their leisure more advantageously.

More free-time activities be directed toward the special needs of the ill and handicapped, whether institutionalized or homebound. . . .

In the concept of adequate income, recreation be recognized as a basic human need and that sufficient income be provided to permit older people to participate in recreation.

Other recommendations of the 1961 Conference on Aging dealt with: (a) the need to develop more public and private areas and facilities for leisure use by the aged, adapted when necessary to their special needs; (b) financing adequate to assure needed facilities and services, whether provided by government or voluntary agencies; (c) the formation of agencies on the federal, state, and local level, to offer recreation services and consultation; (d) the recruitment and training of more effective leaders, both professional and volunteer, including older persons themselves; (e) research and special studies that might be used to determine needs and interests of the aged, extent and type of facilities, special roles of leadership, and appropriate standards and procedures for programing; and (f) a concern that emphasis be placed on *preparing for retirement* through preretirement counseling and early exposure to useful skills and leisure interests.[15]

Exactly why is recreation regarded as having such significance for our older citizens? The problems of the aged involve changes in physical health and ability, retirement from employment and a consequent shifting of economic status and selfregard, change of family responsibilities and ties, often living apart from other people—and, finally, a sense of being old and no longer wanted by a society that worships youth. Aging is not an automatic process. It is dependent on all the factors just mentioned, on the personality structure of the individual, on his previous experiences, and on the opportunities for continuing self-expression and meaningful activity that are open to him. Research carried on at the Age Center of New England, established in Boston in 1954, reveals that many persons find themselves aging in the later 40's and early 50's, while others

[15] See: *Report of 1961 White House Conference on the Aging,* Section 12 (Free Time Activities; Recreation, Voluntary Services and Citizen Participation).

retain a fresh outlook and lively spirit well into the 80's. What makes the difference? One important factor must be the need for continuous stimulation, social involvement, and creative expression. Without these, both physical and mental decline seem to accelerate.

Dr. Howard Rusk describes what he calls the "preventive medicine" of a Golden Age club:

> We are all familiar with the over-65 clubs, the golden age clubs. I saw the first one that was sponsored by the City of New York in 1946. It started for an interesting reason; there was a recalcitrant group of welfare recipients who kept coming in to gripe so often at one of the welfare offices that workers couldn't get any work done. One day, one of the workers with a keen eye said, "You know, I don't believe these people come here to gripe. I think they come here because they don't have any place else to go. The longer you keep them waiting, the better they like it. They bring their lunch and they *like* to stay all day. . . ." He said, "I think if we got a place for them to go and have a little fun, we would get them out of our hair." [16]

To provide a meeting place for this group, the Hodson Center was founded by the New York City Department of Welfare. It met in three rooms near the welfare office, in an old building, furnished with a second-hand piano, a rickety pool table, and a couple of card tables. The program was set up to insure maximum participation of all members. Every member was put on a committee, to serve coffee or tea, to plan programs, put up decorations and send out birthday cards, or to visit sick members who could not attend. Officers were elected every three months, to give more individuals a chance to serve. Within five years, the Hodson Center was attracting 700 aged members, and was running on a daily schedule of six hours, right through the week. It had a varied workshop program, sponsored dances twice a month, and put on a play once a month. Although the average age of those attending was 76, a considerable number of couples meeting at the center have married, since its inception. Rusk comments:

> The thing that interested me was that visits to doctors' offices and to clinics, and admissions to general hospitals for a physical disability from this group, compared to a group who had no place to go and nothing to look forward to, was fifty percent less. . . . Admissions to mental hospitals for senile psychosis was only ten percent of the expectancy.[17]

Today the practice of operating Golden Age, or Senior Citizen, clubs has become widely accepted around the country. At present there are well over 700 such centers, sponsored by welfare agencies, recreation

[16] Howard A. Rusk, M.D., "Recreation Promotes Health," *Recreation,* March, 1963, p. 128.
[17] *Ibid.*

departments, churches, local chapters of national voluntary organizations, labor groups, and service organizations. It should be recognized that a senior center is not just a social club or recreation group. The President's Council on Aging has defined it as "a physical facility open to senior citizens at least five days a week, and four hours a day, year-round, and operated by a public agency or nonprofit private organization with community planning, which provides, under the direction of paid professional leadership, services for the senior citizen." It should include group and/or individual program activities, and at least three of the following services: (a) recreation; (b) adult education; (c) health services; (d) counseling and other services; (e) information and referral services; (f) community and volunteer services.[18]

It is worth noting that the first service listed in this statement is recreation. Among the most common activities provided in senior centers are the following:

Social Clubs	Physical Fitness Activities	Group Singing
Arts and Crafts	Informal Discussion	Hobbies
Sports	Individual and Group Games	Drama
Parties	Group Sightseeing	Camping
Excursions	Conversation	Dancing

Example of Recreation in Senior Citizen Program

Many community recreation departments sponsor varied programs of activity for the aged. One of the best examples is found in Long Beach, California, where over a dozen senior citizens clubs are conducted by the public recreation department. These meet such leisure interests as: chess, checkers, bowling on the green, fly casting, horseshoes, shuffleboard, and similar pursuits. There is a forum program titled "University by the Sea," and an excursion group called the "Golden Tours," which provides inexpensive trips (both short and long) and has a total membership of 2,000 older citizens. In addition, seniors take part in many general offerings of the department, such as classes in square, round, and folk dancing, camera activities, crafts, bridge lessons, and community events.

Camping for the Aged. Another rapidly expanding field for senior citizens is camping. Again, this may be sponsored by many different types of agencies, public and private. It affords a valuable opportunity to break the routine of daily living and provide refreshment of body and spirit, particularly for older persons living in the cramped surroundings of small apartments or furnished rooms, in large cities. This may involve

[18] *Report of 1961 White House Conference on the Aging* (see Sub-Committee Report on the Senior Center).

sleepover camps, or day camping. An example of the latter is the program established by the Older Adult Services of the New York YM-YWHA at Camp Ray Hill, Mt. Kisco, New York. Here, the older person is offered a camp season of six weeks (three days per week) in the country, for a minimal fee. The group leaves from the "Y" center in the city in chartered buses, with pickups at specially arranged points. Campers bring their own lunches and beverages, and the camp provides cool drinks in the afternoon.

The day camp is staffed by trained specialists, and has an average daily attendance of almost 100. Activities include gardening, nature walks, swimming, volleyball and shuffleboard, arts and crafts, dramatics, and choral groups organized by the campers. One camper writes of it:

> Let me tell you why we need this day camp and love it so much. Take, for example, swimming. We have a beautiful pool and specially built steps so that we can walk easily into the water. We have a swimming instructor at the pool who gives personal attention to everybody and who leads water games. As a result, people who have not gone swimming for fifteen or twenty years are doing it again and recapturing the fun of their youth. . . . Can you realize what this means to an older person? There is such a jolly spirit around the pool that every day many people who do not go into the water come to sit around and join in the fun. . . .
>
> This is the same in all our other activities. . . . We have the help of skilled counselors to help us learn these activities and get the most out of them. . . . You can imagine . . . the kind of spirit that we have at day camp. Our big affairs, like birthday parties, campfires, cookouts, and masquerades, are very lively and have a special outdoor flavor we do not get in our year-round club activities. Then, there are the small groups that get together after lunch, each one with a counselor, for discussion and fellowship. We also enjoy the pleasant bus rides to camp, with their singing and jolly spirit.[19]

The importance of skilled leadership in such programs is obvious. Too, between the lines, one sees clearly revealed the role of recreation in maintaining a youthful and vigorous spirit. Certainly, such programs require a degree of special "knowhow," but this is not difficult to obtain. Most of the adjustments that must be made for older participants are based on a thoughtful appraisal of their needs and physical limitations.

For example, the Senior Adult Committee of the Board of Christian Education of the United Church of Canada offers the following guides for overnight camping, for this age group. First, it is important to carefully review camp accommodations to insure the physical health and comfort of the campers. Privacy is important; if larger than two-bed cabins are used, dividing screens or curtains help. Generally speaking,

[19] "Camping for Seniors," *Recreation*, May, 1962, p. 236, n.a.

each older camper likes to be assigned his or her own bed, a place to hang clothes, and the washroom to be used immediately upon arrival at camp. He or she likes to keep the same place at the table throughout. It is recommended that camps for older adults provide:

> Level ground between place of sleeping and eating with no great distance between the two. Minimum of stairs, with banisters. Cabins for sleeping with not more than two beds in a room—some single rooms—with easy access to bathroom facilities under same roof, and with electricity.

> Plenty of bedding—hot water bottles, flashlights, extra pillows for those who sleep propped up, rubber sheeting for beds. Chair beside each bed. Plenty of seating accommodation in various spots around the grounds out-of-doors.

> Arrangements for some special diets—saltfree, skimmed milk, etc. Campers on similar diets might be seated at one part of table. Arrange for nurse to discover needs of each camper for toilet facilities, medical services, and to clear diets with the cook.

> Books, and games, both active and quiet, such as Scrabble, checkers, chess, horseshoes, etc. Provide garden tools, materials for crafts, outdoor painting, etc. Have writing materials, stamps, pens available. Provide music—piano, record player, etc.

> Tags for each piece of luggage with names in big print to eliminate anxiety, and persons available to carry luggage. Have an electric kettle handy for making coffee at any hour, day or night. Have an extra supply of sweaters, shawls, flannel nightwear, raincoats.[20]

RECREATION FOR THE HANDICAPPED AGED

Obviously, a high proportion of aged people who live in the community at large have disabilities which prevent or limit their recreational involvement. Of every hundred persons aged 65 or older, 80 suffer some kind of chronic ailment. Twenty-eight have heart disease or high blood pressure, 27 have arthritis or rheumatism, 10 have impaired vision, and 17 have hearing impairments. Sixteen are hospitalized one or more times annually. If the impairment is great enough, such individuals are likely to be homebound or confined to a nursing home.

Recreation in Nursing Homes

There are many thousands of nursing homes around the country which chiefly serve older persons, although in some cases, younger patients who have suffered from heart attacks, strokes, or similar trauma, may also be long-term residents. The majority of these homes are com-

---

[20] "Overnight Camping," *Recreation,* May, 1962, p. 237, n.a.

paratively small and offer extremely limited recreational opportunities for their residents. Mullen writes:

> Now, on the surface, this (providing for the leisure time of the patient in the nursing home) doesn't seem like such a tremendous task, but, with few exceptions, the most monumental problem is coping with apathy, skepticism and antagonism which completely surround the very suggestion of attempting to provide anything for the aged person in the chronically ill category. The general attitude has been: "Why waste time with such people?" [21]

It is worthy of note that, although financial inability to hire recreational directors is cited by many nursing home owners, the actual reasons are more complicated. Dr. Joseph Lerner suggests that, while many homes *are* too small or lack the finances to provide professional leadership, it is possible for volunteer organizations from the community to fill the gap rather effectively. However, this assistance may be discouraged or even resented by the institution's paid personnel. In some instances, the personnel consider such recreational activities as an additional burden, since they may be called upon to perform additional work in connection with them.

> From the personnel's point of view, it is more convenient simply to allow their aging patients to sit about and be fed and clothed without becoming involved with the need to participate, to even a limited extent, in recreational activities. They feel, therefore, that some programs of recreation are superfluous, if not actually wasteful of their time. In addition, there are occasions when the elderly patient may attend a lecture or concert and become so over-stimulated as to have difficulty in sleeping, with the result that the personnel have an additional problem with which to contend. In some instances, elderly people have been known to wet the bed or have some other mishap associated with participation in recreational activities.[22]

While these may be realistic problems, they certainly do not justify the withholding of enjoyable leisure activities from long-term patients who may otherwise have nothing else to do but sit in a rocking chair month in and month out and gradually deteriorate. Indeed, a number of states have come to the point of requiring that nursing homes *provide* recreation programs, if they are to be licensed. For example, the Connecticut State Department of Health imposes the following criteria for approval of rest homes with nursing supervision.

Under the heading of "Patient Activities Program," nursing homes are required to have appropriate space and facilities (in the form of recreation areas or day spaces) in which to conduct activities.

21 Dorothy G. Mullen, "Re-Animation of the Long-Term Care Patient," *Connecticut Health Bulletin No. 75*, 1961.

22 Joseph Lerner, M.D., "Recreational Activities for the Aged," *Journal of the American Geriatrics Society*, April, 1964, p. 325.

Homes are required to have a recreation director, to be approved by the State Department of Health, who must work a minimum number of hours a week, depending on the licensed capacity of the home. Thus, a home with between 5 and 29 beds must have a recreation director who works up to 20 hours per week; a home with 30 to 59 beds must have a director who works 30 hours a week, etc.

Monthly reports of program activities are required by the State Department of Health, and specific activities, with a stress on crafts, are suggested for inclusion. At least two of the following types of events, for example, must be provided each month: films or slide presentations, birthday parties, entertainment programs, or special holiday parties or picnics. Guides are given for the screening, orientation, and supervision of volunteer leaders, and suggested duties and qualifications for program directors are provided by the state.

In some cases, a number of small nursing homes have joined together, pooling their resources to hire their own professional leader and pay for needed recreation equipment. Thus, between three and six homes may share the cost of a program director, who not only provides direct activity leadership, but also supervises volunteer leadership from the community. In some cases, when an experimental project in cooperative sponsorship of recreation leadership by several nursing homes was organized by the National Recreation Association, it was found that nursing home directors decided to hire their own professional or subprofessional leader, after the project was over.

The National Recreation Association publishes a useful handbook, *"Starting a Recreation Program in Institutions for the Ill or Handicapped Aged,"* [23] which offers guides regarding professional and volunteer leadership, planning activities for the aged, and needed equipment and facilities.

RECREATION FOR THE HOMEBOUND

Somewhat similar, in terms of the limitations that are faced, is the problem of supplying recreation services to the chronically ill or severely disabled homebound individual. Today, a number of different kinds of assistance, including education, medical and nursing aid, and social case work counseling, are available to such persons when needed. Recreation, as a basic human need which homebound patients cannot usually meet independently, must be regarded as an important and parallel form of assistance. This should take two forms:

1. Appropriate activities, hobbies or leisure interests for those who are bedridden, as well as for those who are unable or unwilling to leave their homes

[23] Morton Thompson, *Starting a Recreation Program in Institutions for the Ill or Handicapped Aged* (New York: National Recreation Association, 1960).

2. Arrangements for individuals who, with sufficient encouragement and adequate transportation, are able to leave their homes to take part in recreation in public or voluntary agency programs

In the conduct of such a program, it is usually considered that a professionally trained expert in therapeutic recreation is required to plan, organize, and supervise activities and assignments. Beyond this, because patients must be visited or worked with individually, it is necessary to rely heavily on volunteers. They serve both as counselors or direct leaders with patients, and as clerical assistants or in the transportation phase of the program. Such organizations as the Red Cross, the Gray Ladies, or similar service organizations may be particularly helpful with respect to transportation. The recruitment, orientation, and supervision of volunteers is crucial, if a program for the homebound is to be successful. Their training, according to Thompson, should include the following areas:

1. Group orientation in the physical or social disabilities that may be involved, and in fundamental medical aspects of the service
2. Group instruction and participation in appropriate activities, with stress on individual pursuits that may be carried on by homebound patients under their own direction
3. Techniques for transporting patients, which may involve the use of special station wagons which can accommodate wheel chairs; also, the physical handling of disabled patients
4. Knowledge of facilities and equipment, which may include wheelchair boards, bed easels, magnetic boards for games, prism glasses, oversized checkers, chess and dominoes, long prongs for picking up dropped articles, craft materials, record players and records, books and magazines, and aids for one-handed knitting and crocheting

Four major phases of the organized program for the homebound may be outlined: (a) within the home itself, establishing contact and building confidence; introducing new interests and teaching skills; (b) making arrangements for those who are able to travel to community centers, for participation in activities with special groups of disabled persons; (c) carrying out trips to community cultural resources, spectator events, or recreation centers, on an occasional basis; (d) referral to other social agenices near the home, where the person may go, with or without special assistance, to participate in programs with others who are not severely disabled, such as a day-center for the aged. Obviously, when these final stages are reached, the individual should no longer be considered technically homebound.

A special phase of programing which some social agencies may undertake is the planning of trips of severely disabled patients to nearby farms or bungalow colonies or short-term camps, for summer vacations.

The National Recreation Association has sponsored such ventures on an experimental basis, transporting a group of individuals with varied handicaps (including arthritis, multiple sclerosis, double amputee, cardiac condition, etc.) to a farm in the Pocono Mountains of Pennsylvania. Although successful, and although patients took part in many activities they had never before enjoyed with a high level of sharing responsibility, this represents a difficult and expensive kind of program to develop.

Finally, the homebound may be served by special television programing, as described earlier, which suggests recreational activities and broadens the patient's horizons and interests.

COMMUNITY SERVICES FOR THE RETARDED

In the previous chapter, the special needs of the retarded were discussed. It was pointed out that only a comparatively small number of communities throughout the country have provided recreation programs for retarded children and adults. However, this number has begun to increase rapidly, due in large part to the efforts of the Kennedy Foundation and the National Association for Retarded Children.

Two examples may be cited. The North Carolina Recreation Commission, with the assistance of the North Carolina Association for Retarded Children, has compiled a list of 19 different communities in which public recreation programs, day and resident camps have been established to meet the needs of retarded children and youth. Many of these are on a free basis; others have a minimal charge. In the state of Washington, a survey was carried out in 1964 which revealed that of 47 organized recreation programs with paid professional staff, 10 provided programs for the retarded. This represents an increase over a previous survey carried out in 1962. The publication, *Socio-Recreative Programing for the Retarded: A Handbook for Sponsoring Groups*,[24] provides much assistance for those who are seeking to establish services for the retarded.

Day Camp Program for the Retarded

A useful illustration of effective programing for the retarded may be found in examining a day camp sponsored over a period of three summers by Bronx House, a family-oriented agency in New York City.

Here, approximately 27 youngsters ranging in age from 10 to 13, with varying degrees of mental retardation (several were brain-damaged and several Mongoloid, with such accompanying defects as poor vision, hearing, speech, or motor coordination) were served. Most of the children

24 Elliott M. Avedon and Frances Arje, *Socio-Recreative Programing for the Retarded: A Handbook for Sponsoring Groups* (New York: Teachers College, Columbia University, Bureau of Publications, 1964).

had no previous camping experience and had had limited social contacts and involvement.

They were involved in a regular day camp program serving about 275 boys and girls, who were picked up daily at the agency and transported by chartered buses to a country site. The program is described:

> Mentally retarded campers, like the other groups, were helped to choose a campsite and learn such basic skills as axing, fire building, lashing, and cooking techniques, all of which went into the development of a campsite area referred to as "home base." Then followed emphasis on work projects, such as lashing tables and benches, and developing fireplaces for cookouts. With each successive cookout experience, menus became more elaborate. Before leaving campgrounds, the campers were responsible for cleaning up their site, and equipment had to be returned to the supply store . . . (the program) usually reflected a gradual progression of experiences. . . .[25]

Every opportunity was explored for the meaningful involvement of parents of the retarded children, and, on the whole, they were eager to participate. Prior to the opening of camp and during the season, parents met in small groups to discuss the program and comment on their child's group experience and behavior. Both the campers and their families were pleased with the venture; considerable progress was noted in observational records, in such areas as learning of social skills, improving self-care, and the general mastering of such abilities as canoeing and swimming.

> As the season progressed the initial stage of "good behavior" was gradually followed by some conflict which many began to verbalize. There was evidence of increased sharing of food, supplies, and taking turns in the activities. More and more reference to the group was characterized by "We." Parents noted that the child was able to come to the agency alone and no longer had to be escorted. The child began to verbalize more frequently and was more easily understood by members of the family. Skills learned at camp were carried over into the home. . . .[26]

By the time the day camping program was over, many parents indicated that they found greater relaxation in their homes; they felt less overprotective and also less demanding of their children. Parents found considerable practical help in handling their children's behavior by attending group meetings with other parents of retarded children. Many began to identify more fully with the agency, serving on committees and sharing in responsibilities for parents of nonretarded campers. It was concluded that groups for mentally retarded children in a normal day camp setting conducted by a group-service agency can be developed with effectiveness and considered as an integral part of its total offering.

    [25] Rose Stockhamer, "Day Camp for the Mentally Retarded," *Recreation*, May, 1963, pp. 236–237.
    [26] *Ibid.*

The implications of this program are obvious:

1. A day camp or similar recreational experience, carried out in a sustained way with meaningful goals and tasks under effective leadership, can contribute significantly to the social and intellectual growth of retardates. Often it opens up an entirely new dimension of learning and motivation.

2. In every aspect of community recreation service for the retarded, as well as for those in other categories of handicapped, it is essential to involve the family of those being served. This has two purposes: (a) to help them understand and work more effectively with the handicapped individual; and (b) to give them an awareness that their problem is shared by many others, and that it can be met constructively and without shame or guilt.

AFTERCARE SOCIAL PROGRAMS FOR DISCHARGED MENTAL PATIENTS

It was pointed out earlier in this chapter that mental patients are returning to their homes more rapidly than ever before. People who, 20 years ago, would have been confined, perhaps for many years or even without hope of recovery, in huge, unhappy hospitals on the outskirts of town, are today receiving the treatment they need close to their own homes in mental health clinics, day hospitals, or small intensive care units. New treatment methods, especially the use of pharmaceuticals, have made possible a new concept of treatment that establishes a continuous sequence of care from the point at which illness is identified to the time when the former mental patient completely resumes his place in the community. The social club that is geared to meet the needs of discharged mental patients is a significant part of this sequence.

Such clubs may be defined as follows:

> The ex-patient club can be thought of as a more or less transitional organization of persons who share having had an emotional illness and/or hospitalization. The purpose of such a club should be to help its members achieve and maintain positive social and vocational adjustments in the community by providing opportunities, situations, and experiences calculated to help prevent both social isolation and further social disability. Under qualified leadership, the social club can achieve its purpose by providing activities in the community which combine social interaction, recreation, personal development, and ego support.[27]

They need to be seen in relation to two other types of organizations: (a) the *halfway house,* which is considered to be a residential aftercare

---

[27] *Social Clubs—Yes* (New York: National Association for Mental Health, June, 1963), p. 4, n.a.

facility for discharged mental patients in the community; and (b) *re-habilitation centers,* like Fountain House in New York City, or Horizon House in Philadelphia, which have extensive day and evening programs and rehabilitative services, but which are not residential. Social clubs represent one specific aspect of the program of such houses or centers and may also exist independently, sponsored by other agencies or organizations.

In 1963, the National Association for Mental Health carried out a survey of its 800 divisions and local chapters. Social clubs for discharged mental patients were found in 24 states. Many of them, however, were active on a very limited basis; they were open only one day a week, did not use the services of their state vocational rehabilitation agency, and lacked advisory committees or clear-cut policies for membership. In a report following this investigation, the following guides were presented:

1. Social clubs need basic principles to guide their operation, with clearly understood and defined purposes.
2. They must be meaningfully related to community needs.
3. In terms of "case finding," good channels must be developed for reaching persons who can benefit from the services of the social club. All members should be referred by medical or other professional sources.
4. Criteria should be established for selecting and training volunteers and staff, including a director who has a knowledge of mental illness, an understanding of human behavior, and flexibility and the ability to relate well to people.
5. Regardless of its organizational structure, each social club should be continually under adequate, locally acceptable psychiatric supervision. In formulating its basic philosophy, the club should have a multi-disciplinary advisory committee, including representatives of such fields as psychiatry, vocational rehabilitation, social work, recreation, and occupational therapy. This committee will also be helpful in the referral of ex-patients to the club.
6. There is a need for continuous evaluation of program, with thorough records of members and program activities. Where possible, more formal research projects may be initiated.
7. Club programs may include rehabilitative services or may be limited solely to social activities. Services can be developed on various levels, ranging from unstructured, "drop-in" events, such as movies, picnics, exhibits or coffee hours, to discussion groups, hobby classes, or sessions devoted to preparing for job interviews or similar concerns.
8. A formal administrative structure is desirable; it should make it possible for members to assume personal responsibility for planning and carrying out group activities, through member councils, officers and designated committees.[28]

Clearly, it would be possible to outline recreation programs sponsored within the community setting for a number of other special groups of handicapped individuals, such as diabetics, the deaf or hard of hear-

[28] *Ibid.*

ing, former drug addicts, or cerebral palsied persons. However, the essential principles and methods of organization tend to be the same, with modifications based on the nature of those being served, or on community characteristics. One special problem that must continually be faced by recreation directors providing services to the handicapped is the availability of facilities. Generally, when the group to be served is in the category of the mentally retarded or mentally ill or convalescent, careful planning for control or supervision is all that is required, once the arrangement has been made. On the other hand, when the individuals to be served are physically handicapped to any significant degree, the problems may be more difficult.

USE OF COMMUNITY FACILITIES BY THE PHYSICALLY HANDICAPPED

One of the most serious barriers that prevents millions of handicapped and aged Americans from participating freely in normal community programs is found in simple architectural features that do not permit them to enter or use them conveniently. The needs and basic rights of the handicapped have been ignored in the past by those who have designed and built all types of facilities—churches, schools, government buildings, hotels and motels, airlines and bus terminals, and cultural, recreation, and sports facilities.

Estimates of the number of handicapped persons affected by such barriers as steps, narrow doorways, inadequate toilet facilities, and the absence of safety features, vary from 10 to 20 percent of the nation's population. Schoenbohm and Schranke point out that when the patient leaves the hospital or rehabilitation setting, he is instructed and encouraged to continue a program of constructive activity and recreation. However, as many who have attempted to develop recreation programs for the physically handicapped in the community know, it is extremely difficult to find facilities which meet the simple requirements of accessibility and usability. From a practical point of view, the simple adaptations or preplanned modifications that must be made are comparatively simple to carry out and easy to justify:

> In the long run, the savings on insurance, legal fees and repairs and maintenance more than pay for any small additional costs. As one operator who had a ramp built into his building stated, "After a few years of operation, eighty-five percent of the people entering the building now use the ramp in preference to the stairs, in spite of the fact that it is at a far less convenient location than the entrance with steps."
>
> As the owners and operators of theaters, supermarkets and modern merchandising establishments have learned, barriers to people are barriers to

sales and service. The story is the same with recreation, cultural and sporting facilities.[29]

The American Standards Association, a federation of over 100 trade associations, technical societies, professional groups, and consumer organizations (with some 2,200 companies affiliated as company members) provides the machinery for creating voluntary standards of manufacture, design, or construction of a wide variety of facilities and manufactured articles. These are formulated as single, nationally accepted standards, accepted by member organizations and useful as a guide to others. In 1961, the American Standards Association approved specifications for the design and building of public facilities for the handicapped.[30] These are extremely detailed and thorough, covering such features as walkways, site grading, parking lots, buildings, doors and doorways, floor surfaces, stairs, toilet rooms, public telephones, elevators, switches and controls, identification of facilities (for the blind), warning signals, door handles and knobs.

When construction is carried out, based on these standards, as at the University of Illinois, the participation of physically handicapped individuals is made much more feasible. Often, failure to comply does not represent resistance or disagreement with the principle of making facilities suitable for use by the handicapped. Instead, it may simply represent lack of knowledge or concern about their needs. To this end, it is necessary that professional and civic groups bring pressure to bear whenever new buildings or other facilities are in the planning stage. Usually, compliance is not long in coming, although, when necessary, the public may be asked to state its wishes, or influential groups may wish to support the policy.

As an example of modification of existing facilities, the New Jersey Parkway Authority recently developed special service facilities for handicapped travelers on its Garden State Parkway. Wheelchair access ramps, hand-rails to toilets, and appropriate dining accommodations were installed in all parkway restaurants and service station restrooms.

In terms of thorough preplanning to meet the needs of the handicapped, the Architectural Barriers Sub-Committee of the Florida Governor's Committee on Employment of the Handicapped reported in 1963 that ". . . students returning to the University of Florida found a new 5-million-dollar student union building awaiting them . . . a 470-seat theater . . . a 330-seat auditorium, a 1,200 couple capacity ballroom, 16 bowling lanes, a cafeteria, a barber shop, student government offices. . . ."

[29] Wilko B. Schoenbohm and Robert W. Schranke, "Barriers to Service," *Recreation*, May, 1962, p. 268.

[30] *Making Buildings and Facilities Accessible to, and Usable by, the Physically Handicapped* (Chicago, Illinois: National Society for Crippled Children and Adults, 1961).

All these and many other new college facilities had been made totally accessible to the handicapped. Similarly, in a number of other colleges being built or expanded in Florida, all of the involved architects and administrators have pledged to do their best to assure fully accessible facilities.

Such a policy must be exerted at the planning stage of all public facilities, if the handicapped are to be able to enter and use them freely.

THE SOCIAL INTEGRATION OF THE HANDICAPPED

A major objective in many recreation departments serving handicapped children or adults is that they be integrated into programs involving normal participants, whenever this can be feasibly and constructively accomplished. A number of significant examples of the value of this type of program are described in a pamphlet published by the New York Service for the Orthopedically Handicapped:

> Nine-year-old Richard puts the finishing touches on a ceramic vase. With his left hand, a shiny contraption of steel and wire, he describes an Indian design on the vase's rim.

> "Look," he exclaims, "I don't need the tools." The other children look on in admiration and wonder.

> Richard is a congenital amputee. His left hand and lower arm never developed. When he was first fitted with a prosthesis, he was embarrassed to wear the "hook" in front of his schoolmates. He preferred to let his sleeve dangle empty. He was shy and self-conscious in school, and preferred to sit at home than to play with boys and girls his own age.

> Richard was one of the first children to be placed by the New York Service for Orthopedically Handicapped in a project designed to integrate handicapped children and non-handicapped children in local community center programs. The project, begun early in 1960, was organized to prepare children 8–15 years of age—even those with severe handicaps—for their eventual role in the community at large. It is meant to help the handicapped child to participate in normal community life, and to see himself as a useful and wanted person.

> Richard has been active in various after-school activities at the Lower East Side recreation center where he was placed by the New York Service. He is quite proud of the dexterity he has developed with his "hook." He knows that he is accepted, without derision, by his non-handicapped playmates; and, as in the above quoted instance, he has found that their curiosity may even be tinged with admiration.

> Of course, he has discovered his own limitations, too. Participating in a variety of programs with non-handicapped children his own age, there are

some things in which he cannot compete. He is not likely, for instance, to be "the life of the party" at the piano. But there are so many things he can do, and do well, that Richard has gained a new sense of confidence in himself and joy in living which he might never have found isolated from and fearful of friends and playmates.[31]

This boy, of course, was among the less severely handicapped of the children who were placed in this integrated community center program. Some were severely disabled by polio; others were victims of cerebral palsy, muscular dystrophy, Perthes, or paralyzing spinal deformities or injuries. For example, the case of Janet:

> Janet is confined to a wheelchair, paraplegic as a result of polio contracted when she was an infant. Now 14 years of age, she does not remember the time when she was not in a wheelchair wearing long-leg braces. She never went to elementary school or junior high school, but was taught by special teachers at home. For a while she participated in a special recreation program for disabled youngsters, but remained unhappy and shy.
>
> The New York Service helped to place Janet in an evening teenage program at a community center near where she lived. Here, Janet found a new world and a new life. Whether the boys and girls in her group have a discussion about Cuba, or dating, decide to listen to hi-fi, play cards, or paint, Janet is an active participant. True, when there is a dance, her participation is limited to changing records. In her old program, limited to the handicapped, she could join in a "wheelchair dance"; but she much prefers activities where she can feel part of the mainstream of life to a program where she only can know other children who are as disabled as she is.
>
> Today, Janet is a star student in her high school, specializing in design; and in the community center, her participation and leadership have been so outstanding that she was offered a paid position as a leader in the center's summer day camp program. Janet will never leave her wheelchair, but she has come out of her shell. She has made friends and a real life adjustment in the center and outside it. She has built a solid foundation for a useful, productive and fulfilling life.[32]

It is the belief of the New York Service that programs limited to the handicapped actually tend to hold back these youngsters in making an eventual adjustment in the nonhandicapped community. Such programs reinforce their patterns of anxiety and isolation, prevent them from discovering the many things that are open to them, and keep them from understanding realistically their own limitations.

Does it follow, then, that all handicapped children or adults may readily be integrated into nonhandicapped groups? Based on the degree or nature of the disability, this may not always be a feasible goal.

---

[31] *Children Together* (brochure of the New York Service for Orthopedically Handicapped, n.d.).
[32] *Ibid.*

The program director of a New York group work agency that has provided special services for the mentally retarded for a number of years comments that only within the "segregated" social group, as opposed to the "integrated" group, is the retarded member afforded a full measure of participation and satisfaction. Within the integrated group, he is consistently treated as a *retarded* person; only within the segregated group does he become *just* a person. It is found that, regardless of age, the retarded group members tend to form subcultures within the larger Program Age Division, with little or no interaction with other subcultures. Again, the basic factor seems to be the inability on the part of the retarded to develop and sustain social relationships. The director writes:

> The special groups are not integrated totally into the life stream of our agency. . . . Regardless of their physical proximity to normal groups, they remain on the periphery of the Center's society. Normal members, at best, respond to the retardates with tolerance and, hopefully, understanding.[33]

Based on this experience, this agency therefore takes the view that integration of retardates is an unrealistic expectation. They confine their program goals to: (a) exposing the retarded and normal members to each other; (b) helping retardates participate with normal members in mass programs where they can function on their own level without detracting from the overall program, and (c) helping the retardates adjust to the routines and procedures of everyday agency life.

Even when the integration of handicapped individuals in non-handicapped groups is feasible, in terms of potential degree of acceptance and satisfying involvement, the process is not an automatic one. Thus, one community recreation superintendent writes:

> . . . for several years, I was associated with the Easter Seal Society and Cerebral Palsy Association, during which time our primary interest was in developing a total . . . recreation program that would culminate in the integration of our patients.

> We came to realize rather quickly that there was a significant distance between the indiscriminate casting of a handicapped child into a group of healthy youngsters, and preparing this same child, who has been virtually isolated socially, for integration with children of his age and maturation level. To successfully integrate a handicapped child into a "normal" recreation setup with the non-handicapped requires a structured and gradual sequence of programs, whereby the disabled youngster can prepare and be ready for the final and essential step. We learned rather painfully that, unless this process was practiced, many youngsters were subjected to unnecessary and cruel failure.

[33] Sandra Kohn, "Integration of the Mentally Retarded in a Community Group Service Agency," (New York: Association for the Help of Retarded Children, 1963), p. 18.

I am not inferring that failure is common when the two groups are integrated, but I do wish to stress that individual readiness and preparation
must be of prime concern or the experiment will be fruitless and a *lasting*
adjustment into society may never be realized. In our three years of day
camping and swimming programs for physically handicapped children in
Natick (Massachusetts), many buddy days, family nights, and other integrated special events have been conducted. These activities have helped
bridge the gap from segregated play to total integration into society. . . .
As a result, many disabled children have "graduated," so to speak, from our
programs and are now participating totally in regular Little League, Scouts,
recreation basketball, etc., with their non-handicapped friends.[34]

This chapter has discussed the rationale for providing community
recreation services for the handicapped, homebound, or convalescent
child or adult. It has outlined current trends and given a number of
examples of successful practices. It presents some of the goals that must
still be worked toward, in terms of meeting the needs of specific groups,
enlisting public support and sponsorship, improving facilities for greater
accessibility, and developing integrated programs when this is a realistic
objective.

SUGGESTED QUESTIONS FOR DISCUSSION

1. Discuss the special rationale for providing recreation services for those with
   disabilities in the community setting. What is "tunnel vision," as described
   by Avedon? What are the five levels of service he presents? Can you give
   examples of each?
2. What is the current status of such programs within your community? Discuss
   with respect to the aged, homebound, retarded, blind, and similar groups.
3. "Handicapped youngsters should always be integrated with the nonhandicapped." Discuss this statement from the point of view of a recreation director, both as a desirable goal and as a practical course of action.

[34] Frank Robinson, Letter to the Editor, *Recreation*, September, 1962, p. 331.

Chapter 14

Recreation in the Armed Forces

An important area of recreational service today lies in the programs which are provided to millions of members of the armed forces and their dependents by the federal government. The rationale underlying this program has been clearly stated by the Department of Defense:

> It is the policy of the Department of Defense to promote and provide a well-rounded morale, welfare and recreational program to insure the physical and mental well-being of its personnel. Adequate free-time facilities should be provided, operated and maintained through financial support tendered by the Federal Government.[1]

Recreation first became recognized as an important need of the United States military forces in World War I. At this time, a number of national agencies, including the YMCA, the Salvation Army, the Jewish Welfare Board, the American Red Cross, and others, undertook the

[1] *Department of Defense Directive 1330.2* (Washington, D.C.: Department of Defense, January, 1953).

367

assignment of providing recreation and social services for uniformed personnel in domestic posts and overseas. These agencies operated huts and canteens, planned and organized social, sports, and entertainment programs, and provided personnel and supplies from their own staff and resources. In addition, the War Camp Community Service, founded by the Playground and Recreation Association of America at the request of the War Department, developed more than 500 off-post clubs in nearby communities to serve men in uniforms.

When it became apparent that organized social and recreation programs were helpful in maintaining morale, counteracting fatigue, and reducing other service problems, Special Services divisions were established to meet the need. These were generally conceived as including a wide variety of programs, services, facilities, and activities on regular bases, in maneuver areas, and overseas, to contribute to the total moral, mental, physical, and social well-being of armed forces personnel. Leisure services included recreational sports, libraries, arts and crafts, music, theatrical programs, social events, trips, and many other events and activities, usually centered about local service clubs.

The Special Services recreation program prior to World War II tended to be extremely decentralized, and lacking in both uniformity and professional leadership. Often it was dependent on the personal whims of base commanders and tended to be limited to sports competition on many posts. Financial limitations played a part in this, in that revenues from Post Exchanges often were depended upon to support programs.

During and after World War II, however, armed forces programs expanded greatly, to meet the needs of the rapidly growing branches of the service. Many highly qualified individuals with skills as entertainers, athletes, or recreation specialists in various areas entered the military and were assigned responsibilities in Special Services companies. The newly formed United Service Organizations, Inc., composed of six national agencies (YMCA, YWCA, Salvation Army, National Travelers' Aid Association, National Catholic Community Service and Jewish Welfare Board) became active in providing welfare, religious, educational, and recreational services to armed forces personnel all over the world. In addition, the USO used many of the talented entertainers within the forces, as well as famous civilian performers who contributed their services, to provide touring camp shows. Emphasis during the wartime period was on relaxing forms of recreation and on mass entertainment events. Following World War II, as the nature of military assignments and personnel changed, so the content of recreational programs in the armed forces changed as well. Today there is a greater stress on variety of activity, and on direct participation, rather than on spectator events.

A strong boost to recreation in the armed forces came with the report of the President's Committee on Religion and Welfare in the

Armed Forces. Issued in 1951, this report stressed the contribution of organized recreation services in shaping character, increasing efficiency, and promoting understanding and support of the armed forces both within the United States and in foreign bases.

Today, particularly within the Army (where it is established as a Division within the Adjutant General's office) and the Air Force (where it functions in the Personnel Services Division of the Directorate of Military Personnel), military recreation is a highly professionalized and diversified form of service. Within the Marine Corps, where it is provided as a branch of the Personnel Department, it places great stress on physical fitness and athletics, with less attention given to other forms of recreational activity. In the Navy, recreation is provided by a Special Services Division under the Assistant Chief of Naval Personnel for Morale Services, Bureau of Naval Personnel. Here, as in the Marine Corps, line officers are used to fill Special Service assignments, with a minimum of special training or past interest in recreation.

PROGRAM AREAS IN MILITARY RECREATION

It is within the Army and Air Force Special Services programs that large numbers of civilian recreation personnel are employed, and that the greatest effort is made to provide diversified recreation services, chiefly for enlisted personnel. Basically, the program consists of five major categories: (a) sports; (b) entertainment; (c) crafts; (d) service clubs; and (e) libraries.

Sports. These include both self-directed and/or organized athletic activities. They are usually divided into three phases: instructional, competitive, and self-organized. Program competition is offered in 18 different sports, and leadership is provided by army personnel and civilian specialists with backgrounds in athletics and physical education.

Entertainment. This includes soldier shows (plays, musicals, and informal variety shows); soldier musical events (instrumental and choral groups, concerts, and recorded programs), and touring shows with both military and civilian performers.

Crafts. These are considered to be both recreational and educational in function. Typical activities include photography, woodwork, model craft, automotive, radio, metal work, enameling, jewelry, lapidary, leather craft, ceramics, fine arts, and plastics. Recreation specalists, both male and female, with backgrounds in fine arts and arts education, are employed in leadership positions.

Libraries. These strive to provide reading services comparable to those offered by superior civilian libraries through post and branch libraries and "bookmobiles" which reach outer areas and hospitals. In addition to the normal function of lending books, armed forces' libraries provide reference and reader advisory services, military science reading programs and forums and music hours. Librarians may be male or female, and it is generally required that they have professional training in library service.

Service Clubs. The Army Service Club program is defined as "a facility at any Army installation designed for use during off-duty time by enlisted personnel, their families and friends, which is adequately furnished with supplies and equipment suitable for a wide variety of welfare and recreational activities; and staffed by uniformed civilian service club director personnel." The mission of the service club is to "assist in the development of the efficiency and morale of enlisted personnel by providing a friendly, homelike atmosphere during off-duty hours and wholesome social and recreational activities which function regularly and effectively." [2]

In short, the service club is something of a combination of a living room at home, an informal community hangout, and a well-run and equipped recreation center. Often it includes within its program elements of each of the other Special Services activities: entertainment, crafts, sports, and other cultural activities. Through initial service club involvement, the soldier may become interested in these activities in an informal way, and then may pursue them more fully in a post crafts shop or athletic program. Specifically, the well-rounded club program includes both self-directed activities (individual or small group use of the facility for such activities as pool, table tennis, music-listening, letter-writing, etc.), or planned programs of group activities which require organization and guidance. These may include any or all of the following and may, in some cases, use community resources or leadership:

1. Dances, parties, and social affairs at the military installation and in town
2. Tours, picnics, hikes, and theater parties
3. Music, recorded listening programs, vocal groups, concerts, and musical instruments for use in the club
4. Dramatics, including talent shows and community theater productions
5. Lectures, including discussion groups and special interest groups
6. Photography, crafts, hobbies, and exhibits
7. Volunteer personal services, including gift wrapping, sewing, and shopping
8. Lounges, meeting places for relatives and friends, reading, writing, snack bar
9. Home hospitality arrangements
10. Package shows and professional entertainment
11. Information and publicity center
12. Sports such as table tennis, shuffle board, pool, badminton, and archery. [3]

2 "An Introduction to the Army Service Club Program" (Washington, D.C.: Department of the Army Pamphlet No. 21–59, n.d.), p. 7.

3 *Program Handbook for Army Service Club Personnel* (Washington, D.C., Department of the Army Pamphlet 28–1, 1955), pp. 1–4.

In the Army and Air Force service club program, there is a constant effort to professionalize and improve staff and offerings. To illustrate, each year Service Club workshops are held in a number of regional centers, to upgrade personnel in terms of understanding modern trends in recreation, introducing new program ideas and training in leadership skills. Since 1959, there has been an annual All-Army Contest, titled "Operation Service Club," in which posts all over the world compete with program entries in three categories: (a) complete program over a period of one month, including four phases: social, competitive, creative, and intellectual activities; (b) a special theme program, which may represent a special interest or hobby project; and (c) a four-part program extending over a period of one year, with projects representing the phases just listed.

Depending on the location of the center and other special needs, service club directors may carry out certain unique tasks. For example, when a severe series of earthquakes occurred in Alaska during the spring of 1964, the service club directors at Fort Richardson helped to maintain military and civilian morale by providing emergency recreation and other services. When American families were suddenly evacuated from Panama to the Canal Zone due to rioting in Panama in the winter of 1964, again service club personnel organized many helpful emergency programs and forms of assistance.

European-bound soldiers arriving at Fort Dix, New Jersey, for embarkation have an opportunity to become acquainted in advance with their new duty station through service club activities which give them a beginning familiarity with the country they are being sent to. They learn about the region, take conversational language classes, become involved in nationality parties introducing folklore and customs, and are given other forms of orientation dealing with travel and currency. The emphasis in many service clubs abroad is often on building understanding of the local population, and constructive ties through service programs and joint recreational activities and projects.

Often, the recreation service at a base in foreign countries is designed to help soldiers and their families use the surrounding area's recreational resources to fullest advantage, rather than attempt to meet all needs right on the base. At Aviano Air Base in Italy, for example, military personnel are given informative booklets and counseling advising them of skiing and other winter sports at the nearby Tyrolean Alps, or water recreation and camping opportunities on the sandy beaches of the Adriatic Sea, also close to Aviano. To assist recreation excursions by the families of military personnel, the Recreation Section lends participants skis, poles, and boots, and negotiates special-rate books for skiing. Camping tents, air mattresses, sleeping bags, and other kinds of equipment are lent to families, and a booklet, "Camping on the Austrian and Italian Borders," gives information about selecting clean, safe, and inexpensive camping areas. Picnic kits, games and sports equipment, and party-planning services are also available to the families of Aviano enlisted personnel and officers.[4]

Recreation for Teen-Age Dependents. Both abroad and in the United States, comprehensive recreation programs are provided by Special Services for the teen-age dependents of Army personnel. This is particularly true in the U.S. Army Air Force, which has many bases abroad. Over 30,000 teen-age dependents in various European and Near Eastern countries want and need leisure time opportunities on a year-round, balanced basis—similar to those available in the United States. Thus, the U.S. forces in Europe encourage the establishment of teen clubs on each installation. Since 1958, this program has been assisted by a Teen Forum program, which brings together approximately 300 representatives from 50 U.S. military teen-club programs in countries such as England, Germany, France, Italy, Libya, Spain, and Turkey. At Forum meetings, teen-age delegates share program ideas, fund-raising methods and similar workshop problems. They formulate guides for teen-age behavior and for working with adult advisors on two age levels—grades 7 and 8, and 9 through 12.[5]

Within the United States, one of the important tasks of Special Services has always been to maintain and develop good relations between armed forces bases and nearby communities. An excellent example of interchange and cooperation through a military recreation program—particularly in the area of youth recreation—is found in Dyess Air Force Base, near Abilene, Texas. The Base youth programs make heavy use of the resources of both the military community and civilian organizations in Abilene. The drama program, for example, is assisted by Abilene residents who are active in community theater programs. Air Base youth participate widely in the city's summer recreation programs, and there are various other forms of cooperation.

There is a special youth center at Dyess, under the supervision of the Base recreation direction. Its operation provides a useful picture of a military teen program:

> In addition to four teen clubs, the youth program at Dyess consists of two Boy Scout troops, one Cub pack, one Explorer Post, Little League, Brownies, Girl Scouts, TOPS (Teens Organization for Public Service), a youth committee, teen newspaper, Youth Activities Advisory Council, and many special summer activities: learn-to-swim sessions, fencing, chess and bridge

---

[4] Edward L. Ericson, "Military Recreation: A Family Affair," *Recreation,* October, 1963, p. 373.

[5] Herbert Rathner, "Air Force Launches New Youth Program," *Recreation,* December, 1964, p. 518.

lessons, dance classes, a Children's Theatre production and the Youth Center, which has open house for dependents in the seventh grade or above each afternoon from 1 to 5:30. The Youth Center is closed Sundays and Mondays, and one iron-clad rule is: if you are too sick to go to school, you're too sick to come to the Youth Center. . . .[6]

All groups on the Base use the Youth Center for meetings and planning sessions, but it is never simply open at night as a "hangout." Instead, evenings are scheduled with supervised meetings for various clubs and youth organizations on a weekly or biweekly basis: "Sub-Teens" and "Twix-Teens" on alternate Friday nights, and "Junior-Teens" and "Senior-Teens" on alternate Saturday nights. Each of the Base's four teen clubs (with average memberships of between 75 and 90) elects its own officers every six months, governs itself with its own bylaws, and is self-supporting through dues and special money-raising projects. Each club also elects five adult advisors who serve one year periods.

Other Program Emphases. Dependent on the participants' interests and the leadership abilities of the staff, one form of activity or another may be stressed, within a given base. In one location it may be social activities; in another, creative activities. For example, at Lincoln Air Force Base, near Lincoln, Nebraska, where the total army population, including wives and children, approximates 15,000, there is an extremely heavy program emphasis on arts and crafts.

In addition to sports, entertainment, theater, parties and similar recreation activities, the base service club houses a number of special craft and hobby shops. The photography shop is in great demand by base personnel. Advice and instructions on all photographic problems are provided free by a part-time supervisor; the shop includes two developing rooms, two printing rooms, a dryer-layout room, and a recreation area. Nominal charges are made for the use of the developing rooms, but most supplies for developing are provided without charge. The ceramic hobby shop provides instruction in copper enameling, use of the potter's wheel and ceramics, under professional instruction; it is heavily used by the wives of base personnel. The leathercraft hobby shop offers free instruction in tooling, carving, and assembling of leathercraft.

Other facilities include an automotive hobby shop with more than 30 car stalls for wheel balancing, welding, and other car repair tasks, and a wood hobby shop with a full range of tools and equipment. Here, carpentry hobbyists make items ranging from coffee tables to camping trailers and boats. In addition, equipment used in the recreation program is repaired here.[7]

A similar specialized program emphasis may be found at the Marine Corps' Camp Lejeune, in North Carolina, where a wide variety of water

[6] Mildred Deaton, "Youth in Command," *Recreation,* February, 1962, p. 73.
[7] Robert M. Dula, "Command Performance," *Recreation,* May, 1962, p. 240.

sports, including sailing instruction and water skiing, is made available to military personnel and their dependents.[8] Often in foreign countries, as in Camp Zama, Japan, the emphasis is on programs involving national customs, art, music, and theater, as a basis for promoting intercultural understanding.

PROBLEMS IN MILITARY RECREATION

Essentially, there are two major problems in the area of recreation for the armed forces. The first is concerned with providing activities and services that are sufficiently appealing to potential participants to counteract other types of leisure opportunities which may not be as wholesome. The second is to staff programs with capable and professionally oriented individuals who will view this as a long-term career position.

In terms of motivating participants, the best answer seems to be to provide a range of services and activities that genuinely interest the greatest number of personnel, making use of special leadership resources wherever they may be found. On some bases, there may be a degree of compulsion, particularly with regard to the military athletic program conducted by Special Services. Thus, at one armed forces center in New York State, the following directive was recently issued:

1. The maintenance of high standards of mental and physical health among the members of this command is a primary concern of the Post Commander. The value of organized athletics in the achievement of this goal is undeniable.
2. The proposed athletic program will add significantly to the attainment of this goal. Therefore it is desired that all permanent party military personnel participate a minimum of one afternoon a week.
3. Section supervisors will ensure that all members of their sections participate. The only authorized absences will be for cogent military or medical reasons.
4. The athletic program will consist of 15–20 minutes limbering up exercises and one hour of organized sports such as Volleyball, Softball, Flag Football, Badminton, Tennis and Golf. . . .

While the activities mentioned would normally be part of a recreational sports program, making them required of all personnel tends to remove the element of free choice and recreational spirit. Within most phases of the military recreation program, there *must* be free choice and the activities provided must be so well chosen and presented that military personnel and their dependents participate because they *wish* to do so.

Thus, the quality of professional leadership is extremely important. It is necessary to attract capable young women and men who view this field as more than a brief interlude that provides an opportunity to see the world. Instead, the realization should be brought home to potential

8 "Leathernecks at Leisure," *Recreation,* January, 1963, p. 63, n.a.

candidates, particularly young women, that armed forces recreation provides an important and attractive career opportunity. It seeks individuals who have college degrees in the varied fields of recreation, dramatics, music, art, social sciences, humanities, physical education, and library science. Opportunities for placement include such varied settings as Alaska, Hawaii, Japan, Korea, Okinawa, Germany, Italy, France, the United States, and many other countries.

Sample requirements for applicants are cited on page 49, with starting salary scales running from Civil Service Grades 5 through 9, and promotions to higher grade levels based on merit. Special Service positions in Europe (for which constant recruitment is carried on in colleges and universities) are not in the Federal Competitive system. This means that neither Civil Service status nor Civil Service examinations are required, and applicants may seek information regarding positions directly from the Special Services Unit, IRCB, Department of the Army, in Washington, D.C. Of all the types of openings, positions in service clubs are most frequently available.

This chapter briefly describes the development of organized recreation services within the armed forces of the United States and outlines the components of activity that are provided, chiefly by the Special Services within the U.S. Army and Air Force. Service club programs, both within the United States and abroad, are analyzed in greater detail.

SUGGESTED QUESTIONS FOR DISCUSSION

1. Discuss the historical development of armed forces recreation, with an analysis of the nature of sponsorship in each of the major services, and a presentation of the purposes of this field of activity.
2. Assume that you are a recreation director on an armed forces base. What unique problems might you face, in planning program services and schedules?
3. To what extent is armed forces recreation a professionally staffed field? What steps have been taken to improve the level of service within the Army and Air Force Programs?

Chapter *15*

Religious Sponsorship of Recreation

Distinctly separate from government, yet providing an important segment of organized recreation service, are the religious agencies of our nation. Some of the impressive statistics concerning recreation that is sponsored by churches or affiliated with religious organizations are cited earlier in this text (see page 21). As Meyer and Brightbill point out, religion in our society represents a stable and powerful social institution. The 1960 Yearbook of American Churches lists over 400 separate denominations, with a membership of over 100 million, youth organizations with over 12 million members, and a corporate wealth of over 10 billion dollars.

It is safe to say that each of the major faiths, and a number of lesser denominations, are vitally concerned with the recreational uses of leisure and provide a variety of services and activities as part of their total program. On the national level, this has been particularly true of the National Council of Churches of Christ, the National Catholic

376

Welfare Conference and the Jewish Welfare Board. Such a policy was not always the case. In the early New England colonies in particular, during the seventeenth century, the dominant Puritan church, with its stern Calvinist theology and emphasis on material accomplishment, was rigidly opposed to many forms of play. Gradually, however, through the eighteenth and nineteenth centuries, it came to be recognized that leisure should be viewed as offering the opportunity for spiritual growth and the strengthening of moral values, rather than necessarily a source of evil or degenerative experience.

Thus, in the nineteenth century, a number of religious organizations, such as the Christian Worker's Society of the Church of the Brethren, the Mutual Improvement Society of the Mormon Church, the Young Men's Christian Asociation and the Young Men's Hebrew Association, began to initiate programs of wholesome recreation activities for their membership. Activities took the form of church suppers, picnics, bazaars, lectures, concerts, outings, dramatics, community music, and a host of other club activities for members on various age levels. This practice has spread until the church or synagogue today that does not have a social and recreational program for its membership, or serving a segment of its community's population, is rare.

RATIONALE FOR RELIGIOUS SPONSORSHIP OF RECREATION

What is the justification for the involvement of churches and synagogues in recreation sponsorship? Clearly, this is an expensive and time-consuming task. How is it supported in terms of rationale? There are two kinds of justification: (a) based on the Scriptures; and (b) based on the expanding social role of religious agencies in our society.

The first point is that, from a traditional religious point of view, leisure is assigned a place in our value system; it has deep spiritual connotations. In Genesis, we read:

And the Heaven and the earth were finished, and all the host of them.

And on the seventh day God finished His work which He had made; and He rested on the seventh day from all His work which He had made. And God blessed the seventh day, and hallowed it; because that in it He rested from all His work. . . .[1]

The classical commentaries suggest that this implies that work has no integrity until one enjoys his attendant rest. The religious person who is part of the Judeo-Christian tradition will therefore view leisure as time reserved by God, which must be filled with spiritual meaning—not necessarily in divine worship, but spent according to divine intent.

Thus, leisure and wholesome recreation are both linked to spiritual

[1] Book of Genesis, Ch. 2: 1–3.

celebration and rebirth; the essential religious position is that leisure must not only be seen in negative terms (the avoidance of undesirable play) but as a positive opportunity for spiritual growth and character development.

Strongly supporting the actual involvement of churches and synagogues in sponsorship of recreation has been the expanding social role of religion in our society. No longer is religion regarded as solely a matter of preaching the Gospel or providing the sacraments. Instead, the church has become in the broadest sense an agency which ministers to many of the fundamental needs in our society. Often, ministerial training includes social work orientation and courses involving psychiatric concepts, to prepare individuals for pastoral counseling and similar tasks. Social justice has become vitally attached to religious practice, and it is no accident that in the Civil Rights marches and demonstrations of the early and middle 1960's, white religious leaders of all faiths suffered the same attacks and abuse as did Negro participants.

This concept of social involvement of religion has naturally extended to recreation, as a key aspect of present-day life. E. O. Harbin, a pioneer in Methodist recreation programing, has written:

> There are three reasons why the church must interest itself in community recreation: (1) The members of the church do not grow up in a vacuum. Children, young people, and adults have community contacts that are inescapable. The church must be intelligently concerned, therefore, about what goes on in the community. (2) Then, too, the church's interest in human welfare makes it imperative that it cooperate with other community agencies in providing adequate recreation opportunities of such quality and variety as to meet community needs. (3) The church often has space and equipment that should be made available for community recreation activities, if such space and equipment are not available elsewhere.[2]

In many cases, this has been expanded to the view that religious leaders should go out from the four walls of their churches, to serve the public where it is. A leading officer of the United Church of Christ's Board of Homeland Ministries, the Rev. Truman B. Douglass, urged in 1963 that ministers be posted on "the gambling strip at Las Vegas, the swimming pools of Miami Beach and the ski slopes of the Rockies. . . ." At a meeting of the fourth general synod of the United Church of Christ, he declared:

> Americans in their leisure time are spending more time away from their church homes and we must not assume that people in a resort area will hunt up a church. We feel that the church must go to those places where people who are engaged in leisure time activities usually are.[3]

2 E. O. Harbin, quoted in Reynold E. Carlson, Theodore R. Deppe, and Janet R. MacLean, *Recreation in American Life* (Belmont, California: Wadsworth, 1963), p. 200.
3 Truman B. Douglass, *The New York Times,* July 5, 1963, p. 44.

As a concrete example of the church's growing concern with leisure, in 1964, the National Council of Churches enlarged its ministry to vacationers in the country's national parks, with 195 college and seminary students conducting programs in 36 parks. Working as park employees during the week, on Sundays and in their free time, these students conducted worship services for thousands of park employees and visitors numbering in the millions. Overall, the program was conceived as attempting to "break down partitions between the secular and the sacred in God's great out-of-doors." The program has been directed by the National Council's Department of a Christian Ministry with People in Leisure-Recreation.

TYPES OF RELIGIOUS INVOLVEMENT WITH RECREATION

What are the basic ways in which religious agencies carry out functions related to recreation?

1. *Direct Sponsorship on a Local Level.* Churches and synagogues may sponsor a more or less diversified program of recreational activities on the local level, usually for their own members but in some cases on a nonsectarian basis. When the program is geared to meet the needs of the specific congregation, it may include a certain amount of religious content and may be based on specific denominational beliefs and practices. Thus, church-sponsored camps, meetings or rallies, youth education programs, retreats, and conferences are all likely to make use of pageantry, music, dramatics, reading clubs, and similar activities which relate strongly to spiritual matters. Even when the program that is designed for church members does not have actual religious content, it meets the leisure needs of the congregation in a wholesome way and helps to improve their bond of fellowship. Thus, it is considered to meet overall religious goals. The local church or synagogue may also sponsor such activities as Golden Age clubs, youth canteens, Scout groups, and play schools on a completely nonsectarian membership basis. Here, of course, it must be careful not to give specific religious emphasis to the program, or it may be accused of proselyting in the attempt to attract new members.

2. *Recreation Service on a Broader Scale.* Particularly for young people, a number of religious denominations have organizations that operate nationally, or across a given region of the country. The Protestant churches, for example, have the Methodist Youth Fellowship, the Luther League, the Presbyterian Westminster Fellowship, the Baptist Training Union, and many similar groups. Leading Catholic youth organizations include the Newman Clubs and the Catholic Youth Organization. Jewish youth organizations include B'nai B'rith and Hillel. Each of these associations serve primarily individuals of the particular faith involved,

with a variety of activities, of which recreation represents an important component.

The major faiths also sponsor a number of national organizations which maintain centers throughout the country, such as the Young Men's and Young Women's Christian Association and Young Men's and Young Women's Hebrew Association. These agencies, usually found in large cities and towns, provide nonsectarian memberships with a variety of services, again including recreation as a major focus.

3. *Support of Recreation on a Community-Wide Basis.* In addition to the two preceding forms of involvement, many religious agencies are extremely effective in supporting and improving the total program of recreation service on a community-wide basis. This effort may consist of serving on interchurch or interagency councils, having representation on recreation boards, acting as a base for youth groups, providing facilities where other agencies may offer programs, assisting in fund-raising efforts, or similar forms of participation. Most important, however, is the role of the church or synagogue in promoting desirable moral values and standards for the community at large, in terms of leisure participation. Without acting as censors, or in an undemocratic fashion, religious leaders have the obligation to vigorously present a philosophy that sees recreation as the opportunity for wholesome moral growth and to oppose undesirable leisure activities and trends.

DIRECT RECREATION SPONSORSHIP ON LOCAL LEVEL

Among the categories of activities which are widely found in locally sponsored programs of church or synagogue-centered recreation are the following:

1. Camping and similar outdoor activities, including family camping, conferences and institutes, or retreats emphasizing religious education programs—programs that frequently place heavy stress on recreational activities of all types through the day and evening, including various forms of "inspirational" events, such as campfires, vesper services, singing, dramatics, and rhythmic worship
2. Similar to the above are day camps, play schools, or summer Bible schools, which are conducted by many religious agencies and usually involve many play activities, along with more formal educational content
3. A year-round program of social recreation activities, including family nights, picnics and outings, covered-dish suppers (where each family brings a special dish), game nights and carnivals, bazaars, dances, and informal community singing and dramatics
4. Special interest groups in the arts and crafts area, or in the performing arts of music, drama, and dance that may involve religious pageantry and drama, or secular plays, choruses, choirs, instrumental groups, and similar projects.
5. A network of clubs or Fellowship groups for various age levels, which meet

regularly and have both social and spiritual emphases in their programs and may include youth groups, couples' club, Scout groups, service groups (which perform volunteer service activities in the community) and Golden Age or Senior Citizens clubs

6. Sports activities, in the form of bowling or basketball leagues, or less structured participation in other sports
7. Discussion groups that deal with current events, literature, religious themes, and similar content

In many large metropolitan churches and synagogues, special parish halls or community center buildings or wings of buildings have been developed, with all the types of facilities, meeting rooms, and equipment that are needed for well-rounded recreation programing. Camping, in particular, has been expanding rapidly as a form of church-affiliated recreation. Many religious organizations or associations have purchased large tracts of land, using them both as sites for recreational camping by their congregations and also as centers for religious institutes, leadership training courses, and other types of workshops. Implicit in this practice is the belief that the outdoor living environment, close to nature, is conducive to spiritual growth, and the reexamination of one's moral values. Thus, according to Bone, ". . . statisticians tell us that the number of individual boys and girls attending summer camps sponsored by religious groups is now greater than the attendance at all other camps put together."[4]

In all forms of church-sponsored social recreation, the following point of view is emphasized:

1. Activities must involve people meaningfully; the experience should not be a superficial or passive one but should place them in close contact with each other, developing interdependence and desirable social values.

2. Respect for each other, and the acceptance and understanding of those of different backgrounds, races, and creeds, is a desirable goal of group activities. Often church organizations are active not only in promoting intercultural programs within a community, but in bringing visitors or students from other sections of the country, or other lands, to promote understanding.

4. Religious-affiliated recreation rejects the tawdry, the sensational, and artificial, and places stress on program activities which bring out the more constructive and generous qualities in participants. Particularly in Methodist and Baptist-sponsored programs for youth and adults, there is a great deal of emphasis on folk materials—songs, games, crafts, and the like—because of their traditional backgrounds, and the nature of group involvement they achieve.

[4] Maurice D. Bone, "Church-Sponsored Camping," *Recreation,* March, 1961, p. 126.

RECREATION SERVICE ON A BROADER LEVEL

In addition to programs that are sponsored locally by a specific church or synagogue, there are a number of national youth or adult organizations that are affiliated with major religious denominations, which provide recreation services. Usually, their overall program includes a number of basic components: fellowship, religious education, spiritual development, social welfare, and leadership training. As part of this scheme, however, recreation is viewed as a crucial element. Examples follow, for each of the major faiths.

Protestant: The YMCA and YWCA

Among the most widespread of the youth and adult organizations that are affiliated with the Protestant faith in general, rather than any single denomination, are the Young Men's and Young Women's Christian Associations. Each of these are voluntary organizations devoted to the promotion of religious ideals of living. A descriptive statement published by the National Council of YMCA's describes the "Y" as:

> . . . a movement which helps youth—young men and boys and frequently young women and girls—to develop those Christian qualities which are essential to successful living. In a larger sense, the Y.M.C.A. is a worldwide fellowship dedicated to the enrichment of life through the development of Christian character and a Christian society. The Y.M.C.A. is voluntary, non-governmental, locally run and financed. It is democratically controlled by a volunteer board elected by members. . . .

Typically, program services of the YMCA include camping, educational activities (the "Y" runs 42 formal schools and colleges), personal counseling, and a wide variety of recreation activities: clubs (Hi-Y, Junior Hi-Y and Gra-Y for different age levels), social events, arts and crafts, sports and fitness programs, dances, youth center programs, and institutes and workshops. These are provided in over 1,800 different "Y" centers, with a professional staff of close to 4,000 and volunteer leaders of over 370,000. It is important to note that, although the YMCA is essentially a Protestant organization and is devoted to furthering a Christian way of life, its membership represents all Christian and some non-Christian faiths. A recent study showed the religious affiliation of "Y" members as including 75.2 percent Protestant, 18.9 percent Roman Catholic, and 3.3 percent Jewish.

Similarly, the Young Women's Christian Association is concerned with Christian purpose. The brochure of a major YWCA branch in New York City contains this statement of goals:

To build a fellowship of women and girls devoted to the task of realizing in our common life those ideals of personal and social living to which we are committed by our faith as Christians. In this endeavor we seek to understand Jesus, to share His love for all people, and to grow in the knowledge and love of God.

Apart from a "meditation room" for "quiet thought and spiritual refreshment," an individual counseling service, and a series of Study Group meetings with religious emphasis, there is little direct focus on religion in this YWCA's program, and it is open to members of all races and creeds. It must be assumed, however, that the ideals and purposes of the "Y" pervade the leadership and program content of *all* activities presented. These include the following: a National YWCA Public Affairs discussion program, a World Fellowship program, a Y-Teen program for junior and senior high school girls, interest groups and lounge programs, dance and dressmaking classes for teen-age girls, family forum, good-grooming classes, a sex-education program, coffee hours, dramatics, arts and crafts, language classes, sports and fitness, bridge and photography.

Other Protestant youth organizations on a national scale, such as the Luther League or Methodist Youth Fellowship, tend to be sectarian in membership and more religiously oriented in program than the YM and YWCA.

Roman Catholic: the CYO

The Catholic Youth Organization is the agency which meets most successfully and broadly the spiritual, apostolic, social, and cultural needs of Catholic youth. Since its founding in New York City in 1936, it has grown steadily until, in that city alone, it serves 250,000 members (boys and girls, teen-agers and young adults). As an example of its scope, it operates 5 community centers, 4 settlement houses, 4 summer camps, a CYO Sea Cadet Corps, 17 Delinquency Recreation Projects, 180 teen-age leadership clubs, leadership training courses, swimming classes for the handicapped, and a recreation program for retarded children. Its 600 Boy and Girl Scout troops, 45 summer Day Camps, 36 Young Adult Clubs, Symphony and Music Program and Physical Fitness Council are directed by a core staff of professionals and the assistance of over 10,000 volunteer adult leaders.

Throughout its program, the CYO places a strong emphasis on moral and spiritual values, youth leadership, and patriotism. These are all promoted through the organization's extensive social, athletic, and cultural program, which interacts with Catholic parishes throughout the city.

Perhaps the most unusual example of church-sponsored recreation programing to be found anywhere is the Cresthaven-Whitestone Recreation Center operated by the CYO in the borough of Queens, New York. Initiated as a CYO day camp by the Rev. Michael J. Fleming in 1950, this project has steadily expanded until today it is a sprawling recreation center bustling with year-round activity for the entire family. Operating on a large tract of land within the city limits, it has:

4 large outdoor swimming pools and 4 wading pools
7 clay courts for tennis
1,200 feet of waterfront
recreation halls and dining accommodations for 700 people
facilities for handball, softball, basketball, volleyball, and shuffleboard
day camp facilities for 4,000 children each day
2 yacht clubs in a modern marina, with mooring space for 300 boats

Serving the entire area of Queens County and parts of two other New York boroughs, the Cresthaven-Whitestone Recreation Center operates camping and club activities for children, youth, adults, and families. Its young adult social club, for example, meets throughout the year, planning and carrying on its own program, with such activities as: bowling, skiing, garden club, drama club, travel club, discussion club, sports club, and a varied series of special events.

While this CYO program is unusually large and successful, similar activities on a smaller scale are offered by many other Catholic agencies and centers.

Jewish: National Jewish Welfare Board

Under the overall stimulus of the National Jewish Welfare Board, there is a farflung network of Jewish Community Centers throughout the United States. These include approximately 500 operating units, such as center buildings, camps, and other properties, which employ more than 1,500 professional workers and serve almost 600,000 members of all ages, as well as an additional million persons who come to centers for a variety of activities.

While many YM and YWHA's offer Jewish cultural activities in the form of courses, and music or theater programs based on Jewish history or folk traditions, much of the program is of a completely nonreligious nature. In addition, in many "Y's" and Jewish Community Centers, large numbers of members are not of this faith.

To illustrate, one of the best-known settlement houses in New York City is the Educational Alliance. This agency has been in existence on the lower East Side of Manhattan for over 75 years. It is an integral part of the Federation of Jewish Philanthropies of New York, and its first purpose was to assist Jewish immigrants to the United States by providing educational, social, health, and leisure services. Over the years, the

Educational Alliance's membership has grown to over 6,500 people. Its membership is nonsectarian and today, because of population shifts, it serves a variety of racial groups, including Chinese, Negroes, Puerto Ricans, and a continuing proportion of Jewish persons. The overall program includes camping, mental health consultation, an art school, a religious Hebrew school, a school for handicapped Jewish children, a Cerebral Palsy center, a Mobilization for Youth Program, a street-corner operation for hard-to-reach youth, an aftercare social program for discharged mental patients, and many other social and recreational activities.

All age levels and people of all backgrounds are served in this center, typical of many other Jewish centers throughout the country.

Within such youth organizations as Hillel or B'nai B'rith, however, the membership is a sectarian one, and the focus is more sharply on spiritual and religious values and objectives.

RELIGIOUS INVOLVEMENT IN RECREATION ON A COMMUNITY-WIDE BASIS

The relationship between religious agencies that promote recreational activities and total community programs in this field is a significant one. As indicated earlier, this may take several forms: (a) clergymen serving on interchurch or community councils that are concerned with leisure opportunities; (b) the church providing recreational activities both for its own members and, where appropriate, for the community at large; (c) the church making its facilities available, when needed, for other organizations to sponsor programs; (d) the church cosponsoring institutes and workshops concerned with recreation or leadership training; (e) finally, lending its strength to the support of desirable recreation programs in the community and serving as a source of high moral values with respect to leisure choices.

Clemens, Tully, and Crill have written:

Churches that care for their communities will have representatives on recreation boards, commissions, councils, and/or committees. The church will seek guidance from local recreation departments and auxiliary recreation agencies. The church's recreation program will be integrated with the total community program.

The church can offer its facilities and leadership in the sponsorship and operation of recreation meetings, institutes, workshops, and conferences. If, in the church's judgment, some forms of recreation in the community are unwise, it should oppose them . . . and make worthy substitutions. . . .[5]

It is important that church leaders *not* think of their agencies as *meeting* total community needs. When a service is already provided and

[5] Frances Clemens, Robert Tully, and Edward Crill, Eds., *Recreation and the Local Church* (Elgin, Illinois: Brethren Publishing House), p. 191.

successfully operating, the religious-sponsored recreation program would do well to seek out *gaps* in opportunity, rather than duplicate existing activities. This implies that church or synagogue recreation leaders should communicate frequently with public recreation executives, or leaders in other agencies; if possible, there should be a community calendar or clearing house for activities.

The church or synagogue that wishes to operate effectively in this field must be prepared to carry out the following steps:

1. Organize a recreation committee from the members of its congregation and appropriate staff members, to deal thoughtfully with the problem.
2. Carefully survey and estimate recreational needs, both of the membership of the church or synagogue and of other community groups that might be surveyed.
3. Review available facilities, to determine which can be used by the religious agency itself, or under which circumstances other agencies might be permitted to operate programs within the center. Where feasible, develop a plan for building new facilities; usually this is closely connected with plans for developing facilities for religious education.
4. Develop a separate recreation budget, making use of special fund-raising projects where necessary to support it.
5. Obtain capable leadership to conduct the recreation activities of the church or synagogue. In a large center, this should be directed by a professional individual; under some circumstances it may be necessary to use religious education personnel, who should have background and interest in this field. All part-time and volunteer leaders should receive in-service training in skills and philosophy of education. Often, this can be obtained with the assistance of public recreation departments, which frequently conduct such programs.
6. Coordinate its services and program activities with all other interested agencies within the community.

This chapter deals with the total role of religious agencies in providing community recreation services and activities, and helping to develop overall leisure programs of high quality. The functions of a number of religious organizations, representing the major faiths, are given, and brief guides are presented for program development.

SUGGESTED QUESTIONS FOR DISCUSSION

1. Justify in a thoughtful statement the role of churches and other religious agencies in the provision of recreation services. Indicate how a changing view of the role of religious leaders has played a part in this.
2. What are the three major forms of recreational involvement of religious agencies? Give examples of each, involving programs conducted by various religious denominations which were cited in the chapter.
3. Should the church, under normal circumstances, accept the responsibility of providing programs that meet total community needs? Discuss.

Chapter *16*

Industrial Recreation Programs

Another major, nongovernmental form of organized recreation service is "industrial recreation." This term is generally used to describe "those recreation activities which are provided to satisfy the particular needs and desires of employees of business and industrial firms." [1] Since it is frequently found in companies that are not of an industrial nature, and since labor unions often sponsor recreation programs for their members, the term "employee recreation" is sometimes used.

Historical Background of Industrial Recreation

Recreation designed to meet the needs of employees of a given concern or industry has existed in one form or another since the middle of the nineteenth century. The earliest example is said to have been found in the Peacedale Manufacturing Company in Peacedale, Rhode

---

[1] Jackson Anderson, *Industrial Recreation* (New York: McGraw-Hill, 1955), p. 5.

Island, where, in 1854, a library was provided for the use of the community and musical and religious education activities were offered to children of employees. In the decades that followed, a number of manufacturing concerns began to sponsor trips and annual excursions or picnics for their workers. Some, like the National Cash Register Company in Dayton, Ohio, or the Joliet Steel Company in Joliet, Illinois, built clubhouses or auditoriums for their employees. Others, like the Pullman Company of Chicago and the Conant Thread Company of Massachusetts, provided activities ranging from athletic programs and facilities to outings and social events.

Beginning in 1868, the YMCA initiated program services specially designed for industrial employees. At first the emphasis was on special clubrooms and other facilities for railroad workers. In 1902, the "Y" established an Industrial Department and expanded program services for workers in mining, textile, and steel industrial communities, and even in labor camps.

In the early decades of the twentieth century, the predominant emphasis was on sports programs; indeed, many companies supported baseball or football teams that were almost professional in their skills. Two of these later became the Chicago Bears and Green Bay Packers. In World War I, industrial recreation programs expanded rapidly, as a means of attracting and holding employees in boom war industries. In several cities, industrial recreation associations were formed; one of the first of these was the Industrial Recreation Federation established in New Haven, Connecticut, in 1919. This was a centralized organization which planned, promoted, and administered a variety of employee recreation programs—including athletic leagues, hobby activities, and social programs. Similar federations were developed in Milwaukee, Wisconsin and San Francisco, California.

Industrial recreation programs continued to grow during the 1920's. In 1926, the U.S. Bureau of Labor statistics indicated that 430 companies throughout the country were providing recreation programs for their employees, with a substantial gain over the previous 10 years in varied social activities and recreation facilities. There was a temporary setback during the early 1930's, because of the Depression. However, as unionization spread in the middle and late 1930's, and again in World War II, due to the tremendous growth of war plants, industrial recreation expanded rapidly. The number of companies sponsoring such programs continued to increase in the years after the war. According to the *Wall Street Journal,* estimated expenditures by business and industry for employee recreation amounted to 800 million dollars in 1953, a full 50 percent increase over the amount in 1948.

By 1963, the National Industrial Recreation Association, which had been founded in 1941, had achieved a total membership of over 800 large corporations. Figures compiled by the Philadelphia District Federal Reserve Bank estimated company contributions to employee recreation programs to be in excess of a billion dollars a year.[2]

The NIRA, a nation-wide, nonprofit association organized by industry to assist in the development and coordination of employee recreation programs, describes the current status of this field:

> No longer viewed as a somewhat questionable venture in employee relations, industrial recreation is now firmly established on the basis of objective business judgment as an essential management function. Well-planned, carefully executed employee programs have proved their value both to employer and employee in creating the necessary business atmosphere of cooperation and harmony. To achieve its goals and justify its existence as a corporate policy, industrial recreation must offer a balanced program appealing to all employees and embracing the human needs that a job alone cannot completely fulfill.[3]

Rationale for Industrial Recreation Services

What are the basic reasons why so many large concerns have sponsored or assisted in the development of employee recreation programs? Several key purposes may be cited.

1. *Recruitment Appeal.* It is known that potential employees today desire cultural and recreational opportunities when they consider joining a new firm, both for themselves and their families (see p. 15). Thus, an attractive employee recreation program has significant recruitment appeal.

2. *Improvement of Employer-Employee Relations.* Traditionally (dating from an earlier period of management-labor friction), industrial recreation programs have had as one of their major purposes the goal of establishing harmonious relationships within the plant. Even today, in a period of comparative labor peace, industrial recreation serves to strengthen the loyalty and improve the morale of workers; in this sense it is comparable to employee council, profit-sharing, and similar "incentive-building" plans.

3. *Promoting Employee Efficiency.* The principle is generally accepted that recreation within an industrial concern—just as in a community—promotes physical and emotional well-being. More specifically, it is known that absenteeism is a major concern for American business today. Each day, an estimated 3,500,000 employees fail to show up for work each working day because of "illness," representing a direct cost to U.S. industry of 13.6 billion dollars a year in the form of wages, salaries, and benefits, with many other indirect costs. Leading authorities in industrial management are convinced that the major factor in absenteeism

---

2 "Firms' Outlay Big for Recreation," *Chicago Tribune,* July 27, 1963, n.p.
3 Membership brochure, *National Industrial Recreation Association,* 1964.

is mental and emotional illness; studies have recognized the value of industrial recreation programs in reducing absenteeism of this type. Similarly, it is believed that employee recreation, because it combats fatigue and boredom, helps reduce accident rates.

At one point, industrial recreation might have been viewed as a form of paternalism, and an attempt to fight unionization by voluntarily providing worker benefits. Today, it is regarded as a legitimate and altruistic form of management-labor relations, a morale-building personnel service.

Administrative Patterns in Industrial Recreation

Exactly how is industrial recreation organized? Since companies vary so greatly in their structure, and in the nature of their working forces, no single administrative pattern prevails. The following represent a number of typical arrangements, however:

1. The company takes complete responsibility for an organized recreation program, providing facilities and leadership, and maintaining control of the operation. There may be a fee system for participation, and there may be an advisory council of employees.

2. Facilities, or a capital outlay for developing areas and facilities, are provided by the employer. Management and employees, however, share responsibility for operating the program, usually with a fee system for participation and an employee's council to determine policy.

3. As a variant of the above, the employer may provide the facilities, ranging from clubrooms to gymnasiums or ballfields, but the employees are in total charge of the program.

4. In some companies, an independent employee's association has complete responsibility for the recreation program and uses facilities that it has developed *away* from the plant.

5. When a union operates a program of employee recreation, it may make use of plant facilities, but, more commonly, will use union-owned buildings, campsites, or other facilities for the program. In some cases, the sponsoring agency may be a union local that includes membership from several companies operating in the same industrial field.

6. The program may involve cooperation between the company and the surrounding community or adjacent municipality. In some cases, under contractual agreement, the industrial recreation program may make use of public facilities but provide its own leadership. In others, the company may provide *all* public recreation within the area.

A common arrangement is to have recreation participation based on voluntary employee membership in an employee club, association, or athletic association. When the company itself takes the responsibility for the program, it usually is made a function of an industrial relations or personnel relations division.

Financial Support. It is generally agreed that employees should pay at least a portion of the expenses of the program. This is done through annual membership fees, moderate fees for participation in certain activities, and through use of income derived from canteens, plant vending machines, and similar sources.

Leadership. In the most effective industrial recreation departments, there are professional directors and activity leaders, hired on a full-time basis for this assignment. In others, part-time or volunteer leadership may be relied on heavily.

Administrative Control. No matter which of the six administrative patterns listed earlier prevails, employees themselves should have a voice in establishing policies and carrying out the program. Even when it is operated by a professional director, he should make use of an advisory council for guidance.

Program Content. In general, it may be said that industrial recreation program content falls into the same major categories as community recreation: physical, social, cultural-creative, etc. However, program emphases vary widely from company to company, and there is less of a tendency to have a balanced offering than there is to specialize in certain forms of activity. Examples of such programs follow:

The Delco-Remy Division and Guide Lamp Division of General Motors operates a recreation park that 500,000 sportsmen and picnickers have used since 1956.

Phillips Petroleum, in addition to its athletic program and touring basketball team, also sponsors a full symphony orchestra.

Union Carbide in South Charleston, West Virginia, runs one of the country's largest hunting and fishing ranges. The same company, in other plants, places heavy emphasis on travel, with the recreation association sponsoring a travel club that shows travel films, brings in guest speakers, and charters jet flights for vacation group trips.

The Minneapolis Honeywell Regulator Company has just completed a huge recreation park, including a casting range for fishermen, a ski tow, and 36 holes of golf.

Recent Trends. Carlson, Deppe, and MacLean cite the following recent trends in industrial recreation: (a) there is a greater tendency for employees to share in program costs; (b) there is less emphasis on paternalistic control of the recreation program by management; (c) labor unions have moved increasingly into the field of employee recreation; (d) more activities that are financially self-supporting are being included; (e) the scope of program activities is widening, with cultural and social activities being included, as well as creative; (f) more family activities and senior citizen programs for retired workers are sponsored; (g) some companies or unions are involving employees in deliberately planned preretirement activities with carryover value; and (h) there is increasing cooperation between industry and community recreation agencies.[4]

Examples of Current Practices

To illustrate the scope of industrial recreation programs, several thumbnail sketches which appeared in *Recreation Management* in 1958 are reprinted here; they are followed by more detailed analysis of several current programs.

Allis-Chalmers Manufacturing Company, Milwaukee, Wisconsin. The first recreation program at Allis-Chalmers took the form of parties and picnics. In 1886, the first sports activity—a Rifle Club—was added. Organized activities in baseball, bowling, and basketball were added around 1900. In 1920, a committee with two management and five employee representatives was formed to direct activities. In 1942, the department of recreation was organized as a part of the Personnel Service Section. Since its inception, industrial recreation has shown a steady growth at Allis-Chalmers. Employee participation includes 9,000 of more than 16,000 employees. We use the company's bulletin boards and newspaper to promote activities and utilize over 350 employees as activity leaders.

Eastman Kodak Company, Rochester, New York. The Kodak Park Athletic Association was organized in 1910. It has a present (1958) total membership of 19,700 employees, of which 14,800 are men and 4,900 women. Active participation runs around 35 percent. We increase participation primarily through personal contacts—asking others to "join in." We reach new employees through announcements, personal letters, and individual follow-up.

Armstrong Cork Company, Lancaster, Pennsylvania. The Lancaster Floor Plant of the Armstrong Cork Company has had employee recreation in one form or another since the early 1920's. However, prior to the 1940's, it was essentially an athletic program. Today, the program includes everything from golf to pinochle tournaments, from dances to children's parties. Employee participation runs unusually high. Program director feels that personal contact on the part of committee people and activity leaders, plus plenty of publicity, have been responsible for the high employee interest.[5]

OTHER EXAMPLES

Nationwide Insurance Corporation

The Nationwide Insurance Corporation, in Columbus, Ohio, sponsors an Activities Association with a staff of five employees who are hired and paid by the company under its personnel department, to service

4 Reynold Carlson, Theodore Deppe, and Janet MacLean, *Recreation in American Life* (Belmont, California: Wadsworth, 1963), p. 222.
5 *Recreation Management*, May, 1958, p. 10–11.

2,600 employees. All recreation council meetings and committee meetings are scheduled on the employee's own time, unless there is a brief emergency meeting called, which may be held during working hours. All activities, of course, are scheduled during off-work hours. A recent "Activities Almanac" published by the Nationwide Insurance Activities Association states the following program objectives: (a) development of a spirit of friendliness and unity among employees and their families; and (b) education for leisure through participation in cultural, sports, social and service activities. Specific examples of program follow:

Cultural Council Activities

Amateur Radio Club, Camera Club, Doll Reconditioning, Drama Club, Film Club, Garden Club, Instruction Classes in Cooking, Dancing, Golf, Skiing, Noon Hour Crafts, Press (Political, Religious, Economic and Social Seminar), Stamp Club, Toastmasters, Toastmistress, Informal School

Service Council

Opportunities for service to fellow employees and to the community: Christmas Packaging, Kiddies' Christmas Party, Hospital Hostessing, Purchasing Assistance, Travel Days

Social Council

Dance, Duplicate Bridge, Men's Club, Nationettes, Roller Skating, Style Show, Swim Party, Young Business Folks

Sports Council

Basketball, Fishing, Fun Day, Gun Club, Headpin Tournament, Men's Bowling, Men's Golf, Men's Softball, Pheasant Tail Contest, Physical Fitness, Ski Club, Summer Bowling, Women's Bowling, Women's Golf

In addition, other special activities which are supervised by an administrative Board of Trustees (elected by the membership) include: an annual meeting, an annual show, carnival, displays for trips, and representatives' banquet.

Rockefeller Center, Inc.

An example of a recreation program designed to meet the needs of employees of a large office building complex in a large metropolitan setting may be found in the Employees' Recreation Association of Rockefeller Center, Inc., in New York City. The purpose of this Association, organized in 1939, is to promote good fellowship, cooperate in activities of general interest, and participate in healthful recreation. The program is directed by a board of governors, elected from the officers of the Association. The company itself provides a professional Recreation Director and staff to carry on the program.

In terms of financial support, the program is financed through annual $1.00 membership dues, contributions from Rockefeller Center, and special charges for certain classes and activities. The major facility provided by the company is a gymnasium, in which sports and physical fitness programs are carried on. In addition, members of the Association take part in certain outside activities that are organized through the program, such as softball, bowling, golf, and tennis. Social, bridge, stamp and coin clubs, informal adult classes, and community service projects meet other needs of participants. Other special services provided to employees by the Recreation Association include the arranging of discounts for theater parties to plays and opera performances and obtaining tickets for television and radio programs.

The Rockefeller Center program would suggest that when employee recreation is offered to employees in a large urban center with many existing recreation opportunities, one of its primary functions is to help them take advantage of these opportunities, and to do so in groups based on common interests.

Goodyear Tire and Rubber Company

One of the best-known industrial recreation programs is sponsored by the Department of Recreation of the Goodyear Tire and Rubber Company, in Akron, Ohio. Established in the 1890's, this program is operated under the direction of an Employees' Activities Committee, which is made up of an official representative from each club and activity, and which is incorporated as an nonprofit organization by the state. A 10-member board which is set up by the Employees' Activities Committee serves as an advisory board to the professional Recreation Director.

The program itself is divided into several major categories: Clubs, Divisional Athletics, Varsity Athletics, Special Activities, Music, and Special Services. Examples of each category follow:

Clubs

All Weather Campers	Modern Aircraft
Boats and Yachting	Junior Rifle
Duplicate Bridge	Musical Theater
Engineers Fishing	Photographic
Hunting and Fishing	Wingfoot Bowmen

Divisional Athletics

Archery	Shuffleboard
Badminton	Softball
Bait Casting	Clinics
Basketball	Table Tennis
Bowling	Volleyball
Golf	Pocket Billiards
Horseshoe Pitching	

Varsity Athletics

Basketball   Golf
Bowling

Special Activities

Kid's Basketball   Movies
Concerts   Gardening
Dances   Instruction Groups
Picnics   Clinics
Kid's Golf   Travel Tours
Kid's Bowling   Fish-A-Rama
Camping   Scouting
Christmas Party   Play Nights
Physical Fitness   Fencing
Hobby Displays

Music

Youth band   Musical Shows
Chorus   Quartets
Concerts   Barber Shop Quartets

Special Services

Sale of tickets for non-Goodyear   Departmental Flower Funds
     Athletic Activities and Shows   Bowling and Golf Funds
Sale of State Hunting and Fishing   Investment Clubs
     Licenses   Fund Drives and Civic Programs

Recreational facilities provided by Goodyear for no charge, or for minor service charges, include the following (at Goodyear Hall): bowling lanes, pool tables, steam room, theater, gymnasium, club rooms, kitchen, ballroom, recreation room, horseshoe courts, golf nets, showers and lockers, Little Theater, and shuffleboard. At the Recreational Park at Wingfoot Lake, picnic areas, playgrounds, canteen, shore fishing, and boating are all available. Other facilities include an athletic field and a Scout Lodge.

Industrial Recreation Meeting Community Needs. Perhaps the best-known example of a community recreation program that is conducted by an industrial recreation department is in West Point, Georgia, where the West Point Manufacturing Company operates a broad program of activities. This unusual service makes use of three swimming pools, nine playgrounds, a golf course, and a full-time staff of 16, helped by many part-time and volunteer leaders. West Point and five nearby communities—none of which have public recreation programs—are served by this industrial recreation department.

An excellent example of a recreation program sponsored by employees themselves (without formal plant sponsorship) is the Cornfield Chemicals Club, most of whose members are employees of the United

States Industry chemical plant in Tuscola, Illinois. Operating under a professional Recreation Director, advised by a board of directors who are elected by the plant employees, this club has a total membership of about 1,000 (most of the 200 who do not belong live at a distance from the plant). Also, about 70 employees of two nearby companies have been permitted to join the club. The Cornfield Chemicals Club members themselves have built a large swimming pool several miles from the plant, relying heavily on the volunteer labor of members and with some assistance from management on expenses for materials. The total program is supported by annual membership dues of $6.00 per member, plus charges for certain activities and events, resulting in an operating budget of between 40 and 50 thousand dollars per year. Since public recreation programs do not exist in this area, the Cornfield Chemicals Club, in effect, meets community recreation needs.

UNION RECREATION PROGRAMS

As indicated earlier, labor unions have taken an increasing responsibility for providing employee recreation programs, and for stimulating effective community-wide recreation services. What is the rationale for this trend?

Increased Leisure A Union Responsibility. A primary factor underlying the acceptance of responsibility for providing recreation services has been the fact that unions themselves—through labor contracts that have achieved shorter work weeks, longer paid vacations, and better retirement programs—have helped to *create* vast amounts of leisure. But such advances represent a double-edged sword. One of the purposes of creating a shorter work week, for example, is to spread the amount of work (decreasing due to increased automation) among a greater number of union members.

What has happened, however, is that many workers who are given huge bulks of free time simply go out and obtain another part- or full-time job. "Moonlighting," as this practice is known, was revealed in a Labor Department survey in 1963 as practiced by over 3.9 million workers. Clearly, when the national rate of unemployment is approximately 5.5 percent, but the "moonlighting" rate is 5.7 percent,[6] this represents a major threat to the welfare of organized labor. Three motivations account for workers holding dual job responsibilities: (a) the economic need for added income; (b) the demands of the marketplace for certain skilled types of labor, in short supply; and (c) boredom with the four-day or 30-hour week, and an inability to fill leisure hours creatively and enjoyably.

[6] Sylvia Porter, "Your Dollar," *New York Post Magazine Section,* February 19, 1964, p. 2.

It is to meet the latter motivation that unions are attempting to provide their memberships with attractive leisure programs, and to sponsor conferences and institutes that deal with leisure and recreation as national concerns. Another purpose is to bring to the working classes the amenities of life that formerly were the property of their employers. In an address to the United Automobile Workers' Constitutional Convention in 1964, Walter Reuther stated this point of view forcefully:

> We have to start with the proposition that leisure belongs to us and can be created and used by us; that it is no longer the monopoly of a privileged few in their mink stoles seeking status in the social register. Why should the stage, the opera, the art gallery, the symphony hall, the libraries here in America or anywhere in the world, any longer be regarded as something for the boss and the boss's wife?
>
> The American workers who struggled in the early years for free public education wanted to open up the whole world of learning for themselves and their families. Why should we narrow that world down to a local paper, a picture magazine and a T.V. set? [7]

For this reason too, Reuther continues, labor unions must support community-wide efforts to provide realistically and adequately for growing leisure needs:

> We have the choice of organizing community resources to realize the possibilities of leisure—or allocating larger budgets to a mounting attempt to cope with community problems, such as juvenile delinquency, which could be largely prevented and can be largely solved through the broadest cooperation of public and private agencies, within the framework of public policy. Public policy is essential in this field both to realize the possibilities of leisure and to avoid the traps and tragedies that lie in wait for people who have time on their hands but lack the know-how and resources for turning idle time into creative and constructive living. . . .[8]

A final important purpose of union-sponsored recreation programs is to promote loyalty, team spirit, and a sense of involvement within union memberships. From the fervent allegiance claimed by labor unions during their days of struggle and expansion in the 1930's and 1940's, many unions have declined into a rear-guard holding action, protecting the *status quo* for their members. Often they are socially illiberal or worse. Kirstein documents what he refers to as labor's ebbing strength, by showing how union membership has followed a descending curve and shrunk to new lows for the past 25 years.[9] In many areas, the enlisting of new members has ground to a frustrated halt.

[7] Walter P. Reuther, "The Growing Challenge of Leisure," address at UAW-CIO Constitutional Convention, Atlantic City, N.J., March, 1964, p. 107.

[8] *Ibid.*, p. 107.

[9] George Kirstein, "Labor's Ebbing Strength," *The Nation*, September 1, 1962, p. 86.

Within this context, recreation programs are viewed as a means of providing much needed services to members and as a form of morale-booster. Olga Madar, Recreation Director of the UAW-CIO, nostalgically describes this union's summer children's camp to illustrate:

> . . . the past 16 years of the Children's Camp at "FDR" (Michigan AFL-CIO Labor Center site on Lake Huron) have been the story of brotherhood and swimming, of "Solidarity Forever" and tennis, of democracy and cookouts. It has been the story of "togetherness and belonging" for children of different races and religions; of fathers and mothers who worked in the plants or stood in the unemployment line, walked the picket line or taught in the schools. It has been the story of pleasant memories of the UAW for 10,000 children and 800 staff members who will have a fond image of trade unions that anti-union newspaper stories cannot change.[10]

United Automobile Workers Recreation Department

One of the outstanding unions in the recreation field, as suggested in the preceding passages, has been the UAW-CIO. In 1937 the United Auotmobile Workers established a Recreation Department to provide leisure activities for its members and their families, and help enliven union meetings and other events. The UAW has a professional recreation director assisted by several staff members. Each of these staff members is responsible for a specific region, and works closely with recreation councils made up of representatives from local union recreation committees within the same region. These committees are primarily responsible for the sponsorship of recreation activities on the local level.

The central office in Detroit, Michigan, plans, evaluates, studies, and helps to guide local and regional recreation programs and projects. It also publishes literature in the form of activity manuals and handbooks, and sponsors special recreation institutes and leadership training courses.

Activities. Program activities sponsored by UAW-CIO serve those of all age levels and both sexes. Within a single council, clinics in archery, golf, fly and bait casting, gun safety, pool and billiards, and follow-up classes for those interested in gaining further skill, are offered. Interest clubs in crafts, music, and photography, dance classes and summer camping for children, are popular activities. The UAW also promotes tournament and league competition in baseball, softball, slow-pitch softball, bowling, golf, and archery. Throughout the year, special events, such as carnivals, Christmas parties, family picnics, and square dances are held.

---

[10] Olga Madar, "Report to the President" (Report of UAW-CIO Constitutional Convention, 1964), p. 146.

Finances and Community Relationships. One cent of each UAW member's monthly dues goes to finance the union's Recreation Department which, in turn, allots a half-cent to each of the various regions. In addition, in the local unions, a minimum of one-half cent per month is allocated to the recreation committee. Some funds are collected from league and tournament entry fees, and from "self-sustaining" activities for which moderate fees are charged. A major objective of the union program, however, is to provide activities more cheaply than they could be furnished by commercial concerns.

In many locals, cooperative community-union relationships have been developed. UAW members play basketball in the neighborhood gymnasium, hold Christmas parties in the school auditorium, and play golf on municipal courses. Union recreation leaders frequently are active on local recreation boards, or in stimulating increased public provision for, and concern with, recreation needs.

Focus on Retirement. Unions in general have become increasingly aware of meeting the needs of their retired members. The UAW began a "Drop-in-Center" program in 1951, staffed by retired employees themselves. Beginning with such simple activities as playing cards and watching television, center programs have expanded to include hobbies, educational and cultural activities, counseling on personal problems, and discussion groups. Today, more than 30,000 retired automobile workers and their wives are regularly participating in union-sponsored programs for the retired.

A similar center program for retired members is operated by the International Ladies' Garment Workers Union, which has traditionally been extremely active in recreation programing and which sponsors an outstanding vacation resort, Camp Unity. In some cases, unions have offered courses on preparation for leisure, for their older members. District 65 of the Retail, Wholesale and Department Store Union in New York City, for example, sponsored a preretirement course in 1964 that was attended by a total of 100 union members. Many of these were employees of department stores, and were released by their employers, without loss of pay, to attend the weekly two-hour sessions that dealt with such aspects of retirement as physical and mental health, as well as social and recreational aspects. The course stressed that the end of work does not mean the end of active living, but rather the opportunity for a new and fruitful life. Planning before actual retirement was seen as essential for a successful retired life.

This chapter has described the history of industrial recreation in the United States and analyzed the essential objectives of employee activity programs sponsored by both labor and management. A number of program examples and trends are presented in detail.

SUGGESTED QUESTIONS FOR DISCUSSION

1. It has sometimes been stated that "paternalism" is the underlying motivation for most employer-sponsored industrial recreation. What does this mean, and how true is it today?
2. What are the major forms of administrative sponsorship in industrial recreation, as outlined in this chapter?
3. Discuss the purposes of unions in providing recreation services for their memberships. What element is found in their approach—in terms of philosophy—that does not seem to be found in employer-sponsored programs?

Chapter *17*

The Role of Voluntary Organizations

A final significant area of organized recreation service in the United States is provided by so-called voluntary agencies and organizations. These are nongovernmental in nature, and are financed primarily by voluntary contributions, community fund-raising drives, and membership fees and charges for participation. They tend to be of four major types:

1. Youth-serving organizations, many of which are structured on a national level, with local chapters, troops or councils
2. Special interest organizations, serving both youth and adults, which promote a particular recreational pursuit or hobby interest
3. Community centers to meet a variety of recreational, educational, and social needs, which may be sponsored by local government or religious agencies, whereas others are independently supported through voluntary contributions or civic drives
4. National organizations which are designed to promote the recreation profession itself, or to assist in the provision of organized leisure services

401

Examples of each of these types are briefly described in the pages that follow.

YOUTH-SERVING ORGANIZATIONS

These include a number of organizations with memberships numbering in the millions, such as the Boy Scouts of America, the Girl Scouts, and the Camp Fire Girls. Some are found only in the United States; others are international, with chapters found in as many as 40 or 50 other nations. Usually, they are intended to reach a number of important goals of a character-building nature. Within this total purpose, they rely heavily on recreation and social activities in program development.

Boy Scouts of America

The Boy Scouts of America are part of a world-wide organization with memberships in approximately 69 countries and headquarters in Canada. Founded in England in 1910, and brought to the United States shortly thereafter, the movement spread rapidly until today there are over five million members in the United States alone. The Scouting movement relies heavily on volunteer leadership, although it also has about 3,600 career leaders and executives. It has relationships with many other civic, school, or religious agencies; about half of its 130,000 units are sponsored by churches or synagogues.

Boy Scouting operates on three levels: Cub Scouting, Boy Scouting, and Exploring. Cub Scouts are between 8 and 10; they meet weekly in home-centered programs under the leadership of a "den mother." As they pass simple achievement tests in ·specified skills areas, they move up through 12 membership ranks. Boy Scouting is a varied and vigorous program with emphasis on outdoor adventure, for boys between the ages of 11 and 13. Boys join Patrol units, which are part of larger Scout Troops. As they gain merit badges in any of 100 different Scouting skills and interests, they progress through three ranks: Tenderfoot, Second Class, and First Class. Finally, Explorer Scouts, who are between 14 and 17, undertake advanced projects in community service, citizenship, outdoor activities, and such special interests as boating (Sea Explorer), aviation (Air Explorer), and other types of adventurous challenges.

On all levels, character-building and citizenship are stressed, through the Scout Oath and Law. One of the most important annual projects of the Boys Scouts of America is to sponsor an annual jamboree, attended by many thousands of American youngsters, along with youth representatives of foreign countries. Thus the Scouts work to build world understanding and responsible citizenship.

Girl Scouts of America

As the nation's largest membership organization for girls, with over three-and-a-half million members, the Girl Scouts of America stress a similar group of objectives: good character, conduct, patriotism, and community service. Founded in 1912, the Girl Scout movement is today operated in 12 regions throughout the United States. It has well over 136,000 troop units, about one-fourth of which meet in religious centers.

Girl Scouting serves four age groups: Brownie Girl Scouts (7 and 8), Junior Girl Scouts (9, 10, and 11), Cadette Girl Scouts (12, 13, and 14), and Senior Girl Scouts (15, 16, and 17). All carry on activities in such program fields as sports and games, arts and crafts, music and dancing, international friendship, nature study, and community life. Senior Girl Scouts, for example, may undertake service responsibilities relating to Hospitals, Museums, Child Care, Occupational Therapy, Office or Library Services.

Typical of the goals of youth-serving organizations are these Girl Scout Laws:

1. A Girl Scout's honor is to be trusted.
2. A Girl Scout is loyal.
3. A Girl Scout's duty is to be useful and to help others.
4. A Girl Scout is a friend to all and a sister to every other Girl Scout.
5. A Girl Scout is courteous.
6. A Girl Scout is a friend to animals.
7. A Girl Scout obeys orders.
8. A Girl Scout is cheerful.
9. A Girl Scout is thrifty.
10. A Girl Scout is clean in thought, word, and deed.

Often Girl Scout troops are closely linked to local schools, meeting in school buildings and using their facilities, libraries, buses, and equipment. There is an extensive training program for adult leaders, with a national training school at Pleasantville, New York. In addition, Girl Scouts are joined to girls in 44 other nations, through the World Association of Girl Guides and Girl Scouts.

Boys' Clubs of America

Beginning in the 1860's, when a number of New England communities established centers and program activities to meet the leisure needs of boys from poorer homes, the Boys' Clubs movement spread until, in 1906, about 50 clubs joined to form a national organization. By the late 1950's, there were over 500 clubs, with operating budgets totaling over 15 million dollars. The national organization, with headquarters in New York City, provides assistance in organization and community relations to clubs within seven major districts throughout the country. It also trains leadership, carries on research, consults on building plans, and conducts a public information program.

Separate Boys' Clubs are autonomous organizations, managed by local citizens' boards and supported by voluntary contributions or Community Chest or United Fund Drives. Club memberships consist of boys between the ages of 8 and 20, usually from low-income families in crowded urban centers, although a number of Boys' Clubs have been established in small communities in recent years. The membership is not restricted to boys of proven "good character." Any boy may attend, with none excluded for financial or sectarian reasons. The program places a heavy stress on guidance, vocational assistance, remedial education, and health services, along with social and recreational activities. Today there are over 600 Clubs, with over 600,000 members. Each center is open daily, with game rooms, libraries, clubrooms, and gymnasiums, serving as a "substitute home" for boys and youth in need.

Camp Fire Girls

Founded in 1910, the Camp Fire Girls offer an educational-recreational program with stress on "the application of religious, spiritual, and ethical teachings to daily living." A "love of home and family," and "pride in woman's traditional qualities of tenderness, affection and skill in human relations" are all encouraged. Basically, the Camp Fire Girls' program is individually slanted, rather than organized on a mass basis. There are four age levels:

Bluebirds (7 and 8 years old)—undertake simple craft activities, group activities, creative play, and service projects.

Camp Fire Girls (9, 10, and 11 years old) are involved with seven "craft" areas: Home, Outdoors, Creative Arts, Frontiers of Science, Business, and Sports and Games; there are numerous "honors" activities under each of these.

Junior Hi (12 and 13 years old)—undertake group activities leading to the Group Torch Bearer Rank. Members strive for achievement in one of 25 fields of interest. Leadership and group skills are encouraged and developed in club programs.

Horizon Club (14 through 18) involves activities centered about personality development, social activities, career planning, and community service.

Like both Boy and Girl Scouts, the Camp Fire Girls' movement has an extensive camping program and is open to all regardless of race, creed, or economic status. The national organization offers leadership training and strives to provide special services to socially and culturally disadvantaged girls. Today, the Camp Fire Girls number over half a million members in about 400 units around the country.

Police Athletic League

Another program that strives to serve the culturally disadvantaged youngster in urban slums is the Police Athletic League. Founded in 1914 in New York City as a Junior Police Corps, the organization gradually expanded to include summer recreation programing, with "playstreets," swimming, boxing, and dancing programs. In 1941, PAL was incorporated under the laws of the State of New York. Today, it serves 100,000 children and youth between the ages of 7 and 21, through 35 youth centers, 10 playgrounds, and 45 playstreets. Its extensive program, served by a paid professional staff, includes a variety of sports, arts and crafts, dance, dramatic workshops, hobby clubs, a reading program, and a drum and bugle corps. While recreation is the heart of PAL's service, it maintains a professionally staffed Placement and Counseling Service which assists school drop-outs, provides job training, and makes referrals.

The Police Athletic League is officially sponsored by the Police Department in New York City, and members of its Youth Division work closely with PAL in their precincts. However, the Police Department does not provide funds for the program; PAL must rely on the voluntary contributions of thousands of New Yorkers to support its budget. Working chiefly in high delinquency areas, the program's aim is to keep boys and girls out of trouble wherever possible and, if they get into it, to attempt to assist, guide, and rehabilitate them. It receives assistance and cooperation from neighborhood councils and the New York City Youth Board, and makes ingenious use of a variety of facilities, including church halls, veterans' centers, and store-fronts.

While there is some disagreement as to the wisdom of having police provide recreation services, there has existed for some years a National Police Conference on Police Athletic League and Youth Activities. In over 100 communities throughout the nation, including Milwaukee, Los Angeles, and Washington, D.C., Police Athletic Leagues are sponsored. The Committee on Juvenile Delinquency and Crime Prevention of the International Association of Police Chiefs recommends that police should at all points maintain a strong liaison with public and private agencies. However, when they take the initiative for conducting recreation programs, it is recommended that direct program leadership should be in the hands of experienced, civilian recreation supervisors. Such efforts should be closely coordinated with existing recreation programs through community planning councils and public recreation officials. Further, when police do enter into this field, it is essential that their services meet recognized standards for personnel and program.

Boys' and Girls' 4-H Clubs

Another youth-serving organization with governmental ties is the 4-H Club program. Founded as voluntary groups of rural young people around the turn of the century, and supported today by a system of federal funds that are matched by states and counties, 4-H Clubs also receive the assistance of county agricultural agents and state land-grant college extension services. However, much of the program's leadership consists of volunteer adults trained by agents; it may therefore be considered a voluntary organization.

The membership of 4-H is composed of boys and girls between 10 and 21, chiefly in rural areas of the country. Assisted by two nongovernmental agencies, the National 4-H Service Committee and National 4-H Club Foundation, these young people elect their own officers, plan and conduct meetings and programs, and take part in community activities. The title "4-H" stands for Head, Heart, Hand, and Health, and the National Pledge of Club members is:

I pledge: My Head to clearer thinking,
           My Heart to greater loyalty,
           My Hands to larger service, and
           My Health to better living, for
           My Club, my Community, and my Country.

Club members carry out individual projects relating to livestock and poultry raising, food growing, household arts, conservation and planting, and other forms of constructive tasks centered about home and community. They offer demonstrations, take part in competitions, and in addition to their agricultural education concerns, have a heavy program of recreation activities, including tours and hikes, camping, social recreation, music, dramatics, and other cultural forms of participation. The 4-H Club movement has spread to more than 50 nations and, in the United States alone, reaches well over 2 million boys and girls.

While there are many other youth-serving organizations, including those affiliated with religious denominations, these are typical of the largest and most successful ones—as well as those which meet special needs of youth.

SPECIAL INTEREST ORGANIZATIONS

In addition to organizations which serve the overall needs of youth, there are hundreds of nation-wide associations which promote specific types of recreational interests within the broad realm of sports, outdoor activities, or cultural pursuits. In certain cases, they are established by commercial or other private interests, to promote participation in a given field. In the larger number of cases, they represent the genuine desire of participants to promote their personal areas of interest. A listing of such organizations, compiled by the Department of the Air Force, includes such examples as:

Academy of Model Aeronautics. Washington, D.C. The governing body for model aviation in the United States

Amateur Athletic Union. New York, New York. Organization of volunteer workers interested in the improvement and promotion of amateur athletic sports and games

American Automobile Touring Alliance. Philadelphia, Pennsylvania. Promotes and facilitates touring between nations

American Bowling Congress. Milwaukee, Wisconsin. Men's organization which provides its members with rules and regulations for the game of American tenpins, standardizing playing conditions, and offering tournaments and awards

American Canoe Association. Ramsey, New Jersey. Promotes the use of canoes and kayaks for the purpose of pleasure, health, and exploration through sponsorship of paddling, sailing and slalom regattas, and informal cruises and camping trips

American Contract Bridge League. New York, New York. Association which makes, interprets, and enforces rules and regulations governing the game of contract bridge

American Cryptogram Association. Canton, Ohio. Promotes the science of cryptanalysis as a hobby including the art of analyzing and breaking secret messages or cryptograms

American Numismatic Association. Wichita, Kansas. Promotes the study and collecting of coins, tokens, medals, paper money, and media of exchange

American Turners. Detroit, Michigan. Promotes health and physical education through gymnastics, calisthenics, swimming, and games

American Youth Hostels. New York, New York. Provides youth and adults with opportunities for inexpensive and educational travel at home and abroad principally by bicycle and hiking; also promotes international understanding

Biddy Basketball. Scranton, Pennsylvania. Promotes the sport of basketball for boys up to 12 years old and girls up to 13 years old; cooperates with all youth organizations interested in basketball

Ducks Unlimited. New York, New York. Nonprofit organization for the preservation of waterfowl and the restoration of their breeding and nesting grounds

Garden Club of America. New York, New York. Women's organization which promotes the hobby of gardening

Hobby Guild of America. New York, New York. Nonprofit service organization which assists individual hobbyists and hobby groups, sponsors National Hobby Month, and maintains a "Hall of Fame" of outstanding hobbyists

Izaak Walton League. Chicago, Illinois. Promotes the conservation and restoration of renewable natural resources of soil, woods, waters, and wildlife

Little League Baseball. Williamsport, Pennsylvania. Provides supervised baseball games for boys 12 years of age and under, through neighborhood leagues

National Audubon Society. New York, New York. Advances public understanding of the value and need of conservation of soil, water, plants, and wildlife [1]

These and dozens of similar organizations serve effectively to promote understanding of, and participation in, a wide variety of recreational pursuits in the United States. Usually they are financed through their own membership fees, contributions, and endowments, although a number have the support of private manufacturers who are interested in promoting their efforts.

COMMUNITY CENTERS MEETING RECREATIONAL NEEDS

Particularly in large cities, there tends to be a network of community centers and settlement houses, serving chiefly the needs of disadvantaged youth and adults. Viewed as part of the total social welfare service of such cities, these centers are usually independent in structure, although they may be linked to community councils or associations of neighborhood agencies. Financially, they are usually dependent on fees, charges, contributions, and civic fund drives. In recent years, however, an increasing number of settlement houses have gained a measure of support from urban youth boards that support their efforts, or from other governmental grants that support special projects or services.

Such agencies usually have a social work orientation, and emphasis is placed on case work, group work programs, and community organization methods. However, as in the case of youth-serving organizations, a heavy component of the program is recreational. In most settlement houses and neighborhood centers, the entire age span is covered. Because the program makes use of a center building, with the use of outside facilities somewhat limited, there is usually less emphasis on sports and games, and greater emphasis on social programs, age-level clubs, and the creative arts or cultural forms of participation. In general, the emphasis is less on mass programing than it is on small group memberships, with a deep concern about the nature of the social process and the specific outcomes of the experience for each participant.

To illustrate, the program of the Henry Street Settlement on the Lower East Side of New York City is described in the following terms:

To its neighbors the Settlement is many things: It is an open door where a family can get help in an emergency . . . a friendly clubhouse where

[1] *Directory of National Organizations for Recreation* (Washington, D.C.: Department of the Air Force Manual 34-9, May, 1956).

teenagers can spend safe and happy after-school hours . . . an opportunity extended to every child to develop a creative talent . . . a clinic where an anxious mother can get psychiatric treatment for a disturbed child without cost . . . a lively center where retired men and women can find friends and stimulating activities . . . workshops where family groups can spend time together in "do-it-yourself" home projects . . . a real friend to the youngster who got off to a wrong start . . . a nursery school where a busy mother can leave a child at a fee she can pay.

Specifically, program services at the Henry Street Settlement House include the following, as listed in a recent brochure:

Main House

A combined nursery school and demonstration program in child care is provided where mothers take turns in assisting trained teachers and in helping preschool youngsters develop healthy social behavior patterns.

A credit union, cooperatively run by Settlement members, is a service which for 25 years has offered low-interest loans amounting to nearly 4 million dollars.

There is a pottery studio where professional potters work and teach more than 300 children and adults; classes are free to neighborhood children.

Annex Buildings

A delinquency prevention program is aimed at converting potential street gangs into Settlement clubs, and giving individual guidance to boys and their parents.

Hundreds of neighborhood boys and girls take part in sports program in indoor gymnasium and outdoor playground and playfield areas.

A teen-age center offers after-school activities and evening social events for adolescent boys and girls.

Activity Centers in Nearby Housing Projects

Home planning workshop and craft rooms provide equipment and instruction for budget-saving home-making projects.

In a "Good Companions Center," some 350 men and women over 60 paint, put on original plays, folk dance, participate in discussion groups, and serve as hospital volunteers.

Emotionally troubled neighborhood children and parents are treated at a modern mental hygiene clinic by a team of psychiatrists, psychologists, psychiatric case workers, and teachers.

Within one of the low-rent projects, a model community center equipped with kitchens, clubrooms and an attractive recreation hall offers a nursery school and a program using teen-age volunteer trainees for children's groups.

Other program services include a tenants' organization, a Dance and

Drama Playhouse (where each season 100 performances are offered, and where about 600 students attend classes), and a Music School, where over 650 students attend classes offered by a faculty of 90 teachers. The Henry Street Settlement also operates two summer camps, Camp Henry and Echo Hill Farm, which serve both children and their parents.

While other community center programs may not be as varied or intensified as the activities and services offered by the Henry Street Settlement, its operation illustrates the way recreation is woven into the total program of urban neighborhood centers. The child or adult who attends the settlement participates in all needed or appropriate aspects of program; they, in turn, are interrelated and support each other.

THE RELATIONSHIP OF VOLUNTARY AGENCIES AND PUBLIC RECREATION DEPARTMENTS

Clearly, voluntary agencies which meet recreation needs in American communities have certain administrative advantages, as well as certain limitations. The advantages are as follows:

1. They are free to experiment and try new kinds of program ventures and services to a greater degree than governmentally sponsored agencies would be.

2. They are able to focus their program efforts on the needs and interests of special groups, without feeling the compulsion to serve the total population, as fully as possible.

3. Their hiring policies are usually somewhat more flexible than those of public departments, and they are thus able to use highly skilled specialists in "spot" assignments. Also, because of their social service nature, they often are able to obtain the services of volunteers over a sustained period of time more readily than public departments can.

4. In general, freedom from bureaucratic or political concerns makes them more flexible and able to adapt to changing community and neighborhood needs.

In terms of limitations, the primary disadvantage of voluntary agencies is that they are heavily dependent on funds that must be gathered through contributions each year; until this is done, there is always the possibility that program services which have been planned may not be carried through. Increasingly, federal and municipal funds have been given, as special grants, to a number of voluntary agencies in the social work and recreation fields. However, these usually are intended to support special projects, rather than ongoing activities. A second element of instability is introduced by the fact that, as neighborhoods and ethnic populations change, some agencies have not been able to adapt to new circumstances and needs, and have either moved or gone out of existence. In these cases, a marked gap has been created in available services, which would not be the case if a city-wide recreation agency were responsible for the area.

What should the relationship of voluntary agencies and public recreation departments be? Essentially, it should be a cooperative one, in which:

1. Public recreation departments would assume the task of meeting the *broad recreational needs* of the community, and voluntary agencies would focus on *certain areas of activity,* or meeting the *special needs* of unique groups (in terms of age categories, neighborhoods, physical or mental limitations, etc.) within the community.

2. There would be frequent interchange of ideas, and communication designed to minimize duplication or overlap of services, and to identify gaps in services which should be filled. Both types of groups should be active in social councils or other civic organizations which deal with total municipal or regional concerns, and which mobilize action.

3. Wherever possible, public and voluntary agencies would cooperate in sponsoring recreation conferences, clinics, in-service training sessions, recruitment programs, etc.

4. Mutual interchange of facilities would be established, so that participants in a neighborhood house program are able to use athletic facilities operated by a public park and recreation department, and senior citizens in a club sponsored by the latter are able to use meeting rooms in the neighborhood center.

ORGANIZATIONS SERVING THE RECREATION FIELD

A final category consists of those organizations which, either as professional or service bodies, directly serve the recreation field itself. The most important ones joined together during the 1950's in the Federation of National Professional Organizations for Recreation, including the American Association for Health, Physical Education and Recreation; American Camping Association; American Institute of Park Executives; American Recreation Society; Association of College Unions —International; National Association of Social Workers; National Association of Recreational Therapists; National Industrial Recreation Association; National Conference on State Parks; and Society of State Directors of Health, Physical Education and Recreation. In addition, two service organizations, the National Recreation Association and the Athletic Institute, have served as consultants.

Brief descriptions of each of these organizations follow:

1. *American Association for Health, Physical Education and Recreation.* This organization, founded in 1885 as the Association for the Advancement of Physical Education, is a Department of the National

Education Association, with a total membership today of over 45,000. It has an active Recreation Division, which is chiefly concerned with the promotion of education for leisure in American schools, and enhancing the role of schools as recreation sponsors. At its base in Washington, D.C., it sponsors many conferences and professional meetings, publishes periodicals, and promotes research in health, physical education, and recreation.

2. *American Camping Association.* Incorporated in 1910, and presently based in Bradford Woods, Martinsville, Indiana, the American Camping Association consists of representatives of agencies, institutions, and private camping in the United States. It develops and promotes effective standards for camp facilities, leadership, and programing. It sponsors workshops, provides consultant services, and acts as a voice for the organized camping field in the United States.

3. *American Institute of Park Executives.* Founded in 1898, and with headquarters at Oglebay Park, Wheeling, West Virginia, this organization's membership was drawn from administrative positions in public park departments. It gathered and disseminated information regarding public parks, gardens, zoos, and similar facilities, and their development and maintenance. While its earlier focus was on the facilities themselves, in its more recent efforts, the AIPE also reflected the concern of park executives for recreation as a significant function. Affiliated organizations included the American Association of Botanical Gardens and Arboretums and the American Association of Zoological Parks and Aquariums.

4. *American Recreation Society.* Founded in 1937 at the Atlantic City National Recreation Congress, as "The Professional Workers Division of the National Recreation Association," this organization became an independent association of recreation professionals, constituted as a membership organization. Its purpose has been to promote public understanding of, and respect for, recreation, to upgrade professional competence, improve professional preparation, support governmental programs, and generally assist in all areas leading to the development of recreational service in the United States. It has been based in Washington, D.C.

5. *Association of College Unions—International.* With offices at Cornell University, Ithaca, New York, this organization was founded in 1914. Its purpose is to give directors of College Unions and other student life departments an opportunity to share information, practices, and to hold professional meetings designed to improve their programs.

6. *National Association of Social Workers, Group Work Section.* Based in New York City, this organization consists of workers in community agencies who are primarily concerned with group work practices. Although its focus is on social work, recreation is closely related to this,

and the Group Work Section's members are frequently active in recreational projects and programs. The organization's aim is to raise personnel standards, promote professional education, and encourage research.

7. *National Association of Recreational Therapists.* Founded in 1953 by 23 directors of hospital recreation programs, this organization has become national in scope. It has no continuing headquarters, but operates from the home base of its current president. Its purpose is to establish standards for accrediting recreation workers in state and other institutions; to promote effective teamwork among recreation workers and other institutional personnel; and to improve the in-service and college training of hospital recreation personnel. It works closely with the Council for the Advancement of Hospital Recreation.

8. *National Industrial Recreation Association.* Founded in 1941, the NIRA is based in Chicago, Illinois. It is dedicated to the purpose of helping to develop and improve employee recreation programs. Its membership consists largely of companies and their branches which have employee recreation programs. It acts as a clearing house for program ideas and innovations; it publishes guides for program organizations, consults with industrial concerns, carries out research, and sponsors a number of athletic and hobby contests for industrial recreation participants, on a national basis.

9. *National Conference on State Parks.* The primary purpose of the National Conference on State Parks, established in 1921, has been to provide information for the public on the values and functions of state parks, historic sites, and monuments, and to encourage and promote the development of such areas. Based in Washington, D.C., the NCSP was responsible for publications, conferences, and training courses in this area.

10. *Society of State Directors of Health, Physical Education and Recreation.* Consisting of those officials in state departments of education who have been assigned responsibility for the joint field of health, physical education, and recreation, this association has a professional interest very similar to that of the AAHPER. Its members are chiefly concerned with the development of effective physical education programs; health and recreation are somewhat secondary concerns, and recreational involvement focuses on the school's role in recreation sponsorship and on the development of outdoor education and school camping.

Consultant Organizations

11. *Athletic Institute.* With headquarters in Chicago, Illinois, the Athletic Institute is a nonprofit organization chiefly supported by

manufacturers and distributors of sports and outdoor recreation equipment. Its purpose is to encourage and promote the total field of sports
participation; it thus has considerable interest in the physical recreation
field. It sponsors conferences and demonstrations, and produces films,
pamphlets, and guides on recreation.

12. *National Recreation Association.* Founded in 1906 as the Playground and Recreation Association of America, and with headquarters
in New York City, this national, nonprofit service agency has been concerned with the total promotion of the recreation movement in the
United States. It has cut across the broad field of public recreation and
park departments, private and voluntary agencies, armed forces, and
industrial and religious recreation. It has been governed by a board of
directors and professional staff with national and district advisory committees. Many professionals have been members of the N.R.A., without
a formal voice in its management. It has essentially been a service organization to individuals and agencies in the recreation field, offering
consultation, research, placement, and similar services.

MERGER OF PROFESSIONAL ORGANIZATIONS

Throughout the years of their existence, the National Recreation
Association and the American Recreation Society have had a cooperative
relationship which recognized their separate functions and identity, but
which involved such joint areas of operation as the sponsorship of the
annual Recreation Congress. In 1962, the boards of both groups met to
discuss other areas of possible cooperation; a committee was subsequently
assigned the task of developing a merger plan which would formally
bring the two organizations together.

This process continued for two years. Then, in 1964, the officers of
four leading organizations agreed to a proposal for a merger. These were:
(a) American Institute of Park Executives; (b) American Recreation
Society; (c) National Conference on State Parks; and (d) National Recreation Association. As plans were crystallized in 1965, a fifth organization,
the American Association of Zoological Parks and Aquariums was added
to the merging groups.

The new National Recreation and Park Association became a
reality in August of 1965, with the election of the distinguished Laurance
S. Rockefeller as its president. In accepting this post, Mr. Rockefeller
stated:

> We have entered a new era in this country—an era where parks, recreation
> and the quality of the environment have become a major item of public
> concern. With these developments come heavy responsibilities. So it is
> timely, fitting and important that we strengthen our ties of organization
> and mutual cooperation. Our combined strength will be far greater than

the sum of the individual components. The stakes are great for our organizations, for our professions, and for the public good.[2]

This new nonprofit educational and service organization was fortunate in having as its first executive vice-president and secretary Joseph Prendergast (formerly executive director of the National Recreation Association) and as its executive director and general manager Alfred B. LaGasse (formerly executive director of the American Institute of Park Executives). It was agreed that it would be guided by a combined board of trustees of 60 members (20 lay, 20 professional, and 20 lay members nominated by professionals), and governed by an administrative board of 10 lay and 10 professional members. A number of separate divisions or branches (the first of these being the American Park and Recreation Society) will be formed under the total structure of the National Recreation and Park Association, representing the specialized needs and interests of its members in varied fields. The constitution and other significant details of the founding of the NRPA may be found in the September–October, 1965 issue of the *American Recreation Journal*.[3]

Although the process of effecting a merger was a difficult and painful one, it was clearly the will of recreation professionals throughout the country that it be carried out. The NRPA will now make it possible for recreation workers throughout the United States to speak with a fully unified voice, to work together cooperatively in developing standards and program guides, and to avoid duplication and overlap of services.

This chapter has described and given examples of four major types of voluntary organizations devoted to the promotion of organized recreation service. These include: (a) youth-serving organizations; (b) organizations serving special recreational interests; (c) community centers and neighborhood houses; and, (d) organizations serving or representing the recreation field itself.

SUGGESTED QUESTIONS FOR DISCUSSION

1. What are the four major types of voluntary and professional organizations in the United States today that serve the recreation movement and the provision of organized recreation services? How does each type contribute to advancement in this field?
2. Discuss the scope and function of voluntary agencies, such as settlement houses, in large urban centers. How does recreation program service relate to their fundamental task? Describe their relationship to public recreation departments.
3. What are the implications of the new national organization which has merged five previously existing organizations in the parks and recreation field? In what ways can this organization benefit the American public and the recreation profession?

[2] Statement of Mr. Laurance Rockefeller at National Recreation and Park Association Headquarters, New York City, August 18, 1965.
[3] *American Recreation Journal*, September–October, 1965, pp. 125–138.

Chapter *18*

Research and Evaluation in Recreation

An increasingly important aspect of the recreation practitioner's work consists of evaluation and research which are devoted to the improvement of program and leadership practices. Briefly stated, these two terms have the following meanings:

Research usually is thought of as an organized search for knowledge. Its purpose is to discover answers to questions through the application of scientific procedures. It may involve a wide variety of measurement techniques, but usually includes the following steps: (a) a concise formulation of a problem or hypothesis; (b) the development of a study or experimental design appropriate to the problem; (c) carrying out of the study, including the gathering of data; (d) scoring and interpreting of the data, and (e) presentation of conclusions and possible recommendations for action or further study.

Evaluation is the process of determining the effectiveness of program or leadership in terms of achieving predetermined goals. It is usually concerned with specific situations, and makes use of a number of research techniques, both of a quantitative and qualitative nature.

Practitioners in the field of recreation are usually involved in direct program evaluation. On the other hand, university or government-sponsored investigations usually attack problems of a more fundamental or generalized nature. Both research and evaluation in the recreation field, although carried out in a sporadic and superficial way in the past, are being rapidly improved and intensified. They are viewed as crucial to the improvement of recreation services and the upgrading of the recreation profession itself.

FUNCTIONS OF RESEARCH AND EVALUATION

Typically, municipal or agency recreation departments have been concerned with certain kinds of problems, in an effort to improve services or administrative procedures. These are usually found under the following headings:

1. Determination of needs and interests in programing
2. Analysis of staff functions, roles, assignments, and performance
3. Gathering information needed for the development of facilities, equipment, and physical resources
4. Evaluation of participation; numbers and types of participants, behavior during activity, outcomes of participation
5. Program evaluation: review of a single event, of specialized services, or of the total program

The methods that may be used to gather the needed information fall into several types: (a) surveys, carried on by questionnaire or interview; (b) interviews; (c) case studies, and making use of case records; (d) experimental projects, in which matched groups that have been exposed to different programs or techniques, are compared; (e) use of tests of physical performance; (f) psychological tests or attitude scales; (g) historical analysis; (h) demonstration tests and "pilot" projects; and (i) systematized observation.

A number of practical examples of the kinds of research and evaluation techniques that may be carried out in the effort to improve recreation services and administrative procedures follow.

DETERMINATION OF NEEDS AND INTERESTS

This may relate to a community-wide survey of recreation preferences and needs, to an analysis of the interests and capabilities of a particular group in the population, or to program development within a given agency or specialized recreation service.

Community Surveys

One of the most commonly found kinds of investigation in this field has been the comprehensive survey carried out prior to organizing or restructuring a recreation department in a given community. This may be conducted by a firm of professional consultants operating in the city-planning field, by recreation educators from nearby colleges or universities who are skilled in this task, or by recreation administrators or authorities representing respected recreation agencies or organizations. Usually, they are assisted by residents of the community itself, who may compose a team with representation from various civic, religious, service, and educational groups.[1] Such a team may systematically gather data relating to:

1. Currently available activities, usually offered by voluntary membership organizations or commercial interests, sometimes by public agencies which have begun to operate in this field
2. The nature of existing recreational participation, based on age groupings, socioeconomic class, neighborhood or ethnic breakdowns, and classified according to types of involvement
3. Population factors in the community; how it is distributed and what trends can be discerned; the nature of housing and the needs of specific groups in the population
4. The availability of outdoor and indoor recreation resources and structures; the existing potential for development, based on suitable space and areas
5. The economic potential of the community
6. Expressed needs and interests, voiced by potential participants and community leaders

Based on the data that is gathered, and taking into consideration regional patterns of recreation administration as well as nationally approved standards or guides, the survey team and consultants would then develop a report. This would normally include specific recommendations for action, often based on a plan to be developed over a period of years in gradual stages. These recommendations would cover such areas as: (a) community organization for recreation sponsorship, including a proposed administrative structure; (b) the overall development of resources and facilities; (c) the coordination of public and voluntary agencies within the community; and (d) estimates of costs for program and facilities development, and budgetary guides.

[1] Merrill Krughoff, "What Makes a Good Community Survey?" *Recreation*, May, 1963, p. 221, and June, 1963, p. 264.

Needs and Interests of Specific Groups

Research methods are often used as the basis for carefully determining the needs and interests of specific population groups of actual or potential participants, within a community or agency. Such groups may consist of those within a specific age bracket, those of a certain ethnic group or socioeconomic class, those with certain disabilities, or simply those who are entering a new environment—such as a hospital, armed forces base, or industrial plant. To illustrate two such situations:

Survey of Boys' Club Members. A national study was carried out to determine certain characteristics of adolescent members of the Boys' Clubs of America.[2] With the assistance of the Institute for Social Research at the University of Michigan, a stratified random sampling was developed. The study examined such categories as:

Family and other background characteristics
Interpersonal relationships
Concerns and aspirations; measures of self-esteem, personal values, and goals
Activities and interests; patterns of leisure participation and school involvement
Nature and purpose of membership in Boys' Clubs, and participation in specific
    activities

When completed, the study revealed the major activities enjoyed by boys of different age levels and showed how certain activities increased or declined in the degree of participation as boys grew older. It gave much useful information about dating patterns, the family backgrounds of members, reasons for joining or dropping out of clubs, and other insights which were helpful to those responsible for developing Boys' Club programs.

Study of Handicapped Children in the Community

A study relating to a more specialized youth population was carried out by the Associated YM-YWHA's of Greater New York.[3] This investigation, made possible by a grant from the Association for the Aid of Crippled Children, examined the social and recreational patterns of a group of physically handicapped children who lived within a serviceable distance of a community center. Its purposes were to:

Assess the extent of their impairments, and the relationship of these impairments to their current social and recreational activities

[2] *Needs and Interests of Adolescent Boys' Clubs Members* (New York: Boys' Clubs of America, 1960).

[3] Arthur Schwartz, *Social and Recreational Patterns of Orthopedically Handicapped Children* (New York: Associated YM and YWHA's of Greater New York, 1962).

Examine the feasibility of "integrating" handicapped children with groups of nonhandicapped children

Determine the willingness and ability of parents to cooperate with and make the maximum use of the group work program at the community center in question

Provide the center with other information necessary to the establishment of a pilot program to serve handicapped children, such as costs, transportation and equipment factors, and required staff orientation and adjustments

In carrying out this study, it was necessary to develop reliable instruments to measure such factors as the degree of disability, the existing use of organized recreation services, and the attitudes and expectations of parents. Interview guides, questionnaires, and other classification systems were developed to accomplish these tasks. Throughout the casefinding, sampling, and interviewing process, careful controls were maintained to insure the scientific validity of the findings. When the data was gathered, it was analyzed, coded, and transferred to IBM punch cards; statistical interrelationships were then analyzed with the help of an IBM 650 computer. Again, much useful information was gathered to assist this agency, and others like it, in the effort to provide recreational services for hitherto unreached handicapped children.

Interest Check Lists. The most common method of determining the recreational interests of participants or new members (both to aid them in selecting appropriate activities or to serve as a guide in developing program content) is to make use of interest check lists. Usually, this can be done by preparing a form listing a variety of activities under certain major headings, such as Arts and Crafts, Sports and Games, Hobbies, Dramatics, Social Activities, etc. Respondents are asked to fill out the form, checking those activities in which they have an interest or would like to participate. They may be asked to do this according to their *degree* of interest (on a scale of priority), and may also be asked to indicate whether they have a high level of skill or even teaching experience in the activity. Such forms may be filled out directly by participants or may be filled out during the course of a prestructured interview.

Information gathered in this way gives a picture both of the participant's needs and interests and of the total population that is being served. It may then serve as a basis for revising the program, discontinuing certain activities, and adding or expanding others. Recreational preferences, when measured in this way, are extremely helpful to the hospital recreation director. It has been demonstrated that there is a reasonable expectation of having better participation when individual patients are placed into activities for which they have declared a preference; the same is true of group-preferred activities. The procedure itself, when applied in a mental hospital, may yield useful information about the mental status of the patient, and to some extent his probable length of stay in the institution.[4]

RESEARCH RELATING TO STAFF FUNCTIONS AND PERFORMANCE

Most research carried on within the field of recreational service which is concerned with staff is directed to the following purposes: (a) selecting qualified staff members on various levels of responsibility; (b) reviewing the effectiveness of individual staff members, as a guide to advancement, in-service education needs, and future assignments; (c) evaluating specific leadership techniques and methods; and (d) providing a basis for recommendations designed to improve overall staff performance within a department. Other forms of research have been used to determine per capita costs of leadership assigned to program responsibilities, or have dealt with the improvement of personnel standards.

Usually, the evaluation of a recreation leader on the job is done by a supervisor who observes him in action, and who holds periodic conferences with him. This process is made more objective and thorough when a detailed rating form is used, covering all aspects of the leader's performance. Such a record should be kept on file in the individual's personnel folder, and provides a basis for supervisory conferences as well as a means of judging his improvement over a period of time on the job. An example of such a staff rating form, adapted from a more detailed form used by the Public Recreation Commission in Evansville, Indiana, follows:

Public Recreation Commission—Supervisory Rating Record

Name of Employee _____   Rating Period from   Unsatisfactory
Title _____   _____ to _____   Satisfactory
Date _____   Total score: Outstanding

How to Mark the Service Rating: After each of the traits below there is a line drawn with descriptive phrases placed along it and above the line a numerical rating. Each of the scores describes the degree to which the individual being rated possesses that trait. Place a check mark at the place on the line which you believe shows the degree to which the description applies; Poor Performance on the Left, and Strong Performance on the Right.

1. Attendance   0 10 20 30 40   50 60 70   80 90 100

Can't be depended   Moderate number   Rarely absent
on; often absent   of absences

2. Appearance   0 10 20 30 40   50 60 70   80 90 100
   appropriate
   to job   Unsatisfactory and   Sometimes dressed   Dress always neat
              neglectful   inappropriately   and appropriate

4 William E. Morris and Milton B. Jensen, "Recreational Preferences as Predictors of Participation in Mental Hospital Activities," *Mental Hygiene,* January, 1961, p. 77.

3. Leadership	0 10 20 30 40	50 60 70	80 90 100
	Creates fear; drives instead of leads; creates antagonism	Fairly successful in direction of others	Outstanding leader; has respect of others and brings out their best efforts
4. Organizing ability	0 10 20 30 40	50 60 70	80 90 100
	Unable to organize work; cannot adopt or adhere to a plan	Plans work fairly efficiently	Excellent organizer and planner; delegates authority successfully
5. Ability in instructing	0 10 20 30 40	50 60 70	80 90 100
	Poor instructor; does not prepare material or communicate effectively	Fairly effective; sometimes has difficulty	Highly effective; teaches with clarity and enthusiasm
6. Control and Discipline	0 10 20 30 40	50 60 70	80 90 100
	Discipline weak; lacks effective and consistent control	Moderately successful in discipline	Highly effective; shows skill and courage in difficult situations
7. Judgment	0 10 20 30 40	50 60 70	80 90 100
	Judgment poor or inconsistent	Usually uses good judgment	Exceptionally sound judgment
8. Initiative	0 10 20 30 40	50 60 70	80 90 100
	Little initiative; lacks resourcefulness	Some initiative; fairly resourceful	Dynamic self-starter; highly resourceful and creative
9. Responsibility	0 10 20 30 40	50 60 70	80 90 100
	Poor; cannot be counted on	Usually accepts responsibility; sometimes fails to carry out assignment	Eagerly welcomes responsibility and carries out tasks independently

If different individuals are to apply the same rating form, it is important that they confer in advance to reach an agreement as to the meaning of each score, in order to obtain as consistent a judgment as possible. It may be necessary for them to practice applying the scale and comparing scores for a period of time, to insure reliability. The final "total score" may then be rated according to certain brackets (such as:

0–405 poor, 405–675 fair to good, 675–900 very good to excellent). These might be stated in terms of "unsatisfactory," "satisfactory," and "outstanding." Combined with other judgments, such a rating scale would provide a basis for making decisions as to advancement or retention of staff. Also, it would be generally useful as a means of determining the specific strengths and weaknesses of an individual, offering a basis for advice and an intelligent attempt at self-improvement. Thus used, it would be primarily diagnostic, rather than judgmental.

Other forms of research may deal with the effect of certain approaches to leadership, such as the famous Lewin-Lippitt-White studies,[5] or with the effect of intensified provision of leadership, as in the Skokie, Illinois study.[6] Finally, a number of states, counties, or professional organizations have carried out surveys relating to personnel practices, salary scales in recreation, or required qualifications for individuals at different levels of responsibility. All of these provide a means of helping individual recreation departments establish more desirable practices, or for the profession as a whole to focus on certain problems in order to bring about improvement.

RESEARCH DEALING WITH FACILITIES, EQUIPMENT, AND PHYSICAL RESOURCES

It is extremely important, before developing any major recreation facility, to investigate all the problems related to its construction, potential volume of use, maintenance and costs, as thoroughly as possible.

To illustrate, an increasing number of park and recreation departments are developing such facilities as: (a) ski centers (involving slopes, tows, chairlifts, and snow-making machines); (b) zoos and nature centers; (c) swimming pools and aquatic centers (some with elaborate indoor-outdoor arrangements and other social or sports facilities); (d) ice-skating rinks, convertible for off-season uses); and (e) a variety of new center buildings. Clearly, it is necessary to carry out a thorough analysis of such projects, before they are ever presented as formal proposals before a recreation board or city council. The following areas must be covered:

1. Perusal of the literature and review of architectural plans for similar projects; analysis of cost range elsewhere
2. Field trips to examine similar projects elsewhere, to learn about their antici-

5 Kurt Lewin, Ronald Lippitt, and Ralph K. White, "Patterns of Aggressive Behavior in Experimentally Created 'Social Climates,'" in *Twentieth Century Psychology*, P. H. Harriman (Ed.) (New York: Philosophical Library, 1946), p. 202. See also, Ronald Lippitt and Ralph K. White, "An Experimental Study of Leadership and Group Life," in Guy E. Swanson *et al.* (Eds.), *Readings in Social Psychology* (New York: Holt, Rinehart and Winston, 1952), pp. 340–355.

6 *The Effect of Increased Leadership and Its Relation to Interest and Participation*, Report of Departmental Study (Skokie, Illinois: Skokie Park District, 1961).

pated and actual construction costs, operating costs, experiences in construction, volume of use, methods of scheduling, income from facility, etc.

3. A projection of need and probable use within one's own community, based on population concentration, availability of similar facilities, and experience elsewhere

4. Exploration of possible locations, in terms of availability and cost of land, zoning factors, probable development costs; a priority list of locations that might be developed based on this

5. Analysis of the effect of climatic and other local conditions or factors on attendance, year-round use, maintenance, etc.

6. Needed steps to obtain public support and approval for project

While it will be necessary to involve municipal planning authorities and architectural or building consultants in such a process, it will usually be the recreation administrator who takes the initiative in proposing and exploring the problems involved in the construction of a major new facility. He must obtain detailed, factual answers to questions that may be raised about the project by municipal authorities who are considering it. Indeed, many recreation administrators have developed comprehensive, illustrated, printed reports of their preliminary investigation, before ever proposing the construction of a new facility for expanded program service. And, in some cases, when early research has indicated that the project would be impractical, it has been withdrawn before it could be "shot down."

In general, past research dealing with the construction and operation of the commonest types of recreation facilities has provided standards which may be safely followed by recreation departments and community agencies. In addition, the National Recreation Association has formulated guides with respect to the provision of outdoor recreation facilities.[7] Often, however, an individual community will find it necessary to carry out a thorough analysis, as indicated above, before developing facilities of a more specialized type.

Research Relating to Equipment. A special problem area lies in the field of safety and accident liability. Here, major recreation departments often find it necessary to explore the legal factors involved in protecting themselves against suit for injuries sustained in accidents, or to carefully analyze equipment or program activities, in order to *prevent* accidents for which they might be held liable. Los Angeles recreation authorities, for example, after a series of several fatal accidents caused by falls from equipment on school playgrounds, made a sustained effort to find the best kind of safety padding that might be used under ropes, parallel bars, sliding ponds, and jungle gyms.

In carrying out this study, they did an extended engineering analysis of various materials and products (assisted by an engineering consultation

---

[7] *Outdoor Recreation Space Standards* (New York: National Recreation Association, 1965).

firm), applying 31 separate criteria having to do with safety, cost, maintenance, and durability.[8] In another situation, a municipal recreation
administrator carried out a thorough analysis of liability factors involved
in sponsoring coasting on public streets. Based on the precedents and
decisions that were uncovered in his research, it was decided that the
activity would have to be discontinued by his department.

EVALUATION OF PARTICIPANT BEHAVIOR AND OUTCOMES

Obviously, within a recreation program that has a clear-cut set of
objectives, the key question must be, "What are the outcomes of recreation participation?" In other words, what has really been accomplished
for those taking part? In addition to enjoyment, has there been social
growth, improved emotional adjustment and understanding, or physical
development?

The outcomes of recreational participation represent an extremely
difficult area for the researcher, because: (a) the kinds of changes that
occur as a consequence of involvement cannot easily be identified and
precisely measured; and (b) it is usually not possible to exclude other
causal factors in the participant's background that may be responsible
for change. Indeed, in other areas of social research, efforts to establish
outcomes in terms of behavior changes that have been brought about
through intensified educational or therapeutic service have frequently
proved fruitless.

Nonetheless, the effort must be made. Usually, research and evaluation in this area tends to fall under two major headings:

1. The first consists in data gathering of a statistical type, relating
chiefly to such questions as "Who participates?" "In what activity?" "How
frequently?" and "With what degree of success?" Since this sort of information is useful in viewing the effect of the total program, it is important that attendance and participation figures be based on accurate
head-counts or on actual registration procedures. Often, estimates made
after the session or at the end of the week are subject to guesswork or
even deliberate exaggeration. Attendance reports should be honest and
precise, and should define the meaning of the figure being given: whether
it refers to those involved in single sessions during the week, or the total
of daily attendances, or the number of different individuals registered.

2. More serious attempts to measure the outcomes of participation
must be based on systematic and scientific techniques for gathering information. These may involve keeping detailed case records of individuals
and groups, or developing objective instruments for measuring behavior
change. Examples of this type follow.

At the State Hospital in Jamestown, North Dakota, the Department

8 George D. Butler, "Is Your Playground Surfacing Safe?" *Recreation*, April, 1963,
p. 193.

of Activity Therapies, which includes a strong component of therapeutic recreation services, staff members are required to fill out the following Individual Evaluation Sheet for psychiatric patients under their jurisdiction. Such reports, when placed in the patient's folder and examined over a period of time, provide a means of judging strengths and weaknesses in different areas of personal functioning, interest, and effective participation in different types of recreation activity, and the overall progress of the patient.

Department of Activity Therapies
Individual Evaluation Sheet

Name_____ Ward_____ Date_____

Code: 0—not observed   1—poor   2—fair   3—average   4—good   5—excellent

	Industrial	Recreation	O.T.	Music	P.E.	Manual Arts	Home Arts	Co-Ed	Comments
					Activity Therapies Adolescent Unit				
Punctuality-Constant Attendance									
Personal Neatness									
Concentration									
Attitude toward Supervision									
Attitude toward Other Patients									
Cooperation									
Self-Confidence									
Degree of Supervision Needed									
Interest Sustained									
Ability to Make Decisions									
Flexibility									
Improves with Training									
Takes Instructions									
Takes Criticism, Suggestions									
Initiative/Degree of Voluntary Participation									
Socially Acceptable Behavior									

On a more specialized level, the reaction of individuals to specific types of recreational activity carried on over a period of time may be analyzed. For example, a recent study examined the behavior of a group of retarded children (with varying patterns of ability, disability, and disturbance) who were exposed to square dance instruction.[9] Based on careful observation and case recording of their progress and behavior, with specific reference to social adjustment, a number of conclusions were reached about the value of this activity in working with retarded childred.

A much more detailed and comprehensive attempt to analyze the effectiveness of recreation programing by focusing on an evaluation of the behavior of participants has been carried out by the Recreation and Youth Services Planning Council and the Board of Education of the City of Los Angeles.[10] This has consisted of a major research effort, carried out in three stages, the primary purpose of which has been to develop instruments which might be scientifically used to measure behavior and thus assess the worth of a recreation program. The procedure followed by the Los Angeles researchers was to identify three so-called "domains of behavior," or ways in which major aspects of participant behavior might be classified. These were:

1. the *cognitive domain,* including all the intellectual, knowledge, skills and abilities;
2. the *affective domain,* including behaviors described generally as interests, appreciations, attitudes, and values; and
3. the *psycho-motor domain,* including the manipulative and coordinative physical skills and abilities.[11]

Obviously, both the development of such an instrument and its application requires the involvement of scientifically trained investigators. The department that seeks to carry out an evaluation or research effort of this type must employ skilled technicians in the area of psychological testing or sociological analysis, to devise the scales that will be used, and to supervise their administration.

PROGRAM EVALUATION

Attempts to assess the effectiveness of programs (apart from those aimed at measuring outcomes for participants) fall into several categories. These include: (a) measuring the effectiveness of program techniques

[9] Bertha Eichenbaum and Norman Bednarek, "Square Dancing and Social Adjustment," *Mental Retardation,* April, 1964, p. 105.

[10] Norman P. Miller and Marvin J. Rosen, *School Recreation Evaluative Criteria Study: A Behavioral Approach to Evaluation of Recreation and Youth Service Programs, Phase II* (Los Angeles, California: Recreation and Youth Services Planning Council, 1964).

[11] *Ibid.*

within a single event or activity; (b) within a single specialized branch of service; and (c) total program evaluation. In each case, it is necessary to rely on certain criteria as a means for determining success. If a program has established certain clear-cut goals and objectives, it should be possible to measure the extent to which these are reached. However, recent research by a municipal recreation and parks department indicates that few agencies have so defined their purposes.[12] Lacking these, a set of criteria may be taken from the literature, or devised for this purpose.

Program Effectiveness Within a Single Event. Based on the agreed-on characteristics of a successful program event, it is possible to devise questions which serve to measure any sort of special program. In the area of social recreation, for example, the Bureau of Recreation in Dayton, Ohio, has devised the following "Party Post-Mortem":

General Effect:

1. Was the party good fun for everyone attending?   _____
2. Did all the committees seem to be well coordinated?   _____
3. Did each committee take care of its own clean-up?   _____
4. Was there a sufficient build-up of advance interest?   _____
5. Was there a smooth continuity of theme?   _____

Atmosphere:

1. Was there something easy for everyone to do when he came in?   _____
2. Were there activities that avoided making participants uncomfortable or "on the spot"?   _____
3. Did these activities set the stage sufficiently for the mood of the evening?   _____

Refreshments:

1. Were the refreshments a pleasant surprise that dove-tailed into the party smoothly?   _____
2. Was the group served quickly and easily?   _____
3. Was the best use made of seating arrangements for the refreshments?   _____

Program:

1. Did the party move smoothly from one activity and leader to another?   _____
2. Was there a good balance of program for the kind of people attending?   _____
3. Was there a good balance of leadership?   _____
4. Did the party move at a good tempo?   _____
5. Rate the leaders on the following:
      Did they participate in the activities while leading?   _____
      Did they have control of the group?   _____

[12] *Study of Goals and Objectives in the Recreation Field* (Phoenix, Arizona: Parks and Recreation Department, 1964).

Did they give directions simply and easily? _____

Did their attitudes create a spirit of enthusiasm? _____

6. Did the last activity unify the group and send them home with
a good taste in their mouths? [13] _____

Similar "post-mortems" might readily be developed to appraise the success of other special events, such as carnivals, tournaments, field days, or community celebrations.

Effectiveness of a Specialized Branch of Service. There are many ways of determining effectiveness of a specialized branch of program service in recreation. Brown points out that, within the hospital setting, program techniques may be measured through such devices as personality rating scales, reports of ward activity, reports of patient interaction, and tabulation of frequency of participation and types of activities.[14] For an overall view of the success of a branch of program, it is necessary to state goals and objectives precisely and clearly, and then to attempt to measure the extent to which they have been reached. Often these goals will be unique to the special kind of service being rendered.

To illustrate, in 1963 the National Recreation Association carried out a comprehensive study of center programs and operations in 13 Air Force bases in Germany, France, and England.[15] Various aspects of the program were examined. The major concern, of course, was the ability of recreation centers to provide a broad program for all segments of base populations. More specifically, each base's recreation program was rated objectively on the extent to which it provided: (a) self-directed activities; (b) entertainment; (c) passive activities; (d) miscellaneous services; (e) interest groups and classes; and (f) extension programs and services. Some unique aspects of the Air Force programs which were studied in detail included the effectiveness of recreation center councils, the development of self-supporting recreation classes and interest groups, the use of "interest registers," and the ability of each center to maintain a continuity of program, in spite of the high turnover rate of personnel that was typical of military installations.

Total Program Evaluation. While it is taken for granted that each community recreation department, whether large or small, should subject itself to continuous, ongoing evaluation, it is also wise to plan for periodic major evaluations. This is different from the type of community survey described at the beginning of this chapter, in that it does not involve starting "from scratch." A whole new department is not being

[13] Dayton, Ohio, Bureau of Recreation, "Party Post-Mortem," *Recreation,* September, 1964, p. 362.

[14] Roscoe Brown, "Evaluation of Program Techniques in Hospital Recreation," *Recreation,* January, 1963, p. 38.

[15] Arthur Todd, "The Air Force Assesses Its Recreation Centers," *Recreation,* September, 1964, p. 342.

developed. Instead, an ongoing program is submitting its entire operation to a careful scrutiny. For this to be done most effectively, a team of outside authorities should be brought in. For example, in 1964, the Topeka, Kansas, Recreation Commission contracted with the National Recreation Association to carry out a major analysis of its operation. Forty-four leading citizens of Topeka formed a Citizen's Committee under the direction of the NRA. They were divided into five groups: a General Steering Committee, and four working committees dealing with Administration and Finance, Personnel, Areas and Facilities, and Program.

Under the guidance of the NRA consultants assigned to the study, the Citizen's Committee gathered a mass of relevant data with respect to the city itself (census figures, age groupings, housing, income and employment patterns, land uses) and the work of the Recreation Commission. In evaluating the program twelve guides were drawn from Butler's text, "Introduction to Community Recreation," and used as criteria. In the final report,[16] the study group made major recommendations in each of four areas. These included suggestions with regard to administrative structure, public information practices, agreements with other community agencies, development of new facilities and centers; new supervisory positions, salary scales for personnel and leadership training programs; and revision of programs, including expansion of outdoor activities and nature recreation, and of services for the ill and handicapped.

While there is no rule of thumb as to how often such major self-studies should be carried out by community or agency recreation departments, it would appear that every five years would provide a sensible period. When a community is undergoing rapid change, when there is widespread dissatisfaction or difficulty, or when there is a change of administration, it may also be especially appropriate.

In 1965, the Great Lakes District Program Standards Committee of the National Recreation Association formulated a manual for the evaluation of municipal recreation programs.[17] The product of several years of study and planning, this manual may be used in: (a) self-appraisals conducted by departmental personnel; (b) when a new community wishes to organize a recreation department, or an established department is to be extensively reorganized; (c) when citizen boards or committees wish to carry out a periodic evaluation of the recreation operation; or, (d) when civic organizations concerned with a range of community affairs wish to look critically at recreation.

16 *A Self-Study Relating to the Public Recreation Program* (Topeka, Kansas: Recreation Commission, 1964).

17 Great Lakes District Program Standards Committee, *Evaluation of Community Recreation: A Guide to Evaluation with Standards and Evaluative Criteria* (New York: National Recreation Association Research Department, 1965).

Standards (statements of desirable practice, or levels of performance for given functions) are provided under six major categories: (a) Philosophy and Goals; (b) Administration; (c) Programing; (d) Personnel; (e) Areas, Facilities, and Equipment; and (f) Evaluation.

Within each category, detailed illustrative criteria are provided, to determine whether each recommended standard is being met. This manual, which was scheduled to undergo pilot testing during 1965–66, will undoubtedly prove most valuable to recreation departments wishing to carry out a detailed analysis of their operation.

In conclusion, this chapter has shown how research and evaluation may provide useful and practical tools to the recreation practitioner and administrator. In addition to the kinds of studies and data-gathering techniques that have been described, other researches of a less "applied" nature are being conducted today by graduate students and faculty members at colleges and universities, or by professional or governmental organizations. These may lie within historical or philosophical realms, or may deal with legal analysis, or psychological or sociological concerns. Often they contribute significantly to the understanding and upgrading of the profession.

In 1965, the first National Conference on Research in Recreation was held at Pennsylvania State University, cosponsored by the American Association for Health, Physical Education and Recreation, and the National Recreation Association. This important meeting served to highlight the development of recreation research thus far, and to point to new directions. For recreation to gain a full acceptance as an important form of social service, it is crucial that its contribution to society be clearly identified and documented, and that its organization and administration become as professionalized and efficient as possible. For this to be done, an increasing amount of significant evaluation and research will be needed. It will be important that the recreation professional become fully aware of the findings of ongoing research, including materials not directly within his sphere of interest. In addition, there is a great need to have research findings in recreation made more generally available to the public at large, as a means of improving public understanding.

SUGGESTED QUESTIONS FOR DISCUSSION

1. What are the meanings of the two terms, *research* and *evaluation,* as they are presented in this chapter? How do they differ, and what do they have in common? List the various kinds of information-gathering techniques that may be used in both processes.
2. List and describe at least five types of problems in professional recreation service relating to program planning and leadership development that may be solved through specific research projects or evaluation procedures. Give

examples of each of these, showing the problem, and a related research or evaluation process.

3. In your judgment, how much of the professional recreation administrator's concern should be addressed to research? Apart from carrying on research himself, how can he assist others in the conduct of cooperative research? To what degree should he be knowledgeable in the area of current research findings?

Bibliography

Recreation in Modern Society

Butler, George, *Introduction to Community Recreation* (New York: McGraw-Hill, 1959).

Carlson, Reynold, Deppe, Theodore, and MacLean, Janet, *Recreation in American Life* (Belmont, California: Wadsworth, 1963).

Commission on Goals for American Recreation, *Goals for American Recreation* (Washington, D.C.: American Association for Health, Physical Education and Recreation, 1964).

DeGrazia, Sebastian, *Of Time, Work and Leisure* (New York: Twentieth Century Fund, 1962).

Doell, Charles, *Elements of Park and Recreation Administration* (Minneapolis: Burgess, 1963).

Dulles, Foster Rhea, *A History of Recreation: America Learns to Play* (New York: Appleton-Century-Crofts, 1965).

Fitzgerald, Gerald B., *Community Organization for Recreation* (New York: Ronald, 1948).

Hjelte, George, and Shivers, Jay, *Public Administration of Park and Recreation Services* (New York: Macmillan, 1963).

Hutchinson, John, *Principles of Recreation* (New York: Ronald, 1951).

Kaplan, Max, *Leisure in America: a Social Inquiry* (New York: Wiley, 1960).

Kraus, Richard, *Recreation and the Schools* (New York: Macmillan, 1964).

Larrabee, Eric, and Meyersohn, Rolf, *Mass Leisure* (New York: Free Press, 1958).

Meyer, Harold, and Brightbill, Charles, *Community Recreation: a Guide to Its Organization* (Englewood Cliffs, N.J.: Prentice-Hall, 1964).

Miller, Norman, and Robinson, Duane, *The Leisure Age* (Belmont, California: Wadsworth, 1963).

Outdoor Recreation for America (Washington, D.C.: Outdoor Recreation Resources Review Commission, 1962).

Rodney, Lynn, *Administration of Public Recreation* (New York: Ronald, 1964).

Sapora, Allen, and Mitchell, Elmer, *The Theory of Play and Recreation* (New York: Ronald, 1961).

Slavson, Samuel, *Recreation and the Total Personality* (New York: Association Press, 1946).

Leadership and Group Dynamics

Cartwright, Darwin, and Zander, Alvin, *Group Dynamics, Research and Theory* (New York: Harper & Row, 1953).

Corbin, H. Dan, *Recreation Leadership* (Englewood Cliffs, N.J.: Prentice-Hall, 1953).

Coyle, Grace, *Group Work with American Youth* (New York: Harper & Row, 1948).

Danford, Howard, *Creative Leadership in Recreation* (Boston: Allyn and Bacon, 1964).

Dimock, Hedley and Trecker, Harleigh, *Supervision of Group Work and Recreation* (New York: Association Press, 1951).

Fitzgerald, Gerald, *Leadership in Recreation* (New York: Ronald, 1951).

Kraus, Richard, *Recreation Leader's Handbook* (New York: McGraw-Hill, 1955).

Miles, Matthew, *Learning to Work in Groups* (New York: Teachers College, Columbia University, Bureau of Publications, 1959).

Roberts, Dorothy, *Leading Teen-age Groups* (New York: Association Press, 1963).

Ross, Murray, and Hendry, Charles, *New Understandings of Leadership* (New York: Association Press, 1957).

Shivers, Jay, *Leadership in Recreational Service* (New York: Macmillan, 1963).

Slavson, Samuel, *Creative Group Education* (New York: Association Press, 1948).

Vannier, Maryhelen, *Methods and Materials in Recreation Leadership* (Philadelphia: Saunders, 1956).

Program Planning and the Needs of Special Groups

Anderson, Jackson, *Industrial Recreation* (New York: McGraw-Hill, 1955).

Avedon, Elliott, and Arje, Frances, *Socio-recreative Programing for the Retarded* (New York: Teachers College, Columbia University, Bureau of Publications, 1964).

Bortz, Edward, *Creative Aging* (New York: Macmillan, 1963).

Bossard, James, *The Sociology of Child Development* (New York: Harper & Row, 1954).

Carlson, Bernice, and Ginglend, David, *Play Activities for the Retarded Child* (Nashville: Abingdon, 1961).

Chapman, Frederick, *Recreation Activities for the Handicapped* (New York: Ronald, 1960).

Clemens, Frances, Tully, Robert, and Crill, Edward, *Recreation and the Local Church* (Elgin, Illinois: Brethren Publishing Company, 1956).

Hammett, Catherine, and Musselman, Virginia, *The Camp Program Book* (New York: Association Press, 1951).

Haun, Paul, *Recreation: a Medical Viewpoint* (New York: Teachers College, Columbia University, Bureau of Publications, 1965).

Hunt, Valerie, *Recreation for the Handicapped* (Englewood Cliffs, N.J.: Prentice-Hall, 1955).

Kahn, Alfred, *Planning Community Services for Children in Trouble* (New York: Columbia, 1963).

Kleemeier, Robert, *Aging and Leisure* (New York: Oxford, 1961).

Kleindienst, Viola and Weston, Arthur, *Intramural and Recreation Programs for Schools and Colleges* (New York: Appleton-Century-Crofts, 1964).

Kotinsky, Ruth and Witmer, Helen, Eds., *Community Programs for Mental Health* (Cambridge: Harvard, 1955).

National Council on the Aging, *Centers for Older People, Guides for Programs and Facilities* (New York: National Council on the Aging, 1962).

Pomeroy, Janet, *Recreation for the Physically Handicapped* (New York: Macmillan, 1964).

Robison, Sophia, *Juvenile Delinquency, Its Nature and Control* (New York: Holt, Rinehart and Winston, 1960).

Stafford, George, *Sports for the Handicapped* (Englewood Cliffs, N.J.: Prentice-Hall, 1947).

Williams, Arthur, *Recreation for the Senior Years* (New York: Association Press, 1962).

RECREATION PROGRAM ACTIVITIES

Arts and Crafts

Amon, Martha, and Rawson, Ruth, *Handicrafts Simplified* (Bloomington, Ill.: McKnight, 1961).

Griswald, Lester, *Handicrafts* (Englewood Cliffs, N.J.: Prentice-Hall, 1952).

Hammett, Catherine, and Horrocks, Carol, *Creative Crafts for Campers* (New York: Association Press, 1957).

Ickis, Marguerite, and Esh, Reba, *Book of Arts and Crafts* (New York: Association Press, 1953).

Jaeger, Ellsworth, *Easy Crafts* (New York: Macmillan, 1947).

McNeice, William, and Benson, Kenneth, *Crafts for the Retarded* (Bloomington, Ill.: McKnight, 1964).

Moseley, Spencer, Johnson, Pauline, and Koenig, Hazel, *Crafts Design* (Belmont, California: Wadsworth, 1962).

Reeves, Robert, *Make It Yourself Games Book* (New York: Emerson, 1963).

Squires, John, *Fun Crafts for Children* (Englewood Cliffs, N.J.: Prentice-Hall, 1964).

Camping, Nature and Outdoor Activities

Donaldson, G. W., *School Camping* (New York: Association Press, 1952).

Empleton, Bernard, *et al.*, *The New Science of Skin and Scuba Diving* (New York: Association Press, 1962).

Gabrielsen, M. Alexander, Spears, Betty, and Gabrielsen, B. W., *Aquatics Handbook* (Englewood Cliffs, N.J.: Prentice-Hall, 1960).

Goodrich, Warren, and Hutchins, Carleen, *Science through Recreation* (New York: Holt, Rinehart and Winston, 1964).

Harty, William, *Science for Camp and Counselor* (New York: Association Press, 1964).

Ickis, Marguerite, *Nature in Recreation* (New York: A. S. Barnes, 1965).

Miracle, Leonard, and Decker, Maurice, *The Complete Book of Camping* (New York: Harper & Row, 1961).

Peterson, Gunnar, and Edgren, Harry, *The Book of Outdoor Winter Activities* (New York: Association Press, 1962).

Price, Betty, *Adventuring in Nature* (New York: National Recreation Association, 1951).

Smith, Julian, Carlson, Reynold, Donaldson, George, and Masters, Hugh, *Outdoor Education* (Englewood Cliffs, N.J.: Prentice-Hall, 1963).

Vinal, William, *Nature Recreation* (New York: McGraw-Hill, 1940).

Webb, Kenneth, and Webb, Susan, *Summer Magic* (New York: Association Press, 1953).

Dance

Andrews, Gladys, *Creative Rhythmic Movement for Children* (Englewood Cliffs, N.J.: Prentice-Hall, 1954).

de Mille, Agnes, *To a Young Dancer* (Boston: Little, Brown, 1960).

Duggan, Anne Schley, *et al., The Folk Dance Library*, 5 vols. (New York: Ronald, 1948).

Durlacher, Ed, *Honor Your Partner* (New York: Devin-Adair, 1949).

Hall, J. Tillman, *Dance!* (Belmont, California: Wadsworth, 1963).

Harris, Jane, *et al., Dance a While* (Minneapolis: Burgess, 1964).

Hawkins, Alma, *Creating through Dance* (Englewood Cliffs, N.J.: Prentice-Hall, 1964).

Hipps, R. Harold, and Chappell, Wallace, *A World of Fun* (Nashville: The Methodist Church, 1959).

Jensen, Clayne, and Jensen, Mary, *Beginning Square Dance* (Belmont, California: Wadsworth, 1966).

Kraus, Richard, *Square Dances of Today* (New York: Ronald, 1950).
   Folk Dancing (New York: Macmillan, 1962).
   Beginning Social Dance (with Lola Sadlo) (Belmont, California: Wadsworth, 1964).
   A Pocket Guide of Folk and Square Dances and Singing Games for the Elementary School (Englewood Cliffs, N.J.: Prentice-Hall, 1966).

Latchaw, Marjorie, and Pyatt, Jean, *A Pocket Guide of Dance Activities* (Englewood Cliffs, N.J.: Prentice-Hall, 1958).

Mettler, Barbara, and Carbo, Will, *This Is Creative Dance* (Tucson: Bettler Studios, 1962).

Rohrbough, Lynn, *The Handy Play Party Book* (Delaware, Ohio: Cooperative Recreation Service, 1940).

Rowen, Betty, *Learning through Movement* (New York: Teachers College, Columbia University, Bureau of Publications, 1963).

Shaw, Lloyd, *Cowboy Dances* (Caldwell, Idaho: Caxton, 1939).

Turner, Margery, *Dance Handbook* (Englewood Cliffs, N.J.: Prentice-Hall, 1959).

White, Betty, *Betty White's Teen-age Dance Book* (New York: McKay, 1952).

Woody, Regina, *Young Dancer's Career Book* (New York: Dutton, 1958).

Dramatics

Anderson, Paul, *Story-telling with the Flannel Board* (Minneapolis: T. S. Denison, 1963).

Burger, Isabel, *Creative Play Acting* (New York: Ronald, 1950).

Cummings, Richard, *101 Hand Puppets, a Guide for Puppeteers of All Ages* (New York: McKay, 1962).

Deason, Myrna, *et al., The Modern Skit and Stunt Book* (Minneapolis: T. S. Denison, 1963).

Eisenberg, Larry, and Eisenberg, Helen, *The Handbook of Skits and Stunts* (New York: Association Press, 1953).

Gross, Edwin, and Gross, Nathalie, *Teen Theatre, a Guide to Play Production* (New York: Whittlesey, 1953).

Lease, Ruth, and Siks, Geraldine, *Creative Dramatics in Home, School and Community* (New York: Harper & Row, 1952).

Philippi, Herbert, *Stagecraft and Scene Design* (Boston: Houghton Mifflin, 1953).

Selden, Samuel, *A Player's Handbook* (New York: Appleton-Century-Crofts, 1950).

Simos, Jack, *Social Growth through Play Production* (New York: Association Press, 1957).

Stahl, Leroy, *Simplified Stagecraft Manual* (Minneapolis: T. S. Denison, 1962).

Ward, Winifred, *Creative Dramatics* (New York: Appleton-Century-Crofts, 1950).

Games and Sports

Armbruster, David, and Irwin, Leslie, *Basic Skills in Sports* (St. Louis: Mosby, 1958).

Blake, O. William, and Volp, Anne, *Lead-up Games to Team Sports* (Englewood Cliffs, N.J.: Prentice-Hall, 1964).

Donnelly, Richard, *et al., Active Games and Contests* (New York: Ronald, 1958).

Frankel, Lillian, and Frankel, Godfrey, *101 Best Games for Girls, and 101 Best Action Games for Boys* (New York: Sterling, 1953).

Hindman, Darwin, *Handbook of Active Games* (Englewood Cliffs, N.J.: Prentice-Hall, 1955).

Hunt, Sarah, and Cain, Ethel, *Games the World Around* (New York: Ronald, 1941).

Kraus, Richard, *The Family Book of Games* (New York: McGraw-Hill, 1960).

Mason, Bernard, and Mitchell, Elmer, *Social Games for Recreation* (New York: Ronald, 1935).

McFarlan, Allen, *Book of American Indian Games* (New York: Association Press, 1958).

Menke, Frank, *The Encyclopedia of Sports* (New York: Barnes, 1960).

Mulac, Margaret, *Games and Stunts for Schools, Camps and Playgrounds* (New York: Harper and Row, 1964).

Smith, Hope, *Water Games* (New York: Ronald, 1962).

van der Smissen, Betty, and Knierim, Helen, *Recreational Sports and Games* (Minneapolis: Burgess, 1964).

Vannier, Maryhelen, and Poindexter, Hally Beth, *Individual and Team Sports for Girls and Women* (Philadelphia: Saunders, 1960).

Music

Barton, Fred, *Music as a Hobby* (New York: Harper & Row, 1950).

Carabo-Cone, Madeleine, *The Playground as Music Teacher* (New York: Harper & Row, 1959).

Cheyette, Irving, and Renna, Albert, *Songs to Sing with Recreational Instruments* (Bryn Mawr, Pennsylvania: Presser, 1951).

Landeck, Beatrice, *Children and Music* (New York: Sloane, 1952).

Leonhard, Charles, *Recreation through Music* (New York: Ronald, 1952).

National Recreation Association: Various kits and pamphlets on the following subjects: *Action Songs, Community and Assembly Singing, Approaches to Informal Singing,* and others.

Nye, Robert, *et al., Singing with Children* (Belmont, California: Wadsworth, 1962).

Rosenberg, Martha, *It's Fun to Teach Creative Music* (New York: Play Schools Association, 1963).

Seeger, Ruth Crawford, *American Folk Songs for Children* (New York: Doubleday, 1948).

Wilson, Harry, *Sing Along* (New York: J. J. Robbins, 1948).

Parties and Special Events

de Marche, Edythe and de Marche, David, *Handbook of Co-ed Teen Activities* (New York: Association Press, 1958).

Ickis, Marguerite, *The Book of Patriotic Holidays* (New York: Dodd, Mead, 1962).

Krythe, Maymie, *All About American Holidays* (New York: Harper & Row, 1962).

Millen, Nina, *Children's Festivals from Many Lands* (New York: Friendship Press, 1964).

Sechrist, Elizabeth, *Christmas Everywhere* (Philadelphia: Macrae Smith Company, 1962).

   Heigh-ho for Hallowe'en (Macrae Smith Company, 1948).

   It's Time for Thanksgiving (Macrae Smith Company, 1957).

Spicer, Dorothy, *Folk Party Fun* (New York: Association Press, 1954).

van Rensselaer, Alexander, *The Complete Party Book* (New York: Sheridan House, 1948).

Wackerbarth, Marjorie, and Graham, Lillian, *Successful Parties and How to Give Them* (Minneapolis: T. S. Denison, 1962).

Appendix A

Guides for Working with Volunteer Leaders

In many recreation departments, much responsibility is assigned to volunteer leaders. This frequently causes difficulty when volunteers are more interested in meeting their own needs than in helping others. Some may be unwilling to accept the philosophy or operating procedures of the agency; others may attend irregularly. Therefore, it is necessary to carefully select, guide, and orient volunteer leaders in recreation programs.

1. Volunteers should be recruited to the agency in an organized way, rather than through casual invitation. They should be screened on the basis of: a) having a sound character and attractive personality; and b) having a potential contribution to make to the program.

2. There should be a formal period of orientation, and introduction to the program. In a large agency, separate groups of volunteers may be introduced to the program in this way every two or three months. In smaller departments, individuals are oriented as they enter.

3. Volunteers should be given definite tasks to perform, and should understand the function of these assignments in assisting the overall work of the agency. Tasks should be consistent with their interests and abilities.

4. Volunteers should be given departmental manuals, and should receive whatever forms of in-service education are provided for other staff members. They should be carefully supervised, with regular supervisory conferences.

5. Volunteers should be expected to meet regular responsibilities, and to know that inconsistent attendance or performance is not acceptable. Similarly, they should not be kept waiting for assignments, or permitted to feel that their time is wasted because it is not regarded as valuable.

6. When appropriate, volunteers should attend staff meetings or conferences. Their contributions should be recognized verbally as well as through awards, testimonial letters, or events, and in program reports.

7. The work of volunteers should be evaluated at regular intervals. Those who are particularly capable and devoted should progress in responsibility and level of service.

Under some circumstances, volunteers who are able and wish to do so, may actually become regular members of the staff—assuming that they can meet the formal standards of the agency. Thus, volunteer involvement may serve as preparation for recruitment into the field.

Appendix B

Guides for Training Conference

In-service workshops, conferences, planning sessions or study groups are essential to the improvement of recreation leadership. The following outline illustrates a typical three-day Playground Leader's Workshop, prior to the beginning of a Summer Recreation Program. It is attended by all regular staff members, but focuses on the preparation of temporary summer personnel. It is held in late June, in a large community center with an adjacent playfield.

First Day   *Introduction to Department*

9:00 A.M.–9:30 A.M.   Registration period.

9:30 A.M.–10:00 A.M.   Opening message by Director of Department. He outlines the Workshop schedule and introduces its staff.

10:00 A.M.–11:30 A.M.   Presentation of philosophy of department. Its role in the civic structure is examined, along with other municipal services. Basic procedures and regulations for recreation employees are presented, along with rules for clothing, behavior, public relations, legal responsibilities, and similar topics.

11:30 A.M.–NOON   Questions and discussion.

NOON–1:00 P.M.   Box lunch.

1:00 P.M.–2:30 P.M.   Departmental structure is presented, and key personnel are introduced: supervisors, specialists, maintenance personnel, etc. Each explains his role, and how he will work with summer leaders.

2:30 P.M.–3:00 P.M.   Presentation of color slides of previous summer's program, including highlights in different areas of city, tournaments, special events, and trip programs.

3:00 P.M.–4:00 P.M.   Program objectives and needs and interests of different age groups are analyzed. Then the actual schedule of activities followed in general by playground directors, is presented:
1. daily schedule, with typical time blocks
2. weekly schedule, with special themes and weekly programs
3. special events, trips, and culminating activities
4. use of citywide specialists

440

Second Day	*Program Activities*
9:30 A.M.–10:00 A.M.	Analysis of effective leadership methods and teaching techniques in the area of physical recreation activities.
10:00 A.M.–NOON	Mass demonstration and participation in games and sports: low organization and lead-up games, softball, track and field, volleyball, badminton, and other widely-used activities.
NOON–1:00 P.M.	Box lunch.

Three one-hour workshop-demonstrations in special activities like:

1:00 P.M.–2:00 P.M.	nature programing	arts and crafts	dramatics
2:00 P.M.–3:00 P.M.	dance	trip programing	science exploration
3:00 P.M.–4:00 P.M.	special events	music	rainy day programs

In each one-hour session, a specialist introduces activities, and playground leaders participate in them. At each hour, they attend a different workshop.

Third Day	*Departmental Regulations and Procedures*
9:30 A.M.–11:00 A.M.	Accident prevention, safety, and first aid are presented. First aid procedures for minor injuries are demonstrated by a Red Cross specialist. Municipal attorney outlines procedures to be followed in case of more serious accidents; these include, according to the situation, calling the playground director, police, an ambulance, and the parents of the child.

Proper use of playground equipment, and necessary procedures for trip programs are presented.

11:00 A.M.–NOON	Examination of departmental forms: a. attendance reports, and reports for special programs b. supply requisition forms c. accident report forms d. damage or vandalism report forms e. payroll procedures and schedules f. insurance procedures and forms
NOON–1:00 P.M.	Box lunch.
1:00 P.M.–2:00 P.M.	Analysis of leadership role on playground: 1. maintaining discipline and control 2. providing guidance to children; working with "problem" youngsters 3. working with volunteer leaders or parents 4. community relations role of playground leader

2:00 P.M.–3:00 P.M.	Questions and discussion.
3:00 P.M.–4:00 P.M.	Issuance of materials and supplies.

Announcement of weekly training session, to be held on mid-week evening for all playground leaders, in community center. Includes social hour, for *leaders'* recreation.

Closing remarks by Director—"looking forward to successful summer."

Appendix C

Listing of Films

Theory of Leisure and Recreation

Of Time, Work and Leisure. Problems of leisure in modern society, with commentary by Sebastian de Grazia. 20 min., b&w, 16 mm., rental from Audio-Visual Center, Indiana University, Bloomington, Indiana.

Organized Recreation Service

Town and Country Recreation. Small community develops needed recreation program and department. 20 min., color, 16 mm.

Careers in Recreation. Examines the work of a young recreation professional and the growing need for qualified practitioners. 27 min., color, 16 mm.

Leaders for Leisure. Stresses importance of professionally educated leaders to insure success of community recreation programs. 21 min., color, 16 mm.

These three films, somewhat dated but still useful, are produced by the Athletic Institute and may be rented from offices of Association Films in Ridgefield, N.J.; Oakmont, Pa.; La Grange, Ill.; Hayward, Calif.; or Dallas, Tex.

Recreation and Physical Activities for Special Groups

People Who Care. Career recruitment film for hospital personnel including recreation specialists. 25 min., color, 16 mm. Rental from National Association of Mental Health, New York, N.Y.

Therapeutic Camping. Multidisciplinary approach to working with children with learning and/or adjustment problems in Maine summer camp. 28 min., color, 16 mm. Free rental; Devereux Schools, Devon, Pa., provides sources.

Working and Playing to Health. Examines recreational, occupational, and industrial therapy in psychiatric hospital. 35 min., b&w, 16 mm. Rental from International Film Bureau, Inc., S. Michigan Ave., Chicago, Ill.

Physical Education for Blind Children. Use of modified sports and games with separate or integrated groups of blind children. 20 min., color, 16 mm. Rental from Charles Buell, 2722 Derby Street, Berkeley, Calif.

Camping and Outdoor Recreation

Camping: A Key to Conservation. Demonstrates conservation as focus of summer camp. 23 min., color or b&w, 16 mm. Project of American Camping Association; rental available from Indiana University Audio-Visual Center, Bloomington, Ind.

Beyond the Tooth of Time. Pictures rugged mountain camping and leadership training in Rocky Mountains. 27 min., b&w, 16 mm. For rental, inquire through local Boy Scout Council.

National Parks: Our American Heritage. Comprehensive look at National Park System—why originated, how administered. 17 min., color, 16 mm. Rental from Bailey Films, Inc., Hollywood, Calif.

NOTE: Dozens of other useful films on outdoor recreation are available from state or federal agencies, or national organizations interested in wildlife and conservation. Their availability is usually reported in professional journals.

A wide variety of films on specific sports activities are available from professional film distributors (such as Bailey Films, which distributes films on such activities as archery, swimming, basketball, trampoline, softball, and modern dance), *or* national promotional organizations like the Athletic Institute or the National Association of Engine and Boat Manufacturers, Inc., 420 Lexington Ave., New York, N. Y., which publishes a directory of 300 films of various aspects of boating.

Finally, a number of municipal recreation departments, such as the Youth Services Section of the Los Angeles (Calif.) City Schools, have produced and distributed excellent films of their special facilities or program features.

Photo Credits

The photographs appearing on these chapter pages are courtesy of the following:

Chapter 1. Fontana Village Square Dance, North Carolina. Photograph by Shafter Buchanan

Chapter 2. Phoenix, Arizona, Parks and Recreation Department

Chapter 3. Board of Public Parks and Recreation, Honolulu, Hawaii

Chapter 4. Topeka, Kansas, Recreation Commission

Chapter 5. YMCA of Greater New York

Chapter 6. Camp Handicamp, Idaho Springs, Colorado; courtesy of National Society for Crippled Children and Adults

Chapter 7. Ann Arbor, Michigan, Recreation Department. Photograph by Doug Fulton.

Chapter 8. Creative Art Education Workshop, Rutgers University

Chapter 9. Camp Brace, New York State Youth Division

Chapter 10. Camp Paivika, Crestline, California; courtesy of the National Society for Crippled Children and Adults

Chapter 11. Old Sturbridge Village, News Bureau, Sturbridge, Massachusetts

Chapter 12. Topeka, Kansas, Recreation Commission

Chapter 13. Camp Manitosh, Lake Coeur d'Alene, Washington; courtesy of the National Society for Crippled Children and Adults. Photograph by Hutchison, Pullman

Chapter 14. Fort Sam Houston, Texas; U.S. Army photograph

Chapter 15. Catholic Youth Organization, New York

Chapter 16. UAW-CIO Recreation Department

Chapter 17. Police Athletic League, New York

Chapter 18. National Education Association. Photograph by Carl Purcell

Index

Active games and contests, 78–83
Adolescents, *see* Teen-agers
Adult education, 288–290
Adult recreation, 137–139, 220–221, 264–265, 269, 285–293
AFL-CIO, 296
Aggression, in sports, 95–96
Aging, characteristics of, 293–295
recreation programs for, 167–168, 185, 221–222, 238–239, 265, 348–355
American Association of College Unions, 41, 412
American Association for Health, Physical Education, and Recreation, 18, 23, 33, 41, 127, 300, 411–412, 430
American Association of Zoological Parks and Aquariums, 414
American Athletic Union, 407
American Bowling Congress, 407
American Camping Association, 41, 412
American Institute of Park Executives, 412
American Recreation Society, 32, 37, 41, 299, 412
American Red Cross, 150, 273, 299, 356–357
American Youth Hostels, 407
Aquatics, *see* Boating; Scuba diving; Swimming
Archery, 11, 107, 137
Arlington, Virginia, 168–169
Armed forces recreation, 49, 367–375, 429
Arts, in community life, 17, 160–164, 217–221
see also Arts and crafts; Dance; Drama; Music
Arts and crafts, 213–226, 327–328
Astronomy, 148, 157
Athletic Institute, 11, 413–414
Automation, 10
Avedon, Elliott, *cited*, 332–333, 342–344

Ballet, 196, 198–200
Banks, William, *cited*, 330–331
Baptists, 21
Baseball, 11, 101–102, 105, 263–264
see also Little League
Basketball, 101, 105, 264
Berger, Bennett, *cited*, 277–278
Bicycling, 11, 117, 138

Blind, recreation for, 150–151, 317–321, 346–348
Boating, 11, 105, 132
safety in, 133, 139–141
Bowling, 11, 101, 116
Boxing, 101
Boy Scouts of America, 5, 239, 271, 402
Boys' Clubs of America, 403–404, 419
Brightbill, Charles K., *cited*, 6
Brill, A. A., *cited*, 95
Bureau of Labor Statistics, 12, 31
Bureau of Outdoor Recreation, 16, 49, 129
Butler, George, *cited*, 27

California, outdoor recreation plan in, 134
recreation positions in, 48
Campcraft, 155–156
Campfire Girls, 239, 271, 404–405
Camping, 130–132, 135–138, 351–353, 380
see also Day camping
Canoeing, 138, 150–151
Carlson, Reynold, *cited*, 6, 305–306
Catholic Youth Organization, 379, 383–384
Ceramics, 214, 220, 222, 262–263
Cerebral palsied, 148–149, 222, 302–303, 335–342, 365
Charades, 191–193
Children, recreation needs of, 261–277
Church recreation, *see* Religious recreation
Clawson, Marion, 10
College-age youth, 287
Community, celebrations in, 227–230
facilities for handicapped in, 333, 344–346, 361–363
Competition, 121–128
Conservation programs, 12, 14–15, 132–133, 147
Coral Gables, Florida, 261–265
Council for Advancement of Hospital Recreation, 300
County park and recreation programs, 133–135, 138, 144
Crafts, *see* Arts and crafts
Creative movement, 171–172
Cultural activities, *see* Arts in community life; Arts and crafts; Dance; Drama; Music

447

DATE DUE